Healing

Mother

Earth

Kim Michaels

More to Life Publishing

Healing

Mother

Earth

Kim Michaels

More to Life Publishing

Healing Mother Earth
by Kim Michaels.
Copyright © 2011 by Kim Michaels

Published by More to Life OÜ, Estonia. To contact the publisher, use
the contact information on www.morepublish.com

All rights reserved.

No part of this book may be reproduced, translated or transmitted by
any means except by written permission from the publisher. A reviewer
may quote brief passages in a review.

ISBN 978-0-9825746-2-1

Contents

Introduction 11

PART ONE 19

Key 1
Overcoming the sense of being powerless 19

Key 2
You are consciousness looking at itself 29

Key 3
A new vision for approaching environmental problems 41

PART TWO 51

Key 4
Understanding how the earth was created 51

Key 5
Understanding the basic principle behind all life 69

Key 6
To be a healer, you must overcome your fear of calamity 83

Key 7
To be a healer, you must know your true potential 101

Key 8
Understanding will and power 119

Key 9
Understanding true wisdom 139

Key 10
Flowing with the unconditionality of love 155

Key 11
Accelerating yourself to a higher view of environmental issues   175

Key 12
Bringing a higher truth into the environmental debate   195

Key 13
Overcoming duality in order to give true service   217

Key 14
What it truly means to be free235

PART THREE 255

Key 15
The illusion that there is something wrong with the earth   255

Key 16
A deeper understanding of consciousness   261

Key 17
Understanding the elemental beings 271

Key 18
A deeper understanding of the four elements 281

Key 19
The relationship between humans and elementals   295

Key 20
The process of materialization, of matter realization 311

Key 21
Overcoming the illusion that matter has permanence321

Key 22
Uncovering the central dynamic in human society   335

PART FOUR   353

Key 23
Helping the Earth Mother without doing anything   353

Key 24
Discerning between dualistic and non-dualistic wisdom   371

Key 25
Selfish love will not heal Mother Earth   389

Key 26
Accelerating the environmental debate to a new level   403

Key 27
The immaculate vision for the environmental debate 421

Key 28
Being the open door for peace through oneness   437

Key 29
Individuality is the key to the Golden Age   451

Key 30
Transcending hatred of the Mother   465

Introduction

This book is not for everyone.

This book is released as a gift to those people who have been willing to at least contemplate the old saying that "If you are not part of the solution, you are part of the problem." This book is especially for people who have also been willing to contemplate the saying that "You cannot solve a problem with the same state of consciousness that created the problem."

Once you ascend to the level of awareness, where you begin to realize that all problems seen on earth are the products of a certain state of consciousness, you can then begin to at least glimpse the fact that in order for humankind to find viable solutions to its many problems, there must be a willingness to reach for a higher level of consciousness than the level that precipitated the current problems.

Certainly, there are many people who would instantly object to what I am implying here. They would instantly object to the mere hint that the problems you see on earth could be created by a state of consciousness—for they have been brought up in a thought system which denies the role of consciousness. This might be a religious system, which says that the earth, in its current form, was created by God, and thus it is beyond the powers of man to influence the conditions you see in nature or even on a planetary scale. It may also be people who have been brought up in a materialistic thought system, which says that consciousness is a product of matter, the matter in the brain. And therefore, consciousness does not have the power to influence the matter that is its cause.

So can you begin to see, that this book is not for people who are stuck in the mental box created by traditional religions, nor is it for people who are stuck in the mental box created by materialism? This book is specifically for people who have at least begun to realize that there must be something more to understand about life than what has been defined in either of these mental boxes. And thus, they have begun to realize that in order for humankind to solve the serious problems you see on earth – in anything from natural disasters to environmental problems, to problems in society – well then there must be a new approach.

For these people have begun to realize that the approaches that have been taken so far to these serious problems, have not brought forth a solution. And thus, these people have either already realized – or could very quickly realize – that the only explanation for the fact that no solution has been found must be that human beings have not taken the right approach to these problems.

If human beings are trying to solve a problem from the state of consciousness that precipitated the problem, then is it not obvious why no solution has been forthcoming? And thus, if a solution is to be found, there must be those people who are willing to reach beyond the mental box that precipitated the problem. It is precisely for people who have ascended to this level of awareness and self-awareness that this book is given.

***

Who then is the "I" that is speaking? I am a spiritual being, I am an ascended being. I reside in a realm of energy frequencies that vibrates far beyond the level of what you experience through your physical senses. I am speaking this book through a messenger who has been specifically trained to raise his consciousness and attune it to the higher frequencies in which I reside. Thus, I can use his mind and vocal cords as an open door for bringing forth this message.

If you are open to the existence of spiritual beings and if you are open to the possibility that we can bring forth messages in various ways, then this book is for you. If you are not open to this possibility, then this book has nothing to offer you, as I will not in any way seek to justify or even explain my existence.

It is not my intention with this book to argue for or against certain viewpoints brought forth by the dominant thought systems of the Western world, namely mainstream Christianity and scientific materialism. My purpose for this book is not to present an argument but to present truth that can enlighten those who have already opened their minds to a higher understanding than what has been given in the traditional thought systems. If you are not among these people, simply go in peace, as I am in no way seeking to imply that there is anything wrong with you being in your current state of consciousness.

Introduction   13

The simple reality is that the Word must stand on its own. The Living Word that I give in this book will either resonate with something within you or it will not. If it does resonate with something within your own being, then you will recognize the vibration of truth in the Word I am giving you. If it does not resonate with something in your own being, then you will not recognize it as truth, and you will therefore begin to argue against it with your outer mind. If you desire to engage in this exercise, I respectfully bow to your free will. Yet, I will not in any way seek to cater to those who wish to argue, rather than seeking to know.

Truth is beyond human argumentation—for one simple reason. Those who argue do so because their minds are trapped in a certain mental box. This mental box gives them a certain view, a certain perception, of the world. They believe that their view, that their perception, of the world is either the highest possible one or the only true one. And thus, they are seeking to impose and project their view upon other human beings. They also feel threatened by people who will not agree with their view, and thus they might engage in various uses of force in order to get other people to conform. This is indeed what has created all of the religious or political struggles seen throughout history: One group of people feeling justified in seeking to impose their views upon others, even if it entails using violence or other kinds of force.

I am an ascended being, which means I am above and beyond this dualistic struggle for security. I have security in knowing who I AM, in having attained oneness with the reality that is beyond the mental boxes of human beings.

There are many people on earth, in fact millions of people on earth, who are also at the level – or close to the level – where they realize, that there is a reality beyond the mental boxes defined by human beings, even those defined by the major thought systems of this world. These are the people who have begun to tune in – in their own hearts – to that higher reality. They may have different ways of looking at or defining this higher reality, but they all have one thing in common. They have at least glimpsed that this higher reality is made up of vibrations that are beyond anything in the material world. And thus, they have a frame of reference based on vibration itself, and this is what enables them to tune in to and acknowledge the vibration of truth in my words.

***

I am an ascended being. The name that I have used in most cases, when speaking to human beings on earth, is the name "Mother Mary." This reflects the fact that my last embodiment on earth – my last embodiment out of many embodiments on earth – was as the mother of the being you know as Jesus. During that embodiment, it was my mission to hold the vision for Jesus reaching a certain level of consciousness, and thus fulfilling the mission he came to fulfill.

Despite what you might have been brought up to believe, Jesus' mission had a very specific purpose. That purpose was to demonstrate the potential – that all human beings have – for reaching a higher state of consciousness. What exactly was the state of consciousness that Jesus came to demonstrate? It is a state of consciousness in which you have begun to realize one simple truth, namely that the human mind has the potential to attain power over matter.

Certainly, many people in the modern world have been brought up to look with either indifference or skepticism upon the so-called miracles performed by Jesus. Yet I tell you, that these so-called miracles were not miracles at all. They were the application of a natural law. However, this natural law will not work for people who are below a certain threshold of awareness.

When you are still stuck in a man-made mental box, you will not be able to make use of the natural law that Jesus made use of to perform his so-called miracles. It is only when your level of consciousness reaches beyond a certain threshold, that you become able to put this natural law into motion. And only then will your mind have power over matter.

So this is truly what Jesus came to demonstrate, namely that the human mind has far greater powers than most people suspect. And perhaps you can begin to see how this ties in with my opening remarks about not trying to solve a problem with the same state of consciousness that precipitated the problem?

The problems you currently see on earth were all precipitated from a certain level of consciousness. As long as you look at those problems from within that mental box, the "solutions" you can see will all be defined by the mental box. And thus, you will indeed be seeking to solve a problem with the same state of consciousness that created the problem. This, of course, cannot bring forth a viable solution. For you will inevitably define the cause of the problem as certain other people, and then you will engage in a dualistic struggle to force them to change their

Introduction   15

ways—and thereby – according to your limited vision – bring forth a solution to the problem.

***

Yet, I can assure you that when you look at the history of humankind, it becomes obvious that people who are trapped in this dualistic struggle have never brought forth true solutions to any problems. True solutions have been brought forth only by the people who are willing to reach beyond the mental box of their time and society and look for a new approach.

There was a time when most people on earth believed the earth was a flat disc. Yet there were those who were willing to look through a telescope and study the heaven world. They used the mind's reasoning ability to see that something did not add up, that it simply could not be true that the earth was the center of the universe with the sun and the stars revolving around it. There were those who looked at other conditions known at the time and reasoned that it could not be true that you could sail to the edge of the earth and fall off. And so, these people became the forerunners for a shift in the collective awareness, that eventually caused virtually all people to accept that the earth is indeed round.

This, then, is the only way to bring forth true solutions. You must rise to a higher level of consciousness than the level of consciousness that precipitated the problem. From that higher level of consciousness, you will understand the cause of a problem in a way that you could never do while you were looking at the problem from inside the mental box. And thus, from your higher perspective, the solution to the problem will become obvious.

This is, indeed, the central message behind the mission of Jesus Christ. It was not a mission that was intended to be turned into another dogmatic church, that would do what all the other dogmatic religions have done. It was intended to be a universal mission that could help all people rise beyond their present level of consciousness and continue to do so, until they had finally transcended any and all of the mental boxes created on earth. This was also what Jesus demonstrated, when he gave up the ghost and thus rose above the level of energy that could be perceived by human beings still stuck in their mental boxes.

The entire symbol of Jesus ascending to heaven was indeed meant to outpicture that Jesus rose to a level of self-awareness, that is beyond what most human beings can perceive. Yet this level of awareness is indeed as real as anything you perceive on earth. In fact, it is more real than anything you perceive on earth.

***

My point, then, is that in my last embodiment as Mary, the mother of Jesus, I fulfilled my mission of holding this vision for Jesus and his ascent to a higher state of consciousness. After that embodiment, I also ascended to the higher level of consciousness that Jesus rose to. I have since then been an ascended master, and I have now lovingly volunteered to take on a particular spiritual office for planet earth. The office I hold is that of the Divine Mother for planet earth.

This office has various aspects, which I will explain throughout this book. Yet one of these aspects is, indeed, that I now hold the vision for all human beings that I held for Jesus in my last embodiment. I am holding the vision that all who are willing can indeed ascend to a higher level of consciousness.

I am holding the vision that during this age – during these coming crucial decades – there will indeed be a critical mass among humankind who will raise their consciousness beyond the mental boxes that have created the problems you see on earth. And by these people being willing to be the forerunners, there will be a shift in the collective awareness. There will be an awakening, which will be even more dramatic than what you saw in the Enlightenment, the Renaissance and the Scientific Revolution.

The potential for this present time is indeed an awakening that is unprecedented in human history. This awakening can be an awakening to a greater awareness of the full human potential. Yet, the prerequisite for this awakening happening, is that there must be a critical mass of people who are willing to go beyond their present mental box and consider the full potential of the human mind—or should we say the spiritual mind expressed through human bodies.

If you are concerned about environmental problems, if you are concerned about natural disasters, if you are concerned about the potential for the end of the world, or if you are concerned about the economy or

Introduction   17

other social problems, then I can assure you that the only real solution is to raise your consciousness to a higher level, so that you will gain a different perspective on the problems that you see. By coming to understand the real cause of the problems, you will also gain a new vision of the potential solutions, the real solutions that will not only remove the problem but that will help humankind rise to a higher level of the collective consciousness, so that the problem is no longer created and re-created over and over again.

This, then, is the purpose for this book, namely to offer those who are open, those who are willing, a different perspective on the problems that relate to the physical planet upon which you live. If you are in any way concerned about Mother Earth and about the way human beings relate to Mother Earth, then this book will offer you a different perspective.

May you receive this gift in the same Spirit from which the book is given.

PART ONE

Key 1
Overcoming the sense of being powerless

In this key we will set a foundation that we can build upon, as we continue to explore the connection between mind and matter. And let us begin by considering your situation, as you are reading this book. The very fact that you are open to this book – a book that is claimed to be dictated by a spiritual being through the mind of a human being – demonstrates that you did not fall victim to one of the attempts at social engineering that you were exposed to as a child.

You may look upon many things that happen as you grow up in Western society, and you may think they are relatively innocent. And while they may appear innocent on the surface, I can assure you that there are many hidden things that have the specific purpose of limiting people's ability – and especially their willingness – to think beyond the mental boxes that dominate Western society.

Why are you open to this book? Because you have a natural curiosity about things that are beyond the mental box in which you were brought up. And why do you have this curiosity? Because you refused to submit to the programming that you have been exposed to since childhood. This programming takes many subtle forms, but just take the popular saying that most people have heard as children: "Curiosity killed the cat."

Now my beloved, it may be so that it was curiosity that killed the cat, but it is also so that it was curiosity that elevated humankind from the caveman stage to present-day civilization. When you look at the immense progress that has happened between the time of the caveman and today, you will see that the driving force behind all of this progress has indeed been curiosity, the desire to know, the desire to understand, the willingness to ask questions beyond the current level of understanding held by an individual or a society.

So you do indeed see, I am sure, that curiosity is the driving force behind progress. Yet I am also sure you can see that while there is a force that drives human progress, there is also an opposing force that seeks to hinder, hold back or restrict human progress and human curiosity.

***

I have already talked about the two dominant thought systems of Western civilization, namely Christianity and Materialism. Can you see that both of these thought systems are seeking to limit your curiosity in order to prevent you from asking questions that go beyond what can be explained by either system? So can you see that there is an ongoing force that seeks to expand human understanding, but there is also a constricting force that seeks to limit human understanding to a particular thought system, to a particular mental box?

We will talk more about these forces throughout the book, but for now let me point out two aspects. One is the very personal aspect. There is indeed a force in human psychology that has an insatiable desire for security. This force has been known for a long time to modern psychologists and self-help experts, and it is commonly called the ego. The ego is an element of the human psyche that seeks security above all. One of the ways that people seek to satisfy this quest for security – which is truly a quest for the immortality of the ego – is by adhering to a particular thought system.

In order for a thought system to appeal to the need for security, it must claim to have some ultimate authority. This is what you see in traditional religions, such as the monotheistic religions, which claim to be based on an infallible authority, namely the Bible being the word of God. You see the same tendency in materialistic science, which also claims to have an almost infallible authority based on the so-called objective and undeniable findings of science.

So when people decide to accept either a religious claim to authority or a scientific claim to authority, their egos can feel that these people are now secure in belonging to an ultimate thought system. This, then, allows these people to put aside their curiosity, the questions that are not

Overcoming the sense of being powerless

easily answered. You see, an authoritative thought system offers you a sense of security by defining certain questions as being either beyond what can be known or beyond what human beings are allowed to know. And therefore, you can live a comfortable life in the material world without having to be disturbed by these questions—that cannot easily be answered from the level of consciousness that you currently have.

This, then, allows many people to set aside or ignore their curiosity. Yet I can assure you that this sense of security is bought with a price. For when you set aside curiosity, you will not only abort personal growth but you will also abort growth in society. I am sure you are aware of a period in history called the "Dark Ages." Do you also realize that these dark ages were caused by the fact that the Catholic Church had managed to forcefully suppress all knowledge that went beyond its own doctrines and dogmas? The Catholic Church had effectively created a mental box, and then they had prevented the people of the times from seeking knowledge beyond that box. This is indeed why even the material progress of society was held at a certain level for many centuries.

It was only when this mental box began to be shattered by the early scientists and astronomers, that you saw a revolution in thought that led to the Enlightenment, the Renaissance and the industrial and scientific revolutions. Thus, you see that once the stranglehold of the medieval Catholic Church was broken, then human thought and human invention very quickly caught up to the level it would have been at much earlier, if the Catholic Church had not become a suppressive thought system.

Unfortunately, you will – if you take an honest look at the state of science today – see that even science can be used to create a repressive thought system. There are those who have taken the findings of science and have used them to create a materialistic system, which claims to have proven that there could never be anything beyond the material universe. And thus, this system has simply created another mental box that limits human curiosity. For the system states that while you will not go to hell for eternity for questioning its doctrines, you will certainly be labeled as a person who is unintelligent and superstitious.

***

Now let us take a look at what I said earlier, namely that the original mission of Jesus was to demonstrate the potential for developing the human mind to the state, where the mind has actual power over physical matter. Why did Jesus appear on earth? Well, he appeared precisely because there is indeed a group of ascended beings who have volunteered to take on the task of serving to raise the consciousness of humankind. We who are among the Ascended Host understand very well the dynamics of what is happening on this planet, even though that dynamic is currently unknown to most people.

We understand that the driving force of progress is curiosity, and we understand very well that there is another force seeking to restrict progress by restricting people's willingness to ask questions. It was therefore known to the Ascended Host that at the time when Jesus appeared, there was a need to bring forth new ideas and a new awareness. We are perfectly aware of certain cycles in the evolution of this planet, and we always seek to bring forth new ideas at the opportune moment, when one cycle nears the end and another cycle begins.

If you look at the time of Jesus, you will see that the society in which Jesus appeared was a very restricted and restrictive society. Not only did you have the Roman empire, which had the physical force to restrict people, but you also had the Jewish religion, which had the force to restrict people's minds. And given that the two cooperated to a large extent, you saw a very heavy suppression, both physical and mental. What you basically saw at the time was that the general population were held captive by a small group, a small elite.

This group, this elite, was not homogenous but was indeed divided within itself. Nevertheless, the different divisions were able to cooperate to some extent, in order to maintain their positions of power and privilege. What was this suppression based on? It was based on a particular worldview. There was the view that the world was very limited in size, and thus there was really no way to escape from the society in which you had been born. Then there was the view that the world was a very unpleasant place to be, but that you had the potential to enter a more pleasurable realm after this life. Yet entry into this more desirable realm was restricted to people who fulfilled certain conditions, namely the conditions defined by the prevailing religion of society.

What you see here is, indeed, that there was an elite who had set themselves up in between the people and their God. The people could gain access to God's kingdom, but only by living up to the conditions defined by the elite on earth. Jesus came to challenge this view, and he

Overcoming the sense of being powerless

did so in many ways. He did so by demonstrating that his mind had attained power over matter, and if this had been seen as an example that all could follow, it could indeed have revolutionized society. If more people had understood the essential message behind Jesus' mission – and had indeed learned how to expand the powers of their minds – well, then the dark ages could have been avoided and the Enlightenment could have taken place centuries earlier.

How, then, did the power elite prevent the population from following Jesus' example? Well, they did so by elevating Jesus to an ultimate and superior status as the only son of God—and therefore the only person who could perform such miracles. They created an elaborate doctrine and thought system, which elevated Jesus to the exception instead of the example. And this, then, set the foundation for creating a mental box that made people accept that the powers of their minds were severely limited.

You will see that this mental box survived throughout the Middle Ages without being seriously questioned. It was only with the emergence of the early scientists that some people began to question the mental box upheld by the Catholic Church. Yet unfortunately – as science became more and more accepted in the Western world – the liberating power of science was severely restricted.

***

Once again, you will see that the emergence of science was clearly an expression of the expanding force that gives people their curiosity, their willingness to ask questions beyond the current mental box. Yet you will also see that there was a power elite that did not want people's curiosity to go too far. And so, as the established power elite of the Catholic Church began to lose its power, you saw the emergence of an aspiring power elite who took control over science, or at least the way scientific findings were interpreted. This aspiring power elite then created what is today the materialistic thought system, which claims that there is nothing beyond the material universe.

When you look at how this system was formed, you will see a very clear tendency to suppress knowledge about the powers of the mind. These early materialists attempted to set science up as being in opposition to all religion. They claimed that the obvious flaws of the medieval

Catholic doctrines had proven that all religion is a matter of subjective beliefs that have no objective reality to them. They then came up with the idea that only what was proven through scientific experiments – that could be repeated – could be considered an objective reality. And thus, they managed to make many people believe that the mind was inherently subjective, was inherently unreliable, and therefore should be eliminated from science as much as possible.

This, then, caused a very peculiar condition. The very science that was born from curiosity had now become restricted from exercising curiosity when it came to the human mind. The materialistic paradigm managed to portray the human mind as the product of material processes in the brain. In other words, science – or rather materialism – simply built upon the very paradigm set by the Catholic Church.

As I said, the Catholic Church denied the power of the human mind by elevating Jesus to an exception that no one could follow. Thereby, the church denied the potential that the minds of so-called ordinary human beings could attain power over matter. Materialism simply took this denial to an even higher level by defining the mind as a product of matter.

At least religion was open to the potential that a part of the mind could have been created beyond the material universe and could survive the death of the physical body. Thus, there was at least some opening for the idea that the mind could exist independently of the body. Yet with materialism, it was now seen as an infallible doctrine that the mind is a product of the body and cannot exist before the birth or after the death of the body. It was also seen as an infallible doctrine that the mind does not have the power to go beyond the material universe. And certainly, it follows from there that the mind does not have power over the matter from which it is created.

Do you see the contrast between the true mission of Jesus – which was, of course, an extension of the true mission of the Ascended Host – and what the power elites on earth have been trying to do for millennia? We of the Ascended Host are seeking to raise the consciousness of humankind, to raise the self-awareness of human beings, so they will realize who they are and realize the potential they have for taking command over the matter realm by using their minds.

In contrast, the power elites that seek to rule this world are seeking to prevent people from rising to the level of self-awareness, where they accept that their minds have power over matter. Instead, these power

Overcoming the sense of being powerless

elites are seeking to prevent people from coming to this realization, so that the people will not use the powers of their minds to escape the control of the power elite.

***

This, my beloved, might be a surprising worldview, that you have never heard before. Or perhaps you have heard it in various versions. Nevertheless, I tell you that it is essential for you to begin to ponder this dynamic. It is essential for you to begin to ponder the true nature of the mind and the true powers of the mind. For I can assure you that the current problems you see on Mother Earth were created through the powers of the mind.

You may have been brought up to believe that natural disasters or environmental problems – such as pollution or global warming – have mechanical, physical causes. Certainly, I am not denying that there is a mechanical, physical element. But what I am telling you is that the deeper cause is indeed found in the collective consciousness of humankind.

The reality is that most people on earth have been brought up with a greatly distorted view of who or what human beings truly are. The reality is that you are not human beings, you are spiritual beings who were created for a very specific purpose. You were created not to be passive victims of physical conditions on earth; you were created to serve as co-creators, who would work along with the creators of the earth in order to raise the earth to a higher level than the level at which it was created. Precisely because you were created to fulfill this role, you were given the powers to fulfill this role. And those powers are the powers of the mind.

Whether you realize it or not, whether you believe it or not, human beings are co-creators, and they are constantly co-creating through the powers of their minds. The reality is that human beings are co-creating today, and they have been co-creating for as long as there have been self-aware beings on earth.

The many imbalances and problems you see in Mother Nature today were co-created by human beings through the power of the collective mind. The fact that there are so many imbalances demonstrates one very simple dynamic. The imbalances, that you see outpictured in nature, illustrate the imbalances in the collective consciousness. Human beings have co-created these imbalances, and they are being upheld – and even magnified – through the continued imbalances found in the collective consciousness. If these imbalances are to be removed from nature, then they must first be removed from the collective consciousness. And this can happen only when a critical mass of individuals remove those imbalances from their individual minds.

This is what Jesus came to demonstrate—that one individual can change the world by being willing to raise his or her consciousness. As Jesus said, "If I be lifted up from the earth, I will draw all men unto me." All human beings are connected through the collective mind. Most people on earth are severely restricted by that collective mind, which hangs over them like a heavy weight that limits their curiosity and imagination.

Yet throughout the ages, a large number of individuals have demonstrated that it is possible for anyone to rise above the downward pull of the collective mind. When an individual does so, then that individual will create an upward lift that will raise the collective mind.

Certainly, there is a limit to the effect that can be created by one individual. And that is why Jesus was not meant to raise the world all by himself into some edenic state. Jesus was meant to serve as an example, so that a critical mass of people could follow that example. And when these people collectively raised their consciousness, they would form such an upward momentum that they would be able to raise the consciousness of the whole.

This was the original plan for the mission of Jesus. That plan has not yet come to fruition, but I tell you that there are enough people in embodiment today who have the potential to very quickly awaken to their true mission. And once they awaken to the potential for raising themselves to a higher level of consciousness, well then they can indeed form the critical mass that will cause Jesus' mission to be fulfilled within a surprisingly short period of time.

Part of the purpose for this book is to reach out and awaken these people to see what is the real cause behind their concern for Mother Earth. Your concern is a sign that, deep within your being, you have an inner memory that you have embodied at this specific time for a very particular purpose. And I am now telling you that part of that purpose is indeed to raise your awareness to a higher level, whereby you can become one of the forerunners for raising the collective consciousness to a level that will suddenly expose the essential dynamic I have talked about. This then will enable the population on earth to come to see through the manipulation of the power elite, and thus to throw off the yoke of serving as the literal or virtual slaves for this elite throughout the centuries, and even the millennia.

**

Truly, for Mother Earth to be free from her current burdens, humankind must free itself from the burdens in the collective and individual consciousness. I am aware that many of the people who are concerned about Mother Earth and environmental problems have a tendency to feel powerless. What can one individual do when faced with problems of such enormity as global warming, pollution by international corporations or even the potential for nuclear war? Yet the central message of this book is that there is indeed something that an individual can do.

You are not powerless! You have the power to raise your own consciousness, and thereby you will gain a new vision of the real cause of environmental problems. This will enable you to see solutions that you cannot see at your present level of consciousness.

And thus, I tell you that the sense that you are now powerless is a complete illusion. If you will heed my words and use them to raise your awareness, then the sense of being powerless will simply disappear. Instead, you will feel a new sense of empowerment, for you will realize the truth behind a statement made by Jesus so many years ago: "With men this is impossible; but not with God, for with God all things are possible."

The truth behind this statement is that with the level of consciousness that most people have, then many things are indeed impossible. But when you do raise your level of consciousness beyond a certain threshold, then you will be able to activate the natural laws that Jesus activated when he performed his so-called miracles. And when a critical mass of individuals raise their consciousness to this level, well then you will see a change – even in the physical planet – that from a lower level of consciousness will seem like a miracle. Yet it is not a miracle but the simple result of humankind realizing that the true role of spiritual beings in embodiment is to serve as co-creators and bring the earth to a higher level of balance and abundance. So allow me to take you further into exploring the potential of the mind.

Key 2
You are consciousness looking at itself

I am sure you have heard the saying that history repeats itself. The background for this saying is that we of the Ascended Host use various cycles to present humankind with essentially the same lesson in different disguises. Every time we present this lesson, some among humankind learn the lesson they are meant to learn, while the majority usually does not learn the lesson. And that is precisely why the lesson is then repeated at a future time in a different context.

So with this in mind, take a look at medieval society. The ruling paradigm was the doctrines of the Catholic Church. If you looked at society from an official perspective, there was no alternative allowed. You could be severely persecuted, even tortured and burned at the stake, for questioning Catholic doctrine. Nevertheless, you also know today that there was an underground movement of people who did indeed dare to question Catholic doctrine. They existed in certain secret societies and they existed in the form of the early scientists that had begun to actually investigate the heavens.

Now look at the society you live in today. There is again, at least in many areas of society, an official paradigm, namely scientific materialism. This paradigm says that there is nothing beyond the material world, and therefore all beliefs in some kind of spiritual reality are simply superstitions that are created by the processes in the physical brain. Yet even today you also see a kind of underground movement of many people who are daring to question this official paradigm. Fortunately, the punishment for questioning the official paradigm is not as severe as it was during the Middle Ages. Nevertheless, it still requires some courage – especially for people who hold any kind of position in society – to question that paradigm.

Yet you will see that even though many scientists are not willing to officially question materialism, there are scientists who have for decades been conducting research that clearly points beyond the materialistic paradigm. So let us take a look at some of the findings they have come up with.

**

If you go back to the 1800s, you will see that science had a clearly dualistic view of the world. The world was made of two separate elements, namely matter and energy. They could interact in various ways, but one could not be converted into the other. You will notice that this is very similar to the monotheistic view of two separate compartments, namely heaven and earth.

Then, in 1905, Albert Einstein created the first serious challenge to this dualistic worldview. His Theory of Relativity essentially says that matter does not exist, because everything is made from energy. What most people have not understood is that, beginning in 1905, the official materialistic paradigm has essentially been shattered.

This, again, is very similar to what you saw in the Middle Ages. When Galileo, Copernicus and Kepler started publicizing their findings that the earth could not be the center of the universe, the official Catholic paradigm was effectively shattered. Yet because so many people would not abandon the Catholic faith, the church still survived and maintained a grip on society for a long time after these initial discoveries. And of course, even today the Church has a strong hold of the minds of millions of people around the world.

Nevertheless, can you see that when Albert Einstein published his simple formula e=mc2, then materialism began to crumble? The reason why this happened is that Einstein proved that matter is simply a construct of the human mind and the human senses. The dualistic paradigm of a division between matter and energy is clearly born from the physical senses, which are designed to detect only the energy vibrations that make up physical matter. And thus, to the senses matter seems real. However, there is a reason for this.

As a simple example, you might have seen movies of an airplane propeller, which seen from a certain distance seems to spin so quickly that it forms a solid disc. Yet if you take the movie and slow it down, then you become able to see the movements of the individual propeller

You are consciousness looking at itself   31

blades, and then your eyes can see that there is indeed space between the blades. And so, it is simply a rotating propeller and not a solid disc.

This is the same way your physical senses work. Your senses are designed to detect energy vibrations that vibrate within a certain spectrum of frequencies. Yet your senses are not designed to detect the individual movements, the individual energy waves. Your senses are designed to provide you with the bigger picture, that shows you the forms made up by these individual vibrations.

Thus, when you look at your physical body, you cannot see that your body is made up of smaller units, called cells. Neither can you see that the cells are made up of smaller units, called molecules. And you cannot see that the molecules are made up of atoms or that the atoms are made up of subatomic particles.

So you see, your senses show you a picture of the material world that is focused on the kind of vibrations that make up physical matter. And your senses are not able to see beyond that level of reality. Yet science has undeniably proven that there is a level beyond what your senses can detect, and that this level is completely real. Science has proven the existence of cells, molecules, atoms and subatomic particles.

***

Yet when you take Einstein's finding that everything is made from energy, you will – if you apply simple logic – see that this has shattered the materialistic paradigm. The reason is very simple.

If everything is energy and if everything is vibration, then is there really any limit to what kind of vibrations can exist? As an example, take your physical eyes. They can detect light rays that vibrate within a certain spectrum of frequencies, between red and violet. They cannot detect light rays that vibrate at higher frequencies, such as ultraviolet or many other frequencies detected by science. So you now see that there is only a narrow spectrum of vibrations that can be detected by the senses, but science has discovered that there is a continuum of vibrations beyond the spectrum that can be detected by the senses.

And you know very well that science has also discovered many areas where there is a continuum that goes on indefinitely. For example, take a simple idea, such as numbers. There is no limit to how far you can continue to count. Literally, the numerical scale is infinite, as far as science knows today. So with this in mind, is it not also logical that there is a virtually unlimited continuum of possible vibrations? And when you realize that such a continuum exists, how can science then say that there is nothing beyond the material universe?

Do you see that when scientists define the material universe, they define it in a very narrow way. They define it based on what they can detect with the instruments they have developed up until this point. This is really not that different from the medieval Catholic theologians, who had defined the limits to human knowledge based on their interpretation of Scripture and their definition of doctrine. Can you see that what materialists have done is to simply artificially create a barrier, a boundary, and then they have said that human curiosity is not allowed to go beyond it. And this is exactly what medieval theologians had done.

Therefore, it should be no surprise that many scientists, philosophers and even many spiritually minded people have indeed dared to think beyond the mental box created by materialism. Yet let me stay with science. Based on Einstein's discoveries that everything is energy, a new branch of science was developed. It is normally called quantum mechanics, or quantum physics. This branch of science studies the very small, namely the atom itself.

Originally the word "atom" came from the Greek philosophers, and it signified the smallest possible particle that could not be divided into smaller units. Yet modern scientists have discovered that what they call the atom can indeed be divided into units, namely subatomic particles. They have also discovered that these particles have some very strange properties. One of them is what is called the wave-particle duality, namely that a particle will sometimes act like a wave and sometimes act like a particle.

Thus, you might realize that it would be more practical to no longer talk about subatomic "particles" but something else, such as subatomic "entities." It turns out that if scientists conduct an experiment that is designed to detect particles, then the subatomic entity will behave like a particle. But if they conduct an experiment that is designed to detect waves, then the same subatomic entity will behave like a wave.

Scientists are still baffled by this today, but it is because they have not been willing to think outside the mental box that goes all the way back to sensory perception. The senses can only detect something that has substance, that has mass. And scientists are still thinking based on

You are consciousness looking at itself 33

this form of perception. What they need to realize is that the wave-particle duality proves the need to go beyond sensory-based thinking.

It is not that a subatomic entity can change shape and be either a particle or a wave. It is that a subatomic entity is an entirely different construct, that is neither a particle nor a wave. This subatomic entity needs to be conceived of in an entirely new way that goes beyond particle and wave.

***

Before I go deeper into that, we need to take another look at some of the startling findings of quantum physics. One of the cornerstones of materialism is that science is entirely objective, whereas all spiritual or religious beliefs are entirely subjective. This claim is based on conducting scientific experiments that will yield the same results regardless of the beliefs of the person performing the experiment. It is therefore believed that the consciousness of the scientist has no influence on the outcome of the experiment.

What quantum physics has proven beyond any doubt is that this assumption is not true at the level of subatomic entities. When a scientist studies a subatomic entity, then it is inevitable that the consciousness of the scientist will influence the outcome of the experiment. The outcome of the experiment is a product of three factors: the subatomic entity, the instrument used to study it, such as a particle accelerator, and the consciousness of the scientist.

What most scientists have not been willing to do is to look at the philosophical consequences of this discovery. One of them is obviously the fact that scientists can no longer afford to ignore consciousness. Certainly, at the macroscopic level of visible things, you can conduct an experiment that is not in a visible way affected by the consciousness of the scientist.

Yet you also know that everything that you see is made up of subatomic entities. And therefore, the deeper laws that govern the behavior of subatomic entities will also have a fundamental influence at the level of macroscopic things. And since it has now been proven that the consciousness of the scientist can interact with subatomic entities, then it is no longer feasible to say that objective science can be conducted while ignoring consciousness.

The artificial construct that science decided to ignore the human mind cannot be upheld, when you truly apply the logical consequences of quantum physics. And this, then, proves that it is absolutely necessary that science begins to study consciousness and the potential of the mind.

***

However, there are other philosophical consequences of the discoveries of quantum physics. One of these is that subatomic entities have no physical substance or existence. It has been proven that such entities can appear seemingly out of nowhere and disappear back into nowhere. From a logical viewpoint, this is not a feasible conclusion. Something cannot appear out of nowhere. So given that it has been observed that a subatomic particle can suddenly appear where there was "nothing" before, the only logical consequence is that there must be a realm beyond what is currently detected. In this realm, the subatomic entity can exist as a potentiality, but then something causes it to cross a threshold or boundary and appear as a physical particle.

Certainly, there are already many scientists who have begun to speculate about this realm. Some have called it a ground state, a quantum field or other names. The point I want to bring up here is that what science has discovered is completely parallel to what mystical and spiritual people have been saying for thousands of years, namely that there is a realm beyond the material world. If you take Einstein's findings, it becomes very easy to see that this realm is simply made up of vibrations that are of such high frequencies that they cannot be detected by physical instruments.

As you know, there is a limit to what any instrument made out of matter can detect. A telescope can only see so far into space. You also know that science has realized, for example, that the universe is so vast and so old that there are stars and galaxies that cannot be seen from earth because the light has not had time to reach earth. And thus, scientists are aware of something called an observation horizon.

My point being that there is indeed a realm of vibrations that has not yet been detected by science—and that will never be detected through instruments made out of matter. However, this does not mean that this realm needs to remain undetected. For human beings have another instrument that is designed to detect vibrations that are beyond what can be detected by the senses or even the physical instruments that essentially extend the range of the senses.

That instrument is the human mind. The human mind does indeed have the potential to liberate itself from the body and the physical senses. This does not mean that the mind loses awareness. And thus, the mind can travel into the realms that are beyond the material universe. Throughout the ages, many people have developed this ability to a larger or smaller degree. I would say that all who are interested in this book have already developed this ability to the degree that they know – through an inner knowing that is beyond outer proof or intellectual reasoning – that there is a reality beyond the material realm.

Certainly, the person who is speaking these words has developed the ability to tune in to a higher realm and receive energy impulses that are, then, translated into words through his lower mind, brain and nervous system, and vocal cords. Yet of course, many other people have developed similar or different abilities to detect what is beyond the material world. If scientists would be willing to study this phenomenon – as some, of course, have already started to do – then there could be an entirely new field of scientific study that would bring about a fundamental paradigm shift.

***

Let me briefly describe certain other findings of science. Quantum mechanics studies the very small, but the science of cosmology studies the very large, namely the universe as a whole and galaxies. What cosmology has proven is that the universe is not fixed in size. Medieval theologians believed that the entire universe was a very small dome that extended over the flat disc of the earth. Yet science has, of course, proven that the universe is far larger, in fact almost unlimited in size. Science has also proven that this universe is not only expanding, but it is expanding at an accelerated rate. Now my beloved, put this together with another current theory of science, namely that of the Big Bang.

The theory says that at some point in the distant past, about 15 billion years ago, the entire material universe was compressed into what is called a singularity. Then, supposedly, a giant explosion occurred that hurled all matter out from a central point. This matter then gradually began to form various particles that organized themselves into atoms and molecules, and gradually – through a completely mindless evolutionary process – formed the incredibly vast and complex universe you see today.

Scientists believe that this happened according to certain laws of nature, one of which is the first law of thermodynamics, which says that energy is always conserved. In other words, the total amount of energy that is available to the current universe was released in the Big Bang. No energy has been added to the universe since the Big Bang.

Now my beloved, if it is really true that no energy has been added to the universe since the Big Bang 15 billion years ago, how can you then explain that the universe is expanding at an accelerating rate? What drives this acceleration?

According to science, everything must be driven by energy. Yet if the total amount of energy available was released in the Big Bang, does it not stand to reason that the universe should be gradually running out of energy that is available for expansion? If you take a bullet being fired by a gun, then all of the energy available to drive that bullet is released in the initial explosion. And as the bullet travels away from the gun, it will gradually lose energy and therefore eventually fall to the ground. So if all of the energy available for the expansion of the universe had been released in the Big Bang, then it should not be possible that the universe could be expanding at an accelerated rate. The acceleration should have slowed down, and the universe should have started contracting.

There is, of course, a way to explain this, and it is to take a look at what science has already discovered about the Big Bang. Scientists are aware that in the first milliseconds after the Big Bang, the laws of physics, the laws of nature that you see today, did not exist. They had "broken down." This means many things that scientists have not yet fully understood. But what it truly means is that the singularity that preceded the Big Bang could not have been part of the material universe that you see today. There literally was no material universe before the Big Bang. There was no time, there was no space, there was no matter, there was no energy. There truly was nothing before the Big Bang that has any resemblance to what you see in the universe today. So what, then, did exist before the Big Bang?

***

You are consciousness looking at itself

This is a question that scientists cannot currently explain. Yet there is a logical explanation—but only if you are willing to go beyond materialism. The logical explanation is that before the Big Bang, there was no physical, material universe, but this does not mean that there was nothing. There was "no thing" but there was not "nothing." Because what existed before the Big Bang was a realm of frequencies that is beyond any of the frequencies used to construct the material universe.

This level of frequencies is what I would like to call the spiritual realm. In this realm you find conscious self-aware beings who have existed for a much longer time span than the material universe. This is not inconsistent with the consequences of quantum physics and cosmology. What quantum physics has proven is a clear connection between the human consciousness, the human mind, and the very basic building blocks of the material universe.

Today, you live in what is called an information society, but there are scientists who have begun to speculate that you actually live in an information universe. I have talked about a subatomic entity that can take on the form of a particle or wave. Yet what determines what form this entity will take on, what tells the entity to take on the form of a wave instead of a particle? Well, when you begin to ponder these questions, you see that what Einstein did was to take one step towards a deeper understanding of reality, but he did not take the full step.

When you look at the world through the perception of the physical senses, you see a world made out of solid matter, and this matter appears very real to the senses. When you go to the deeper level of perception that was opened up by Einstein's findings, you see a different world, a world where matter has no reality or independent existence, because everything is made out of energy—vibrations. Yet when you go to the even deeper level of perceiving at the level of quantum physics, then you see that the world is not truly made out of energy. The world is made out of information.

***

Yet it does not end there. There is an even deeper level of perception. For what, my beloved, is information? Does information have an existence independently of consciousness? There are, of course, many people who will immediately say that information can exist on its own. For example, they will say that the libraries of the world contain billions of books that store information. They will say that the world has millions of computers that store vast amounts of information on their hard drives and servers. Yet does a computer truly store information, or does it simply store data? Does a book store information, or does it simply store letters and numbers? Does the computer know what is stored on its hard drive? Does a book know what is stored on its pages?

You see my point, do you not? What is in a book is not information—any more or any less than what is in a rock or a galaxy. One of the old Greek philosophers, named Pythagoras, said that everything is numbers. He might as well have said that everything is information.

What scientists have already proven is that there is information encoded in everything. And what scientists are attempting to achieve is to decode the information in nature, so they can understand why nature works the way it does and why it takes on the form that it does. This is the entire purpose of science—to decode the information that is stored in nature.

Yet what is it that scientists are using in their attempts to decode this information? You might say they are using scientific instruments, but does a telescope really reveal information about a distant star? Or does the light rays passed on by the telescope become information only when they enter and are processed in a conscious mind?

When you open up your computer and the computer displays data on the screen, even the data on the screen is not information. It only becomes information when it enters your mind and is processed there, by you attaching some meaning to what is otherwise meaningless data. Do you not see, my beloved, that what I have previously called curiosity is the desire for meaning, the desire to find patterns and meaning in everything you see around you in the material universe?

This is humankind's oldest quest. But where does this quest come from, where does this quest take place? It comes from a deep inner desire to know, a deep inner desire to find meaning. And the quest itself takes place within the human mind!

Why is this so? It is so because the fundamental building block of everything that exists is indeed consciousness—consciousness itself. Everything is created out of consciousness. And what you experience in yourself, as the drive to know and understand, is consciousness longing to experience itself through you.

What drives the quest for both a spiritual understanding and a rational, scientific understanding is the drive of consciousness to look at itself through you. This has some important ramifications that we will explore in the following key.

Key 3
A new vision for approaching environmental problems

Let us begin by looking at your experience as a human being on earth. You live in a very exciting time, when humankind has made immense progress, and where it seems as if every day new discoveries are made, new forms of technology are developed. Yet what is it that drives this immense progress? It is indeed that humankind has expanded its understanding of the world.

Yet what is the basis for this expansion of understanding? Well, from a superficial viewpoint you might say that it is information. Human beings today have infinitely more information about the material universe and how it works than the cavemen of only a few thousand years ago. And it is certainly true that information has driven progress, but as I have just explained, there is a deeper dimension. For where does information exist? It exists only in the human mind. It becomes useful only when processed by a human mind.

You may take all of the information discovered about the physical universe and encode it into a computer. You can get the computer to organize and manipulate this information in various ways, but you cannot get the computer to understand what this information means to a human mind. So can you see that even though people have made tremendous progress, this progress has been made only on one side of the coin of life?

Human beings, at least in the Western world, have so far ignored the other side of the coin of life. They have attempted to gather information about the material world, but they have not attempted to study the very instrument that allows them to gather and apply this information, namely the human mind.

So can you also begin to glimpse that if people would indeed start studying the mind, then even more progress could be made than what you see today? What I am giving you here is an alternative to the worldview of both religion and materialistic science. What I am giving you is a vision that everything in the material universe, including Mother Earth, is truly made up through a process that has not yet been understood by either mainstream religion or science.

***

Let me give you a deeper description of this process. Let us begin by going beyond the material universe. I have said that the material universe exists in a certain spectrum of frequencies and that there are energy frequencies beyond the material universe, namely a spiritual realm.

If you continue to go towards higher and higher frequencies, you would – from a logical, linear viewpoint – think you would end up at the ultimate frequency. This is both true and not true. There is indeed a highest frequency in what we might call the world of form, but this highest frequency is not the ultimate reality. For you see, for there to be a frequency, there must be a wave, and for there to be a wave, there must be something that can vibrate. A wave in the ocean propagates through the medium of water, a radio wave propagates through a medium, as does sound.

So what you realize is that for there to be any kind of vibration, there must be some basic substance or reality that can be put into vibration. Where does this basic substance come from? Well, if you go beyond the realm of what vibrates, you go into an entirely different realm that cannot be fathomed by the linear state of consciousness and cannot be described by the linear medium of words. Yet this is nevertheless a state of consciousness. It is a unified, omnipresent state of awareness, which is what people for many thousands of years have been calling God, although most of the people who use the word "God" have not even begun to understand the state of consciousness I am talking about.

Any time you see people talk about a God and then apply some kind of form, some kind of linear form to that God, they have not understood the true nature of God. In reality, God is beyond anything that has form, anything that vibrates. When you go beyond the level of vibration, then you go into the pure awareness that is God. This is a self-aware being, which I would like to call the Creator.

A new vision for approaching environmental problems   43

This Creator is the source, the origin, of the entire world of form in which you live. Yet this Creator is nothing like the Old Testament God, or the many other images of God found in religions around the world.

The Creator has no form; the Creator is the source of form. The Creator is a self-aware being with a state of consciousness – self-awareness – that is beyond what anyone on earth can even begin to fathom. You can, however, use the mind's ability to get at least a glimpse of this state of awareness, and throughout the ages many people have indeed had such mystical experiences.

The Creator is a self-aware being with a desire to create, to express itself. This is not something that was forced upon the Creator. It is driven by love, an unconditional form of love that wants to be expressed and that finds ultimate joy in expressing itself. Thus, the Creator created the world of form, in which you live, out of pure love, out of pure joy.

***

Yet how did the Creator create the world of form? We have released another book, given by Lord Maitreya,[1] that explains this in more detail, but I will give a brief summary here. In the Creator's self-awareness there can be no distinction, no separation. Thus, it actually is not possible for the Creator to create something that has a distinct or separate form. So in order to create anything, the Creator must begin by creating a void in which forms can exist and appear to be separate. Thus, we might say that the Creator withdrew its own Being, its own Presence, and created a space, a void.

The Creator, then, created a sphere in the center of this void. This sphere was created out of the basic substance of creation, which is what I, in another book,[2] have called the Ma-ter light. This is a substance that cannot be detected by any material instrument, for the simple reason that it has no form. It does not even have vibration, but it has the potential to be stirred into vibrations. If you want a linear illustration – which, of course, can only be inaccurate – then consider the ocean when it is completely still and without any waves. This ocean can be said to have no waves, but when a wind starts blowing, then the ocean can be stirred into waves. And the waves can be detected, but the ocean itself cannot.

1   Master Keys to Spiritual Freedom
2   Master Keys to the Abundant Life

This Ma-ter light, however, is not something that exists separately from or independently of the Creator. The Creator fashions the Ma-ter light out of its own Being, out of its own consciousness. For at the level of the Creator, there is nothing but consciousness.

After having created the initial sphere and having created certain structures, certain forms, within that sphere, the Creator then projected extensions of itself into that sphere. These extensions took on the form of separate beings with a localized sense of self-awareness. This is in contrast to the Creator, which has an omnipresent, non-localized sense of self-awareness. We might say that the Creator is able to look at its creation from every single point at the same time, but it cannot look at its creation from one single point exclusively. It attained this capability only by creating extensions of itself that appear as separate, individual beings that look at the world of form from a particular, localized vantage point.

After this initial sphere was created, the self-aware extensions of the Creator began the process of expanding their sense of self-awareness, until they no longer saw themselves as separate, localized beings but had become aware of themselves as extensions of the omnipresent Creator. And when they had attained that level of self-awareness, their entire sphere was raised to a higher level of vibration. Their entire sphere ascended and now became part of what you today – from your vantage point – see as the spiritual realm.

***

The initial sphere was not the only sphere. There have been several of these spheres, and your material universe is part of the latest of these, which is the seventh in number. The latest sphere in which you find yourself has not yet reached the ascension point, because there are not enough beings within it who have reached the level of self-awareness, where they see themselves as extensions of the Creator.

Do you see that the purpose for the entire world of form is not, as traditional religion might have it, that the Creator desires to be worshiped and admired? The deeper purpose is that each self-aware extension of the Creator has the potential to expand its self-awareness, until it reaches the same level of awareness as the Creator.

A new vision for approaching environmental problems 45

In the New Testament there is a situation, where Jesus is accused of blasphemy, and he refers to a statement from the Old Testament, which says: "Ye are gods." The reality is that each human being is a God in the making. Regardless of the level of self-awareness you have today, you have the potential to expand your self-awareness and to continue to do so.

The first threshold that will be passed for you is when you reach the level of the ascension, where you can ascend from the material realm and become an ascended, immortal being in the spiritual realm that is right above the material universe in vibration. Yet even from there you can continue to grow through all of the previous spheres, until you reach the highest of these spheres. And then you can cross another threshold and attain the self-awareness of a Creator. Thereby you become able to create your own world of form, your own universe. This is the purpose of life, the purpose of creation: the growth in self awareness.

What has happened on earth – from the caveman stage to the present civilization – is that there has been a growth in self-awareness. And this growth could take a quantum leap if the people who are ready – and who have taken embodiment for this purpose – would become more aware of the potential of the human mind.

For when you take what I have told you here and in the previous keys, you realize that everything is created out of one basic substance, that I call the Ma-ter light. This Ma-ter light has the potential to take on any form, yet it cannot take on form by itself. It takes on form when a self-aware being envisions at particular form and then projects that form onto the Ma-ter light.

Do you recall I said that the so-called miracles performed by Jesus were not miracles but the application of a higher natural law? Well, the reality is that when you reach a certain level of self-awareness, you become able to activate this natural law. Thereby, you will be able to consciously formulate an image and consciously project it onto the Ma-ter light, whereby you will instantly see the Ma-ter light conform to the image and thereby manifest the form that you envisioned.

When Jesus looked at a man with a withered hand, his consciousness did not see what the consciousness of most human beings would have seen. He did not see a withered hand; he did not see any imperfect state as real or permanent. Jesus saw beyond the outer form of the withered hand. He saw that the withered hand was made up of a basic substance that had only temporarily taken on the form of the withered hand. Yet Jesus also saw that this substance, this Ma-ter light, could as easily take on the form of a perfectly healthy hand as the form that it had temporarily taken on.

Jesus saw that the withered hand was simply a manifestation of the man's imperfect and unbalanced state of consciousness. And thus, what Jesus did was that he held the vision for a healthy hand, and he super-imposed that vision upon the Ma-ter light that made up the withered hand. And because Jesus' consciousness was so much higher than the consciousness of the man with the withered hand, Jesus' consciousness could override the other man's consciousness and thus instantly heal the hand.

Yet be careful to realize that there were people that sought healing from Jesus but Jesus did not heal them. The reason is that Jesus did not come to do everything for everyone; he came to show people what they have the power to do by developing the same state of consciousness that Jesus had attained. Thus, he only performed certain healings as a demonstration of what was possible. And it was, of course, the intention that people should then use this to develop the powers of their own minds, instead of looking to Jesus to do it all for them.

And this is, indeed, the shift that needs to happen among the spiritual and open-minded people in today's world. If you are truly concerned about planet earth and the future of planet earth, then the most important thing you can do is to begin to expand your understanding of the human mind and its true potential.

***

You may, right now, look at environmental problems or natural disasters and think you are powerless to change them. But as I have said before, this is because you are looking at these problems through the filter of the same state of consciousness that created them. That state of consciousness is very much focused on the material world, and it tends to see material conditions as real. Therefore, to this state of consciousness material conditions form a real limitation, a real boundary, for human capabilities. Yet, as I have attempted to explain, once you raise your consciousness beyond that level, you begin to glimpse – gradually and over time – that there is a deeper understanding of life.

A new vision for approaching environmental problems 47

Matter is not truly as real as it appears to the senses and a certain level of awareness. And once you begin to realize that matter is not ultimately real, then you also begin to accept that matter does not form an impenetrable boundary. Matter is not beyond change.

You may look at planet earth today, and you may think that pollution or global warming has gone beyond a threshold from which there is no way back, and things can only get worse. But once you raise your awareness, you see that every condition that could possibly exist in a physical form can be changed by applying a higher vision. Once you begin to realize that every physical form is the outpicturing of information that has been applied to the basic substance of the Ma-ter light, well then, my beloved, you realize that any physical form can be changed by applying different information to that same Ma-ter light.

***

This is not unlike what you have experienced when working on a computer. You know that what appears as images on your computer screen does not have an ultimate reality. You can, in various ways, change the appearance of any image on your computer screen, and how is this accomplished?

The image on the computer screen is made up entirely of information. On the computer's hard drive or in its memory, the image you see does not exist; there are only "zeros" and "ones" arranged in different sequences. So by applying a different sequence, a different form of information, you can change the image on the computer screen, and you can do so instantly. The computer screen has the capability to display any image you can imagine, but of course it cannot imagine images on its own. So it can only outpicture what you apply to it.

This is the same with Mother Earth. Mother Earth has the potential to outpicture the abundant life and a completely balanced state of nature. The current imbalances – in the form of natural disasters, pollution or the lack of resources or food – are brought about because Mother Earth is outpicturing the imbalances in the collective consciousness of humankind. Yet if a critical mass of people will attain a higher vision – and use the powers of their minds to superimpose that vision upon the physical planet – then you will indeed begin to see changes.

Take note that I am not hereby saying that those who are concerned about the future of Mother Earth should not take physical actions. I am not trying to say that you should sit in a cave in the Himalayas and meditate all day and that you should withdraw from society. On the contrary, it is not my intention here to say that people who have been engaged in the environmental issue or social or political issues should withdraw.

However, it is indeed my intention to say that if you will make an effort to raise your level of consciousness, you will find that you will gradually begin to attain a new understanding, a new vision, of the problems that you today might see as being beyond change. And thus, you will gain a new foundation for engaging yourself in society. You will become one of the forerunners for taking the debate in society to a new and higher level, where indeed people will begin to see solutions that they cannot see today.

Can you see, my beloved, that there was a time when people had not discovered bacteria, and therefore many diseases seemed completely incurable. Yet with the simple discovery of bacteria as the cause of many diseases, there was – instantly – a shift in the debate around health. Suddenly, people could see ways to cure diseases that had not been seen before. Is it therefore that difficult to understand, that if the environmental debate, and the general debate in society, could be lifted to a higher level, then people would begin to find ways to combat pollution and global warming that simply cannot be seen today?

It is not that the solutions are not there; it is simply that they have not been discovered. But the reason why they have not been discovered is that so far the debate has been centered on superficial conditions that are not the real cause. Yet, if the debate was to be expanded to include the deeper causes, then the solutions would become apparent.

This, then, is the vision I wanted to give you in order to set a foundation for the coming sections of this book. We have now set a sufficient foundation, and I would therefore like to take the book in a slightly different direction. It may seem as if what is going to follow will go in a different direction than you might expect. Yet I assure you that I have good reason for making this shift. For it is indeed our intention to give you a deeper understanding of how the material universe was created, before we then again begin to talk more specifically about the state of Mother Earth, including environmental problems and such problems as the fact that two thirds of the world's population is living beneath

A new vision for approaching environmental problems 49

the poverty level, with millions and millions of people living one meal away from starvation.

So allow me to build upon the foundation and give you a deeper understanding of the spiritual causes behind the material phenomena with which you are concerned.

PART TWO

Key 4
Understanding how the earth was created

It may seem as if what I am advocating here is a worldview that is similar to the one presented by most religions for thousands of years on this planet. This, however, is not the case. If you look at especially Western Christianity, you will see that this religion is based – as is all of the so-called great monotheistic religions – on a fundamentally dualistic worldview. Christianity makes it clear that the world can be divided into two separate and distinct spheres, namely the material world and the heaven world. Christianity also makes it clear, that there is an impenetrable barrier between the two worlds, so that only people who live up to certain conditions will be allowed to enter the kingdom of God.

Although it is not my intention here to go into a deeper description about the shortcomings of this dualistic worldview, I will point out a very simple reality. The dualistic worldview presented by the Christian religion – in the name of Christ – is in direct opposition to the non-dualistic worldview presented by Jesus himself. Jesus did not say that there was an impenetrable barrier between the heaven world and the world in which you live. Jesus was killed by the orthodox religious people of his time, precisely because he challenged the worldview that says there is a barrier—and therefore you can enter the kingdom of heaven only by living up to certain conditions defined by an external religious authority on earth.

If you look at monotheistic religions, and even many other religions in the world, you will see a distinct pattern. They all present the view that you are separated from God by an impenetrable barrier, a barrier that you cannot go through on your own power. Yet there is a way for you to get through this pearly gate into the kingdom of heaven, but only if you blindly follow the leaders of the external religion. This is the view that Jesus challenged, when he said that the kingdom of God is at hand and that the kingdom of God is within you. Do you see that in this foundational statement – often overlooked ignored or interpreted away by Christian preachers – Jesus challenged the dualistic worldview?

Instead, he said that there is no fundamental barrier between you and God's kingdom, because the only real barrier is found in your own consciousness. It is possible for you to enter the kingdom of heaven by going within yourself and doing what Jesus told all people to do, namely to stop looking at the splinter in the eyes of their brothers and instead look for the beam in their own eye.

Can you begin to sense that this is not a dualistic worldview? What Jesus gave was a view which says that you are not separated from God's kingdom by any external barrier. In fact, you are not separated from God's kingdom at all, for did not Jesus say "I and my father are one?" So you see, what orthodox Christianity has done is essentially the same that the priests of the materialistic religion are attempting to do today, namely to say that you are confined to the material universe and that your mind does not have the power to go beyond the material universe on its own.

The religious authorities said that you have no ability to know truth on your own, and therefore you should blindly believe in their doctrines. And the priests of materialism are likewise saying that you cannot know truth on your own, and therefore you should blindly follow their doctrines—which they claim are not doctrines but are based on the undeniable, indisputable and objective findings of science. Yet it is not objective to look at the world through a materialistic instrument – and fail to see anything beyond the material world – and then interpret this as proof that there is nothing beyond the material realm. This is not objective science. This is a political interpretation that is no different in nature than many of the doctrines constructed by medieval Catholic theologians in order to control the minds of the people.

Do you see that if you look at world history, there has always been a small elite who has been seeking to control the population? And the most effective way to control the population is not through physical force but through mental force—by controlling people's minds and thinking. And thus, this power elite has always been seeking to force people to limit

Understanding how the earth was created

their imagination, to limit their thinking – their reasoning, their intuition – to the mental box defined by the system constructed by the elite, be it a religious, a political or a scientific-materialistic system.

***

Now, I am not hereby trying to say that all of the people who are advocating a particular system as the ultimate source of truth have an evil intent, or even that they are knowingly seeking to control the thinking of the people. Many of these people are indeed well-meaning, but they do not understand that they are being used by a small elite who is intent on controlling every aspect of life on this planet. And thus, it is understandable that many scientists will balk at what I am saying here and will indeed deny that they are in any way seeking to control people's thinking. Yet, the deeper reality here is that being well-meaning is not the same as being aware of what one is doing in a larger context.

There is an event horizon, an observation horizon, beyond which you cannot see. But there is also a psychological equivalent of this observation horizon, which is the fact that there are certain things people are not willing to see, even though they might be capable of seeing it—either with their physical eyes or with the deeper senses of the mind itself.

You will see, for example, that medieval Catholic leaders were fully capable of looking through a telescope and observing the movements of the stars in the sky, the very same movements observed by Galileo, Kepler and other early astronomers. Yet they were not willing to see that these findings invalidated the Catholic doctrine that the earth was the center of the universe and therefore the earth was extremely important to God and to God's plan for the universe.

Likewise, you will see that there are scientists – or scientifically minded people – who are not willing to look beyond the observation horizon defined by the materialistic paradigm. They are not willing to look at the findings of quantum physics and realize and acknowledge that these findings have proven that there is indeed something beyond the material universe. And therefore, the fundamental doctrine of materialism has been disproven as effectively as the fundamental Catholic doctrine about the earth being the center of the universe.

This, then, brings us to a dividing line. I need you to start considering whether your upbringing has imposed an observation horizon upon your mind, beyond which you are reluctant to venture. Is it possible that as you grew up in whatever society and culture you encountered, your mind has been programmed to take certain things for granted and consider them to be such self-evident truths that there is no reason to question them, no reason to look beyond them?

Why is it so essential for you to consider this idea? I have said from the very beginning that this book is aimed at those who have the potential to awaken and become part of the solution, part of the people who will bring humanity to a new and higher level of awareness—that will then allow humanity to transcend some of the physical limitations and problems that you currently see on Mother Earth. Yet what is the basis for you becoming one of these forerunners? How can you help humankind transcend the old level of consciousness, if you have not yourself transcended that level of consciousness first? And how can anyone transcend a certain level of consciousness without going beyond the observation horizon, the mental box, defined by the old level of consciousness?

**

My beloved, consider what I mean when I talk about a certain level of consciousness, and let us use an obvious example that I have mentioned before. If you go back around 500 years on the European continent, virtually every human being on that continent accepted the ideas that the earth was a flat disc and that it was the center of the universe. You may look back today and think that this was a ridiculously limited worldview. You may even reason that medieval people therefore were ignorant or less intelligent than you are today. I will not deny that there has been somewhat of a growth in the intelligence level of humankind as a whole, which means that there are people in today's world who have a higher level of intelligence than the people of medieval times. Yet it would be extremely naïve to believe that medieval people in general were more stupid than people today.

There were many people in medieval times whose intelligence was far beyond that of the average population of today. And yet, when you go back to medieval society, you will see that even the most intelligent

Understanding how the earth was created

people in the population believed in these ideas of a flat earth and an earth-centered universe. Why did they believe in these ideas? Simply because they had been brought up to see them as so self-evident that there was no reason to question them. They had therefore simply accepted these ideas and had then gone on with what they saw as their life's mission, whatever that might have been.

And so, what you see is that it took a few individuals who were willing to question what hardly anyone else questioned in order to bring society out of the mental box, and up from the level of consciousness represented by medieval society. And even after the few started questioning these unquestionable paradigms, it took quite some time before the population at large began to open their minds to the possibility that these unquestionable truths needed to be questioned. And actually, it took that the old generation passed away, before there was a widespread acceptance of the idea, or should we say the reality, that the earth is round.

Yet in today's world, there is the potential that many more people can awaken much more quickly and therefore bring society to a new level of awareness more quickly than it happened in medieval times. If you have read this book up until this point, you should count yourself among the people who have the potential to become part of this shift in awareness. Yet in order for that potential – your personal potential – to become a manifest reality, you need to open your mind to the need to question some of the paradigms, some of the self-evident truths, that you have grown up to believe. You need to open your mind to the need to question the unquestionable, to realize that the self-evident may not be as evident when you take a closer look—but may indeed either be an incomplete or a completely incorrect view of reality.

***

Let me now explain to you an even deeper layer of why this is so important. Let me begin by explaining to you how planet earth was actually created. A very long time ago, in a "country" far, far away – as many fairy tales begin – there was a group of beings who came together and decided to exercise their creative powers in creating a new solar system.

My beloved, you may have grown up taking for granted the planet upon which you live, the sun that gives you light and life and the solar system that allows your planet to stay at a distance from the sun that makes material life possible. Yet I can assure you that starting with "nothing" and creating such an intricately balanced system is not an easy task.

First of all, you need a driving force, which is the equivalent of your physical sun. This driving force was represented by two beings who had attained a very high level of consciousness. These beings had not attained that level of consciousness in the sphere in which the material universe is found. They had attained it in a previous sphere, and they had attained that level of consciousness by helping to bring that sphere to the ascension point, where it became a self-sufficient, self-sustaining aspect of the Creator's unfolding world of form. These beings had then volunteered to lay down their attainment in the bringing forth of the very next sphere, in which the material universe is found. Because of their attainment, they were able to become the open doors between the higher sphere and the newly created sphere that has not yet reached the ascension point and become self-sustained, selfluminous.

You see, when a new sphere is created, it is created by the beings in the sphere that has just ascended. It is created by them extending their own beings to form the spiritual energy or substance that is the very basis for creating the new sphere. You will notice from your own world that even physical movements have two aspects. There is momentum, which is the driving force that causes an object to move. And then there is direction, which is the information that directs the movement of the object in a certain direction or to a certain result.

You see, then, that when a sphere has gone through the process of the ascension, there are beings in that sphere who have reached a level of consciousness where they become self-luminous, they become able to tap into the flow of the Creator's Being that is sustaining the world of form. These beings become the open doors through which the River of Life, that is the Creator's Being, can flow into the next sphere that is being created.

**

The material universe, as we have seen, is created out of a basic substance, a basic form of energy, that vibrates within a certain frequency spectrum. Yet contrary to the view presented by traditional religion, this

Understanding how the earth was created

basic substance is not fundamentally different from the substance that makes up the higher realm, what we might call the spiritual realm, or as traditional religion calls it, the heaven world. Instead, the reality is much closer to that discovered by modern science, namely that there is only one basic substance – call it light or energy, if you will – that simply vibrates at different levels.

So you see the point, that when a new sphere is created, it is created from the very same substance found in the newly ascended sphere. Only that substance is now lowered in vibration, so that it enters the vibrational spectrum that makes up the newly created sphere. And even in the newly created sphere, there will be several levels of vibration, so that the material universe is not actually the fullness of your current sphere.

The reality is that in your current sphere, there are several levels of vibration, several spectra of vibration, beyond the material realm. I will later discuss these levels in more detail, because for now my point is to show you the process of how a planet and a solar system is created. What we see now is that for the material universe to even exist, there must be a flow of energy from a higher realm that is lowered in vibration into the spectrum of frequencies that makes up the material universe.

This lowering of high-frequency energy into a lower vibrational spectrum is indeed the very driving force that started the process which science today describes as the Big Bang. Yet what science has not yet recognized is the fact that this lowering of energy to the material frequency spectrum was not a one-time event. It is indeed an ongoing, continuous process.

If you take an honest look at the entire mindset, the paradigms, out of which the theory of the Big Bang came into being, you will see that it is intricately – and in very subtle ways – affected by the desire to uphold the materialistic paradigm that there is nothing beyond the material universe. Thus, the theory of the Big Bang states that all of the matter and energy found in the current universe had been compressed into such extreme density that it formed a singularity. And then, in the Big Bang event, all of the energy was hurled outwards in a giant explosion.

My beloved, this entire worldview is based on a desire to uphold the idea that there is nothing beyond the material universe. It is supported by a law that was formulated centuries ago as what is called the first law of thermodynamics, which says that in any interaction, the total amount of energy is conserved. Yet if you take a closer look at the first law of thermodynamics, you will see that it was formulated at a time when science was in a much more primitive state than you see today. It was formulated based on the observation of steam engines, which means that it was done before there was even the imagination that it was possible to split the atom and release immense amounts of energy from what was at the time seen as the smallest building blocks of matter.

So if you take an honest look at this law, you will see that while it is correct for certain so-called macroscopic events, it cannot be uncritically transferred to what scientists call microscopic events, namely at the level of the atom and subatomic particles. Yet because of the unwillingness to question the materialistic paradigm, few scientists have been willing to question the first law of thermodynamics. Were they indeed willing to question this law – and apply current experimental findings and theories – they would see that the first law of thermodynamics indeed does not apply at the level of atoms and subatomic particles, nor does it, for that matter, apply at the cosmological scale of suns, black holes, supernovas and dark matter.

Thus, you see the danger of assuming that we have now discovered an absolute truth, an absolute principle that can never be violated. Let me assure you that there are no such absolutes in the entire universe. If there is one absolute statement that could be made, it would be precisely this, that there are no absolutes in an unascended sphere. In an unascended sphere everything is in flux, for everything is subject to the consciousness of the beings who created the sphere and those who now inhabit the sphere. Even the so-called laws of nature or laws of physics are not absolutes in the sense that people conceive of them today. They are subject to change over time, or rather as the material universe evolves towards its ultimate purpose, its ultimate outcome.

My point here is to show you that scientists have already discovered certain phenomena that point to the fact that in the universe as a whole, energy is not conserved. If scientists were willing to employ precise enough measurements, they would notice that when they split the atom in a nuclear reaction, slightly more energy is released than can be accounted for by the energy that holds the atom together. If scientists were able to make precise enough measurements, which currently is not possible, they would discover that in your physical sun more energy is released than can be accounted for by the nuclear processes of the sun. In other words, both the atom and the physical sun are openings

Understanding how the earth was created

through which energy from a higher realm is streaming into the material universe.

***

And this brings us back to my intent of explaining to you how a solar system can be constructed. As I said, there are beings in a higher realm who volunteer to become the open doors for delivering the driving power, the driving energy, for creating the next sphere. A long time ago, two such beings volunteered to hold the spiritual focus for what then became your physical sun. Without a sun, no solar system could exist. Planet earth could not exist, and it could not bring forth any lifeform that could be the basis for the expression of self-aware beings—what you today call human beings but which are far more than what you currently conceive of.

So the driving force, the very foundation, the very keystone, for the construction of your solar system was that these two beings volunteered to extend a part of their beings into forming the open door, through which energy from the spiritual realm can stream into the material frequency spectrum and be directed out into all directions, as the driving force behind the very nuclear processes that power the physical sun.

This, then, was the foundation that allowed other self-aware beings to step in and become the builders of the planets in your solar system. These beings had not attained the same level of consciousness as the two beings that volunteered to be the focus for your sun. They had attained a level of consciousness, which I would like to call the elohimic level of consciousness. This is to tie it in with one of the names used in the Old Testament for God, namely that of "Elohim." There are certain biblical scholars who realize that the name Elohim is not a singular name, but a plural name. Thus, the consequence is that Elohim is not a name that refers to the ultimate God, the one Creator. It refers to a plurality of beings, and these are the beings who became what we might call the "builders of form" and who combined their creative powers to create the planets of your solar system.

There are seven levels of the Elohim, but on each of the seven levels there are to beings, one holding the masculine polarity, one holding the feminine polarity. These seven Elohimic levels represent seven distinct levels of high-frequency spiritual energy. They have in esoteric teachings often been referred to as the seven rays. This name indicates that they are light frequencies of a certain vibration, and when these seven light frequencies are combined, they are able to bring forth what you experience as material phenomena. In other words, the entire material universe is created out of the combination of these seven spiritual energy frequencies, these seven spiritual rays.

Thus, the beginning of the creation of the earth was that these seven Elohim – these 14 beings – came together in the common decision to create the planet upon which you live. This was done for a twofold purpose. Partly to give the Elohim the opportunity to experiment with their level of creative ability in creating a planet. But also in creating a platform that would allow other spiritual beings to descend into the material frequency spectrum, take on bodies made of the substance that makes up that spectrum, and therefore experience that world from the inside. This has, as I have mentioned before, the twofold purpose of allowing these beings to grow in self-awareness, so that they can expand their self-awareness, expand their co-creative abilities and expand their appreciation for the intricate and infinitely beautiful world created by their ultimate Creator and the spiritual hierarchy out of which they are extensions.

So the Elohim then met in a higher realm and formulated the blueprint for planet earth, including what lifeforms this planet would be able to bring forth—and thus what learning opportunities it would afford the beings who would descend upon it. After having formulated the blueprint for the earth, the Elohim then began to use that blueprint as a foundation for applying information to the basic substance provided by the beings who hold the focus for the sun. In other words, the sun radiates the basic energy out of which planet earth is made, and the Elohim then superimposed their blueprint, superimposed the information in the blueprint, upon that energy. And over a long period of time, the blueprint then caused the energy from the sun to coalesce into the denser matter that makes up the physical planet.

This was a very gradual process, and it was not the instantaneous creation described in the Bible. Nevertheless, if you are willing to interpret the story of Genesis creatively, you can conceive of the seven "days" of creation as seven time periods that correspond to the seven spiritual rays I have just mentioned.

Understanding how the earth was created

Thus, the Elohim started by projecting the energies of the first ray, the blueprint of the first ray, onto the energies from the sun. Then the blueprint of the second ray was projected onto the energy from the sun, and so forth until finally the physical planet started appearing—as if out of nowhere. Yet it did not appear out of nowhere, as I have explained that even a subatomic particle does not appear out of nowhere. It came into being, it appeared out of, the higher frequency energy that cannot be detected by your physical senses and by material instruments. Thus, in a way one might say that the blueprint that existed as a potential in a higher realm was brought into manifestation by being lowered into the material frequency spectrum.

***

Now, my beloved, I earlier promised you to explain why it is so important for you to reconsider the paradigms found in your consciousness. Do you begin to see that when the Elohim created the physical planet earth, they did so through their own consciousness? Each level of Elohim, the Elohim for each ray, held a blueprint of the earth in their minds, and it was this blueprint that was superimposed upon the basic energy coming from the sun. If the blueprint held in the minds of the Elohim had been different, then the earth would have been different, as indeed is proven by the other planets in your solar system that are very different from the earth and therefore can sustain a very different lifeform than what you see on the earth.

Now then, after the earth was created, it took a certain time before the earth had reached the level of manifestation that was able to support intelligent lifeforms. In other words, at a certain time in the very distant past – far beyond what science currently considers the origin of life on this planet – there were self-aware beings that started to descend onto planet earth and take on a form of life on this planet. Take note that I am not saying these first self-aware beings took on the kind of physical bodies that you are currently wearing. Yet this is a topic I will not go into at this point.

My aim is to show you that a very long time ago, self-aware beings started descending into the thoughtform of planet earth. And from that moment, they then started co-creating the earth along with the Elohim. Thus, the earth started becoming a combination of the creative powers of the Elohim – working from a higher level – and the beings who were working from within the frequency spectrum of planet earth itself.

For a very long time, the self-aware beings who descended to planet earth were in complete unity with, in complete alignment with, the vision of the Elohim. Thus, what they added to the earth, what they co-created on the earth, was indeed an extension of and an expansion of the blueprint created by the Elohim. At that time, planet earth was in an ascending spiral of reaching greater and greater levels of beauty complexity, harmony, balance and sophistication.

In those past, what we might call "golden," ages, there was none of the limitations and imbalances you currently see on Mother Earth. There were no natural disasters, so-called. There were no earthquakes, no volcanic eruptions, no tsunamis. There were no extremes of weather, such as hurricanes or droughts. There were no meteors that were able to penetrate the protective shield around the planet and create mass upheavals or extinctions. The beings who lived on planet earth did not have the physical limitations you see today. They did not have diseases of their bodies, they did not ever lack for food or other sustenance. And thus, they did indeed live in a state that is hardly conceivable for the people who today inhabit this planet in physical bodies.

So my beloved, can you now see where I have attempted to take you? Can you see that if you want to help bring the earth to a higher level, where some of the current limitations have been transcended, you need to begin to question the paradigms and beliefs that make these limitations seem like the inevitable consequences of natural laws that are beyond human control?

**

My beloved, consider the fact that most of the religious philosophies found on this earth – and I am here talking thousands of such philosophies found in many different cultures over the time span you call recorded history – consider that most of these myths or thought systems contain the concept that in the distant past, there was a more ideal state. And then somehow, human beings fell out of that ideal state. And thus, what you see today is not the original ideal state, whether you call it paradise or something else.

Understanding how the earth was created

Now, of course, for you to even begin to entertain this idea, you need to first overcome the paradigms imposed by both orthodox religion and materialistic science. For even though orthodox Christianity does talk about a state of Paradise that human beings fell out of, they are not connecting that state to the physical earth. Instead, they see the physical earth as being separated from the kingdom of heaven, and therefore planet earth is not able to outpicture the perfection of the kingdom of heaven. Instead, you need to rise into the heaven world in order to experience this perfection.

Yet, what I am telling you is that planet earth in past ages has indeed outpictured a state of beauty, balance and harmony that people today can only conceive of as belonging to the heaven world. And thus, it is indeed possible – and indeed the intention of the Elohim – that the earth will again outpicture this state of balance, beauty and harmony. Yet for this to happen, human beings must be part of the co-creation of this new state. And how can human beings do this? They can do this only by raising their consciousness.

On the other hand, materialistic science will also deny that the earth in the past has manifested a greater state of complexity and perfection than what you see today. Yet this is due, again, to the desire to uphold the materialistic paradigm, which is so based on the theory of evolution. This theory says that evolution can only go in one direction, namely from less sophisticated, less complex, lifeforms towards more sophisticated, more complex lifeforms. And thus, in order to truly understand the role of human beings on this planet – the potential of human beings on this planet – you need to look beyond the scientific paradigm and realize that evolution can indeed go in both directions. Because evolution is not a mechanical, mindless process; it is a process that takes place in consciousness. And thus, it is indeed affected by consciousness, including the consciousness of human beings.

***

In other words, the Elohim did not create the earth in one instant creation event. They set in motion an evolutionary process, and they are continuing to guide that evolutionary process, along with many other non-material beings, to this day. Yet the evolutionary process of planet earth is fundamentally affected also by the beings who inhabit bodies in the frequency spectrum of planet earth. These beings, by combining the creative powers of their minds, are indeed able to change the physical environment on earth within the limits defined by the Elohim.

In other words, human beings do not have the creative powers, even if they combine the minds of all human beings on the earth, to create planet earth. Nor do they have the power to destroy planet earth. Yet they do indeed have the power to take the earth into a downward spiral that eventually ends up destroying the civilization human beings have created, even to the point of obliterating all physical traces of past civilizations.

And thus, you see that the history of the earth has been a process that has two distinct elements. In the distant past, waves of lifestreams descended to planet earth and created very sophisticated civilizations. And then – after these lifestreams had learned the lessons that they could learn from planet earth, after these lifestreams had mastered their creative abilities as these abilities could be expressed on planet earth – well, all of these waves of lifestreams ascended back to the spiritual realm from which they had descended. It is as Jesus says in the New Testament, "No man can ascend back to heaven, save he that descended from heaven."

And thus, you see that in the distant history of planet earth, waves of lifestreams descended to this planet and then ascended back. And as they ascended back, all traces of their civilizations were raised into a higher frequency spectrum, and that is why you will not ever find physical traces of these past civilizations. Do you see, my beloved, that this is another example of the observation horizon beyond which you cannot go? There simply are no physical traces of the civilizations that have ascended from earth in past epochs of history.

Yet there is also another process, and it is that after a certain point, a shift happened on earth. There now was a wave of lifestreams that descended, and they also brought forth a sophisticated civilization, far more sophisticated than what you see today. Yet in the end, a very large number of these lifestreams were not able to ascend. And therefore, instead of creating an ascension spiral for their civilization, they created a descension spiral that gradually took their civilization and their level of consciousness into a self-destructive spiral.

These lifestreams were able to affect even the physical environment on earth to the point, where they precipitated various events that literally

Understanding how the earth was created 65

obliterated most physical traces of their civilization. You will notice that even today archaeologists have found certain signs of past civilizations that seemed to have a level of sophistication that cannot be explained even by today's technology. Yet I can assure you that in the not-too-distant future, other traces of such civilizations will be discovered, until it will be impossible to uphold the current historical paradigm that past civilizations have been more primitive than current civilization. This, of course, is another outcome of the materialistic desire to uphold materialism as the ultimate source of truth.

So my point is that in the past, civilizations have self-destructed and even precipitated events that have been carried on in mythology as the biblical flood, or even the physically proven events of various ice ages. My beloved, just consider for a moment that where the great city of New York is situated today, there was not too long ago a very thick sheet of ice. Imagine that if such a sheet of ice again moved down and covered the area, then the current city of New York would be ground into dust. And when the ice retreated, it would seem as if there had never been a city in that location.

So you see, indeed, that Mother Earth has certain physical processes that are quite capable of extinguishing most traces of past civilizations, that could have been as sophisticated or more sophisticated than what you see today. Human beings in the modern world may think they have built great monuments that will last forever, but you would be surprised at how quickly the natural processes of earth could extinguish these monuments to the human ego and its desire for immortality in the material realm. There is no such thing as immortality in the material realm—that is: until the material realm itself ascends and becomes a self-luminous sphere in God's creation.

***

So again, let me return to my premise of why it is so important for you to reconsider your paradigms. I have explained that the Elohim created a perfectly balanced and harmonious planet by superimposing the blueprint they held in their consciousness upon the basics substance that makes up matter. I have explained that the self-aware beings who descended to earth and took on bodies here then started to co-create based on the original blueprint. And I have now explained that the earth in its current condition is far below the original balance and harmony envisioned by the Elohim. And this lower condition is a creation of the fact that, over a long period of time, human beings have co-created by superimposing the images and beliefs held in their minds upon the basic substance that makes up matter itself.

So can you see, now, that the current unbalanced conditions found on earth are a product of the mental images, the blueprints, that human beings have superimposed upon the original blueprint of the Elohim? This original blueprint has not in any way been destroyed; it still exists in the mind of the Elohim. Yet it has, so to speak, been covered over by the lower images superimposed by the minds of human beings. And therefore, that original blueprint is not what you see as the actual reality on earth.

It only exists, now, in the realm of potentiality, in the realm of probability. What is the actual reality in the current time-space realm of earth is the unbalanced and inharmonious blueprint created and held in the minds of human beings. And thus, the absolutely only way that Mother Earth can shake off its current limitations is if human beings – at least a critical mass among human beings – are willing to take a critical look at the blueprints they hold in their minds—and then question what they see as the unquestionable aspects of those blueprints.

Only if a critical mass of human beings will begin to question their beliefs about the earth and the material universe, will they be able to throw out some of the limiting mental images they hold and replace them with the higher mental images currently held in the minds of the Elohim and other spiritual beings. And only when human beings begin to accept and internalize these higher mental images – and therefore direct their awareness through those mental images – well my beloved, only then will the basic substance that makes up the earth begin to take on those higher images.

And thus, do you now see why it is so essential for you to begin to question what you have been brought up to believe cannot or should not be questioned? You must overcome the fear that by questioning the dogmas of your childhood religion, you will be condemned to hell by an angry God in the sky. You must realize that, instead, the loving God in the spiritual realm will only welcome you to question any limitation and instead realize and accept what Jesus meant when he said "Fear not little flock, for it is your father's good pleasure to give you the kingdom."

Understanding how the earth was created

It is indeed the pleasure of the Elohim to give you a planet that has complete harmony and balance, so that it can meet all of your physical and spiritual needs. It is not the design of the Elohim to have a planet where people have a limited lifespan due to diseases or old age, or where two-thirds of the population live below the poverty level with millions of children starving to death every year. The Elohim hold a much higher vision for this planet, and they would be happy to see it outpictured instantly. And indeed, it could be outpictured almost instantly if enough people were to accept this higher vision with the same sense of reality that they currently accept the limited conditions that they see around them.

And thus, you must also be willing to question the scientific projection that the earth is a material, mechanical creation that must obey certain laws that are beyond the power of the human mind. You will not become an unintelligent, superstitious idiot by questioning the materialistic paradigm, for it is indeed as limiting as the idea that the earth was flat. You will become a much more free, a much more aware, being by realizing that the fundamental reality of the material universe is that everything is a creation of consciousness. And thus, your consciousness can indeed affect your material circumstances, and the collective consciousness of humankind can indeed affect the material circumstances found on this planetary home.

I can assure you that in the not-too-distant future, people will be looking back at the current materialistic paradigm, and they will see it as being just as primitive as the belief in a flat earth. Thus, if you are willing to be a forerunner for the shift in consciousness that is already beginning to happen – but has not yet broken through in the awareness of most people – then come along with me, as I will take you on a journey that will help you question what you have been programmed to believe cannot or should not be questioned.

Key 5
Understanding the basic principle behind all life

Let me take you on a journey into the heart of Elohim, that you may gain an understanding of who the Elohim are and how they looked at their task of creating planet earth. The first thing you need to consider is the difference between the state of consciousness of most human beings on earth and the consciousness of the beings I call the Elohim.

You may look at planet earth and see some of the manifestations of selfishness and self-centeredness that can be found virtually anywhere on this planet. As a spiritual person, you might very well have seen these manifestations your entire life, and you might have realized that this simply cannot be the full potential of human beings. There must be something more, there must be something higher, and what you have really sensed in the inner levels of your heart – in the innermost recesses of your being – is indeed that it is possible to rise above the state of consciousness that is so blinded by selfishness and the lower desires— that are almost animalistic desires, insatiable desires. For you can never have enough of this or that or the next thing.

And so, the reason why you are open to this book, open to the spiritual side of life, is that you carry with you from past lifetimes an understanding – a knowledge, an inner knowing – that there is a higher potential for human beings. It is possible to rise above this state of selfishness, of spiritual blindness, and come to truly understand what life is, how life works and how the ultimate and ultimately benign Creator created the world of form. It is possible to understand the principles and the vision that the Creator had, before it made the first impulse towards actually manifesting the world of form. And when you do come into the oneness of this understanding, then you have escaped the human, the self-centered, the animalistic, the carnal.

You have therefore risen to a state of consciousness, where you are not really an individual being, as most human beings look at this today.

You realize the underlying truth behind the old statement that "No man is an island." And of course, that is equally true for any woman.

You realize that beneath the seeming differences and divisions found on earth, there is an underlying oneness, an underlying, unifying principle that ties all life together in this giant web of life. And when you do, indeed, reach the level of consciousness of the Elohim, you have not only understood this underlying oneness as a theoretical or intellectual concept, you have risen to a state of consciousness, where you have become one with that unifying consciousness, that unifying principle that ties all life together in this giant web, which we might call the Antahkarana of life.

The Elohim, then, are beings who are beyond all selfishness. They are so far beyond what you see expressed today on planet earth that most human beings would not be able to fathom the consciousness of the Elohim, nor would they be able to withstand being in the Presence of the Elohim. For the consciousness of the Elohim has become the open door for the light from a higher sphere, and therefore the light in their beings is so intense that few people can even stand to be in their Presence.

And thus, although the Elohim are not able, as I explained, to bring forth enough light to be the driving force behind creating a solar system – for beings of an even higher level of awareness need to do this – the Elohim are still the open doors for bringing forth the vision and the driving force in their own beings in order to superimpose that vision upon the light provided by the beings in the sun.

Thus, the Elohim have come into such a oneness with the creative principles that are defined for this particular sphere, that there is not even a question of whether they will follow them or not. This does not mean that the Elohim have given up free will; it means that they have given up a separate will. For truly, what most people on earth see as free will is not truly a free will, for it is a will that is based on the illusion of separation, the illusion that makes people think that they are separate beings and that they can do whatever they want to others without affecting themselves.

***

Understanding the basic principle behind all life   71

Do you perhaps begin to sense that if there truly is an underlying one-ness to all life, then this belief in separation is a complete illusion? If all life is interconnected, then you are never an island. Even though you may see yourself as an individual being here on earth, you are still not a separate being. You may think, based on your observation or experience with life on earth, that you can do certain things that affect other people, but if those things never come back to you here on earth, then you might think you have gotten away with this. You might think you have man-aged to do something to other people, and yet it had no consequences for yourself. This, of course, is indeed one of the greatest of all illusions found on earth, and it is precisely the same illusion that has caused all of the burdens on the body of the Earth Mother.

Just look back a few decades at how there was a consciousness in the Western world that was completely unwilling to recognize the phe-nomenon of pollution, and the possibility that letting out certain tox-ins in nature would one day have profound effects upon human beings, even upon the entire human population. Can you see that the entire at-titude towards pollution that was rampant up until the 1960s and beyond is indeed based on this basic illusion, that human beings are separate be-ings and that human beings, therefore, as a race, are separated from the planet upon which they live—human beings are separated from nature. "We live 'in here' in our big cities; nature is somewhere 'out there.' And what we let slip into the water and the air from our big cities will only affect nature out there. Or maybe it will have no effect at all on nature, but it certainly will not come back to haunt us one day. We can get away with polluting all we want without it ever coming back to hurt us."

Do you see, that this very consciousness was indeed the founda-tion for all of the environmental problems that you currently see on this planet? Do you then see that if there is ever to be any real progress in transcending environmental problems, it is absolutely necessary that humankind as a whole will overcome this illusion of separation?

Yet this process of overcoming the illusion of separation must start somewhere, and it must start with individuals. First with one individual: you, and then with other individuals, until gradually a critical mass has been built. Do you see, my beloved, that this was exactly what hap-pened during the 1960s and beyond, when first a few people started be-coming aware of the potential impact of pollution upon the human race? And then, gradually, this awareness spread like rings in the water, until a critical mass was reached. And now, even the governments and the media and big industrialists could no longer ignore the need to change the attitude, the behavior and the policy towards pollution.

Yet do you see that truly solving environmental problems will not be done by simply enacting laws that restrict the behavior of people or corporations? If the underlying problem is indeed the sense of separation, well then a true breakthrough will not happen until that sense of separation has been challenged completely. And therefore, more human beings must begin to understand and uncover the underlying principles that the Creator defined, when it decided to create the sphere in which you live, when the Creator decided to create the world of form.

These are the underlying principles behind every sphere that has ever come into being, and it is what we might call the Alpha aspect of the laws of God. There is, however, also an Omega aspect, which is a set of principles that were designed by the beings who brought forth the creative impetus for your particular sphere. These Omega principles, what we might call the laws of nature or the laws of physics, are of course not in any way separated from or in opposition to the Alpha principles of God's law. They are simply the extensions of these principles but given a specific form in order to bring forth the sphere in which you live, with its particular characteristics.

Again, the Elohim were in complete oneness with both the Alpha of the Creator's laws and the Omega of the principles of those who defined the design for your particular sphere. The Elohim, then, are working from within your sphere to create solar systems, and even organize them – at the higher levels of the Elohim – into entire galaxies. And then – at an even higher level of consciousness – in the sphere that has ascended most recently – you have beings who organize even the galaxies into one coherent system that moves in unison, like the players in a giant symphony that all play to the same music.

And thus, there is harmony. Harmony between all levels of the whole—and that is precisely why the whole carries such beauty. Look at the beauty of the night sky and realize that were it not for the fact that there are beings with a higher level of consciousness than human beings that have created this beauty, well then none of this could even exist. For the universe itself would long ago have self-destructed, or it would never even have gotten started.

Understanding the basic principle behind all life

***

You see, my beloved, there is one unifying principle that underlies all creation, that underlies the entire world of form. It is a principle that can be described in many ways—and has indeed been described in various ways through various religious, or spiritual, or esoteric teachings. Yet given that I have started out by talking about the discoveries of modern science, let me once again use science as the metaphor for describing this principle.

Once again, as I said in my remarks about the first law of thermodynamics, it is necessary to realize that this principle was discovered at a time when science was in a much more primitive state than today. This refers both to the philosophy of science and to the actual instruments that scientists used to make their measurements. As a result of this, scientists formulated what is generally called the second law of thermodynamics. This law states that in a closed system, disorder will increase, until the system reaches the lowest possible energy state, where there is no difference in temperature, where there are, consequently, no organized structures possible.

As an example of the kind of closed system that is talked about in the second law of thermodynamics, take a bathtub filled with water. Now apply a force to the water by moving your hand back and forth until you create waves in the bathtub. Then remove your hand and watch as the now closed system of the bathtub relatively quickly finds its way towards an equilibrium, where the water is no longer moving. For it has reached its lowest possible energy state.

This is a very simple demonstration of the principle discovered in the second law of thermodynamics. Of course, with the current knowledge of science itself, it is obvious – or at least it should be obvious to most scientists – that the second law of thermodynamics has certain limitations. For given that scientists today know that everything is energy – that everything is vibrations, and that everything is interconnected – then it should be obvious that there truly is no closed system. There is no system that can be entirely closed.

It is simply not possible to create one system, anywhere in the material universe, and say that this system is completely isolated from the rest of the universe. You may look at the immense space between various galaxies or between solar systems, or even between the earth and the sun, and you might think that it is possible for some "body" in this universe to be isolated. But you know that your earth is affected by the gravity of the sun, receives rays from the sun and even receives so-called cosmic rays that come from far beyond the sun. You know that your sun moves in a larger system, called a galaxy, and you know that even your galaxy moves as part of the entirety of the universe.

And thus, you see, there can be no truly closed system. This is a concept that I will return to later, but for now what I want to focus on is that regardless of the fact that there is no truly closed system, the second law of thermodynamics is based on the discovery of a true principle, namely the one underlying principle behind the world of form.

You see, in the very beginning – before there was any world of form – there was only the Creator. When I say "only," of course this is somewhat of a misnomer, for the Creator is Allness, the Creator is a state of consciousness far beyond the Elohim, so far beyond that there is no point in even using words to try to describe it. Yet the consciousness of the Creator can be experienced; even human beings can have a glimpse of that experience. And thus, when only the Creator existed, when there was no form, what drove the Creator to create form was indeed the very principle discovered in the second law of thermodynamics.

***

That principle might be expressed more poetically as love, but a love that is beyond human possessive love, and is a truly unconditional love that never accepts any conditions as finite or ultimate. Thus, here you have a Creator, which is completely self-sufficient, which is complete and whole in itself. What would drive such a being to create a world of form and invest its own Being in that form?

Well, it is the very principle that even brought the Creator into existence, namely that of self-transcendence, continual and perpetual self-transcendence, the transcendence into a higher state. What I have called love could also be called the drive to be more, and even the Creator is an expression of the drive to be more. And thus, as an expression of that drive, the Creator desired to be more.

And how does a complete and whole self-sufficient Creator become more? Well, the Creator becomes more by creating a world of form out of itself, by sending extensions of itself – localized extensions of itself –

Understanding the basic principle behind all life

into that world, so that they might become more by interacting with the world of form. And thus, in the process of the extensions of the Creator becoming more, then the Creator itself becomes more.

You see, this is the most fundamental principle behind all form, and it has been described in the second law of thermodynamics precisely by saying that there is always a drive to become more. And if this drive is suspended, then things must self-destruct.

Even though there strictly is no closed system, we can reformulate the second law of thermodynamics by saying that if a particular system or unit in the world of form is not in the process of transcending itself, then that system or unit will go in the opposite direction and self-destruct. It will go towards a lower and lower state of energy and organization and sophistication, until it can no longer maintain any existence in the world of form. So we might say that the second law of thermodynamics makes it clear that nothing can stand still.

There is no such thing as still-stand. Anything in the world of form must be either transcending itself and becoming more, or it must be self-destructing and becoming less. There is nothing in between. It may seem – I am well aware – that there is something in between, but this is an illusion created by a particular aspect of the human mind, called the ego, and we will later talk about it in greater detail. Yet the underlying principle discovered in the second law of thermodynamics is precisely that nothing can stand still, nothing can remain the same.

However, we can even go to a deeper level in our understanding of the second law of thermodynamics, for what is it that makes something self-transcend, the absence of which makes it self-destruct? Well, it is indeed that there must be a driving force—that nothing can exist that has form unless there is a driving force that creates that form, that sets it apart from the lowest possible energy state and that continues to keep it apart for as long as it exists.

So you see, then, that for anything to exist, for anything to continue to exist, it must be in tune with, it must be flowing with, this driving force behind the entire world of form. This driving force can be conceived of as a flow of energy, although not energy as you understand it in a physical, material sense. Therefore, I would like to call it the "River of Life," which is a metaphor meant to illustrate that the entire material universe can be seen as one giant river.

If you picture in your mind the immensity of the Amazon River – not only near the ocean where it is wide, but even in the smallest areas of the jungle, where it begins as small creeks and streams – if you look at this entire river, you can conceive of it as one giant system that is moving in unison. As the water near the ocean flows into the ocean, it creates a space, and the water behind it flows into it—and so on and so forth until the very farthest drop in the mountains is now affected and flows into the space created by the drop before it.

As another example, you might picture the entire universe, where all of the galaxies, according to modern science, are constantly expanding away from each other. And this, then, might also be seen as a river, although it does not flow in a linear fashion; it flows in a spherical fashion, expanding outwards, outwards, outwards, ever transcending itself and becoming more in the process.

So my point is that even beyond the material universe, into other spheres, there is this giant driving force, the River of Life. And the Elohim, of course, are completely one with that river. They flow with it, they allow the river to express itself through their beings, and as they then become the open doors for the river to flow, then they also become the directors of the river over their area of influence.

It is not that when you unify your being with the River of Life that you lose individuality or self-awareness. On the contrary, your individuality, your self-awareness, is expanded. And then, as you direct the River of Life and see the consequences of how you directed, then your self-awareness is expanded even more. And thus, you become more by flowing with the River of Life and letting it flow through you.

This is, then, the Alpha and the Omega pull that truly is the driving force behind all creation, where, as I said, even the Creator as the Alpha becomes more by seeing the Omega of its own creation unfold—and by allowing its own Being to be embedded in that creation and thus unfolding with it.

***

Yet we now need to take this to a deeper level. For you see, the purpose of creating a world of form is not simply that the Creator becomes more. This is the Alpha aspect of the purpose, but the Omega aspect is that *you* become more, or rather that all self-aware extensions of the

Understanding the basic principle behind all life

Creator become more. And to that end, it is absolutely essential that each self-aware extension of the Creator's Being is endowed with the ability to make choices, and is then given complete freedom to make any choices it wants and then experience the consequences of those choices.

My beloved, in order to understand this principle, you need to be willing to step back and question one of the most fundamental beliefs that is promoted by many of the religions found on this planet. This is the belief that it is possible for human beings to make a mistake so grave that they are forever condemned to an eternity in a fiery hell or some other very undesirable place, as defined by each individual religion. Nevertheless, most religions on this planet do contain the idea that whereas you have at least some freedom of will, there is some epic importance to the choices you make. And thus, some choices will give you eternal life in some heaven world, whereas other choices will give you an eternity of punishment in some lower realm.

Let me now endeavor to explain the reality behind these ideas. You are, as I have hinted at before, a God in the making, a Creator in the making. You are designed to start out as a very localized extension of the Creator's Being who has a very limited sense of self-awareness. You are aware of yourself as an individual being that exists in a very localized environment. For example, you might be aware of yourself as one human being, as one physical body, on this little planet, called earth.

Surely, there was a time when human beings thought the earth was the center of the universe, and therefore being even a small human being on earth was still important in God's plan. But given that you today have the knowledge of the immensity of the universe, you can see that, truly, being a human being on this planet is a very localized sense of self-awareness.

Yet even so, you have the potential to grow in self-awareness, and this is indeed the process that has been demonstrated by the Buddha, by Jesus and by other spiritual beings who are today ascended and comprise the spiritual teachers of humankind. And even beyond that of the immediate state of ascending from the earth, there is an ongoingness to the expansion of your self-awareness, that can take you up, not only from the sphere in which you currently live, but through other spheres beyond it, until you actually reach the very level of self-awareness of the Creator from which you came.

This means that instead of there just being one Creator, there will now be two creators, two beings, two individual beings with the self-awareness of a Creator, and thus capable of creating their own universes. And this, of course, can be repeated indefinitely, and is being repeated indefinitely in the existence of an unfathomable number of universes, worlds without end, way beyond what most human beings are able to fathom with their current linear state of consciousness. Thus, let me just hint at this reality, rather than going into it in any great depth, so as not to overwhelm your mind at this early stage of the book.

Yet what you need to take away from this discussion is indeed that the greater purpose behind the creation of the world of form is the growth in self-awareness, where you start out with a very localized sense of self and gradually expand that self, until you reach the level of the Creator. Now, what exactly does this mean? How can you complete this process of the expansion of self-awareness?

Well, can you see that the Creator that started the very world of form in which you live is beyond its own creation? The creator is more than the creation, is more than anything in the world of form. And thus, in order for you to reach the level of self-awareness of the Creator, you need to continue to transcend your current self-awareness until you reach the ultimate level. And that means you can never allow yourself to stop at any point, you can never allow yourself to identify yourself with anything in the world of form. You can never allow yourself to identify yourself as a being who has reached some kind of ultimate state from which you cannot transcend yourself.

This, my beloved, is the reality, the deeper reality, behind the second law of thermodynamics. For you see, in this world of form, the underlying principle is self-transcendence, but the Omega aspect of that principle is self-transcendence through free will. Thus, we might say that everything in this world of form – when it comes to the form aspect of it – is subject to free will. This means that in the material universe – which, as I have explained, is part of a sphere that has not yet ascended – every aspect of this universe is subject to the free will of the beings who inhabit it.

As I have said, the earth was created by the Elohim in a very high state of purity, because the Elohim are one with the River of Life. Yet since then, the beings who live inside the system of the earth have used their free will to enter a lower state of consciousness. And thus, they

Understanding the basic principle behind all life

have actually been allowed to outpicture a lower state of balance, harmony, beauty and abundance than what was originally envisioned and manifest by the Elohim.

Yet while free will is the ultimate law, free will does not exist alone. Free will itself is not a closed system, for free will exists within the larger principle of self-transcendence. And thus, if you look at planet earth today – and realize that many of the limitations you find on earth today are the products of the state of consciousness of humankind – well, then you might ask yourself a question. Once a group of beings living on a planet have created a lower state than was originally envisioned by the Elohim, how can these beings escape that state?

***

Just for a moment, think about yourself and how – as you grew up on this planet – you have come to take certain things for granted without even thinking about questioning them. Consider how you have been brought up to believe that there are many aspects of life on earth that are the products of the laws of nature and that these laws are immutable and invariable, meaning that you as an individual, or even humankind as a whole, has no power over them whatsoever.

This has many ramifications, for example you might believe that there are limits to how many people can live on planet earth, that there are limits to how much food can be produced on this earth. And therefore, the fact that there are many people today who are living near the starvation level is caused by there being too many people on earth. Or you might even have been brought up to accept that because of a principle called "survival of the fittest," there is a law of nature which mandates that some people form an elite who have special privileges beyond the ordinary population.

If you go back in time, you will see that during the Middle Ages there were societies, called the feudal societies, in which the vast majority of the population were the virtual slaves of a small noble class. What kept this society alive for centuries was that the noble class, the elite, had managed to prevent the population from being educated to the point, where they could even envision a different society.

Thus, do you see my point? Everything is subject to the free will of humans beings. Many conditions on earth are subject to the free will of human beings, yet human beings exercise their free will according to their vision. And so, once humans beings have entered into a certain state of consciousness – that gives them a limited vision – how will they ever rise beyond that state of consciousness?

If there was no mechanism that would work against the status quo, well then people could remain trapped at a certain level of self-awareness for an indefinite period of time. Can you see that this is not in accordance with the overall purpose of the universe, namely the growth in self-awareness?

Free will mandates that you have a right to enter into any state of consciousness you like, but the Law of Free Will also states that you do not have a right to remain in that consciousness for an indefinite period of time. You can remain in a state of consciousness for a long time, as measured with earth time, but you cannot remain in it indefinitely or forever, for then you would not be able to self-transcend and reach the ultimate goal for this universe.

What is the mechanism that makes it impossible for self-aware beings to remain in the same state of consciousness for an indefinite period of time? Well, it is the mechanism behind the second law of thermodynamics, which simply says that the moment you lock yourself at a certain level of consciousness, at that moment your environment will become subject to the second law of thermodynamics that seeks to return everything to the lowest possible energy state. Which means that everything in your environment will start breaking down, until you once again open your mind and become willing to transcend your state of consciousness.

So do you see that the spiritual meaning behind the second law of thermodynamics is that the very definition of a closed system is a being or a group of beings who are refusing to use their free will to transcend their current level of consciousness? Thus, these beings are no longer flowing with the River of Life, because they have created a closed system in their minds. Do you see that the only system that can be somewhat closed is, in fact, the mind of a being with free will? Because that being has the right to temporarily set itself apart from the River of Life. Yet in order to prevent that being from becoming permanently trapped in that sense of separation, the River of Life will make sure that when a being sets itself apart, everything it co-creates can only break down.

Understanding the basic principle behind all life

This is indeed why you see a tendency that closed societies will create so many problems that they eventually end up breaking down the entire civilization. Cast a quick glance back at the history of humankind, as it is currently known, and you will see many civilizations that rose, sometimes too great levels of sophistication and organization, only then to stagnate. And as soon as they stagnated, the downward slide began, and it is amazing how quickly this could result in the total collapse of a sophisticated civilization—that actually thought it would endure forever.

Do you not see that the current environmental problems experienced by Western civilization are one example of this process? Precisely by becoming a closed system – by believing that human beings were separated from the nature around them – Western civilization started creating environmental problems that then started very quickly having effects on the civilization itself. Fortunately, some people were alert, and it has now been a growing awareness that Western civilization is not a closed system. And therefore, it is necessary to understand how nature works in order to avoid destroying the civilization that has been built.

Yet what does this ultimately mean? Is it just a matter of discovering a few principles, and then we can create a civilization that can last forever? Nay, my beloved, what I am telling you here is that for any civilization to be sustainable, that civilization must be in a constant process of self-transcendence. It is not possible to discover laws or principles, and once you know and apply those laws, you can remain at a certain state for an indefinite period of time.

As I have now tried to explain to you, the very underlying principle behind the entire world of form is self-transcendence. And thus, only when you are in alignment with that fundamental law, will you – as an individual or an entire civilization – be sustainable.

Sustainability means constant self-transcendence. If you attempt to attain sustainability by maintaining a certain state, then the second law of thermodynamics will break down that state until you end up having nothing left.

This is not some angry and judgmental God who is seeking to punish you. This is a loving God who wants you to attain the fullness of God's kingdom, which means God's self-awareness, God's state of consciousness. And in order to make sure that you do not use your free will to settle for less, God has set up a law that will make it impossible for you to be permanently trapped in a lesser state of self-awareness.

***

This, then, is what the Elohim know; they are one with that self-transcendence of the River of Life. And they designed a planet based on that principle, so that the very planet itself is designed to give humankind the best possible platform, not for remaining in some edenic state for an indefinite period of time, but for remaining in the true paradise of constant self-transcendence.

As long as humankind was willing to transcend, as I said happened in the first civilizations, then the earth was continually transcending itself. But when that desire and drive for self-transcendence was lost – and humankind became obsessed by the desire to attain permanence in the material world – then the second law of thermodynamics immediately began to break things down and manifest the many forms of imbalances you currently see on planet earth.

This, then, is an idea that I am well aware will be in contradiction to almost everything you were brought up to believe, whether you had an upbringing that was dominated by a particular religion, or no religion, or even the materialistic religion. There is hardly any philosophy on earth today that truly understands and incorporates this principle. And thus, I am aware that it might require some adjustment on your part before you are able to truly lock in to what I have explained to you.

So I will talk, in the coming keys, about more concrete aspects of how the Elohim used the seven spiritual rays to design planet earth, so that you may come to a gradual understanding of the qualities and the perversions that make up planet earth. And then, I will later come back to this principle of self-transcendence, this principle of the River of Life, of the unconditional love that causes all life to flow. And we will see if we cannot, then, attain a higher understanding of exactly why this principle is so important for those who are willing to be the forerunners for healing Mother Earth.

Key 6
To be a healer, you must overcome your fear of calamity

So far, I have given you certain hints in this book, hints that were meant to awaken your understanding and point you towards the realization that current conditions on earth are so far from the original vision and design of the Elohim that it almost defies comprehension. I have also attempted to give you hints to make you see that the reason why there is such an immense difference between the current reality and the original creative vision, is that humankind has descended or fallen into a state of consciousness that is so much lower than the consciousness at which all co-creators came into being.

You see, what I have given you here is the idea that planet earth can be considered a giant schoolroom. In fact the entire material universe can be considered a giant schoolroom for lifestreams that have come into being in order to descend into this world, yet into many different parts of this world—we might say on many different planetary systems.

Yet when you look at planet earth today and consider the current theory of evolution, you might get the idea that co-creators started out at a very low state of consciousness, such as what we might see represented in the animal kingdom in the form of certain predators who are only out to kill other animals, and who will do so without any form of emotion. One might therefore think that co-creators came into being at what is currently the lowest state of consciousness outpictured on earth, and then had to work their way up from there.

Based on this thinking, one might get the idea that the lowest state of consciousness outpictured on earth was the beginning point, and that what you currently see as the highest consciousness outpictured on earth is the highest possible level of evolution available to human beings. This, however, is very far from reality.

There is certainly a very small percentage of people on this planet who have reached a higher state of consciousness than that at which co-creators came into being. Yet when you look at the vast majority of humankind, they are not even close to having returned to the state of consciousness at which they came into being. In other words, even though we might set up a scale and apply it to the majority of humankind, defining the lowest possible state of consciousness and the higher states of consciousness, even what would be the highest state of consciousness on that scale is still lower than the point at which co-creators came into being.

***

So you see, this gives you some sense of how far below the original vision and design the earth has actually fallen. This might also give you some sense of why several religions contain myths about the collapse of past civilizations, about the punishment of God that supposedly wiped all people from the earth, such as the biblical flood and other myths about disasters on a large scale.

In fact, this fear of large-scale disasters is actually in the collective memory from past ages. There have, as I explained earlier, been certain civilizations in the past that did not descend below a critical level, and therefore the majority of the members of those civilizations ascended to the spiritual realm after their sojourn on earth. Yet there have also been certain civilizations in which the majority of the members could not ascend, and therefore the civilization self-destructed according to the second law of thermodynamics.

Thus, there have been quite a number of such events. Yet, I must tell you that as severe as these events have been, they have always been localized and have not had a global scope. Even the biblical flood is not a myth about an event that affected the entire earth. There were certain localized areas that were flooded rather suddenly and caused many people to die, and even certain civilizations to disappear. Yet it was not that the entire landmass of the earth was flooded, as most Christians today believe.

Thus, what I endeavor to explain to you is a very simple reality, and the reason I explain it to you is that before we really move into considering the creative powers and the creative vision of the Elohim, we need to face and confront the fear that many people have of a worldwide calamity of some sort. This is a fear that has been programmed into the collective consciousness, partly because of past events and partly because there are certain forces – that I will describe in detail later – that are seeking to control the collective consciousness. And thereby control the individuals who have the potential to be the forerunners for raising that consciousness to a higher level, where it is beyond the control of any forces that are not coming from the level of love. Thus, it is absolutely necessary for those who aim to be the forerunners for the shift in consciousness, that they look at and deal with this fear of some worldwide calamity.

I have already stated that no man and woman is an island, and that all life is interconnected. I have stated that the entire earth is one interconnected system. In fact, the entire material universe is an interconnected system. Yet you must also understand that this does not mean that the earth, in its current state, is a complete system that must either go up or down as a unit. The earth was certainly designed as an unfractured, an unbroken, whole. Yet, when the beings embodying on earth began to descend into a lower state of consciousness, that whole began to be fractured into separate compartments.

***

I have said that free will is the basic law of the material universe. Free will means, among other things, that any self-aware being has the right to experiment with any level of consciousness that it desires to experience. When a self-aware being is first created and descends to any planetary home in the material universe, it descends with a certain level of consciousness. This level of consciousness is very localized, very focused on the self and its immediate local environment.

As an example of this, you might take indigenous people from around the world who live in small tribal units, that are scarcely aware of anything beyond their local area, meaning the area where they can walk by their own power. Yet if you look at such people, you will also find that they often have a quite unselfish approach to life. They feel very much connected to nature and the environment, they have a certain code of honor and they are very much connected to the whole of their tribe, seeking to help the whole to the best of their ability. So although these indigenous people might be said to have a limited knowledge compared to what you see in Western civilization, one cannot truly say that they have a low or a selfish state of consciousness.

My point being that a new co-creator has a very localized awareness and sense of self, but it is not a selfish being. It has a certain sense of being connected to something beyond itself, and it has a certain sense of principles and honor for how to behave in a way that is not what we would call selfish, or ruthless, or inconsiderate of other beings in its environment.

Yet, in the original design, there are two options that such a being can choose. It can continue to grow and expand its consciousness from the level at which it is created, gradually expanding its awareness of its environment, of its own capabilities, of its own mind. Gradually attaining mastery over its own mind and entering a state of consciousness, where it seeks to work for raising the All instead of only raising itself. Yet the other option is that a being can choose to go in what we might call the opposite direction, of becoming more and more focused on itself, even beginning to see itself as a separate being. And then seeking to expand its ability and power to act as a separate being.

This means that a being now seeks to raise itself in comparison to others, and therefore in many cases seeking to put down others instead of raising the All. It means that the being now takes on a selfishness, a self-centeredness, an insensitivity, even a ruthlessness in how it deals with other forms of life. The goal of this being is to create the impression, the appearance, that it is above and beyond other beings in its environment, and it is willing to do virtually anything in order to attain this goal.

This is the goal you might see embodied in what today would be called an egomaniac, such as some of the dictatorial leaders you have seen in the past. This might be a Hitler, a Napoleon or some of the Roman emperors or other great conquerors, who were willing to kill thousands if not millions of people in order to attain what they had defined as their goal—which in most cases would always elevate themselves to some ultimate status on earth.

So do you see, here, the essential choice faced by new co-creators? Will they expand their sense of self until they realize that all life is connected, and therefore their ultimate self is the All—meaning that the only way to raise up your self is to raise up the All? Or will they go in the opposite direction and begin to define themselves as a self that is separated from the All? And therefore, it will seem as if the ultimate way to raise up the self is to set the self apart from the All, by some appearance that defines the self as being somehow superior to all other beings in its world.

***

Now, as I said, the Law of Free Will gives any self-aware being the right to go in both directions and have either experience. And indeed, as I have explained, in previous civilizations where most beings ascended, it means that most beings in those civilizations chose the upward path of expanding the self, until they obtained that sense of oneness, where every member of a certain group saw themselves as being in oneness with the whole and with each other. And therefore, each member worked only to raise up the whole, until the whole was indeed raised up and the civilization ascended.

This does not mean that the civilization ascended as a group, for the ascension is a process that takes place at the level of each individual being. Each individual being in a civilization must earn its own ascension and must ultimately ascend alone. Yet a group of beings can indeed come together and build and reinforce a collective ascension spiral that will make it easier for the members of the group to ascend, although in the end each individual must face the same tests in order to qualify for the ascension on an individual level.

What happened in the civilizations that did not ascend was that in these civilizations you had a majority of the members that chose to go in the opposite direction and instead reinforce the separate self. When a critical mass of the members of a civilization go into this self-centeredness and selfishness, then they obviously cannot form an ascension spiral.

However, as I have attempted to explain, there is no standing still. You are either transcending yourself and ascending, or you are not transcending yourself, becoming a closed system and therefore becoming subject to the second law of thermodynamics and descending. And so, the civilizations in which a majority of the members refused to enter the ascension process, naturally formed a descension spiral that caused those civilizations to eventually self-destruct.

The question then became: where will these beings go who did not ascend? And this, of course, is where a new mechanism came into place, so that instead of ascending after one lifetime on planet earth – which in the early civilizations truly could be several hundred years as even hinted at in the Bible – it was now necessary that beings would come back to earth over several lifetimes. The Law of Free Will is not the black-and-white, all-or-nothing law that is depicted in many religions. Indeed, most religions in the Western world give you the impression that you have one shot at salvation. If you do not ascend, if you do not qualify for salvation after this lifetime, then the only alternative is an eternity in hell.

However the true alternative is re-embodiment on earth, which truly for some lifestreams has so far been close to an eternity in a hellish world of selfishness and self-centeredness—and the resulting struggle to raise oneself by putting others down. Certainly, this struggle to always raise the self in comparison to others can only lead to conflict with other beings, who are likewise seeking to raise their selves and therefore want to put you down or even prevent you from raising yourself up. And when this struggle continues and continues lifetime after lifetime, it can indeed be conceived of as a hell that is worse than the fiery hell envisioned by the Christian religion and certain other religions.

So what you truly see on planet earth is that there are lifestreams who have been embodied here for a very long time span. In fact, there are many lifestreams embodied on earth today who were among those in the first civilization that did not ascend, and who have continued to reincarnate here – in some cases with brief stints on other planetary systems – until today, still being stuck in that warring consciousness, where they seek to raise themselves by struggling against others who are likewise seeking to raise themselves to a superior status.

And given that this planet is small enough that it is possible for a person to know whether he or she is really the superior person on the planet, then it becomes obvious that there cannot at the same time be many beings who attain this sense of superiority. And thus, the inevitable result is this struggle that you have seen in past civilizations and that you can even see outpictured today in political systems, in nations or in large corporations and their attempts at world dominance.

***

To be a healer, you must overcome your fear of calamity   89

My point for giving you this knowledge is to help you see that even though the earth was conceived based on a unified vision, then, what has happened since the descent into selfishness, is that the consciousness of humankind is no longer a unified system. Certainly, we can look at the entire planet as a whole and we can talk about a collective consciousness of humankind. Even if you go back to the civilizations that did ascend, you can look at a collective consciousness.

Yet what you would see in those civilizations was that all of the inhabitants in those civilizations were at the same level of consciousness. There was still some beings that were at the lower end of the spectrum, and other beings that had worked their way towards the higher end of the spectrum. Yet there were hardly any beings in those civilizations who had taken that lower road of going into the selfishness and the self-centeredness of seeing themselves as separate beings.

Yet once a majority of the members of a civilization began to descend into that level, then you now had a distinct division between the few beings who were still above the level of selfishness and the beings who had descended below it. So in the beginning you had a division into two distinct levels, one we might call unselfishness and one we might called selfishness. Yet over time, even the level of selfishness has been expanded, so that there is now quite an enormous range between the higher levels and the lower levels of complete and utter ruthlessness and what we might call the lower aspects of selfishness.

So if you look at the collective consciousness of planet earth today, you cannot simply talk about one level of consciousness or one spectrum of consciousness. You certainly still have a division between selfishness and unselfishness, but even at the level of selfishness, you now have several levels. In fact, at the level of selfishness you have seven distinct levels that correspond to perversions of the seven rays, represented by each of the Elohim.

***

My point for bringing this up is to show you that the possibility of this division into seven perverted levels of consciousness is an expression of the Law of Free Will. At the highest level of selfishness [the less selfish] you find beings who have perverted only one of the seven rays. At the next level down you find beings who have perverted two, and so forth and so on, until you reach the very lowest level, where you find beings who have perverted all seven of the spiritual rays.

Contrary to what you might think, these beings are not necessarily what you will call obvious egomaniacs or psychopaths. In fact, the beings who have perverted all seven rays often appear to be either sophisticated or at least very powerful beings. Some of the most powerful people you have seen throughout the history of the world – and even see in the world today – are precisely beings who have attained a momentum on perverting all seven rays, and therefore are skilled at subjecting other people to their will through the misuse of each of the seven rays. This is why they are able to make so many other people submit to their authority and work for their purpose.

So what you see, then, is this division into seven distinct levels of the selfish consciousness. Now, if there was to be a worldwide calamity – that would wipe out most of the people on this planet – then I trust you can see that this would be an injustice towards not only the beings who are not in the level of selfishness but also towards the beings who have only perverted one or a few of the seven rays. My point is, therefore, to show you that the Law of Free Will makes it highly unlikely that there would be a worldwide disaster that would kill most people on earth.

Each distinct level of the perverted consciousness has created its own downward spiral. It is possible that in a particular civilization there can be a majority of the people who are trapped in the same perversion. For example, you might see a civilization where the majority of the people have perverted all seven rays. It is therefore possible that such a civilization could create a downward spiral so intense that it leads to the destruction or the falling apart of that particular civilization. This has happened in the past, but as I said, always in localized areas.

In other words, even if a civilization creates such a downward spiral that it manifests as some physical calamity – be it a natural disaster or a man-made calamity such as a war – then this will not have global consequences. Even in today's world – although it has become more unified through communications technology – there are still civilizations that are an outpicturing of a certain state of consciousness. And thus, although there can be certain localized calamities that may affect a great number of people, there is currently no possibility of a worldwide calamity that would wipe out most people on earth.

To be a healer, you must overcome your fear of calamity 91

***

My beloved, it is extremely important – if you want to be one of the forerunners for healing Mother Earth – that you begin to contemplate these ideas. I am well aware of a psychological mechanism that may make this difficult. But I will make you aware of this mechanism as well, so that you might make your decisions based on this awareness.

When you look at the past, of how civilizations have declined, you might see a very simple mechanism. If you go, for example, to the Roman civilization, you will see that a substantial part of the people in the center of that civilization were completely blind to the possibility that the civilization might be conquered and go into decline. The downward spiral lasted for quite some time, before an outside enemy managed to conquer Rome. When you look back at it today, this downward spiral is obvious. Yet you also see that for the people who were caught inside the downward spiral, it was not obvious at all. They were so blinded by the spiral they had created, that they could not see where it was leading. This, then, is the pattern you will see repeated, even in today's civilization where, as I already described, during the 1960s the vast majority of people in Western civilization were unable to see the potential dangers of pollution.

So here is now the mechanism that I wish to make you aware of. As I have said, a shift in consciousness always begins with a few individuals. Yet how do these individuals begin to wake up and see what the majority of the people in their civilization cannot or will not see? Well, truth be told, the awakening will for most people begin with a sense of realism, a realization of the potential dangers of the current downward spiral.

And for most people, once they come to the realization that there is a downward spiral and that it can lead to some very disastrous outcome, well then that realization will give rise to fear. This is not necessarily the way we in the ascended realm want people to awaken, but the reality is that this is the way that most people awaken.

Thus, if you look at yourself, you might indeed realize, that the reason why you are open to this book is that you have gone through such an awakening, where you came to the realization that there are certain aspects of the current civilization that, if they are allowed to continue unchecked, will lead to disastrous results. And you might very well have felt a certain fear as a result of this realization.

Yet what I hope you can begin to see is that when the Elohim designed planet earth, they were in a state of consciousness completely beyond the level of selfishness. Therefore, the Elohim had no fear whatsoever. The reality is that fear is not an emotion that can exist in the higher realms. Fear is an emotion that is born out of the illusion that you are a separate self.

In other words, while you still see yourself as connected to a larger whole, you will know that you are not alone. And as a result of not feeling completely alone, you cannot experience what most people call fear. Fear is the inevitable companion of going into the illusion of seeing yourself as a separate self. Truly, in reality, no man or woman is an island, and when you realize this, you cannot feel fear. But when you go into the illusion of seeing yourself as an island, then it is inevitable that you will feel fear.

Fear, then, is the product of – and the inevitable companion of – the separate self. It is not truly you who feels fear; the fear is felt by the separate self. But as long as you identify yourself with or as that separate self, you experience the world through the filter of that separate self, and thus you experience fear.

***

So can you begin to see the vision I am seeking to impart to you here? You may have awakened to the potential for some major calamity, be it as a result of war, be it as a result of pollution, be it as a result of other aspects of what you see as the limitations of civilization or the behavior of human beings. Yet can you begin to see that the limitations you see are the products of the state of consciousness that I have called selfishness?

The limitations are caused by the fact that most people on earth see themselves as separate beings, and therefore they have entered into the inevitable struggle against other people, who also see themselves as separate beings. It is this struggle that has brought humankind into a lower state of consciousness, and it is this lower state of consciousness that has precipitated the current imbalances that you have become aware of. Thus, the calamity that you might fear is a direct product of the lower state of consciousness, which means – very simply – that the only realistic way to avoid the calamity is for a critical mass of human beings to transcend the state of consciousness out of which the calamity might be precipitated.

Any calamity is the result of a downward spiral, and the downward spiral is created by people at a certain level of the perverted consciousness. The only way to break the downward spiral is for a critical mass of people in a society or group to raise their consciousness beyond the perversions that created the spinal.

Yet do you see that raising your consciousness beyond the perversions means that you raise your consciousness beyond the self-centered consciousness? You must question, see through and then transcend – through your conscious choices – the illusion of the separate self. Yet in order for you to be willing to question this illusion – even to be capable of questioning the solution – it is essential that you first attain at least some freedom from the fear that accompanies the illusion.

My beloved, consider again the people that I said have perverted all of the seven rays. I have said that they have often appeared on the world stage as very powerful individuals who could subdue other people and get them to follow their will. Yet if you look more closely, for example at a person like Adolph Hitler, was he truly a powerful man, or was he driven by an extreme fear? What drives a man to want to have power over the whole earth? What drives a man to want to control every person on earth? Wanting power over other beings, wanting to control them, is the direct outcome of fear. If you have no fear whatsoever – as you see exemplified in Jesus and the Buddha – you have no need to control others at all. The more fear you have, the stronger the need to control others.

Thus, can you see, fear is a crippling emotion, a paralyzing emotion? Most of you have probably never truly considered the psychology of individuals such as Adolph Hitler. But if you take a closer look, you will see that throughout his career – if we might call it that – there was one characteristic that made the eventual outcome, namely his self-destruction, virtually inevitable. That characteristic was his tunnel vision, his lack of vision.

Whether it was Adolph Hitler, or Napoleon, or the Roman emperors, you will see that they were blinded by a particular outlook on life. And the reason why they could only continue to act based on that outlook was that they were never able or willing to question it.

Yet why were they not willing to question their basic outlook on life? Well, it was precisely because of their fear. They were afraid to question it, and thus they could not see through it, could not see beyond it, could not free themselves from it. And as a result, they continued to blindly follow the same track. When you look at this track from the outside, when you look at the events in retrospect, it is obvious that it was the track of self-destruction. What Hitler attempted was completely impossible, and thus his downfall was given from the very moment he set his war machine in motion. Nevertheless, he could not see this until the very end, and most of the people who supported him or worked under him could not see it either, even though a few began to wake up towards the end of the war.

So my point for telling you this is to show you that if you want to really become one of the forerunners for healing Mother Earth, then you must have the courage to look at the fear that has accompanied your personal awakening. It may have been necessary for you to experience this fear in order to be awakened. Thus, I am not trying to say that this is wrong or that it is a sign of some kind of fault of yours. As they say, ignorance is bliss, meaning that while you are ignorant of the avalanche coming down the mountain, you might continue happily making merry and living as if nothing bad could ever happen. And thus, when you awaken to the potential for changes or calamities, there will be, in most cases, a fear.

Yet for you to truly be a forerunner, you must transcend the level of consciousness that has created a downward spiral. And for you to truly transcend that consciousness, you must transcend the illusion of separation. And it is precisely this illusion that gives rise to the fear—and the fear makes you afraid to question the basic state of consciousness that has created the downward spiral.

It has been said, and wisely so, that all fear is a fear of the unknown. The unknown is that which you are not willing to look at. Once you look at something and understand it, you will also understand how to overcome it, how to transcend it. Knowledge is power, the truth will set you free. It is lack of knowledge that keeps you trapped, whether it be in a physical prison or in a mental and emotional prison, where you are trapped by your fear.

Fear paralyzes you, so that you are afraid to take a look at what you fear. And if you do not take a look at what you fear, you cannot come to understand it, and therefore you cannot acquire the truth that will set you free from the fear.

***

If you are willing to take an honest look at people you know or at people in your society, you would see that there is currently a great number of people in the Western world who have started to awaken to the potential that Western civilization is in a self-destructive spiral. Yet you will also see that a substantial number of these people have then entered into or been trapped in a spiral of fear.

Many of these people, for example, believe in various conspiracy theories or they believe in various doomsday scenarios, painted by those who either want to control people or who simply love to scare others because it makes them feel superior that they can get other people to believe in this scenario they have dreamt up. Can you perhaps begin to sense that the people who are trapped in conspiracy theories and doomsday scenarios are paralyzed, because the underlying psychological mechanism is either that there is nothing that can be done to stop the calamity or that there is no point in trying, because what is the point of striving for something better when the world anyway is going to hell in a hand basket?

Yet can you see that if you go into this reaction, you are essentially using the potential for a calamity as an excuse for not raising your own state of consciousness, for not questioning the state of consciousness that has caused a downward spiral? You are not willing to look at how you, as a member of the civilization that has gone into a downward spiral, has been affected by the very consciousness that has caused the downward spiral. You are not willing to look at the beam in your own eye, and thus you sort of throw up your hands and give up. Or you hunker down and build shelters or food storage, or what have you, to prepare yourself for the worst, so that you might survive when all of the other people die because they are not willing to go into the state of fear that you are in.

So can you see, my beloved, that the people I seek to reach with this book are the people who are willing to question their fear, to look at their fear and look at why they have this fear? I am seeking to reach the people who are willing to see the need to transcend their fear, to see the need to raise their consciousness.

What is it that will pull Western civilization, or even humankind as a whole, out of the downward spiral? It is that one individual here, one individual there, and eventually a critical mass of individuals everywhere dare to raise their individual consciousness beyond the level of the collective consciousness that has created a downward spiral. And as sufficient numbers of people do this, then indeed an entire civilization, an entire society, will be pulled up higher and transcend the consciousness that created the downward spiral. And this is the only way – the absolutely only way – that downward spirals can be broken.

I have attempted to explain to you the Law of Free Will. Do you see how this law works? If all people in a civilization do nothing to transcend the current level of consciousness, then this downward spiral will continue until the civilization self-destructs. Yet when even one person begins to reverse the trend, then there is a force that pulls in the opposite direction. And as more and more people join that ascending movement – and eventually create an ascending spiral within the larger collective descending spiral – then there will eventually be a shift, where the entire civilization can be pulled out of the descending spiral.

My beloved, I am not here trying to say that you should over-interpret these stories and myths from the Old Testament. Yet I might refer you to the myth of Sodom and Gomorrah, where the question was asked whether God would spare the city if 10 righteous men could be found within it. And then, when 10 could not be found, it was asked if God would spare the city if even one righteous man could be found.

The reason why I do not want you to over-interpret this myth is that there is not the angry God in the sky who is deciding whether a civilization should be spared or whether it should be destroyed. This is all decided by the Law of Free Will. Yet, do you still see the principle that if only a few people within a civilization are pulling the opposite way, then they can indeed delay and eventually reverse the downward spiral?

Yet for you to become one of the people that pulls in the opposite direction, you must overcome the fear that the downward spiral is irreversible. If you are trapped in this fear – that nothing can be done, that the problems are too big and beyond the reach of any individual or group of individuals – then you will be paralyzed. And you will, in fact – through your fear – only contribute to the downward spiral.

Again, as I have said, there is no standing still. You are either in the perversion of selfishness that causes people to act out in selfish ways, or you are in another perversion of selfishness, namely fear—and therefore you are contributing to the downward spiral. Or you are in the process of transcending both the fear and the perversions, and therefore you are in an ascending spiral. There is no in-between, as the Bible also says: "Choose ye this day whom you will serve." It does not help to heal Mother Earth that you have awakened to the dangers of current civilization, if you have simply entered into a consciousness of fear. For the fear that you produce will only reinforce the downward spiral.

***

Thus, for you to be one of the forerunners for healing the earth, you need to question the fear. And you need to question it based on the knowledge I have given you, the knowledge that can – when you truly internalize it – set you free from all fear. For you will realize that even if a civilization goes down, those individuals who have entered an ascending spiral will not go down with it. Irregardless of what might happen in the physical world, those who are in the ascending spiral will transcend any downward spiral and therefore rise to higher levels of awareness. Which means that you will either ascend permanently from the material realm and not have to come back into embodiment, or if you do have to come back into embodiment, you will come back in a higher state than the downward spiral you might have been born into in this lifetime.

Thus, you can only benefit from being willing to question your fear and from being willing to question the very consciousness, the level of selfishness, out of which the fear comes. And to this end I will, in the following keys, give you further insights into the seven spiritual rays used by the Elohim to create planet earth, and the perversions of those rays. For once you see the positive vision of the true potential of the rays, and also see the perversions of those rays, it will be much easier for you to choose whom you will serve—whether you will continue to serve the perversions or whether you will transcend them and serve the positive qualities, the positive potential of the seven rays.

All beings on earth have all seven rays within their minds and beings. Yet all have one ray that is stronger than the others, that is their primary ray. Once you discover what your ray is, you will feel a new sense of freedom, a new sense of joy. And you will gain a new vision of how you can express that spiritual ray in a greater measure, that will indeed make an invaluable contribution to the raising of the consciousness of humankind. And precisely by expressing your spiritual qualities, you will also give the most effective possible contribution to breaking the downward spirals of humankind and of your own civilization, so that you can avoid the very things that you might fear, but that are truly not nearly as threatening as you might think.

My beloved, we in the ascended realm are eternal optimists. There are those on earth who will say that they are not being pessimistic, they are being realistic by pointing out the insurmountable problems that exist. Yet we who have ascended have ascended because we realized that there are no insurmountable problems on earth. As Jesus said 2,000 years ago: "With men this is impossible, but not with God, for with God all things are possible."

The way to overcome fear is to realize that all of the problems you see on earth are created out of the selfish state of consciousness. The problems are precipitated by the second law of thermodynamics, yet the way to raise yourself above this second law is to stop being a closed system that is set apart from the whole, from the River of Life.

When you instead enter an ascending spiral, you join that River of Life, and now you are with God, with the Creator, the Creator's intent. And thus, as Jesus said, with God – in oneness with the River of Life – all things are possible. When you transcend the perverted consciousness that makes you subject to the second law of thermodynamics, then it is easy – effortless – to transcend the downward spiral and the potential for calamity.

Any problem you see on earth, any imbalance you see on earth – be it in nature or in human society – can be transcended by transcending the level of consciousness that precipitated it. My beloved, do you begin to sense that what I am giving you here is an entirely new approach to solving human problems? Do you begin to catch a glimpse of my enthusiasm, my realistic optimism, my joy that I have because I have become one with the River of Life? And thus, I know its full potential.

Do you begin to sense your own potential and how it is indeed possible for you to become part of the ascending spiral and to leave the descending spiral behind forever? Can you not begin to sense how catching this ascending spiral is the ultimate antidote to fear? And can you then not begin to sense that it might be worth your while to at least question your fear, so that you might get a more clear vision of how to transcend it?

If you begin to sense this, then take my hand, as I, who hold the office of the Mother of God for planet earth, am indeed willing to lead you by the hand into a greater understanding of how the planet upon which you live is truly put together. When you know how things are put together, then you will see how the earth has been taken apart. But then you will also see how to put it back together again.

For whereas all the Kings horses and all the kings men cannot put Humpty Dumpty back together again, I can assure you that all of the spiritual people on earth – working together with the spiritual beings in the ascended realm – can indeed put planet earth back together again.

Key 7
To be a healer, you must know your true potential

Now that we have addressed the issue of fear, let me address the Omega aspect—that forms another polarity, designed to keep people in a state of passivity. That Omega polarity is the sense of hopelessness or despair, the sense that one person cannot make a difference, that one individual cannot stand up against the mass consciousness or even the ruling elite, who has such a firm grip on power—or so it seems.

Why should you – as just one individual – be able to do anything that will make a difference on a planetary scale? Well, my beloved, if everyone had said that throughout history, then you would still be living in caves, and the book certainly would not have been invented. When you do look at history, you will see that there have indeed been numerous cases where one individual made a difference, by being the open door for bringing forth some new idea or invention that took society one or even several steps higher.

The reality is, however, that individuality has always been seen as a threat by the ruling elite. And therefore, when you look at history, you will see that the ruling power elites of any society have attempted to discourage individual expression, individual creativity.

My point, therefore, is that if you do, indeed, look at history, you will see that history is on your side. Why did the fate of humankind change from the caveman level to that of modern civilization? Well, because, as I have said, it is one of the basic forces of nature, one of the basic laws of the universe, that self-transcendence is a mandate.

I have talked about the desire for growth, the drive for growth, and I have talked about the second law of thermodynamics, which takes effect when the desire for growth is halted. When an individual or society stops self-transcendence, well then they become subject to the second law of thermodynamics. Which will break down whatever structure they seek to maintain—as opposed to allowing that structure to transcend itself and become more in the ongoing creativity of the River of Life. Yet if you step back and think more deeply about this, you might have an inner revelation, that will allow you to know exactly what I am saying here. The deeper reality is that there is an upward trend, an upward force, in life that propels all life to transcend and become more.

***

Let us take a look at where this force comes from. I have explained that your Creator started by withdrawing its Being and creating a void. The Creator then extended part of its Being to create a sphere inside that void, a sphere that had certain structures and forms, and could therefore serve as the basis for the growth of self-aware extensions of the Creator. I have explained that the first sphere eventually ascended and became part of what is now the spiritual realm.

After the first sphere ascended, the beings, who had been instrumental in bringing that sphere to the ascension point, decided to serve once again by being the open doors for creating the very next sphere. These ascended beings now sent extensions of themselves into the next sphere. And as these extensions grew in self-awareness, they raised up the vibration of their entire sphere until it too could ascend. This has continued, as I said, for several spheres, and you are now in the seventh of these spheres.

You may look at the material universe in which you live, and you may see that it is almost infinite in size. You know very well that there are millions of galaxies that can be seen from earth, but you also know, as I have said before, that there is an observation horizon beyond which you cannot see from earth, because the light from distant galaxies have not had time to reach earth. And so, I can assure you that beyond the huge number of galaxies that can be seen from earth, there is an even greater number that are not visible.

My point here is to show you, as I am sure you already suspect, that in the immensity of the material universe, there are many other intelligent lifeforms besides human beings. Now, what science has proven is that everything is interconnected. When you go to the deeper levels of subatomic particles and even beyond to pure energy, everything is intricately connected in a giant web of life. This means that the entire material universe is an interconnected whole. What this specifically means

To be a healer, you must know your true potential

for planet earth is that even though it may seem as if human beings are isolated in a vast empty space, this is not the case at all. Human beings are – in the invisible realm of pure energy – deeply connected to all other self-aware beings in the entire material universe.

I can assure you that there are many other planets with intelligent, self-aware lifeforms. They all form a giant web of life, what we might call an Antahkarana of life. Out of the millions of planets with similar lifeforms as you see on earth – and the millions more with lifeforms that are not at all similar to what you see on earth – the vast majority of them are in an upward spiral. Thus, we might indeed say that the entire material universe is in an upward spiral, and this is proven by the very fact that, as science has observed, the material universe is expanding at an accelerated rate.

This expansion, this acceleration, is driven by the fact that the vast majority of the self-aware beings, who live in the material universe, are in the process of transcending themselves. Therefore, their interconnected consciousness has formed what I call the River of Life, which can be seen as a giant creative movement that causes the vibration of the entire material universe to be constantly raised up.

Yet when you look at the universe, you will indeed also see that there are certain areas that have not yet fully joined this upward movement. This is not to say that they are not part of it, for truly the entire universe is accelerating, which means that everything within it is being pulled upwards by the River of Life. Nevertheless, because of the Law of Free Will, there is room that there can be planets, even some solar systems, within the material universe, that are not accelerating at the same rate as the rest of the universe. Therefore, there are indeed units within the material universe that have fallen behind the general, upward, accelerated movement of the whole.

This is, of course, allowed, according to the Law of Free Will. The inhabitants of a planetary unit can collectively slow down the acceleration of their unit to the point, that it falls behind the rest of the universe. However, what these beings cannot do – again in accordance with the Law of Free Will – is to set their unit, their planetary unit, outside of the material universe. In other words, you can slow down the acceleration of your unit, but you cannot prevent that unit from being pulled upwards by the magnetic pull of the rest of the universe.

Think about what this means. It means that in order to slow down the growth of a particular planet, the inhabitants of that planet must fight against the upward pull of the entire rest of the universe. This is an immense force, and you can see, by simple mathematics, that it is not possible that the inhabitants of a given planet can completely slow down the growth of their planet against the upward pull of the rest of the universe.

This is indeed part of the reason why you are no longer living in caves. Planet earth has been pulled up by the force generated by the rest of the universe, and humankind cannot slow down this growth beyond a certain level.

This is not to say that the growth of the earth has been entirely caused by what we might call the background acceleration of the universe. For indeed, there have been many people on earth who have also been willing to become the open doors for the creative force of life to flow through their minds and beings. And this creativity, this creative flow, is indeed part of the reason why society has transcended the cave man stage and has reached the level of modern civilization.

**

Let us, then, take a look at the dynamics of the earth itself. If you look at the human population, you can actually divide it into three distinct groupings. There is, first of all, the majority of the population, which make up around 80% of the total. These are the people who are neither particularly good nor particularly bad, if you want to apply such a relative, dualistic standard. It would, however, be better to say that the majority of the population are people who have not yet developed a strong individuality. They are therefore more likely to follow along with whatever trends are currently dominating the mass consciousness. You might see this, for example, in how many people go along with fashion trends, or how they are pulled into various forms of entertainment or fascination with particular events. You might also see how many people spend most of their lives seeking to accumulate material possessions in the race to keep up with the neighbors.

So my point is this. The majority of the population have not yet developed the strong individuality that makes them leaders. They are therefore likely to follow along with the strong leaders that dominate

To be a healer, you must know your true potential

their society. So who are these leaders? Well, if you set up a linear scale – where you have at the bottom of the scale the lowest possible consciousness that you see on earth and at the top of the scale the highest possible consciousness – you can then use this scale to realize, that when I say the lowest possible consciousness, I am talking about beings who have the greatest degree of selfishness and self-centeredness. In other words, I am not talking about people who are barely conscious, I am talking about people who are indeed very self-aware and have a very strong "individuality" and personality—only their entire lives are focused on themselves and the goals that they see for themselves.

This is not to say that the people who have the lowest consciousness are necessarily only focused on their own lives. Many of them do indeed serve in leadership roles in society or in business, but they do so out of a completely self-centered focus. It is a matter of what is in it for them personally or for what they see as the supreme cause for which they are fighting. You will, therefore, see that many who are at the lowest levels of consciousness have indeed been the strong leaders of history, such as the many dictators found throughout the world in every historical epoch. Adolph Hitler, Napoleon, Stalin and many such leaders were indeed some of the most selfish and self-centered people to ever walk the earth. And therefore, they had the lowest level of consciousness according to the scale I am proposing.

On the other hand, you can, of course, also see people who had a higher level of consciousness. These are people who were less self-centered but who nevertheless also had a strong individuality. They might be the inventors, the thinkers, the humanitarians, those who did something selflessly in order to serve the onward progress of society in various ways.

So what you see now is that, based on this scale, we can divide humankind into three categories. First, there is the 10% who have the lowest level of consciousness, or should we say the highest degree of selfishness. Then there is the general population, which makes up the 80% in the middle. These are people who range from being fairly selfish and self-centered to being very much aware of what goes on in society and the need to do something for others. And then above this, you find what we might call the top 10%, namely those who have the highest degree of selflessness and altruistic approach to life.

So my point here is simply this. The majority of the population tend to follow strong leaders. So who are the strong leaders? Well, when you look at history, you will see that in most cases they have belonged to the bottom 10%. And the reason for this is very simple. Those who are in the bottom 10% are very focused on themselves. They see themselves clearly as separate beings, and they are therefore willing to go to great length to further the interest of themselves as separate beings. Now, as I said, these bottom 10% can also seem to work for a cause, yet you will see a very simple characteristic. When the bottom 10% work for a cause, it is always a cause that is defined in a dualistic way.

This means that you have a group of people who are right or good and you have another group of people who are the scapegoats. A typical example of this is Adolph Hitler, who would himself have claimed to be working for the ultimate good cause, namely the purification of the human race and the creation of an ideal society as he saw it. Yet of course, you know that Hitler's vision was clearly dualistic, in the sense that he had appointed another group of people as the scapegoats. And therefore, he saw it as perfectly necessary and perfectly justifiable to eradicate this group of people in order to purify the race and create an ideal society.

This, then, is the characteristic that is typical for the bottom 10%. They may claim they are working for a good cause, but their cause is always defined so that another group of people are the scapegoats that stand in the way of the fulfillment of the cause. And thus, it now becomes justifiable to use various means, including murder, in order to pacify the scapegoats. This is what you can see throughout history, even in the Old Testament, where the Jews often claimed to be God's chosen people and claimed that their God had not only justified but even mandated that they kill other tribes.

So do you see that this is the overall characteristic of the bottom 10%? They are extremely aggressive in promoting their self-interest, even the self-interest that is camouflaged as a greater cause. And in order to do this, they are willing to violate one of the basic laws that govern human behavior, as expressed in the unconditional command "Thou shalt not kill." Even though these people may claim to be religious, as for example the inquisitors behind the Spanish Inquisition, they are nevertheless able to justify killing because of the greater cause. Their modus operandi, therefore, is that the ends can justify the means.

To be a healer, you must know your true potential   107

***

Now, on the other hand, if you look to the top 10%, you will see that these are people who in many cases have virtually no self-interest left. They are completely focused on actually serving a greater cause, and they have also realized that this greater cause cannot be defined in a dualistic manner. It is not a matter of dividing humanity into two separate spheres – the good people and the bad people – and then eradicating the bad people. It is a matter of finding ways to raise up all life.

If you want to see a modern example of a person in this category, you might look at Mahatma Gandhi in India and how he managed to free India from the clutches of the British empire by using a philosophy based on non-violence. It would have been extremely easy for Gandhi to become a strong leader, that could lead India in a violent uprising against the British. Yet he resisted this temptation and instead insisted on a course of non-violence.

So do you now see the fundamental difference between the leaders in the bottom 10% and the leaders in the top 10%? It is the aggressiveness with which they are willing to pursue their goals. And this, of course, is precisely why, in many cases in history, the leaders from the bottom 10% have been able to take over and dominate society. They have done so through violence and force.

Yet as you can also see from history, a shift has indeed occurred on this planet. Violence and force are no longer seen as acceptable means by a large percentage of the population. What this demonstrates is that among the 80% of the general population, a larger and larger percentage has begun to realize that violence is not an acceptable means of promoting a cause. More and more people are beginning to realize the fallacy in the ethos that the ends can justify the means.

This is what paved the way for the emergence of democracies and the concept that all human beings are created equal, and that they have certain rights that no force on earth can take away from them. And so, with this in mind, you can see that even though there are clearly many problems on earth, there has been a general upward trend.

***

We might say here that when you take a look at history, it is easy to focus on the strong leaders, it is easy to think that it was either the aggressive leaders in the bottom 10% or the creative leaders in the top 10% that brought society forward. This however, is not a true understanding of history.

The reality is that any society will be a reflection of the consciousness of the 80% of the general population. No matter how strong a leader a society has, it cannot go beyond or below what the 80% are willing to do. You may have a strong aggressive leader, like Adolph Hitler, but he would not have been able to pull Germany into a major war unless the 80% of the German population had been willing to support it. Likewise, you may have a strong creative leader such as Gandhi, but he still would not have been able to prevent India from erupting into violence if the 80% of the population had not been at a certain level of awareness, where they were willing to look for non-violent solutions.

So my point is to show you that there has been a growth in the collective awareness of humankind. What has brought about this growth is partly the upward pull of the entire material universe and partly the upward pull of the top 10%. Which means that if you desire to be one of those who are the forerunners for healing Mother Earth, you must look at yourself as belonging to the top 10%. And you must therefore realize that whereas you alone cannot change society, there is indeed something you can do to bring about such change. For when you raise your own consciousness, you will indeed add to the magnetic pull that will pull up on the 80% of the population.

As I said, it is indeed the 80% that determine the fate of a civilization, but the 80% are not strong enough to take their society in a particular direction. They will follow the pull of either the bottom 10% or the top 10%. And therefore, if there is to be an accelerated growth in Western civilization, it can happen in only one way. It can happen only if the top 10% – those who are the most spiritually aware people, those who are the least aggressive, the least self-centered – will indeed begin to exercise their right to take dominion over society.

This, of course, does not mean that you need to become the strong, aggressive leaders that you see in the bottom 10%. You are not meant to rule with an iron fist. You are meant to rule by pulling the 80% of the general population upwards through the power of your mind.

Western civilization has already reached a level, where the general population is ready to be pulled upwards by the top 10%. Yet the breakthrough has not yet happened, and it has not happened for one simple reason, namely that the top 10% have not yet awakened to their role as the forerunners. They see themselves as just individuals who are striving for personal growth, but they have not yet awakened to their potential for bringing forth change in society by creating or adding to the upward momentum. And thereby pulling the 80% over that critical boundary, that suddenly shifts the public debate and creates an entirely new awareness about the relationship between human beings and the planet upon which they live.

***

So can you see that by you, and many other spiritually aware people, becoming more aware of your potential to raise the collective consciousness, there can indeed be a dramatic shift within a relatively short period of time? Yet in order for this shift to reach its full potential, there are two things you need to know. First of all, you need to be aware of where the bottom 10% came from. You see, the Law of Free Will makes it possible for beings to go in two directions. You can, as mentioned before, accelerate upwards towards a higher level of awareness or you can decelerate downwards towards a lower level of awareness.

What you have seen in every previous sphere, including this one, is that the majority of the self-aware beings in a sphere have always chosen the path of acceleration. In the first three spheres that were created, no being chose the downward path at all. Yet beginning in the fourth sphere, there were indeed beings who chose that downward path. These were not beings who were in an obvious way evil, as you might think when you consider the myths about a devil that appears obviously evil. On the contrary, many of the beings in the fourth sphere who were not part of the accelerating spiral, had leadership positions. They were, indeed, as you see on planet earth today, the aggressive leaders who thought they were so qualified to rule others that they had deliberately sought out leadership positions.

Now, my beloved, it is important that you understand an aspect of free will here. Free will gives any self-aware being the right to pursue any experience that it thinks it needs. Free will, therefore, goes far in order to accommodate a being having any experience that it desires. So in the fourth sphere there were indeed certain beings who had been allowed to assume leadership roles, even though they were still trapped in a self-centered approach to life. They truly thought they knew better than anyone else in their sphere. The reason why these beings were allowed to assume leadership positions was that it was hoped that by having the experience of being leaders, they would eventually have enough of that experience. They would eventually be able to transcend the self-centered desire to be leaders and instead adopt a less self-centered approach to leadership.

This did, indeed, happen for many beings, but there was a relatively small group of beings who did not transcend their self-centeredness. Instead, they added on to it, until they became more and more convinced that their perception of the world was not only right but was the only right one, meaning that it was superior to all others. These beings, therefore, lived in what we might call a "mental box" of their own making, and they saw everything through the filter of that mental box.

This condition was allowed to exist for a very long time, but there does come a point, where such a condition can no longer be sustained. That point came when the entire sphere was very close to the ascension point. In other words, a being or a group of beings have the right within free will to go into their own mental box, but they do not have the right to uphold that for an indefinite period of time.

For when the majority of the beings in their sphere are ready to ascend, then there comes a point, when the beings who are not part of the ascension spiral must make a choice. They must either choose to change their ways and join the ascension spiral, or they must choose to continue in the descension spiral. Yet as I am sure you can see, the fact that some beings choose to remain apart from the ascension spiral cannot justify that the ascension of an entire sphere is held back. I am sure you can see that if the millions of planets with intelligent life in the material universe were ready to ascend today, then it would not be justifiable that the inhabitants of planet earth would be able to hold back the ascension of the entire universe.

So there did come a point in the fourth sphere, where the beings who were not part of the ascension spiral were confronted with the need to make a choice. Some of these beings did indeed choose to join the ascension spiral, and they were then given assistance by the spiritual

To be a healer, you must know your true potential   111

teachers of that sphere to very quickly catch up to the level of awareness attained by the rest of the beings in their sphere. Yet there was a group of beings who refused to do this. These beings had become so convinced that the universe was – or should be – functioning according to their perception, that they were not willing to question their perception and bring it into alignment with reality.

The question now became what to do with these beings. Obviously, they could not ascend with the rest of their sphere, for only beings who have given up all sense of a separate self, all selfishness and self-centeredness, can ascend and reach immortality in the spiritual realm. The solution, therefore, was that these beings would continue their descending spiral, until they literally fell into the next sphere that was being created as the fourth sphere was ascending.

***

Now my beloved, you might take a look at many of the religions found on this planet, and you may see that a considerable portion of them contain some kind of mythological story about a fall. In the Western world, you have the story of the Garden of Eden and Adam and Eve, who fell by eating the forbidden fruit. All of these stories have a basis in reality, and they all go back to what I have just described, namely the original fall that began in the fourth sphere, when a small group of beings decided to remain apart from the ascending spiral. This is not to say that these many stories were formulated based on a complete awareness of what I have just told you. But it is to say that in the collective memory of humankind, there is a rudimentary awareness of the possibility of a fall.

Yet what you also need to realize is that this fall is not the result of some angry God casting beings out of heaven because they have made a seemingly innocent mistake. The deeper reality is that the fall is a product of the Law of Free Will, which mandates that a small group of self-aware beings cannot hold back the vast majority in their own sphere or even their own planetary unit.

Why is it important for you to be aware of this dynamic? Well, it is important because when you realize that there are certain beings who have fallen into a lower state of consciousness, then you can gain a new understanding of human history. Suddenly, it now becomes possible to understand why there have been leaders, such as a Hitler or a Stalin, and why they have for a time seemed almost invincible. These are leaders who have a very long momentum on misusing power in order to subdue the population.

I can tell you that some of the most aggressive leaders you have seen in human history are indeed among the original fallen beings that fell in the fourth sphere. They first fell into the fifth sphere, and again they sought to attain dominant positions in that sphere. When that sphere had reached the ascension point, they again refused to come up higher, and so they feel into the sixth. And some of them fell into the seventh, which is your sphere. And they have again attempted to set themselves up in dominant positions as best they could. And therefore, these lifestreams have kept incarnating over and over again in many different societies, where they have attempted to attain leadership positions and do what they have now done for so long that they cannot see any other way.

So the question now becomes: why are these lifestreams allowed to reembody and continue to reembody on earth? Well, they are allowed to embody here because the 80% of the general population did in past ages descend to a level of consciousness that was also highly dominated by the illusion of separation and the focus on the separate self. This meant that the majority of the population were not open to any higher ideas or ideals. They were, for example, not open to the concept of human rights and equality among people.

And therefore, the general population were not open to the guidance of the Ascended Host, who serve as the spiritual teachers for planet earth. And as I have said, when you turn yourself into a closed system, the second law of thermodynamics becomes your teacher. And the second law of thermodynamics then mandated that now these very self-centered lifestreams could begin to embody on earth, so that they would become the visible teachers of humankind.

In other words, these very self-centered lifestreams became substitute teachers, that would outplay the tendencies in the collective consciousness to such an extreme that people could finally begin to see the fallacy of this approach. You may look at Adolph Hitler, and the last thing you would consider was that he was a teacher. Yet if you step back from the deep emotions that might be involved, you can see that what Adolph Hitler did was to make evil so obvious that many people finally saw the need for a new approach, so that this planet never again would see a situation like the Holocaust.

***

So what you realize here is that there is a force, a magnetic force, that is pulling the entire material universe higher and higher. You can resist this force, the inhabitants of an entire planetary unit can resist this force. Yet as the force becomes stronger and stronger, it takes more and more effort to resist the force of transcendence, the River of Life. And what does this mean? It means that those who do resist the force of transcendence must outplay their self-centeredness in more and more extreme forms.

You might look at the Middle Ages and the feudal societies and the Inquisition and see that this was an extreme example of a power elite subduing the population. And then you may see that when the stranglehold of the Catholic Church was finally broken by the early scientists, there was a clear upward trend which brought society forwards towards democracy, freedom and equal rights. Yet you can also see that at the same time as this upward trend, there was a tendency for the creation of dictatorships that became even more extreme than what you saw during the Middle Ages. The dictatorships of Hitler, and Stalin, Mao or Pol Pot were even more extreme than the dictatorship of the Catholic Church, the Kings and the noble class.

So can you see that even though, from a certain perspective, it may seem as if things are getting worse and worse, this is actually a product of the fact that there is an underlying trend that pulls society up higher? You might, as an illustration of this, consider a room that is in total darkness. There is no differentiation, for everything is dark. Yet as the sun slowly starts rising, more and more light comes into the room. At first, everything still appears gray, but as the sun rises above the horizon, there comes a point, where there is now a very strong light shining into the room. But at first, the effect of this light is to create a sharp contrast between the light and the shadows. Do you see that from a grayness, in which there is little differentiation, there comes a period where there is a very strong differentiation? And then, there comes a period where the light becomes so strong that the shadows begin to fade away.

Planet earth is right now at the point, where the shadows are at their strongest. But they are beginning to fade away. Planet earth is ready for the emergence of a greater light that will make the shadows disappear, so that all is seen in the light of a new day.

***

Now, let me make you aware of of another force that is part of this picture. I have talked about the entire material universe having numerous planets that have formed an upward spiral. Yet the material universe is not an isolated unit. As I have said, everything is made out of energy and energy is vibration. There is a continuum of vibrations, ranging from the densest level, which is that of physical matter, to the very highest level that is very close to the Creator.

Beyond the material frequency spectrum is the spiritual realm. But between the material frequency spectrum and the spectrum of the spiritual realm, there are three distinct levels. The highest in vibration is what we might call the etheric level or the identity level. It is where you find the blueprint held by the Elohim. The blueprint for planet earth is stored at the highest level of the etheric realm, and from here it was gradually lowered into the level below the etheric realm, which is the mental realm, the level of thought. From the mental level, the blueprint was lowered to the next level down, which is what we call the emotional level. And from here it was then lowered into the physical frequency spectrum.

So do you see that there is a flow of energy from the spiritual realm, first into the etheric realm, then into the mental, then into the emotional and then into the physical? This is not unlike what you experience personally, if you think about your own mind and being. You will see that at the very deepest level, there is your basic sense of identity, your sense of who you are. I am not here only talking about your name, your national origin, your race or religion. I am talking about your sense of whether you are a spiritual being or a human being.

And then, from this level of identity, your awareness flows into the mental realm which is the level of thought, where you have a more clear sense of your environment, your potential, what you can do and what you cannot do and how you can do what you can do. Yet you will also see that the mental level is a level that is good for making plans, but it is

To be a healer, you must know your true potential 115

not sufficient to carry out those plans. For in order to take action, there must be an impetus, a momentum, that propels you into action. And that momentum comes from the emotional realm. There must be a feeling that triggers your action, and then an impulse breaks through to the physical level, where you actually do something.

So my point is that the material universe is part of this greater whole. The material universe is connected, is intertwined with, the emotional realm, the mental realm, the etheric realm and even the lower levels of the spiritual realm. These four levels of the physical, emotional, mental and etheric form the totality of the unascended sphere in which you live.

Yet even this is not an isolated unit, for it is connected to the spiritual realm as well. So my point for telling you this is to show you that there are numerous beings in the material realm that have entered an upward spiral, but there are also numerous self-aware beings in the emotional realm who have entered an upward spiral. There are more beings in the mental realm, more beings in the etheric and there are more beings in the spiritual realm who are also part of the ascending spiral of your sphere.

***

My point, therefore, is that you who are members of the top 10% on earth are not alone. You are part of this greater continuum of billions and billions of lifestreams who are part of the ascending spiral of your sphere. And if you will follow the example of beings such as the Buddha or Jesus, you can indeed become a very powerful force for raising the collective awareness of humankind.

Take the example of Jesus who said clearly, "With men this is impossible, but not with God, for with God all things are possible." What he meant was that when you look at yourself, even when you look at the spiritual people as a group, you can see that you do not have the human power to change society, to change the course of civilization. Yet you do not have to do this with human power. You simply have to align yourself with the immense upward momentum formed by the entire ascending spiral of your sphere. In order to align yourself with this spiral, you have to go through a personal transformation that was also demonstrated by Jesus. Jesus said, "I can of my own self do nothing," because he realized that he could not do anything by his own power.

Jesus said that "it is the father within me who is doing the work," because he knew that there was the flow of the River of Life, the flow of the Spirit, through him that was able to accomplish what I have earlier described as a higher natural law. The miracles performed by Jesus were not truly performed by Jesus as a human being. They were performed by the upward momentum of the River of Life, working through Jesus.

Why was it necessary for this upward momentum to have someone in embodiment to work through? Well, it was necessary because of the Law of Free Will. The people who are in physical embodiment on earth are the ones who have the responsibility for determining the fate of the earth. We who are the Ascended Host cannot override the free will of human beings in embodiment, and that is, indeed, why there is a need for those in embodiment to do what Jesus demonstrated when he said, "I am the open door which no man can shut."

When you become an open door for the upward movement of the River of Life, then no man, no force on earth, can shut that open door. This is truly the example that Jesus came to demonstrate. This was his true mission—to demonstrate that all human beings have the potential to be the open door for a far greater power, and therefore activate a natural law that can indeed produce what seems like miracles to the human level of awareness.

Now, my beloved, I sincerely hope that I have not overwhelmed you. I hope that you are able to follow me, so that you do not think I am giving you a completely unrealistic, utopian view of the world. I hope you are able to see that what I am giving you here is indeed a deeper understanding, a deeper realism of how change comes about on this planet.

Those who are the fallen beings do not want you to understand this, and that is why they have done everything possible to limit your understanding, to limit your imagination, so that you think that the future of this planet will be determined only by physical power, the power that they are seeking to control. What the fallen beings do not want you to understand is that you have access to a higher power. You see, they themselves do not have access to this power, because beings who are trapped in selfishness cannot access the higher power I am talking about.

Only when you transcend the illusion of the separate self and begin to work for raising the All, can you be the open door for the River of Life. This is, again, what Jesus demonstrated. This is your potential, not only as an individual but as a group of the top 10%, the most spiritually aware people. And so, having given you at least a glimpse of this potential, I will move on to help you understand it in greater depth and detail.

Key 8
Understanding will and power

Before we go any further and talk about practical aspects of how to heal Mother Earth, and how to solve the many human conditions that are affecting the health of Mother Earth, I would like to give you a deeper understanding of how the earth was created. This understanding might seem to be a bit esoteric for some readers, who would like to get into the more practical stuff as soon as possible. Yet I assure you that by giving you this understanding early, I set a foundation that we can build upon. And as we go through the book, you will see that it will be highly fruitful in terms of giving you a deeper understanding, that can shed new light on many aspects of the environmental debate and the political factors that relate to the environment and to life on earth.

You will see that many of the things you have been brought up to believe about the environment are simply not correct. They are out of touch with the basic reality of how this planet actually functions. Therefore, devoting your life to promoting particular political solutions will do very little to actually heal Mother Earth.

The simple reality is that current political conditions on earth are, as everything else, the consequences of a particular state of consciousness. So seeking to supposedly solve environmental problems from the same level of consciousness that has created those environmental problems in the first place, is simply not going to work. It is not a realistic solution, and therefore I will do what I can in this book to help those who have open minds and hearts to come to see beyond the illusions, which most people on this planet have been brought up to believe in without question.

You will, then, begin to see exactly why humankind has created so many environmental problems. You will begin to see the underlying consciousness that has created the problems. And therefore, you will also begin to see how so many of the proposed solutions are completely out of touch with reality—and therefore are not solutions that will work for the environment but only solutions that will work for certain people, who have specific human interests at heart and not environmental or natural interests.

So what I would like to do is to give you an introduction to the seven spiritual rays that the Elohim used to design and manifest planet earth. Yet although it was the Elohim that built the physical form of planet earth, the introduction I will give you in the next keys will not come from the level of the elohimic consciousness. There is for each ray a certain hierarchy, where the highest being representing the ray is the Elohim and the Archangel of that ray. Yet there are also lower levels, reaching down to masters who have recently ascended from planet earth and therefore still have a clear memory of what it is like to be in physical embodiment in the density of the energies that you currently find on this planet. These masters have elected a particular master to serve as the leading master for each ray, and the technical term for that master is the "Chohan" of the ray. Thus, we will now give you, in the following keys, an introduction to each of the seven rays, given by each of the chohans of that ray.

And thus, we will begin with the first ray and the Chohan for that ray, whose name is Master MORE. Master MORE has been known in several ascended master teachings and esoteric traditions under different names, such as the name El Morya or the Master M. Yet he has decided to change his official name to Master MORE, in order to express not only what he is about but what the first ray is about. It has been understood by students of previous organizations and teachings that the first ray is the ray of power and will. Yet this is a somewhat simplistic understanding, and so I will let Master MORE expound upon the true characteristics of the first ray.

Master MORE:

I am indeed the Master M, the Master El Morya, the Master MORE— for MORE I AM. Whatever you think of me, I am more than that.

If you have known me in decades past, I am now more, for I have transcended myself many times. If you have known me 10 seconds ago, I am now more, for I have transcended myself in the past 10 seconds. Thus, by the time I am done giving this discourse, I will have transcended myself at least 144 times, corresponding to the 144 different levels of consciousness that are possible in the material frequency spectrum.

Understanding will and power

And thus, if you want to have the full understanding of the discourse I will give, then you also need to transcend yourself 144 times as you study this discourse – perhaps many times – and therefore absorb the full meaning. This is, of course, not limited to my discourses but to the discourses of any ascended master. There are always many different levels of consciousness, and only those students who are willing to open their minds to an understanding that goes beyond their present level, will gain the full understanding of any discourse we give.

This is not to say that you can instantly understand all of the 144 levels of a discourse. You are currently at a present level of consciousness, and if we say that that level of consciousness represents level I, then obviously you will not be able to understand, instantly, the level that represents the 144th level of consciousness.

Nevertheless, what you need to focus on is to understand the level that is above your current level of consciousness. For that is how you grow, and once you have grasped that level, then you reach for the next. And so forth and so on, until you do indeed go around the entire wheel that has 144 facets, 144 sides. And then, when you have seen a particular problem, a particular issue, from 144 different perspectives, well then, my beloved, you can claim to have the full and complete understanding of that topic.

***

So this might be my opening words here. For one of the major blockages that prevents the solution to virtually any problem on earth, including the problems related to the environment, is precisely that fools rush in where angels fear to enter. Human beings rush in with snap judgments, with limited knowledge—that they think is full knowledge. And therefore, they throw themselves with great enthusiasm at solving problems that they have not even begun to understand.

And therefore, most of the solutions they can see will only make the problem worse, or will create other problems that will mushroom into other problems—until you have a society that is so burdened by problems that it seems like there is no way out. There is nothing you can do, and thus the civilization goes into a downward spiral, where everything gets more and more chaotic, more and more disorganized—until the civilization perfectly outpictures the second law of thermodynamics.

Because the internal friction of that civilization has broken down the civilization, until there is no order left.

So it should be obvious that this discourse that I give – as the discourses given by Mother Mary before me and as those that will be given by other chohans after me – have only one purpose. And that is to expand the understanding of those who have open minds and hearts, those who are open to realizing that there could be more to understand about a particular issue than what they currently know and see.

Progress in human affairs has never – ever – occurred or been promoted by those who think they know everything. If you think you know it all, how could you possibly be open to learning something new? And if you are not open to learning something new, how could you possibly be in touch with the underlying purpose of all creation? Mother Mary has already explained that purpose: it is the growth in self-awareness.

Yet what exactly does it mean to grow in self-awareness? Ah, here is a topic that few people have ever even considered. For of course, it is not part of the common discourse in current Western civilization.

And why is it not part of the common discourse, my beloved? Well, it is indeed because Western civilization has become a battleground for people who think they know everything. And therefore, they seek to promote their self-elevated systems, that they think can define life and can answer all of the questions that one should ask about life.

Such has been the fate of the Christian religion, which at a very early stage in its history became hijacked by those who wanted to use that religion – and who will use anything – in order to gain power over the people. Thus, the Christian religion became a tool for controlling the thinking of the people, as can be seen by anyone who is willing to study the history of the Middle Ages.

Then, suddenly, a new trend began to emerge, a new movement in human thought. There were those who dared to say, "Well, why can we not ask the questions that go beyond church doctrine, why are we not allowed to consider certain aspects of life? Why can we not look at the movements of the stars in the heavens and then draw the conclusion that they contradict the Catholic doctrine that the earth is the center of the universe? If the earth, truly, is not the center of the universe, what meaning does it have to say that because of a certain church doctrine, we are not allowed to ask the question of how the universe really functions?"

Understanding will and power

And so, you see, for a time science – which was indeed sponsored by the ascended masters – became the movement for opening the minds and hearts of human beings. Yet as it happened with Christianity, it also happened with science. Gradually, those whose desire is to control the population, to control people's thinking, started influencing science. And soon you saw the emergence of a concept called scientific materialism, which is as restrictive for human thought and for human curiosity as was the Catholic doctrine of the Middle Ages.

As a scientist today, you may not be pulled before the Inquisition and tortured on a rack or burned at the stake, but there are certainly many barriers that prevent scientists from, at least openly, addressing or discussing questions that go beyond the prevailing materialistic doctrine. Scientists have, as Mother Mary has eloquently explained, discovered an undeniable link between the basic level of matter and the consciousness of human beings. Yet so far, too few scientists – or even philosophers for that matter – have been willing to ask the logical questions that follow from this discovery.

My point is simply this. Do you want to become one of the forerunners for changing the current conditions that are threatening to destroy the body of the Earth Mother? If you do, then my question is, "Are you willing to think beyond the mental box in which you have grown up?"

Are you willing to truly ask the questions that both church, and state, and science tell you you are not allowed to ask or that you do not need to ask? If you are, then you can benefit much from these discourses. For of course, as I have said, each issue, each problem, can be understood from 144 different perspectives. And only when you see it from 144 different perspectives do you have that full, spherical understanding of the topic.

***

Currently, the environmental debate in the Western world is not at the bottom of those 144 levels of consciousness. Indeed, there are many both scientists, politicians, journalists and others in the Western world who have climbed up the ladder, if we might talk of a ladder, of these 144 levels of consciousness.

Yet there are very few who have risen above the bottom third of these possible levels. For too many are still stuck in looking at environmental problems and the entire environmental issue from a strictly materialistic perspective.

I am not thereby saying that I encourage anyone to develop a so-called Christian perspective on environmentalism, for that is not likely to be true progress. What I do encourage is that people take the current scientific understanding of environmental issues and then build upon it by using the universal spiritual understanding that we will release in this book, and have released in many other teachings through this messenger. Then, by building upon the foundation set by science, you will be able to take the spiritual understanding and climb the ladder of the remaining levels of consciousness, until you see the problem in its full complexity.

And while it may seem as if seeing a problem from 144 different perspectives might make everything very complicated, the deeper reality is that when you do see it from every angle, then it actually becomes much more simple to see the true nature of the problem and therefore the possible solutions.

So let us begin by setting a foundation for your understanding of the relationship between human beings and the planet upon which they live. This understanding must begin by acknowledging what Mother Mary has already spoken about, namely the purpose for the entire existence of the universe: as I have said, the growth in self-awareness.

***

Growing in self-awareness is not the same as growing in knowledge. There is currently a perception in the Western world that the people who have the most knowledge about a problem must be the ones who are best suited for defining the solution to the problem. Yet knowledge is horizontal, whereas growth in self-awareness is vertical.

It is when you rise from a certain level among the 144 different levels of consciousness to the next level up that you have grown in self-awareness. You see, rising to another level of consciousness is not simply a matter of acquiring factual knowledge that can be learned by heart. It is a matter of internalizing, of integrating, knowledge, of integrating understanding until it is not simply something that is put into the container of your mind. But rather, it becomes part of how you see life in the material realm.

Understanding will and power

In order to truly understand what this means, I would like to introduce a few concepts. Some of you may be familiar with them, but I will give them from a slightly different angle that might still give you deeper insights than what you have gained before.

The inevitable conclusion from a spiritual outlook on scientific discovery is that you are not a product of your physical brain. Your mind, your being, your sense of self is not produced by chemical or electromagnetic processes in the brain. You are a spiritual being who has entered into the vehicle of your physical body. It is comparable, although far more complex, to when your physical body gets into a car and uses the car as a vehicle for getting from Point A to Point B more quickly than you could do on your own two legs.

Thus, the body is the vehicle for expressing yourself in the denser energies that make up the physical planet, called earth. Yet the unfortunate problem that has occurred on earth is that most people have come to identify themselves so fully with the physical body, that they think they either are the physical body or that their abilities are limited by the physical body. It is as if a driver thinks he is the car or cannot do anything beyond what the car can do.

Obviously, if you are open to this book, you are open to the spiritual side of life. Therefore, you realize that you are a spiritual being, inhabiting a physical body for a time and that you, the spiritual being, will continue to exist after the physical body can no longer be sustained. Nevertheless, have you actually fully realized what it means that you are a spiritual being inhabiting a physical body? I think not, so let me give you a few pointers.

It has been my experience as a spiritual teacher – who now for over a century has been teaching students through various messengers and organizations – that even the people who are open to the spiritual side of life are still very much trapped in a certain view of themselves and their own abilities. They are very much trapped in the programmed mindset that your physical body is a limitation to you expressing yourself as a spiritual being. Most people believe that their primary means of expression on planet earth is the physical body. Thus, what is possible for you is what is possible for the body. What you can do on planet earth is limited to what your physical body can accomplish.

Nothing, of course, could be further from the truth. The primary means for expressing yourself on planet earth is not your physical body, nor is it your physical brain—it is your mind. Your mind has several aspects. As science has shown, there must be a part of reality that is beyond the frequency spectrum currently defined as the material universe. Thus, there is a part of your mind, a part of your self, that is beyond the material universe.

You are a spiritual being, which means that there is a part of you that is not residing in or limited to the physical body. It is not that the totality of your being, your spiritual self, has descended into the physical body. On the contrary, only a small portion of your total being has descended into the physical body. What has happened is that most people on earth have become blinded by the density of the vibrations found in the material frequency spectrum, so they have forgotten that greater part of their beings. They have lost the contact between the conscious part of their minds and the greater part of their minds.

$$***$$

The greater part of your mind resides permanently in the spiritual realm, which, as we have said, is a realm of higher frequencies than those found in the material frequency spectrum. This being is what we in certain past teachings have called the I AM Presence, in order to signify that it is connected to, that it is an extension of, the Creator itself.

You might recall that in the Old Testament there is a section where Moses ascends a mountain in order to get a new covenant directly from God. Moses asks God for a name to give to the people, and the only name that God will give is the "I AM" or the "I AM THAT I AM." Thus, in order to connect your spiritual being with the Creator itself, we have named your spiritual being the I AM Presence.

Yet it would be extremely helpful for you to understand that words have certain limitations. You will understand this by simply observing how easy it is for people to get into arguments. One person says something to another, and the second person understands those words in a completely different way than intended by the person who spoke them. The reason is simple: words do not convey a clear and unequivocal message, as for example do the numbers used in mathematics. Words can be interpreted, and indeed will be interpreted, by each person who reads or hears the same words. Thus even the name "I AM Presence" can be interpreted in ways that convey a certain limitation.

Understanding will and power

Many people who have grown up in the Christian tradition, and have been exposed to the Christian view of God, will think that God is the never-changing perfect creator somewhere up there in the sky. If God is already omnipotent and omniscient, then why would God need to change? Yet, as Mother Mary has already explained, the Creator is constantly transcending itself, and therefore the Creator is not the same I AM or the same I AM THAT I AM today as the one who appeared to Moses on the mountain so long ago. As I transcend myself every second, well certainly the Creator transcends itself even more than I do—which is why I have not yet risen to the level of consciousness of the Creator.

So my suggestion for this book would be that we instead make use of the realization, known by some biblical scholars, that the translation of the name of God given in most Bibles is actually not a correct translation of the original Hebrew. "Yod he wav he" is not best translated as "I am that I am" but actually as "I will be who I will be." The reality is that the Creator did not give Moses a fixed name but simply said, "I will be who I will be at any moment," and that is precisely why the first two commandments given to Moses were: "Thou shalt have no other gods before me" and "Thou shalt not take unto thyself any graven image."

For the moment you take onto yourself a graven image of God, well then you have lost touch with the real God, the Living God, who is constantly transcending itself. And so, even the concept that you have an I AM Presence in the spiritual realm that stores your divine individuality and is always there for you, might give you the idea that your I AM Presence is always the same. Yet your I AM Presence is constantly transcending itself, and one of the ways that it does transcend itself is through you, through your experiences and the decisions you make here in the material realm.

Thus, I would suggest that instead of talking about an "I AM Presence" we talk about an "I Will Be Presence," a Presence that is constantly flowing with the River of Life, eternally becoming more as the entire universe is becoming more. Your mind, your being, then, is an extension of this I Will Be Presence, and it is precisely because the Presence willed to be more that it extended itself as you into the material realm.

***

Thus, as Mother Mary said, the first ray has often been seen by spiritual students as the ray of the will of God or the power of God. Yet the first ray is called the first because it was what started the process of creation. And what did start the process of creation? It was indeed the drive, the desire, to be MORE, the desire for self-transcendence. And thus, what is the highest will of God? It is the will to be more, the will to transcend, the will to express itself. And it is from this desire that the power of God begins flowing.

The reason why you need to understand the dynamic nature of the first ray is again the interpretation of words. For too many people, when they hear that the first ray is the ray of will and power, naturally compare it to how they see will and power be expressed on planet earth. Yet what you see expressed on planet earth is in most cases perverted will and perverted power. It is not the real power of the first ray.

You see, what has happened on earth is that too many people have lost touch with the reality of the River of Life, with the ever-flowing, ever self-transcending nature of creation. This is especially true for those beings who rebelled against the purpose of God in a higher sphere and have thus descended, fallen, into this sphere and have not yet overcome that sense of separation from the River of Life. When you lose the connection to the River of Life, you no longer see self-transcendence and growth as the very source of life, as the very purpose of life, as the very joy that is the motor of life. Instead, you begin to see growth and self-transcendence as threats. Threats to what? To your sense of being in control.

You see, once you separate yourself from the River of Life, you can no longer flow and constantly self-transcend. If you are not constantly self-transcending, what must you do instead? Well, you must seek to hold on to something, you must seek to own, you must seek to possess. You must seek to stop the clock, to stop the river, to freeze the river, so it cannot continue to flow towards the ocean of God's Being.

Thus, can you see how this consciousness has affected almost every aspect of life on earth? Can you see how you have grown up in a culture that is almost completely infused with this mindset of wanting to own, wanting to possess, wanting things to remain the same, wanting to control, wanting to stop the clock?

Yet when you take a closer look, you see that the perversion of will and power has two distinct aspects. As Mother Mary has explained, ev-

Understanding will and power

erything has an Alpha and an Omega aspect. The Alpha is the expanding, the Omega is the contracting, and whenever you have a perversion of any God quality, it takes an Alpha and an Omega form.

So let us take "will." What, really, is will? In its purest form, will is an expression of the creative drive. Will is paired with power because it is impossible to express will without power. Yet power in itself must also the paired with will. For if you have only power, you will not be able to create any particular form.

To understand this, let us take a look at the scientific concept of the Big Bang. The current prevailing wisdom is that at some point about 15 billion years ago, the entire universe was compressed into what is called a singularity. One might ask a simple question here. It is acknowledged by science that in this singularity the laws of nature that you see today had broken down. It is even acknowledged that time did not exist. So given that there was a point where time did not exist, how can scientists be so sure that the Big Bang took place 15 billion years ago? Well, my beloved, they calculate this by looking at the current conditions in the universe. They look at the current expansion rate of the universe. Then they reverse the direction of that expansion rate and calculate the point where the universe would have begun, if it had always expanded at the same rate as it does today. In other words, the concept is a linear concept.

Yet if you go back to the time right after the Big Bang happened, scientists realize that there were no matter particles. The subatomic particles that today make up all matter had not yet come into existence, for in the first milliseconds after the Big Bang this was, according to science, a completely uncontrolled explosion, a raw expansion, a raw expression of power.

When you look at an explosion on earth created by a bomb, you will see that it is an uncontrolled, unplanned expansion that simply blows apart everything. So my point is that the uncontrolled expression of power simply creates an outward thrust but cannot cause that outward thrust to start forming specific structures. This is why you see that an explosion on earth only blows things apart. You never see that by placing a bomb inside a house and blowing it up, then spontaneously the house will reassemble after the initial explosion.

So what was it then that caused this initial explosion of the Big Bang to gradually start producing organized structures out of the initial chaos? Well, it was indeed will; will that has an intent.

Instead of the Big Bang being an uncontrolled explosion, aimed merely at expansion, the fact that you today live in an ordered and structured universe proves that there was a will, there was an intent, behind the process that started the Big Bang. In other words, the very fact that there today are laws of nature that scientists can study, proves that there was more to the Big Bang than an uncontrolled explosion. There was will, the will of God. And what is that will? As I have said, it is the expansion of self-awareness. And how does this expansion happen?

***

It happens when a self-aware being formulates an intent, executes that intent and then sees the result. The entire purpose for your existence, as an individual being with self-awareness and free will, is that you use your self-awareness to formulate an intent for what change you want to affect in the world of form. You then use your power to flow through the matrix of the intent, until you actually produce a visible, noticeable change in the world of form. And yet, as you produce that change and see the result of that change, you learn something about yourself in the process. And when that lesson is fully learned and integrated, you will expand your sense of self as a result of formulating an intent, projecting that intent outside yourself and observing and integrating the result.

Do you see, then, that when you are in tune with this process, there is no such thing as a "right" thing to do or a "wrong" thing to do? In the mind of the Creator, there is no "right" and "wrong." This is quite simply the greatest injustice ever projected upon God by human beings. Only it was, of course, not projected by human beings but by the fallen beings who in a previous sphere rebelled against God and God's plan for growth through free will.

The Creator gave you self-awareness and free will. The Creator intends you to use those abilities to grow, to transcend yourself, until you reach the same level of awareness as the Creator, and can then become a Creator in your own right.

What is the purpose for the entire world of form? It is the growth in self-awareness. Thus, in God's mind anything you do – any intent you

Understanding will and power

formulate, any intent you project – has the potential to teach you something about yourself and therefore expand your self-awareness. If doing something expands your self-awareness, then it was not an error, it was not a mistake—it was part of the process that is life.

Yet the fallen beings desired to prove God wrong, to prove that the Creator was wrong in giving self-aware beings free will. For it would cause them to misuse that free will, so that they would not expand in self-awareness but would contract in self-awareness—and thus become subject to the second law of thermodynamics and self-destruct. So they decided that the best way to prove the Creator wrong was indeed to cause people to misuse their free will in a way that would separate themselves from the River of Life.

And thus, these fallen beings took council in order to see how they might accomplish this purpose. And they came up with a very simple idea. They realized that all they had to do was to create a standard based on the dualistic concepts of right and wrong. Instead of allowing all potential choices to be simply choices that could lead to growth in self-awareness, they now divided all potential choices into two distinct categories. One that represented "right" choices and one that represented "wrong" choices.

***

When you believe in the validity of such a standard, then you are trapped in a dualistic view of the world. You are trapped in a view that sets you apart from the River of Life, for now you are no longer able or willing to simply experiment with the River of Life. You are not willing to experiment with your will, with your power, with your creative abilities and learn from everything you do, continuing to expand your self-awareness so that you make ever more refined and sophisticated choices.

Instead, something very subtle and very profound happens to you. What happens is that a distance, a chasm, opens up in your mind. A chasm is an empty space that divides two sides from each other. What is it that the chasm in your mind divides? Well, it divides the conscious part of your being from the I Will Be Presence in the spiritual realm. You no longer see yourself as an extension of the Presence, you see yourself as a separate being with a separate will. Instead of simply acting upon any impulse that comes to you from the Presence, you now feel the need to evaluate – in your lower mind – before you take action.

This may seem like a subtle and insignificant difference, and I am fully aware that even most spiritual students will find it hard to wrap their minds around this concept at first. Yet I trust that as the other chohans expand upon the foundation I have set, you will come to see this more clearly. Until hopefully, at some point it will suddenly snap into focus, and you will experience the reality of what we are talking about.

You will suddenly see that you are more than this outer mind, which we have called the human ego—that believes it needs to know and analyze and evaluate everything before it acts. So that it can be sure before it takes action that it will not make a mistake. Yet look at a scientist who is attempting to discover a new procedure or a new material. What is it that has been the driving force in the success of science? It has been the willingness to experiment.

The nature of an experiment is that you do not know the outcome ahead of time, and that is precisely why you can learn from an experiment. For if you already knew the outcome, what was the point of conducting the experiment? Yet if you do not conduct the experiment, how can you learn?

So do you see that if you refuse to experiment with life, you lose touch with life itself, with the River of Life that is constant experimentation? Self-awareness can be expanded in only one way; by experimenting with the co-creative abilities you have, wherever you are at in this immense continuum of the world of form. Whether you are in the highest levels of the spiritual realm or in a faraway galaxy or in a physical body right here on planet earth, it does not matter. For wherever you are, you have the potential to expand your self-awareness.

And even though you may think that conditions are very primitive on earth – and certainly they are primitive compared to the spiritual realm – yet I tell you an eternal truth. It does not matter how primitive conditions are in a given environment, for by making the best possible use of those conditions, you can nevertheless transcend your state of consciousness. In fact, the more primitive conditions are, the greater the potential for expanding your self-awareness.

***

Understanding will and power 133

My beloved, there are beings in the spiritual realm who have great respect and admiration for those of you who have descended into physical embodiment on planet earth. There are some beings in the spiritual realm who do not feel they are quite ready to take this step. And there are those who have great respect – I will not say "envy," for that emotion does not exist in the spiritual realm – but they have great respect and admiration for those who have been willing to experiment with the density of this realm. Yet why is it that some beings have taken this step of volunteering to descend into the dense world that you see on planet earth? Well, it is precisely because the denser the world, the greater the opportunity to self-transcend.

If you can come into a world as dense as planet earth, if you can start out with the low level of consciousness that beings take on in order to descend into the material realm, then you have an immense opportunity to transcend your sense of self by rising above that initial state of consciousness. It is difficult to use words to adequately describe the spiritual realm, for it is so easy for people to interpret words in a linear fashion. Yet let me give you a simple concept. When you look at planet earth today, you see around you certain forms that have a certain density and have certain colors.

You know, obviously, that colors are created by the vibration of the light rays, and the lower vibration corresponds to certain colors and higher vibrations correspond to other colors. And you see that most things on earth are dense, are solid, and have somewhat muddled colors. Yet you also see that there are a few things on earth that have brighter colors, more transparent colors. You see this in light from the sun, you see this in light filtering through the leaves of the trees on an early spring day.

If you were to compare the material universe with the lowest level of the spiritual realm, you would find that in the spiritual realm there are also forms, there are also materials, yet these materials are not as dense as the ones you see on earth. They do not appear as solid and tangible and their colors are lighter, more transparent, more translucent.

What you see is that the reason why things appear solid on earth is that matter has a lower vibration than the substance that makes up the spiritual realm. So can you also see that for a spiritual being to come into embodiment on a planet like earth, you need to enter into and thus take on a certain state of consciousness that corresponds to the density of physical matter?

Take note that I have said that your mind, your being, is not produced by the physical brain. Yet your mind interacts with the physical brain and uses the brain and nervous system to direct the physical body. And in order to do this, your mind must enter into – your pure spiritual being must enter into – a state of consciousness of a certain density. And this is what makes it so easy for human beings to identify themselves with the physical body and think that the limitations of the physical body are also the limitations for what they can do with their minds.

Thus, do you see that the lesson, the primary lesson, you are meant to learn by taking embodiment on planet earth is precisely that your mind is not limited by your physical body and that you can, indeed, express your creative powers on earth without using the physical body, but using the mind directly—and therefore manifesting results that could not be produced by the physical body? This is the greater lesson that you are meant to learn on planet earth.

It is not a great mystery to understand.

Your physical body is naturally made from the kind of vibrations that the earth is made from. The density of these vibrations defines the density, and thus the abilities, of the physical body. Your mind begins by descending into this physical body and therefore taking on a sense of identity as being the body. Yet your potential for growing in self-awareness is to rise above this identification with the body.

***

Thus, I have talked about 144 different levels of consciousness. Well, on planet earth with its current density, you can define these 144 levels and you can define that the lowest level of those 144 levels is indeed that of identification with the physical body, where the mind thinks it is simply the body and nothing more. Yet as you climb the ladder of the 144 levels of consciousness, you begin to dis-identify yourself from the body. You begin to realize that you are more than the body, that your mind is not dependent upon the body but has an existence outside of and independently from the body.

And eventually, as you rise higher and higher, you begin to demonstrate the level of the mastery of mind over matter that was demonstrated

Understanding will and power

by the Buddha, by Jesus and by other spiritual teachers who have come for one purpose only, namely to awaken people from this lowest state of complete identification with the physical body and the material world.

Do you see that you are here for the greater purpose of the growth in self-awareness? And so, to facilitate this purpose, you have descended into a certain environment. And you grow in self-awareness by mastering the environment, but what does it mean to master a certain environment? Well, it means, precisely, that your mind realizes that it can express its co-creative abilities independently of the limitations of the environment, meaning both the limitations of the physical body and the density of matter itself.

This is when the mind begins to realize that it has mastery over matter, and I can assure you that once you realize that your mind has power over matter, you take a giant leap forward in self-awareness. Of course, realizing that your mind has power over matter requires you to overcome the entire consciousness that wants to stop self-transcendence, that wants to maintain things as they are on earth. You need to overcome the entire consciousness that wants to control your mind and keep it within the mental box, where a small elite, namely the fallen beings who are currently embodying on earth, can control the majority of the population.

For the population are so identified with the physical body that they think they are dependent upon the physical body – and therefore certain conditions in society – for their very existence. And thus, can you see that the desire to control is not what you might think is the physical desire to control in order to gain riches or privileges or get the people to fight your wars—it is far more. It is the desire to prevent the people from starting to attain the mastery of mind over matter.

And that is, indeed, why you see that both traditional religion and materialistic science have been – and are being – used to make people believe that they are either miserable sinners or sophisticated monkeys. But in either case, they have no ability beyond a certain level—and certainly do not have any abilities to affect matter directly with the powers of the mind and without going through the physical vehicle.

***

Thus, I have given you a sufficient sense of the characteristics of the first ray and the perversions of that first ray, the desire to control, the desire to make things stand still, the desire to control the people—or even the perversion that wants to create an uncontrolled explosion, such as anarchy or unrest that blows apart the existing structures of society.

For you see, we of the Ascended Host desire to see gradual growth, not a destructive, explosive anarchy that blows society apart. We desire to see Western civilization rise up many levels in order to manifest a Golden Age, but we realize that this cannot happen in one giant leap. It must happen in a gradual process, so that people preserve their sense of continuity.

Yet do you also see that the more closed-minded you are, the more identified you are with the physical body, well the more you will cling to the sense of continuity? Whereas when you free yourself from that identification, you will be able to flow with the River of Life and thus make progress much more quickly towards a higher sense of self.

And thus, everything is a delicate balance, a delicate balance that has, when you look at human history, always decided progress. What are the people able to deal with in their minds? How many changes can they handle before they lose their sense of equilibrium, their sense of continuity, their sense of identity?

And what you see in today's world is that never before in recorded history have so many people been either already open or at the point of becoming open to the need for rapid change and the willingness to go through those rapid changes in their own minds and beings. So that they can indeed be the forerunners for lifting up the collective consciousness to an entirely new level. Change must happen gradually for a time, but there can come points in history, where a critical mass of people are ready to take a quantum leap forward. And thus, you see a revolution, such as what you saw in the Renaissance, or with the industrial and scientific revolutions.

You are ready, the world today – humankind – is ready for another quantum leap in a universal spiritual revolution, a revolution in consciousness, that will suddenly awaken a very large number of people to the true potential of the human mind. Thus making people realize that the ultimate, the final, frontier is not space; it is indeed consciousness. Consciousness is the ultimate human frontier. "Human know thyself, know thy mind." For it is in the mind that you will discover the keys, not

Understanding will and power

only to the healing of Mother Earth but to the transcendence of Mother Earth into a new state, where the current problems simply can no longer exist. For there is not the limitations in the collective consciousness that cause those problems to be projected onto the Ma-ter light itself.

Thus, I bid you a fond adieu, as I have had my say and set a foundation that the other chohans can build upon. And I have given you a sense of how the Elohim started with the first ray and built upon it, yet for each ray integrating the other rays in a harmonious whole that eventually manifested the planetary home with all of its complexity, a complexity that scientists have only begun to uncover.

For there is so much more to discover, when you recognize that science cannot ignore consciousness, but that, indeed, consciousness is the key to answering the many unanswered questions of science. The questions that keep popping up as scientists know more, and thus can use that knowledge to formulate even more questions. And thus, there comes that wondrous phase of discovery, where you in a sense feel overwhelmed, but nevertheless also feel the excitement of discovery. Where you acknowledge that the more you know, the more you realize you don't know, but that it is because there is something you have not yet seen.

And when scientists realize that the reason why they keep finding more and more questions is that they are ignoring consciousness, well then they will be able to take that giant leap, where now instead of discovering more and more questions, they will begin to find answers to those questions. And then, suddenly, everything will shift until in the not-too-distant future, people will look back at today's time and think it was as primitive as the time when people thought the earth was flat.

For today most people think the mind is flat. They have not begun to realize the spherical, non-linear nature of consciousness.

Key 9
Understanding true wisdom

I am the Chohan of the second ray. Lord Lanto is the name I have used in previous dispensations, given by the ascended masters, in our continuing attempts to enlighten humankind and awaken our unascended brothers and sisters to the same level of self-awareness that we have attained. What is it that drives the ascended masters to seek to awaken humankind? Is it a self-centered desire?

Well, that depends on how you define "self-centered." Indeed, when you are still in embodiment on earth, you tend to see yourself as a separate self. And therefore, you tend to see that you can have a self-interest as a separate self. Yet when you ascend and become an ascended master, you do so by completely transcending that sense of the separate self. You literally let the separate self die, and you therefore become one with the higher being that you are.

Yet in this process of becoming one with your higher being, you also see that you are one with all life, you are one with all expressions of the Creator. For you see that the Creator is all and in all, and so how can there be a separate self-interest? For when you realize that your greater self is the All, you see that it is in the interest of yourself to raise up the All. And thus, you naturally express that greater self-interest in an attempt to raise up those who are still trapped in that lower state of consciousness, of identifying themselves with the physical body and thinking their minds have no abilities, no powers, beyond those of the body.

***

And thus, as my illustrious brother, MORE, has explained, it all begins with the drive to experiment and to express your God-given individuality. Yet the fallen beings have managed to cause most people on earth to almost completely turn off the will to experiment. And they have done this by creating this false wisdom, this false standard, that there is something that is right and something that is wrong. And thus, most people have come to believe that life is not a matter of experimenting, life is not a matter of trying the unknown and learning from whatever the result may be. Instead, life is now a closed process of seeking to avoid doing what is wrong, so as to avoid this terrible punishment of the angry God in the sky. Or even avoid the "natural" punishment of becoming extinct because your choices make you unfit for survival.

Do you see that the process started by the Creator itself is an open-ended process? But what has happened on earth is that most people have come to believe in the illusion that life should be a closed process. Instead of seeking to experiment, one should seek to avoid error and do what has been predefined as the "right thing to do."

This, my beloved, is what most people currently see as the highest wisdom on earth. Yet it is indeed the lowest possible wisdom; it is a false wisdom. It is based on a false image of God as the angry being in the sky. But beyond that, it is based on a false image of God as an external being that is separated from the conscious self that now feels itself trapped in a physical body on earth.

Thus, instead of looking at life as a grand opportunity for self-transcendence, most people look at life as somewhat of a burden, from which they can only hope to escape in one of two ways. One is that the angry God in the sky has mercy upon them, and thus elevates them to living in its own kingdom. And the other is that after the death of the physical body, there is the cessation of self-awareness and thus nothingness. Yet in both cases – be it the salvation pictured by orthodox Christianity or the cessation of awareness pictured by materialistic science – it is actually much the same mindset behind it, namely the desire for a non-existence. This is a state in which you have no awareness, where you have no will, where you have no responsibility to experiment and learn from the results.

What is really behind the two models of "salvation" presented in Western society? It is the unwillingness to apply what is the true wisdom of the second ray. So then, let me give you at least a glimpse of the infinite, nonlinear, spherical wisdom of the second ray.

***

As my brother MORE has explained, the driving force behind life itself is the willingness to experiment, the willingness to formulate an intent

Understanding true wisdom

in the mind and then to allow the power of the life force itself to flow through the mind and take on the form envisioned in the intent. Yet this is only the beginning of the process that can lead to an expansion of self-awareness. For what is the point in formulating an intent, imagining and envisioning a certain matrix, and allowing the life force to flow into it? For there to be learning, that can result in an expansion of self-awareness, there must be a willingness to look at the result and to evaluate it in such a way that it leads to an expansion in self-awareness.

Can you begin to see that if you look at your life, and the life of most people on earth, there are indeed only very few people who have this willingness to look at the result and learn from it? Most people act, and after experiencing the result of their actions, they seek to either escape the consequences or they seek to escape having to evaluate the consequences.

Now, I am in no way saying this to blame you or other people for this reaction; it is quite an understandable reaction. But it is understandable only when you realize that it is based on a false approach to life. The false approach comes in, of course, because of the standard of right and wrong imposed by the fallen beings. It is in no way pleasurable or comfortable to evaluate the results of your actions based on this dualistic standard, where certain things can be so absolutely wrong that they condemn you to an eternity in hell. Certainly, anyone with common sense would want to avoid this experience, and that is in large part why so many people do not want to exercise their ability for self-observation and self-evaluation.

What has happened – as a result of the false standard imposed by the fallen beings – is that most people have come to believe that self-observation and self-evaluation is a process that must be based on the prevailing wisdom of their society. For example, people who have grown up in a Christian culture and uncritically believe in the dogmas and doctrines of the Christian religion, will believe that there is a standard, defined by Christ himself, for how they should act. If they make the choices that are defined as right according to this standard, then something good might happen to them, either in this life or in whatever existence comes after this life. Yet if they make the choices that are defined as wrong based on Christ's standard, then they are sure to go into an eternity in hell.

Can you perhaps begin to glimpse that this evaluation based on an external standard cannot, and never will be able to, give you growth in self-awareness? When you think that your experimentation with life should be evaluated based on an external standard, you also come to believe that your experimentation with life should live up to an external standard. Yet if the self that you currently think you are believes that it must conform to a standard imposed upon it by an external force, how can the process of attempting to live up to this standard possibly lead to a growth in self-awareness?

What does it mean to be self-reliant, to be self-sufficient? Does it not mean that you see yourself as being complete and whole within yourself, and therefore needing nothing from outside yourself? So what is self-awareness? Is it not an awareness that exists inside the self and therefore is independent of any opinion or standard that exists outside the self?

Where exactly is your sense of self-awareness located? It is located inside your self—it is not located on the back side of the moon or in the mind of your father, or mother, or brother, or sister, or aunt or uncle. No one else can hold your self-awareness, for your self-awareness must inevitably be inside your self. I am not hereby saying that other people cannot influence your self-awareness. Yet even if other people have influenced your self-awareness, your self-awareness is still located within the self—and you are the one who is looking at life through your self-awareness.

Can you look at life through the self-awareness of another human being? You know you cannot, and therefore it follows that no other human being can look at life through your self-awareness. Your self-awareness is yours. Right now, you are looking at life through the filter of your current sense of self-awareness. This self-awareness encompasses what you know and believe about yourself and what you know and believe about the world in which you live, or at least in which you are currently focusing your attention, your sense of self. Who you think you are, what you think you can do on planet earth, is determined by your sense of self-awareness.

***

I am perfectly aware that in the current conditions found on earth, it is inevitable that anyone in embodiment will grow up with a sense of self-awareness that is heavily influenced by the prevailing wisdom in his or

Understanding true wisdom

her society. Take note that I am not here trying to find fault with the fact that you currently have a limited or warped sense of self-awareness. I have been in embodiment on earth, and I have been under the heavy weight of the collective state of consciousness. I have felt the weight of the fallen consciousness and their false wisdom.

Yet I have also, through a number of embodiments, transcended the sense of self that could be affected by the mass consciousness or by the fallen consciousness. And thus, I know it is possible to free yourself from the limitations of the sense of self as a separate being. And I know that when you do free yourself from these limitations, you experience an incredible sense of freedom and joy, that compares to nothing else on earth.

Do you see, perhaps, that we of the Ascended Host are like salesmen who have a very great disadvantage. We are trying to sell you something, but the problem is that in your current sense of self-awareness, there is nothing that compares to what we are trying to sell you. Thus, it is difficult for us to communicate to you exactly what it feels like to transcend the limited sense of self that you currently have.

It is almost impossible to use words to communicate the difference between the state of consciousness currently experienced by most human beings and the state of consciousness that we experience in the ascended realm. It is not like comparing one apple to another apple and saying that one apple is far sweeter than the first. It is like trying to sell a piece of merchandise that you have no foundation for understanding, much like a person born blind has no foundation for understanding what it feels like to see. And if you cannot understand the benefits of what we are trying to sell you, well then why should you even accept our offering, even when it is actually free. For it requires no payment, although it does require an effort on your part.

***

"Wisdom is the principal thing, and with all thy getting, get understanding." Yet let me attempt to explain to you at truth, a reality, that for many people – even many spiritual seekers – will be an inconvenient truth that they will be reluctant to accept.

Most of the people who are open to the spiritual side of life, to the spiritual path, are so because they are curious about life. They want to know about life, they want to know about the spiritual side of life, and they have attempted to satisfy that quest for knowledge by studying the spiritual teachings that are currently available on earth. There is nothing in itself wrong with this approach. You have to start somewhere. You have to start with the very limited knowledge of spiritual concepts with which most people were brought up in Western society, and then you have to seek to expand your understanding from there.

Yet what I desire to impart to you is at least the beginning of a sense that studying outer spiritual teachings is not in itself the same as acquiring wisdom. We might say that there is a difference between having knowledge and having wisdom. Knowledge, for example, can be seen as a linear intellectual knowledge, such as what scientists acquire through material instruments and studies.

A scientist, for example, might use material instruments to study the sun and thus will acquire great knowledge about the material aspects of the sun. Yet how can studying the sun through a telescope reveal anything about why the sun is the way it is? You will know, I assume, that scientists are very good at answering the "how" questions, such as how the sun works. But they are not very good at answering the "why" questions, such as why the sun even exists or why it functions the way it does.

As both Mother Mary and Master MORE have explained, the real issue here is that scientists have already discovered the undeniable link between consciousness and matter, but they have not been willing to fully look at and evaluate what their discoveries mean. In other words, they have not been willing to truly look at the deeper meaning behind the results of their experiments.

The consequence of the scientifically discovered fact that everything is energy is that there is a deeper reality, which means that everything is consciousness. So if you really want to understand the "why" questions about the sun, you need to realize that the physical sun is an expression of a certain state of consciousness. Scientists say that everything has a corresponding quantum waveform. Yet behind that quantum waveform, there is an intent and a vision. There is a matrix in the mind that has formulated an ethereal blueprint for how the physical sun should be manifest and what qualities and characteristics the sun should express in the material frequency spectrum.

Understanding true wisdom 145

If you truly want to understand the sun, especially if you want to understand the deeper "why" questions, you need to tune in to that consciousness. Yet the matrix for the sun cannot be found in the material frequency spectrum; it is found in a higher realm. And it is only as the life force itself flows through that matrix, that the physical sun is manifest.

Thus, can you see that you can look at the sun through a telescope, or any other material instrument, for an eternity without even understanding that there is something more to know than what is detectable in the material realm? As Mother Mary has already talked about, there is an observation horizon for what you can see with your physical senses and material instruments. Yet there is also an observation horizon for what you can see and understand with the outer, analytical, intellectual mind.

So my point is that you can keep studying spiritual teachings for a lifetime, and you can acquire great intellectual and linear knowledge about spiritual concepts, yet that is not the same as acquiring wisdom.

***

You will, if you are honest, see that there are many spiritual seekers who have acquired a great intellectual knowledge of certain spiritual teachings. They can remember them and they have an intellectual understanding that allows them to recite the right concepts or the right passages to always seem to get the long end in an argument or discussion. Yet if you take a closer look, you will see that while these people have a great understanding of spiritual concepts, they often lack in the application of these concepts in their personal lives. You will, for example, see many people who have a great intellectual understanding of spiritual ideas, yet have very little ability to use this knowledge to control their own emotions, to control their own state of mind.

Thus, if you truly want to make progress beyond a certain point on the spiritual path, you need to begin to realize that true wisdom does not come from understanding with the outer mind. It does not come from acquiring intellectual, linear knowledge. It comes from integrating the knowledge into your entire being, so that it is not something that exists only in your mind but infuses your entire being and therefore is naturally and effortlessly expressed in your actions.

Can you see, for example, that many of the people who are following a traditional Christian church have accepted an outer standard for how a "good Christian" should behave? This outer standard prescribes certain "dos" and "don'ts." For example, many Christians believe that they are not allowed to drink alcohol, or smoke tobacco or say swear words. Thus, they believe that if they follow this outer standard, they are living up to the standard of Christ. And therefore, they are guaranteed to be allowed entry into the kingdom of heaven.

Yet did not Christ say that the kingdom of God is within? And what did he mean? He meant that the kingdom of God is a state of consciousness. It is not a matter of following a few outer rules, and then you are guaranteed entry into the kingdom of heaven. It is a matter of changing your state of consciousness in a fundamental way, so that you transcend the state of consciousness in which you see yourself as being separated from the kingdom of heaven—and instead rise to a state of consciousness in which you know you are in the kingdom and have never been separated from it. Separation being only an illusion created in your mind, an illusion that you have now transcended, because you have allowed the separate self to die for the sake of following Christ into the eternal life of oneness with the All.

So then, this is why you see so much hypocrisy in the Christian religion, where some people think they are good Christians, yet others can see that they have not lived up to certain of the teachings of Christ, such as the command to love your enemy, to turn the other cheek, to love your neighbor as yourself. They think that if they do not drink or swear, then they do not have to love their neighbor as themselves, but they can talk about their neighbors behind their backs or condemn a neighbor because he does not believe as they believe or follow the same rules as they follow. This, of course, is not an internalization of the teachings of Christ, and thus it will do little to bring these people into the kingdom of heaven, as Jesus himself described in many of his parables—for example, the parable about the man who entered the wedding feast without a wedding garment.

So my point here is that if you are to truly know the second ray, you cannot simply strive to be thought wise among men, according to the prevailing wisdom of your society. Seeking to live up to the external standard created by the fallen beings – by always doing what is defined as right and never doing what is defined as wrong – will not give you

Understanding true wisdom

entry into the ascended state. You will gain entry into the ascended state only by transcending the sense of self as a separate being—and how can you do this?

Well, you can do it only by making the decision to reignite your willingness to experiment and then be willing to observe and evaluate the results of your experiments, no matter what they are compared to the external standard. It is a complete fallacy, created by the fallen beings in a deliberate attempt to prevent people from ascending, that there is an external standard defined by God. And if you live up to that external standard, then God will accept you into his kingdom, and if you fail to live up to it, then God will condemn you to an eternity in hell.

There is no external standard for human behavior, and you will begin to understand this when you begin to understand what Mother Mary and Master MORE have already explained, namely that the purpose of life itself is the growth in self-awareness. You do not grow in self-awareness by living up to a standard that you see as being forced upon the self from the outside. There is no standard for how you should grow in self-awareness, because it is an entirely individual process. You grow in self-awareness by expressing the unique characteristics of the self, and in expressing them, discovering them and then multiplying the talents you have been given originally from your higher self.

***

Do you see what Master MORE said about your spiritual self? Instead of calling it the I AM Presence and signifying something that is never-changing, he calls it the I Will Be Presence, to signify that it is always transcending itself. Thus, for you to fulfill the purpose for which your I Will Be Presence sent you into this world, you need to always be transcending yourself. You need to adopt the attitude that you are not a fixed self that has to live up to a fixed external standard. You are an ever-flowing self, who will be who you will be at any moment, for no matter what you may have done or not done before, you are willing to experiment and try something new. You are willing to be what you will be at this moment, regardless of what you were a moment or 10 years or 10 lifetimes ago.

Do you see that behind the concept of an outer standard for right and wrong, there is another more subtle concept? It is the concept that choices in the material realm can have consequences that are permanent, and therefore have a permanent impact on your self. What the fallen beings managed to do was to cause almost everyone on earth to go into the state of separation. This was not that difficult to accomplish, partly because many of the lifestreams that are currently on earth saw this as simply another experiment with their self-expression.

They said, "Well, it is possible to see yourself as a separate being, and so in order to fully understand what it means to be in embodiment in a dense sphere, why not go into that experience and see what it is like?" Let me assure you that there is no law that necessitates you going into the sense of self as a separate being, yet there is no law that seeks to prevent it either. For if you desire to have that experience, it is open to you according to the Law of Free Will.

Yet the issue here is that once you see yourself as a separate being, it is difficult to overcome that sense of being separate. And the fallen ones have done everything they can think of to prevent you from transcending that sense of self, so that once you step into it, you will be trapped in it for an indefinite period of time. And they think that if they can cause enough lifestreams to be trapped in the sense of separation for an indefinite period of time, then they will eventually force the Creator to change its design for the universe.

One of the ways in which they have attempted to prevent you from transcending the sense of separation is indeed by saying that the choices you make on earth have consequences that you can never escape through your own choosing, through your own power. In other words, they want you to believe that once you have made certain wrong choices, those choices can never be undone by yourself. Instead, you must wait for some external power to save you from those choices.

My beloved, it is indeed not wisdom to believe this concept. I realize that most people have been brought up, have been programmed, to believe in this concept without ever even questioning it. Yet it is time for you to question this idea, if you want to climb higher on the ladder of the 144 levels of consciousness. For indeed, I can tell you that this particular idea is found at the level that represents the two-thirds level of the 144 levels of consciousness.

Many of the spiritual seekers that today have the potential to be the forerunners for healing Mother Earth have reached that level. They are now facing this precise initiation of having to deal with the false belief

Understanding true wisdom

that although you could make certain choices in the past, you cannot undo them by your own power to choose. This is the two-thirds level, and you might know that if you look at the great pyramid in Egypt, the King's chamber is at the two-thirds level of the complete height of the pyramid. This is the level where the Christ appears, where the student is meant to begin glimpsing what it means to rise to the consciousness of the Christ mind.

Yet in order for you to make that quantum leap, you need to deal with the lie that although you could make past choices through your power to choose, you cannot transcend the consequences of those choices through your power to choose.

You need, then, to contemplate the workings of the Law of Free Will. The Law of Free Will states, very simply, that you have a right to make any choice you want, because you have a right to experiment with anything that is possible on earth. As we have said, there are 144 levels of consciousness possible in the material frequency spectrum. You have a right to enter into any of those levels and then experience life through the filter of the sense of self-awareness that corresponds to each level. This is perfectly in accord with the Law of Free Will.

***

You do not start at the very lowest level; you actually start at the level that is one-third up on the ladder of 144. Thus, your choice is to either start ascending towards the two-thirds level, where you begin to put on your Christhood, meaning the ability for the mind to have mastery over matter. Or you can choose to descend into the lower levels of consciousness, until you eventually reach the very lowest level, where you think your mind has no power over matter, even is a product of matter.

Any of these 144 levels of consciousness are available for your experimentation. There is nothing wrong – seen with God's eyes – in you descending to the very lowest level. Yet what does it take to descend to a lower level? It takes that you make a choice. It is your power to make choices that gives you the ability to descend to a certain level.

So does it make any logical sense whatsoever to say that even though your power of choice allows you to descend to a certain level, once you have reached that level, your power of choice has somehow been suspended? And thus, you cannot exercise your power of choice to once again transcend the level to which you have descended.

Of course, you have never been presented with this line of reasoning, and thus it is understandable that you have not thought about it. But yet, now that I have presented it to you, do you see that it is indeed a higher form of wisdom?

Any choice you can make in the material realm can be transcended by making another choice. You cannot possibly descend to any place in the material universe at which you are permanently trapped. The only way to descend is to make choices, and thus it follows that by making different choices you can also ascend. I am not thereby saving that you can undo what you have done in the past—or am I?

Let us look at this in another way. What is the entire purpose of creation? Well, as we have now said many times, it is the growth in self-awareness. How do you grow in self-awareness? Let us say that you make a choice in your current lifetime that has a consequence that most people would label as undesirable. In other words, you have now created a physical, material consequence. Once that consequence is manifest in the material frequency spectrum, most people would say that because you cannot turn back the clock, you cannot make undone what you have done, you cannot erase that consequence by hitting the "undo" command on your computer's keyboard. Thus, most people would say that your consequence is permanent and that you cannot rise beyond it.

Yet what have I just expounded upon earlier? Have I not said that studying spiritual teachings is not the same as internalizing them and that until you do internalize them, you do not increase your self-awareness. So let us say that you take a physical action on earth and that you produce a certain consequence. Does the physical consequence itself change your self-awareness?

When you think about this more deeply, you will see that even though you have made a choice that produced a certain physical consequence, the physical conditions themselves will have no permanent impact on your sense of self. Your sense of self, as I have explained, does not exist outside your self. Thus, your sense of self does not reside in the physical consequences. Your sense of self exists inside your mind, and therefore the real question is how the physical consequence affects your state of mind, affects the way you look at yourself and life.

Understanding true wisdom

***

Now, let us go to a deeper and more subtle level, that will require you to stretch the mind beyond what you may have possibly done before. Let us say that you make a certain choice that produces an undesirable consequence. Why did you make that particular choice? You made that choice as an expression of your current state of consciousness—your awareness of how you see yourself and the world in which you live.

For example, if you are completely identified with the physical body and perceive that another person is threatening the life of the physical body, you may instinctively strike out and kill that person. You may later find out that your evaluation of the situation was incorrect and that the other person had no intent of threatening you. And thus, you might realize that killing the other person was unnecessary and see it as an error. And therefore, you might think that you have made a terrible mistake of killing another human being and that this makes you a murderer and puts a stain on you from which you can never escape. After all, you cannot bring the other person back to life, and thus you cannot undo what you have done.

Yet here is where we need to go to the deeper, more subtle level. The purpose of life is to increase your self-awareness. So let us look at a situation where you have killed another human being for no good reason. You cannot choose to simply make this undone, so how can you choose to undo the impact it has had on your sense of self? Well, you can begin by realizing, that your action was an expression of a certain state of consciousness, of a certain sense of self.

It was your identification with the physical body, that caused you to react to defend that body against what you perceived as a threat. Thus, can you begin to see, that if the purpose of life indeed is the growth in self-awareness, then what you can do in this situation is to seriously begin to question the state of consciousness that makes you feel so identified with the body. You can begin to reconnect with the reality, that you are a spiritual being who is more than the body. And when you do indeed transcend the level of consciousness where you are so identified with the body, you have truly undone the impact that your former action had on your sense of self.

Yet, here is the subtle point that most spiritual seekers have not understood. When you make a choice based on a certain state of consciousness, what is the deeper reason why you made that choice? It is that you look at life through the filter of that state of consciousness. So can you now see that when you made a choice that had a certain material consequence, you will also inevitably look at that consequence through the filter of the very same state of consciousness that caused you to make the choice? And can you therefore begin to see that when you looked, originally, at the consequences of your choice, you evaluated – or rather judged – yourself based on the level of consciousness that caused you to make the choice?

Can you then begin to see, that the very reason why you would even contemplate killing another human being in self-defense was that you were identified with the body? But even beyond that, you saw yourself as a separate being, as a separate self that was being threatened by another separate self. Can you therefore see, that in order to see yourself as a separate self, you must have come to believe in the false wisdom of the fallen beings, namely that you are a separate self that will be judged based on an external standard? Can you see, that when you act as a separate self, you will also judge yourself based on this very standard of right and wrong? And thus, you will do exactly what the fallen beings want you to do, namely judge yourself as a being who has now committed such a grave error that you can never be redeemed, that you can never rise above it through your own powers?

Can you see that what the fallen beings are attempting to do is to first tempt people to descend into a lower state of consciousness? And then, as people inevitably act out based on that lower state of consciousness, they know that people will inevitably take self-centered actions. And then the fallen ones come in with their false standard of right and wrong and seek to make people judge their actions based on that standard. And when you judge your actions based on the standard of right and wrong, you will inevitably be susceptible to the projection that you have now done something so wrong that you will be condemned to hell—unless you can somehow be saved by an external force.

And of course, if you look at traditional religion, you will see that a particular religion and its priesthood have always set themselves up as if they were that external force that could guarantee your salvation. Of course, the price that you must pay to earn this salvation that they offer you, is unquestioning obedience to them. And thus, can you see that this is simply the fallen ones who attempt to make you make a mistake and

Understanding true wisdom

then make you believe that the only way to overcome that mistake is to follow them blindly, as the blind leading the blind that Jesus talked about?

This is the fallen beings creating a problem and then setting themselves up as the only ones having the solution to that problem. Thus attempting to manipulate the people into following them blindly—a theme we might return to once or twice before the book is completed.

***

So can you now see the difference between false wisdom and the higher wisdom of the second ray? The perversion of the second ray is to judge according to a dualistic standard with right and wrong. It is to condemn yourself or others as being beyond redemption. The higher wisdom of the second ray is that you are never beyond redemption.

The purpose of life is your growth in self-awareness. You grow by experimenting in the material realm, by formulating an intent and projecting it into this world. And then, you see the result. And by evaluating that result, you grow in self-awareness.

However, how do you truly grow in self-awareness? You grow when you recognize that whatever choice you made was an expression of your current sense of self-awareness. And thus, when you see that a choice had an undesirable consequence, you realize and acknowledge that the very fact that you could produce such a consequence shows that you are currently expressing yourself through a lower state of consciousness. And when you then use this realization to take an honest look at yourself, you can transcend that state of consciousness.

And when, indeed, you do transcend the former state of consciousness, you will also stop judging yourself and your actions based on your former state of consciousness. And when you no longer judge your actions based on the lower state of consciousness, you are free from that state of consciousness.

And therefore, whatever actions you have done in the past were simply experiments. The consequences of those experiments are no longer important, for what is important is the lesson you have learned and have now integrated into your being.

In order to fully understand how you integrate a lesson into your being, you need to have a deeper understanding of how exactly you learn lessons and how exactly you can come to make the highest possible decisions. Yet, I will be content with having given you a foundation and then letting my brother, the Chohan of the third ray, expound upon it. For certainly, in order to truly apply the wisdom of the second ray, you must also know and experience the love of the third ray.

Thus I, Lanto, thank you for your attention, as I truly appreciate the opportunity to give a teaching for those who are willing to grapple with the subtle concepts of the difference between what seems to be the universally accepted wisdom in their environment and the higher wisdom for which there is no outer proof. Yet the proof can be known when you are willing to transcend your current sense of self.

At the lowest level of the 144 states of consciousness possible on earth, there is no way you can grasp, or even begin to grasp, what I have given you in this discourse. So the very fact that you have now read this discourse to the end proves that you are not at the lowest level. So take some encouragement from this, and use it to spur you on to continue to question your current mental box. Until, as my brother MORE said, it suddenly snaps into focus and you see the greater wisdom we are seeking to impart, the greater wisdom that I AM.

Key 10
Flowing with the unconditionality of love

Paul the Venetian is the name I have used in my office as the Chohan of the third ray. The third ray has in previous dispensations been named as the ray of God Love, but what then is God Love? For surely, you can see – can you not – that God's love cannot possibly be the same as the human love that you mostly encounter on earth? God's love cannot be possessive and seeking to control those that it claims to love. God's love cannot be given based on artificial or ever-changing conditions, or personal likes and dislikes, personal idiosyncrasies, personal moods.

Thus, you have a choice to make. Are you content with the human love that you have encountered so far in your life, or do you want more? Do you want a higher form of love, the true love of the third ray? If you do want more, then I, Paul the Venetian, will guide you on a little journey into the higher realms of love, that you can glimpse a higher love— when you are willing to step outside of the separate sense of self that thinks it needs to control everything. And thus, in its attempt to control, it wants to reduce everything to something that can be quantified and therefore grasped with the outer, intellectual, linear mind.

Do you fully understand that in order to control something, you must be able to predict that something? Have you ever truly considered this? What does it mean that you want to control something? Does it not mean that you want to control what happens in the future, so that you limit the options for what can happen in the future into a framework defined by you. In order to have the desire to control, you must then have a vision of what should or should not happen, according to your current state of consciousness and the way you see life through the filter of that sense of self.

***

Do you see, then – as my brothers Lanto and MORE have explained, and as my most esteemed sister, Mary, has explained – that the desire to control is precisely in contradiction to the original vision and design for the material universe? I know well that your mind has been programmed to believe that there are invariable laws and conditions. Traditional Christianity has programmed you to believe that there is a will of God, namely the will of the angry, judgmental being in the sky, who has defined what is right and what is wrong, what will get you to heaven and what will condemn you to an eternity in hell. Likewise, science has defined a set of natural laws that they claim no force in this universe can violate or go beyond.

Yet can you begin to sense, that this all comes down to what Lanto explained as the external standard for right and wrong? Can you begin to see that this standard was defined by the fallen beings after they fell into a lower state of consciousness? This state of consciousness is lower because it is a state of consciousness that is identified with, and thus confined to, a certain spectrum of vibrations.

We have said that there are 144 levels of consciousness possible in the material universe. We have said that you start out, or rather that a new co-creator, starts out its sojourn in the material universe at a level of consciousness that is a third of the way up, in other words at the 48th level of consciousness. Yet this is the case for a new co-creator, who takes embodiment for the first time in the material universe in which you currently abide.

As we have already hinted at, and as Maitreya explains in greater detail in his book, the fallen beings fell in a higher sphere than the one in which the material universe is found. Thus, they fell from a different level of consciousness that was actually a higher level of consciousness than the 48th level at which new co-creators start in the material universe. You must therefore understand, that before they fell, these beings had attained a level of consciousness that was higher than what the vast majority of human beings on earth have attained today. What this means is that these beings, even when they first descended into the material universe, had a higher level of consciousness than the level at which a new co-creator starts on earth. This means, on the one hand, that these beings saw themselves as being superior to virtually all other beings on earth, and they still see themselves as being superior. It also, on the other hand, means that most human beings on earth will indeed experi-

Flowing with the unconditionality of love

ence these beings as being superior to themselves. Yet what is the sense of superiority based upon?

It is based upon the perverted wisdom of the second ray, which has been raised up as the ultimate way to guide the attainment or the level of consciousness of a lifestream. Yet this perverted wisdom is not the highest wisdom of the second ray; it is a lower form of wisdom, in the sense that it has descended below a critical level of vibration.

You are aware that your eyes can see only the forms of light that vibrate within a certain frequency spectrum, called visible light. You are also, most likely, aware that visible light is made up of light rays that have a certain wavelength. You may, if you have studied physics, also be aware that if an object is smaller than the smallest wavelength of visible light, then there is absolutely no way that your eyes can see this object. Even the most powerful microscope ever constructed can only work with visible light, and thus you cannot see an object that is smaller than the shortest wavelength of visible light. This is a physical impossibility.

Can you now transfer this to what I said about wisdom? Everything in the entire universe can be conceived of and understood in terms of vibration. The higher wisdom of the second ray vibrates above a certain level. In order to grasp that higher wisdom, you must raise your level of consciousness, your sense of self-awareness, to that level. Only when your state of consciousness vibrates at the same level as the higher wisdom, can that wisdom be grasped by your mind.

I trust you can see that this is comparable to what I said about your physical eyes, so once you take wisdom below a certain level, you go below that level of the true wisdom of the Christ mind. Now, in order for you to grasp that lower wisdom, your mind needs to vibrate at that same lower level. But can you see that, at the moment you lower your mind to that level, you will no longer be able to grasp the higher wisdom of the second ray?

***

If you step back for a moment and think more deeply about this, can you begin to sense the deeper truth behind what we have explained? We have said that you are an extension of the spiritual being that we have called your I AM Presence or your I Will Be Presence. Yet what exactly does it mean that you are an extension of this spiritual being, what exactly is the "you" that we are talking about?

Your I Will Be Presence is a being that was created out of other spiritual beings in a higher realm than the material realm. It was created as an individualized extension of these beings and then sent into the current sphere, in which the material realm is simply the most dense part. We have used the concept that there is a spiritual realm and a lower realm. The material universe is the lowest part of this lower realm, but there are higher realms in this sphere that has not yet ascended.

In fact, we have previously talked about four levels of the current sphere, namely the highest level, which is the level of etheric forms, which is also the seat of your sense of identity. And then the next level down is the mental level, which is the seat of ideas and concepts. The third level down is the level of the emotions, which is the energy in motion. And then, the lowest level is the actual material universe, the material realm itself.

The concept I wish to give you, then, is that when the Elohim started creating the earth, they themselves were spiritual beings in the newly ascended sphere. They started the process of creating the earth by projecting their beings into the etheric realm. Here they formulated the basic will and intent to manifest planet earth. They also formulated what we might call the etheric blueprint, as the overall ideas for what kind of planet should be created and what kind of lifeforms it was meant to provide a home for.

Then, after the etheric blueprint was set, they took the next step of projecting themselves into the mental level, where they created an even more detailed plan, that included every detail of the physical composition of the earth and the process that gradually brought forth an environment with various lifeforms that could eventually manifest a sophisticated enough brain and nervous system that it could allow self-aware beings to descend into the vibrational spectrum of this world.

After this mental blueprint was set, they then projected their beings into the emotional realm, where they began to actually set in motion the energy waves, the rhythmic almost musical progression of energy that would form the rhythmic cadences and harmonies that would bring the etheric and mental blueprints into the material vibrational spectrum and that would gradually manifest – as wave upon wave upon wave – the physical planet.

Flowing with the unconditionality of love

If you could see this process, you would see a process of such beauty that it defies even the beauty you see in nature. Even the beauty seen through the best of your telescopes from the birth of suns and galaxies, cannot quite compare to the full beauty of seeing not only the material creation but the progression from the etheric to the mental, to the emotional and physical. It is a process of immense beauty, my beloved. Such incredible beauty that I wish I could impart it to you in an instant vision, for it would change your outlook on life forever.

Are you not open to the spiritual side of life precisely because you have an incredible attraction to beauty, a fascination with beauty, a love for beauty? Does not your heart grow within you, when you encounter something of extraordinary beauty? Are you not stunned in admiration by the beauty and intricacy of nature, or the human body or even certain things created by human beings? Is there not a stirring in your heart, when you feel the early morning air, see the rising sun filtering through the mist and hear the birds greeting that sun with the pure joy of their hearts?

How is it possible that a being born on a planet as dense and coarse as earth can have this inherent sense of beauty, this inherent longing for beauty? Well, it is because you were not born out of matter, your inner being is not a product of matter. And therefore, your inner being has a longing for something beyond the matter world. You long for that realm out of which you came, out of which you are an extension. You long back to union with your source, with that I Will Be Presence, that extended part of itself as the you that is now experiencing the material world from the inside.

What is, then, this "you?" Is it the person you see yourself as being? Nay, it is not. It is so much more—or we might even say it is so much less, and I mean this in the best possible way. You see, your I Will Be Presence has a unique individuality. In the entire world of form, there are innumerable spiritual beings. Yet out of this huge number, your I Will Be Presence is absolutely unique. There is no one else, no other being like your Presence. That uniqueness, that individuality, is permanently anchored in the Presence in the spiritual realm. You are an extension of that individuality, but nothing you do, nothing that happens to you, in the material realm could possibly destroy or even lower and water down the individuality of your Presence.

***

What can happen through your experiences in the material realm is that the individuality of your Presence is expanded and grows—it transcends itself and becomes more. Why is this so, how does anything become more? Well, it does so by the process that Jesus described in his parable about the three servants who were each given various numbers of talents. And then two of the servants multiplied the talents, whereas one servant refused to multiply it.

So you see, this is indeed the very driving force behind life, the drive to be more. And therefore, the mandate of life is to multiply what you have been given, and thus you will be more. And so, your I Will Be Presence followed that calling to multiply its talents by extending itself into the material realm as you. And as you experience whatever you experience in the material realm, the "talents," the individuality of your Presence, will indeed be multiplied.

I know that based on what you have been programmed to believe, this can be difficult to grasp, but the fact is that even the worst possible experience you could have on earth will multiply and expand the individuality of your Presence. For your Presence does not look at that experience from the inside, as you do. The Presence looks at it from the outside, and thus is not emotionally involved with it or even identified with it, meaning that your Presence can see it as simply a learning experience. And even if your Presence learns that this is not the highest possible experience, this is still a valuable lesson that allows the Presence to become more through that experience.

So what is the "you" that experiences the material world from the inside? Well, it is an extension of the Presence. Yet in order to understand this self that descends, it might be helpful to consider an analogy. We have in previous books and teachings used the analogy of a movie projector, but in this case I will use it slightly differently.

You know that a movie projector consists of several elements. One is the light bulb, which is the driving force in the projector. This is comparable to the very core of your Presence, the I AM level of your Presence. Then, you have the film strip in the projector, through which the light from the light bulb passes. That film strip is in this version of the analogy comparable to the individuality of your Presence. We might say

Flowing with the unconditionality of love

that this is the I Will Be aspect of your Presence, the desire to project something into the material world.

Yet if the movie projector had only the light bulb and the film strip, it would not be able to actually project an image onto a movie screen. For the image to be directed and focused on the movie screen, the projector needs the very front piece, namely the lens. This lens is a clear piece of glass. It is therefore able to transmit the light and the images onto the movie screen, yet the lens needs to be adjusted in a precise way in order for the images on the screen to be sharp, to be in focus, instead of being blurred.

And thus, you see the function of the lens is to transmit the images from the film strip and to focus them on the movie screen. This, then, is comparable to the self that the I Will Be Presence extends from itself into the material realm. Mother Mary has, in her magnificent book about the abundant life, named it the "Conscious You." This is to signify that it is a self that is comparable to the lens in a movie projector. Your true individuality is anchored in the I Will Be Presence. As the light shines through that individuality, it is meant to be projected onto the movie screen of the material universe, the movie screen of the Ma-ter light, through the lens of the Conscious You. The Conscious You is truly the seat of free will, yet this is a topic that has given rise to much confusion among human beings.

***

We will, all of us together, comment on this, so what I will give you here is only the beginning. Yet, if you look at the ideal scenario for the descent of the Conscious You into a physical body on earth, this ideal scenario is that the Conscious You functions as the perfect lens through which the individuality anchored in your Presence is then projected upon the Mater light and expressed through your mind and physical body.

This means that the highest use of the free will of the Conscious You is that it is, as Jesus said, the open door which no man can shut. It is the open door which no power in this material universe can shut. In other words, the Conscious You will not allow any condition in the material universe to shut down the flow of light – filtered through your divine individuality – that comes from your Presence.

This, then, is what happens when a new co-creator descends into the material universe at the 48th level of the 144 levels of consciousness possible here. Such a new co-creator has an openness to the flow of light and individuality from its Presence. It is not fully aware of what this means, but it has enough awareness to know that it is not a separate being acting alone.

In fact, the new co-creator knows already what Jesus expressed when he said, "I can of my own self do nothing; it is the father within me who is doing the work." The new co-creator knows that even though its physical body has certain abilities to act, those physical abilities are not the highest potential for its expression in the material world. It knows that its real potential for self-expression is through the mind, but not a mind that is separated from its source. It knows that the driving force for its self-expression truly comes through the Presence. And therefore, it knows that by multiplying that connection – by remaining the open door, by becoming more and more able to transmit the light and the power and the love from the Presence – then it can expand its self-awareness, its sense of self, and experience greater and greater levels of the mastery of mind over matter.

Do you see my point? A new co-creator that comes into embodiment in the material universe for the first time has an awareness that it has the potential to attain the mastery of mind over matter. Yet the question becomes how this ability will be exercised. For you see, the purpose of the descent of the Conscious You is not only to be the open door for the flow of light and energy from the Presence to the material world. A lens is a clear pane of glass. It can indeed transmit light from the light bulb to the movie screen, but it can also allow light to flow the other way. Likewise, the Conscious You is a clear pane of glass that allows the Presence to experience the material world. You are, so to speak, the magnifying glass through which the Presence looks at the material world. And thus, impressions from the material world flow through the lens of the Conscious You back to the Presence.

Now, my beloved, here comes the subtle part, that it may take some contemplation for you to grasp and internalize. As long as the Conscious You stays at the 48th level of consciousness or rises above it, it will fulfill its original mission. It will be the clear pane of glass for light streaming from the Presence and being superimposed upon the Ma-ter

Flowing with the unconditionality of love

light. And it will be the clear pane of glass for impressions going the other way, allowing the Presence to experience the material realm.

Yet it will only be that clear pane of glass. How, then, does that allow the Conscious You to exercise free will? Because it is the Conscious You who decides which parts of the material realm to focus its awareness upon. The Conscious You directs, for example, the eyes of the physical body and decides what to look upon, what to focus its attention upon. This, then, is what gives the Presence an opportunity to experience what the Conscious You focuses upon, and it also gives the Presence an opportunity to affect positive change in whatever the Conscious You is focusing its attention upon.

You might say that as the Conscious You is the lens that focuses the images on the film strip so they are sharp on the movie screen, the opposite flow of impressions is a process whereby the Conscious You acts as the lens in a camera, that allows the Presence to get a clear and focused image of what is going on in the material realm. Thereby, the Presence can see where the expression of its divine individuality can have the most effect in multiplying the talents of whatever is currently manifest on earth.

Do you see the greater wisdom behind this design? When the Conscious You fulfills this role, it will never feel alone, it will never feel abandoned by its source. It will always feel connected to the Presence, and therefore it can never come to identify itself with the material realm. It will always know it is a spiritual being who is only temporarily abiding in and expressing itself in the material world. But even more profoundly, the Conscious You will also know that being in the material world is an immense opportunity for growth.

The Conscious You can never feel that being on earth is some kind of punishment; it cannot even feel that this is a negative experience. For it will know that whatever it experiences – no matter how limiting conditions might be – to the Presence they are an opportunity for self-transcendence and for the expression of individuality to cause the transcendence of conditions on earth.

Thus, the Conscious You, when connected to the Presence, will never fall prey to the illusion that conditions in the material realm are permanent and beyond change, beyond its own power to affect change. The Conscious You will know the reality of what Jesus said, that with men this is impossible but with God all things are possible. It will know that while it is connected to the Presence, the power of the Presence can transform any condition that it is experiencing on earth. And therefore, it does not need to allow any condition on earth to permanently affect its sense of self.

In fact, in its original form, one could say that the Conscious You has no sense of self, at least not in the sense of a separate self. It sees itself as the "I" of the I Will Be Presence. As Jesus said, "I and my father are one."

***

Now then, how does the Conscious You descend below the 48th level of consciousness? It does so by projecting itself below that level of consciousness, which is where we begin the lower third that is represented by the levels of consciousness that are possible when you go into the illusion of seeing yourself as a separate being, a being that is not an extension of the I Will Be Presence, a being that is not a spiritual being but is somehow disconnected and separate.

There are, obviously, 48 levels that are possible in this realm of separation. When I say that the sense of separation is an illusion, it is because, as we have already explained, everything is created out of the Creator's own Being, and thus nothing in the world of form could ever be separate from the Allness of the Creator. The Conscious You can never in reality be separated from the Presence, but because it is the focus of self-awareness, it can come to see itself as separated from the Presence.

It is, as Lanto described, perfectly within the Law of Free Will that the Conscious You formulates a desire to experience what it is like to go into those 48 lower levels of possible states of consciousness. There is nothing inherently wrong or unlawful about the Conscious You deciding to do this. Yet it is important to understand that this decision is not made at the level of the Presence. It is a decision that is made at the level of the Conscious You, and thus the decision must be undone and transcended at that level.

There is no power in heaven that can undo for you your decision to descend into separation. Neither is there, as Lanto explained so eloquently, any force on earth that can prevent you from undoing your decision to descend into separation. Yet there are, as we have said, forces on earth who will attempt to make you believe that it is not possible

Flowing with the unconditionality of love

for you to undo that decision, and thus – once you have descended into separation – you cannot escape that condition by your own power.

This is a lie that has been projected at humankind by the fallen beings for a very long time. In your current civilization, the earliest recognized account of this lie is actually in the story of the Garden of Eden and the fall of Adam and Eve, including the entire concept of original sin that says that you were conceived and born in sin and therefore a sinner even without making any choices to sin. Implying, of course, that you cannot choose to undo what you have not chosen to do. Yet the reality taught by the ascended masters – now through several organizations – and taught by all true spiritual teachers, including the Buddha and Jesus, is that you have indeed chosen, and therefore you can choose to undo what you have done.

Now, the first thing you need to understand here is that the illusion of separation forms the "perfect" trap for the mind. It is truly a spiritual Catch-22, where – once you are blinded by the illusion of separation – you cannot see, as I explained earlier, the higher wisdom of the second ray. My beloved, please try to mentally step back and see the overall picture of what I am attempting to convey. Once the Conscious You has stepped into one of the 47 lower levels of consciousness, you literally cannot grasp the higher wisdom with the mind itself. You cannot intellectually understand what I am saying, at least you cannot understand it in a way that will make a difference and that will propel you beyond those lower levels of awareness.

So what is it, then, that can propel you beyond? For are we not telling you constantly that you do have the potential to transcend? Well, the force that can propel you beyond is not will or power, nor is it wisdom. The only force that can propel you beyond is love, but of course not the human love, but the higher vibration of the pure love of the third ray. As Master MORE explained, the beginning of your self-expression is to will, to formulate an intent, a vision for how to carry out the intent and then to project that intent into the matter realm. As Lanto explained, the next step in the process that leads you to raise your self-awareness is then to evaluate the results.

As long as you have not descended below the level of separation, you can evaluate the results by referring to your Presence. The Conscious You is not actually evaluating, as you would think by hearing the word. For in your present state of consciousness, you think that evaluating means using your intellect. But the intellect is a comparable faculty; it must have something to compare to before it can analyze. And in your current state of consciousness, the standard that you will compare to is precisely the standard defined by the fallen beings, the dualistic scale with right at one end and wrong at the other. Yet this is not God's standard, this is not the higher wisdom of the second ray. For as Lanto explained, in the higher wisdom any result, any consequence on earth, is an opportunity for self-transcendence, and thus there is no need for a value judgment.

So when you are in the pure state, the Conscious You has no external standard created in the material realm for evaluating its results. It simply allows the experience of those results, those consequences, to flow through its clear lens back up to the Presence. And then, the Presence will evaluate the results and send back that evaluation to the Conscious You. Which now has the best possible foundation for making the choice to transcend its current level of consciousness, so as to manifest a higher, more sophisticated, consequence than what it is able to manifest at its current level. So do you see that if the Conscious You stays the open door that works both ways, then the Conscious You will quickly learn that the results it has manifested so far were a consequence of its present level of consciousness, namely the 48th level at which it started.

And as it then sees the higher potential, it can make the decision to accelerate itself beyond the 48th level to the 49th level of consciousness. It will then become the open door for a higher expression of individuality anchored in the Presence, and as a result it will produce even higher results. When the evaluation has come through, then it can transcend to the 50th level of consciousness, and so forth and so on, until it reaches the 144th level of consciousness that is complete control by mind over matter. And thus, it is ready to ascend from planet earth and perhaps even the material universe.

***

Yet, as I said, once the Conscious You descends into the illusion of separation, the Conscious You is no longer the clear lens that functions both ways. You see, my beloved, when the Conscious You becomes tempted, as Eve was tempted by the Serpent, it becomes subject to a very subtle illusion. Take note of what is stated in the Book of Genesis, where it is said that there was a forbidden fruit that Adam and Eve were not allowed to partake of, for if they did – according to the Serpent – then they would become as gods knowing good and evil. This is precisely the illusion that the fallen beings believe in, and that they are trying to make everyone else believe in as well.

These fallen beings, in their spiritual blindness and their spiritual pride, truly believe that by rebelling against the Creator's purpose, by separating themselves from the River of Life, they have become as gods in their world. Do you see what I said earlier, that when these fallen beings fell to planet earth, they had a higher level of consciousness than the other beings on earth? And thus, they believed that they were literally gods on earth, for they were so much more sophisticated than the average person found here. You will see, if you look at some of the most so-called powerful people of history, past and present, they literally think that they are like gods on earth who can get away with anything or who should be allowed to get away with anything. For they are so above the ordinary human being as to be in a completely separate category.

Do you see that when you understand the original intent of the Creator, you see that it was actually the Creator's intent that each self-aware being would eventually – through the process of self-transcendence – become a God in heaven. Yet the fallen beings decided that they were not willing to self-transcend and become a God in heaven, and thus they have ever since attempted to become a god in whatever realm they have fallen into. And that is precisely why they want to set themselves up as gods on earth, or as the beings who are worshiped as gods by human beings, even if they are not in a physical body.

What, then, was it that caused the fallen beings to fall? Well, as Mother Mary explained earlier, truly it was a perversion of each of the seven rays. But given that I am the Chohan of the third ray of love, let me explain the perversion of love. What, then, is the perversion of love?

The true love of the Creator is the love of self-transcendence. The Creator wants to see all life transcend, until it rises to its highest possible potential. It wants to see you transcend your sense of self until you reach the highest possible potential, which is the level of the Creator out of which you have come. This is pure love. In the Creator's mind, there is nothing that could ever prevent you from taking the next step towards the ultimate level of consciousness.

Take note that when I talk about the consciousness of the Creator, I talk about a consciousness that is far beyond the 144 levels possible on earth, so please do not confuse the two. Yet my point here is that the Creator realizes fully that the process whereby you expand your sense of self-awareness is the process of experiencing the world of form. Now, when you think about this, you realize that in the world of form you have forms that are distinct from one another. And what sets forms apart? It is that there are specific conditions that define each form.

In the most simple possible illustration, you have a circle and a square. No form can be both a circle and a square at the same time, for a form must live up to either the conditions that define a circle or the conditions that define a square. Yet you, as I have now explained, are a self-aware being who can experience any condition in the world of form. But because you are a clear lens, a clear pane of glass, the open door, then you will never be confined to or defined by any of the conditions in the world of form. You are the open door which no "man," as a metaphor for the conditions in the material realm, can shut. The only thing that can shut the door of the Conscious You is the choices made by the Conscious You, the choice to see itself as a separate being.

So do you now see what is the perversion of love? The pure love of the Creator is the love that will not accept any conditions that limit your sense of self. Therefore, we might say that the greatest love is unconditional, although it is truly beyond conditions. So the perversion of the greatest love is to say that there are indeed conditions in the material realm that can not only limit your expression in this realm, your ability to express yourself in this realm, but also should limit how you see yourself, the sense of self that you accept.

And in order to create this illusion of conditional love, once again, the fallen beings only had to make use of the duality consciousness, which defines a scale with two opposites. It now becomes possible to say that if you live up to certain conditions, then you are worthy of God's love, whereas if you do not live up to those conditions – but instead are characterized by other conditions – then you will not be worthy of the Creator's love.

Can you see the fallacy? The Creator knows what you can do on earth. The earth is like a sandbox, where you can never really do anything to permanently hurt the Presence, or the Conscious You, or the Ma-ter light out of which everything on earth is made. So the Creator

Flowing with the unconditionality of love

will never condemn you permanently for anything you do. In fact, there is nothing you can do on earth that would make you unworthy of the Creator's love.

That is why we say that God's love is unconditional, for no matter what you have ever done on earth, you could never lose the possibility to transcend that state of consciousness and come back to a state of righteousness, where you can experience the Creator's love. As Jesus said, it is the Father's good pleasure to give you the kingdom and he lets his sun shine upon the evil and the good.

God's love is constantly flowing to all extensions of itself, to all self-aware beings. You may go to the lowest possible place that you can experience – be it in the very bowels of hell – and you may look at the demons that howl there and blaspheme God all day. Yet the Creator's unconditional love is constantly being extended to those beings. The only difference is that these beings have put themselves in a state of consciousness, where they firmly believe that they are unworthy of God's love, and therefore they cannot accept it.

You too are likely, as a human being on earth, in a state of consciousness where you think you are not worthy of God's love because of something you have done on earth. And therefore, you do not believe that you can simply ignore your past actions, ignore your sins and accept God's love. Yet I tell you that nothing you have done on earth has changed the Conscious You. The Conscious You is still the open door, and if you are willing, you can indeed experience God's love—that is streaming from your Presence 24 hours a day, 365 days a year.

You can, if you are willing to step outside of your current state of consciousness, experience God's infinite, unconditional love for you right at this second. As you are reading these words, I am extending my personal momentum on the third ray of God's love to you. I will add it to your own, so that you might have an ability to transcend the words and snap out of the sense of identity that makes you think you are unworthy of God's love and separated from God's love.

***

Do not despair if you cannot step out and experience God's love. I know that some will be able to do so, while many will not. But my point is that even if you are not able to experience God's love, can you not at least sense that there is a potential for transcending your current sense of self? And that it is, indeed, your current sense of self that is the only factor that prevents you from experiencing God's love.

It is not what you have done or not done; it is the way you have allowed what you have done to affect your sense of self that blocks the experience of God's love. And that sense of self is not the true sense of self with which you descended into the material realm. It is a false sense of self that you have built because you came to believe in the lies, the serpentine lies, of the fallen beings. By partaking of the forbidden fruit, which is the sense of separation and the dualistic state of consciousness, you have not become as a god. You have become the powerless subject of those who think they are gods on earth.

Can you perhaps sense that somewhere in your being is a determination, that you will not continue to allow these fallen beings to define your sense of self? I am not here asking you to go into a state of anger against the fallen beings, but I am asking you to tune in to the fact that somewhere in your being is a sense of determination to be free from the influence and the lies of these fallen beings, to be free of that conditional love.

That inner determination is actually an expression of love, the true love of the Creator that drives all extensions of the Creator to constantly transcend themselves. What you are longing for, as a freedom from the fallen consciousness, is an expression of the desire for self-transcendence. Whatever level of consciousness you are at, the true love that is the core of your Being – the true love of the Creator – will drive you to transcend that level of consciousness. This is how all life progresses.

How, then, will you even begin to transcend the lies of the fallen consciousness concerning love? Well, you must begin by understanding what Jesus meant when he talked about the multiplication of the talents. I have said that when you see yourself as a separate being, you begin to identify yourself based on the conditions of what you have done on earth. And thus, you think that because you have done certain things – that are defined by the external standard as being wrong or sinful – you are no longer worthy of God's love. This illusion you must begin to question, but you must also begin to question the Omega aspect of perverted love, namely that you should not express love freely and without conditions—but that even your expression of love should be based on conditions defined by an external standard in this world.

Flowing with the unconditionality of love

Do you see that the standard with which you have grown up has conditioned you to believe, that your receipt of love is dependent on conditions? But it has also conditioned you to believe, that your expression of love, your giving of love, should be based on conditions. You have been programmed to evaluate how you express love and to only express it when your evaluation – conducted with the outer, linear mind based on a standard defined in this world – determines that people are worthy to receive your love. In order to truly begin to raise yourself beyond this illusion, you must realize a simple fact.

You cannot own love!

It is a complete fallacy to think that you are giving your love to someone else. You cannot give your love, for there is no love that is yours; you cannot own love. What have I said about the Conscious You? It is simply like the lens in a movie projector; it is a clear pane of glass. It has no love to give; it can only be the open door for God's love to flow into and be expressed in this world.

What most people mean, when they talk about giving love, is not giving God's love; it is giving a perverted love, a human love that is not love at all but simply a psychic projection aimed at controlling other people. You think you own love, and once you make someone the worthy subject of that love, you begin to think you own them. And thus, you give your "love" conditionally in an attempt to control them. This is the simple reality of human love.

So if you wish to raise yourself beyond this illusion of perverted love, there is only one way for you to do so. It is to realize that you are the Conscious You, you are a clear pane of glass. You cannot give love to anyone. What you can do is choose to make yourself the open door for God's love to flow and express itself in this world.

And then, you can begin to examine your conditions – the conditions that you have allowed to be programmed into your mind – for how to express love. And then, when you see those conditions for the dualistic, self-centered, perverted conditions that they are, you can consciously choose to transcend them and thus allow God's love to express itself, despite any conditions you might have had or any conditions found in your society.

***

Few things on earth have been more perverted than love and people's understanding of love. If you want to be a forerunner for healing Mother Earth, it is inevitable that you begin to question the conditions for the expression of love. What is it that will ultimately heal Mother Earth? It is that a critical mass of people become the open doors for a stream of God's love, that can accelerate the earth beyond present limitations and problems. Yet for you to be an open door for that transformation, you must begin by questioning your conditions—that say you should shut off the flow of God's love through your being. You must begin by giving love, even when you think that you should not.

You must begin by doing unto others what you want them to do to you, even when they do the opposite and continue to do the opposite of what you want them to do. As Jesus said, love your enemies, love those that hate you, love your neighbor as yourself—but then also love yourself by opening yourself up to an experience of the love that God has for you.

You cannot, my beloved, intellectually come to an understanding that will help you overcome the perversions of love. It is not a matter of understanding spiritual teachings in great detail and depth. There is no amount of understanding that will propel you beyond the perversions of love. You can transcend the perversions of love not through understanding, but only through doing, by allowing the flow of love to express itself through you, even when your outer mind thinks it is not appropriate.

This does not mean that love is always expressed in the way human beings want it to be expressed, namely as a soft and gentle love that accepts people for who they are. God's love is unconditional because it does not accept any conditions, meaning that when you begin to allow God's love to be expressed through you, you will not always be soft and gentle.

There will be some people who have such a limited state of awareness, that God's love will want to shock them and shake them out of that limited awareness by challenging the very conditions that define their limitations. Thus, God's love can be very direct, very challenging, and it is indeed not always pleasant for people in a lower state of consciousness to experience God's love.

Yet you must be willing to be the open door for that expression of God's love whenever needed, whenever it desires to express itself in helping another transcend a limited level of consciousness. Of course,

Flowing with the unconditionality of love

you must also be open to allowing that love to flow into your own being and challenge your own conditions, so that you can no longer ignore them but must look at the beam in your own eye and decide to finally transcend it.

***

My beloved, as you can possibly sense, I, Paul the Venetian – as the Chohan of the third ray – have a great love for human beings. And in my great love, I am so eager to express my love that I sometimes get carried away and forget about the limitations of space and time. There is so much more I could express, that I desire to express. Yet in this particular volume, we have a clear goal. And thus, to avoid overwhelming you, I will end here.

I will end by expressing my most tender love for you. You are my spiritual brother or sister. There is nothing you could have possibly done that would make me judge you according to the standard of the fallen beings.

You may judge yourself, as Lanto explained, according to your present level of consciousness, but I am not at your present level of consciousness. I have transcended it, and thus I do not judge you based on your present level of consciousness. Neither does, of course, God.

If you could grasp this one idea – that God is not at your level of consciousness and therefore does not judge you based on your present level of consciousness – then I think it would give you a new approach to life, a new vision of the future. Perhaps even a sense of the love that God has for you, precisely because God is at an infinitely higher level of consciousness and only wants to see you rise to that same level of consciousness.

Thus, take comfort, take hope, for the essence of love is that self-transcendence is always possible. This is true love. No conditions in God's love, ever flowing from Above.

Key 11
Accelerating yourself to a higher view of environmental issues

Serapis Bey I AM, and I am the Chohan of the fourth ray. This ray has traditionally been called the ray of purity, but what exactly does that mean? You may look upon the earth and you may see any number of things, which you would consider impure. You may also look upon the earth and see any number of things, which you would consider pure. But the key is how you determine, how you discern, the difference between pure and impure.

For as the chohans of the first rays and our beloved Mother Mary have already explained, what the fallen beings have done on earth is to set up this dualistic standard for evaluating everything. And so, even if you think you are a spiritual student, even if you have followed certain spiritual teachings for years or decades, it does not necessarily mean that you have raised your level of consciousness to the point, where you know the true purity of the fourth ray. You may indeed only have grasped the dualistic standard for dividing purity from impurity, and this simply will not take you beyond a certain level on the spiritual path.

Let me thus endeavor to explain what is true purity, the non-dualistic, unconditional purity of the spiritual realm, the purity that does not accept any conditions on earth. And thus, you cannot simply say that as long as I do not do the things that an earthly standard has defined as impure, then I must per definition be pure. It is not a matter of doing or not doing certain outer things, it is not a matter of living up to conditions defined by the dualistic state of consciousness. It is a matter of going beyond the level of duality. And then, what is the level of duality? It is precisely a level of vibration, as we have explained.

***

And so, then, let us look at this from the perspective of the fourth ray. We have explained that a new co-creator descends to earth at the 48th level of the 144 levels of consciousness possible in the material realm. We have explained that if a co-creator follows the original vision, it will for a time experiment with its co-creative abilities according to that 48th level of consciousness. It will experience the material world through the filter of that 48th level of consciousness. And then, as it gets feedback from the Presence, it will multiply the talents and accelerate itself beyond the 48th level to the next level up.

As we have explained, the Elohim used the seven spiritual rays to manifest the physical planet earth. Thus, as a new co-creator first descends into the material realm, it begins by being initiated in the first ray. Thus, we might say that at the 48th level, you are initiated by the Chohan of the first ray as your primary spiritual teacher.

You now have seven levels up for mastering the initiations of the first ray, and this is to be understood as follows. No ray is separated from any other ray. The rays do not exist independently of each other; they are very much intertwined with each other. So at the first level of initiation, under the first ray, the Alpha aspect of your initiation is indeed the first ray and the Omega aspect is also the first ray. Yet on the next level up, the Alpha aspect is the first ray and the Omega is the second ray—and so forth and so on, until you reach the seventh level, where the Alpha is still the first ray and the Omega is the seventh ray. Then, of course, you climb to another level, where the Alpha is now the second ray and the Omega still goes through the seven rays. And finally you reach the level where the third ray is the Alpha and the other rays the Omega.

Yet what happens then, when you have gone through those first three levels? Well, at that point you will – if you have successfully followed the initiations administered to you by the first three chohans – you will have reached a level, where you now have the potential to accelerate yourself to a distinctly higher level. This is the level of the fourth ray, and what will it take for you to be able to accelerate yourself, accelerate your state of consciousness, to the level where you can begin to receive the fourth-ray initiations? Well, it will take, quite simply, that you have attained a state of balance in your being, a balance between the three first rays of power, wisdom and love—as they have traditionally been seen.

Accelerating yourself to a higher view of environmental issues 177

***

We have in previous dispensations said that as the light descends from your Presence, it first enters into the secret chamber of the heart, which is an energy center located along the spine behind the center of your chest, at the height of the physical heart. There are, as you are probably aware as a spiritual student, eight of these major energy centers. There is one for each of the seven rays, and then the eighth center is the secret chamber of the heart, behind the heart center or the heart chakra. It is in this secret chamber of the heart that the light from your Presence descends into your four lower bodies, the four bodies that correspond to the etheric, the mental, the emotional and the physical level. As the light descends from your Presence, it is first split into the first three rays, that we have traditionally called power, wisdom and love.

This is what gave rise to the teaching that you have a threefold flame in the secret chamber of the heart. This flame was illustrated as three plumes, a blue representing the first ray of power, a yellow representing the second ray of wisdom and a pink representing the third ray of love. And it was depicted that the three plumes of the threefold flame emerged from a sphere of intense white light, which of course represents the fourth ray. It has also been explained that if you did not have balance between the three plumes of the threefold flame, then you could not raise your state of consciousness beyond a certain level.

Thus, what you will indeed see in most of the co-creators who have taken embodiment on earth is that they have one plume which is larger than the other two. For example, you might see some people that have a great momentum on exercising power and tend to set themselves up as leaders in various fields. Yet they do not have the balance of the other two plumes, so they are lacking in wisdom on how to exercise that power, and they are lacking in the love that allows them to avoid misusing their power in order to control other people.

You may also see many people who have great momentum on the yellow plume of wisdom, and they are often the intellectuals that set themselves up as leaders in fields such as science, theology or philosophy. Yet again, many of them do not have the developed blue plume that allows them to actually do anything beyond discussing in their academic circles. And likewise, they do not have the pink that allows them to go beyond and realize that there is more to know about life than what can be known through the intellect.

Finally, of course, you will see many spiritual people who have a great momentum on the pink ray of love, the pink plume of love, and thus would never dream of harming anyone. And although these people can be conceived of as the gentle people who have the potential to bring peace to earth – for they have attained some peace in their own beings – they do not have the wisdom or the power to actually go out and make an impact upon society, preferring in many cases to retreat into spiritual settings, where they are removed from the power plays of everyday life.

And thus, what I endeavor to illustrate here is that when a co-creator has been taken through the first 21 levels of consciousness, beginning with the 48th level and rising from there, then it should ideally have attained this balance of the threefold flame. So that all three plumes of power, wisdom and love are developed to the same intensity and thus can harmoniously blend together—and in their blending together can then be accelerated into the purity of intent of the fourth ray.

Let me for the sake of clarity refer to what Mother Mary has explained, that some of the most powerful people you have seen in Earth's history had perversions on all seven rays. Most of these people were not lifestreams that started out as co-creators on earth; they were lifestreams that fell in a higher sphere. And thus, from that higher sphere and their fall through succeeding realms, they have ended up perverting all seven rays. The vast majority of the co-creators who started out on planet earth, or even in the current material universe, have only perverted one, two or three of the seven rays, corresponding to the power, wisdom and love of the threefold flame.

***

Thus, the original design is set up so that a new co-creator will start out being initiated on the first three rays. And then, only when the co-creator has attained balance in those three rays, will it rise to the level of the initiations of the fourth ray, for which I am the Chohan.

What, then, will it take to successfully pass the initiations of the fourth ray? Well it will take that you accelerate your intent away from seeking to raise yourself as an individual being and go to the higher level of seeking to raise the All. We have said that as you descend at

Accelerating yourself to a higher view of environmental issues   179

the 48th level, you do have a sense of connection to your Presence. You know that although you are an individual being, you are not a separate being. Yet you still very much have a sense of self as an individual being, and you are very much focused on the characteristics that set you apart from other individual beings in your surroundings.

This is perfectly natural and in order. And it is still different from what happens, when you descend below the 48th level and go into the level of separation. For even though you may see yourself as being different from other individuals, this is not the same as seeing yourself as being in opposition to or competition with them. Nevertheless, your task on the first three rays is indeed to multiply the individuality that you have been given. And thus, we might say that as you go through the initiations of the first three rays, you are indeed focused on yourself, and you are focused on raising yourself beyond what might be the level of the collective consciousness in your environment.

The wisdom of this design becomes apparent on a planet like earth, where so many people have descended into the level of separation. How can a new co-creator come into embodiment on earth without being pulled down by the mass consciousness? Well, it can do so only by being focused on its individuality and seeking to raise that individuality independently of the mass consciousness. Which, by the way, it can attain only by attaining balance of the threefold flame. For it is precisely when there is not balance, that a co-creator is open to being pulled into following the mass consciousness.

Yet one of the essential characteristics to understand on the spiritual path is that it has several distinct levels. While you are, for example, being initiated on the first ray, there are seven levels of consciousness that you go through. Yet these seven levels are gradual progressions from one to the other. Then, as you come to the seventh level of the first ray, you need to make what has been popularly called a quantum leap to the initiations of the second ray. Yet the quantum leap from the first to the second and from the second to the third is not as great as the quantum leap you must make from the third to the fourth.

As I have said, even on the first three rays you are still seeking to raise yourself as an individual being. Yet on the fourth ray you must begin to question what brought you to the level of the fourth-ray initiations. You must begin to question whether you truly are an individual being, in the sense that it is only your job to raise yourself without being concerned about others.

This, then, becomes a very profound and a very subtle initiation, that it can be difficult for many lifestreams to pass. And in what might seem like a paradox, it is precisely the lifestreams who have been the quickest at attaining mastery on the first three rays that find it difficult to pass the initiations of the fourth ray. For you see, the fourth ray is the first ray that begins to initiate a lifestream into what we might call the Christ levels of initiation.

I am well aware, as we all are, that the word "Christ" will for many spiritual people have a certain negative connotation because of the many misuses of power seen in the Christian religion. Nevertheless, the reality is that Christ is a universal term, and thus we have decided to continue using it. For again, it is necessary for any spiritual student to stretch the mind beyond its current mental box in order to be ready, so that the teacher can appear and take the student to a higher level. Thus, those who insist on clinging to a particular view of Christianity and are not willing to question that view – and accelerate their understanding of Christ beyond that of the outer religion of Christianity – are simply not ready for the initiations of the fourth ray—and must therefore take another round in the levels of the first three rays.

The Christ, then, is a universal term that represents a state of consciousness in which you attain awareness of the underlying oneness of all life. As we have explained, you live in a world of form, where each form is set apart from other forms by specific conditions, characteristics and appearances. Thus, when you look at the many forms at the level of the senses and the outer mind, it might easily seem as if there is no connection between them. And this is precisely what makes it possible for you to believe that there is no connection between you and other people, or between yourself and God, or that there is no connection between humankind and the planet upon which they live.

This is what has given rise to the current approach to life on earth, which has created numerous environmental problems. It is unfortunately also what has given rise to the approach that most people have taken to solving these environmental problems, which is precisely why they have not been solved but are only becoming worse and worse as the population and the level of industrialization increases.

Accelerating yourself to a higher view of environmental issues 181

Thus, if there is to be an effective solution to environmental problems, it will be necessary for a critical mass of people – those who want to be the forerunners for healing Mother Earth – to begin to understand the need to accelerate their consciousness to the level of the Christ consciousness, where they begin to see beyond the illusion of separateness.

For you see, when you begin to rise to the level of the Christ consciousness, you begin to see the fallacy of separate forms. You begin to see that separate forms are not really separate, for they are only varied expressions of the same underlying reality. Science, of course, has already provided you with evidence of this. All of the different matter forms that you see on planet earth are made from smaller building blocks, called molecules. Molecules are made from atoms, atoms are made from subatomic particles and subatomic particles are truly energy waves. And as Mother Mary has explained, even the energy waves are not the fundamental building blocks of matter. For when you truly understand the findings of science, you realize that the ultimate reality is consciousness.

***

And thus, at the level of the Christ initiations of the fourth ray, you begin to understand that everything is consciousness. And therefore, everything you see on planet earth is an expression of a certain state of consciousness. This has many implications, but one obvious one in this context is that any environmental problem you see on earth is not caused by the physical conditions that may seem to cause it—and thus it cannot be solved by seeking to change those physical conditions.

In order to manifest a truly effective solution, it is necessary to see that the environmental problem is truly a physical outpicturing of a certain state of consciousness. And it is only when the collective consciousness is accelerated beyond that level of consciousness, that the environmental problem will be ultimately solved.

For example, we can go back to the 1960s, when most people in the Western world were unaware of the effects of pollution. Most people had no idea that the seemingly ingenious and convenient solution of seeking to kill harmful insects with DDT would cause that substance to enter the food chain, where I could eventually come back to them through their food and thus have wide-ranging effects on their physical bodies—and of course also on the natural environment. What did happen in the 1960s was that there was an awakening to the physical effects of DDT and other toxic substances being spread into nature and the food chain. Yet this only led to a partial solution to the problem. As you will see, even countries who forbid a certain chemical substance cannot prevent companies and corporations from constantly seeking to come up with other substances, that will do what the forbidden substance did without having any side effects that are known as of yet.

So do you see that making it illegal to use DDT did not provide a permanent solution to the problem of chemical pollution? It simply started at race that is much like the race you see in certain sports, where athletes attempt to use chemical substances to boost the abilities of the physical body. As athletes are being tested for known substances, there are those who are seeking to create new substances that are not yet known and thus cannot be detected by standard tests. Of course, these new substances have side effects, which are not known either—and thus the athletes are playing Russian roulette with their health.

Likewise, society is playing Russian roulette with the health of the earth by outlawing a certain substance, which only causes corporations to attempt to come up with other substances. They may not have the exact same side effects as the outlawed substance, but could have other more subtle side effects that are not yet known. And they will not be known for some time, thus allowing the corporations to make a profit until the side effects become known.

Is it not obvious that for a permanent solution to this problem to be found, there must be a shift in awareness? So that humankind finds ways to solve particular problems without having to use dangerous chemical substances that are spread in the natural environment. And thus, can make the body of the Earth Mother so ill, that it eventually cannot fulfill its function of providing a platform for the evolution of humankind.

Can you perhaps begin to see, that if there was a willingness to step back and look at the deeper cause of consciousness, it might be possible to find solutions to certain problems that would not create other problems? For example, let us take the issue of harmful insects that affect the crops that are meant to feed people. In their present state of mind, people seem able to see only one solution: we must use force to kill the insects that are destroying the crops. And so far the main method for

Accelerating yourself to a higher view of environmental issues 183

doing this is to take a chemical substance and spray it onto the crops, thereby killing the insects.

Yet what if this particular approach is actually driven by a certain perversion of the first ray of power, the second ray of wisdom and the third ray of love? What if this perversion drives certain people and certain corporations to want to use force because they have a momentum on force? And thus, if they can persuade society to implement their force-based solutions, then they can make a profit by thus attempting to solve a problem through force. And as long as society believes that this is the only, or at least the most effective, way to solve certain problems, then few people will ask the deeper questions of whether there actually was a way to solve those problems without using force.

As you are no doubt aware, nature has its own ways of limiting the size of all populations. For example, you may find insects on one continent that originally came from another continent and were imported by human beings who were not aware of their potential harmful effects. The reason people were not aware of the harmful effects of these insects was that in their original environment they were not a problem, because they were balanced by certain other natural conditions. Yet because these predators, be they other insects, birds or diseases, were not present on the new continent, the insects could suddenly multiply without the normal restrictions. And thus, when you realize this, you see that if people could discover the balance of nature that keeps certain populations in check, they might be able to limit the size of insect populations without having to use chemicals—that will always have side effects one way or the other.

***

Yet for those who are willing to step even further back, one might begin to question whether the existence of harmful insects was part of the original design of the Elohim? Is it possible, given that everything is an expression of a certain state of consciousness, that the insects themselves are an expression of a lower state of consciousness? Is it possible that when the Elohim designed planet earth, it was able to provide sustenance for its inhabitants without the interference of harmful insects, or diseases or any other "natural" conditions that could threaten the food supply?

Do you see the point I am aiming to introduce here? I have said that the attempt to solve certain environmental problems with force is an expression of a lower state of consciousness. Yet what if the problems that people attempt to solve are also an expression of a lower state of consciousness?

You now have a situation where humankind – by going into the consciousness of separation and duality – has manifested certain conditions that threaten the food supply. Yet in their attempt to solve these problems, they use another lower state of consciousness. Can two wrongs make a right, can a problem precipitated by one lower state of consciousness be solved through another lower state of consciousness?

Well, if you think it can, then you are not yet at the level, where you are ready for the initiations of the fourth ray. For those who are indeed ready for the initiations of the fourth ray, and the beginning of the journey into the levels of Christ consciousness, will indeed be open to seeing that it is self-evident that in order to truly solve a problem, we must understand the cause. And in order to truly understand the cause, we must step back and ask questions beyond the very mental box, the very state of consciousness, that precipitated the problem. This is what becomes obvious for those who have attained some balance on the first three rays and who begin to grasp the initiations of the fourth ray.

***

It has been stated in previous dispensations that I, Serapis Bey, run a spiritual retreat that is located in the etheric realm above the physical location of the temple at Luxor, Egypt. It has been stated here that when lifestreams come to my retreat, the first initiation they encounter is that they are put into groups with other lifestreams with whom they have the greatest potential for conflict. It may be differences in personality, karma, astrology and what have you.

Yes, I put lifestreams into groups with others, and they are selected based on their potential to have conflict. They will then stay in these groups and work in what we might call a spiritual sandbox – where they cannot harm themselves or each other – until they begin to grasp precisely what I have just talked about. Namely the need to step back and look beyond the outer differences. And even more importantly, the

Accelerating yourself to a higher view of environmental issues   185

need to realize that you cannot solve a problem with the same state of consciousness that created the problem.

As I said, on the first three rays you are making progress by accelerating and raising yourself as an individual being. This will often cause lifestreams to become very strong and determined in expressing their individuality. And it may cause them – even though they have made progress and have attained some balance of the threefold flame – to be very forceful or strong and to have relatively little consideration for the fact that other people are also here to express their individuality.

And thus, what you typically see at my retreat – and what you for that matter often see in spiritual movements and groups on earth – is that you have certain individuals with very strong individuality and strong opinions that clash with each other and cannot find out how to cooperate. Thus, the initiation faced by the students at my retreat is that they must learn to balance the expression of their individuality with the expression of the individuality of other lifestreams. They must begin to see that it was never the Creator's intent or design that only one lifestream should be raised up as being superior to all others.

The Creator's design and intent is to raise up all self-aware extensions of itself. And thus, the lifestreams who come to my retreat will remain in this spiritual kindergarten initiation until they begin to see the deeper truth behind Jesus's words: "He who would be greatest among you, let him be the servant of all." This, then, shows you the foremost perversion of the fourth ray of purity. It is the impure motive, but it is not impurity in the sense of what you might think by looking at the earth. Where you might say that certain actions are clearly impure but others are pure—yet this evaluation is based on a dualistic standard.

As an example of this, let us look at the many religious people on earth, such as many Christians who believe that by being a member of their particular church, by never questioning its doctrines and by following its various prescriptions for how to live, they have put themselves in a category that is above and beyond the categories where you find those who are not members of their church, or who are not following the outer rules as strictly as they are. What you see in such people is admittedly not the lowest level of consciousness possible on earth.

These people are not complete egomaniacs who go out and use violence against other people in order to get what they want. Yet what you see is not what these people claim it to be, namely a higher or more pure form of consciousness that is fundamentally different from the lower manifestations. As we have explained, everything has an Alpha and an Omega aspect. The Omega aspect of the perversions of purity is surely the many perversions you see on earth, such as the use of force to get what one wants and many others. Yet the more subtle Alpha perversion is indeed the attempt to raise oneself up as being superior to others based on a standard defined on earth, and not the true standard of the Christ mind.

What is the subtle difference? It is very simple, really. The Christ standard seeks to raise all life, and thus there is no need for one self-aware being to raise itself up in comparison to others. The Christ is greatest among you because the Christ is the servant of all, seeking to raise up others before raising up its individual self. The being who has begun to grasp the Christ consciousness has been willing to do what Jesus said, to lay down his life for a friend, to let the individual sense of self die in order to be reborn into the greater sense of self and realizing that you are part of the All but so are all other self-aware beings. And therefore, beyond a certain point, you can actually raise yourself only by seeking to raise others, by seeking to raise the All.

***

And this, of course, applies to the planetary home as well. When you begin to grasp the levels of the Christ consciousness, you realize that you are not simply a disconnected being, living on a planet. For the planet is an energy system, but more than that it is a matrix of consciousness. And when you took embodiment on earth, you became a part of that whole. And thus, in order to truly raise yourself up and pass the initiations of reaching the 144th level of consciousness possible on earth, then you need to seek to raise the All, including all other people but also the body of the Earth Mother, so that you are working only to accelerate everything beyond current problems.

The perversion of purity is that you seek to raise yourself up in comparison to others, which absolutely must necessitate that you put other people down. For you see, there cannot be comparisons and value judgments in the Christ consciousness. Only in the duality consciousness, only in the consciousness of anti-christ, can there be a comparison based on a relative scale, which says that certain conditions are impure

Accelerating yourself to a higher view of environmental issues 187

whereas certain other conditions are pure. And thus, those people who meet the conditions for what is impure, are less valuable, less worthy, than those people who meet the conditions for what is pure.

Do you see, or at least begin to see, that in the Christ mind such a standard simply has no meaning? Those students who sit in their groups in my retreat and argue with others, seeking to make themselves right and make other people seem wrong, they have not begun to grasp the Christ perspective. And thus, they must stay in those groups until the light bulb does start shining within their heads.

When you do begin to grasp the true purity of the fourth ray, you see that the idea of defining purity and impurity based on a standard that springs from the duality consciousness is based on the duality consciousness itself. It has no reality in the Christ light, and thus you will begin to see through it. You will begin to see how this tendency to set up relative opposites – and then to say that one is better than the other – is indeed the one underlying problem that has given rise to all of the many different problems that you see on earth.

You begin to grasp that there really is one cause that has simply led to the expression of many seemingly individual and disconnected problems. And thus, you begin to realize that you cannot simply look at environmental problems as physical problems, as material phenomena. If you really want to find a solution, if you really want to heal Mother Earth, you must go to the deeper level and look at the reality that everything is consciousness. And therefore, every physical manifestation seen on earth is the expression of a certain level of consciousness, a certain perversion coming from the duality consciousness.

Until you do see this, you only have one approach to solving environmental problems, and it is to take the same approach as the Christians I just described, who have used their Christian religion to define a certain outer standard for what is pure and impure. And thus, they impose a value judgment that they themselves are better – because they live up to certain conditions – than the people who do not live up to those conditions. And some of them even take the further step of saying that the threat to the future of planet earth is precisely that certain other people are not living up to the conditions they have defined. And thus, very easily comes the subtle reasoning that in order to prevent the greater calamity of God destroying the earth, it might be justified that we kill these other human beings and get them off the earth.

And thus, you see the cause of religious war. But can you also see that many people in the current environmental movement are taking a similar approach? They are only looking at environmental problems from the level of material conditions. Thus, they say that the people who are actually causing the material conditions do not live up to their own self-created standard for right and wrong, for pure and impure.

Many people in the environmental movement have defined a certain standard for how people should live and what they should do or not do in relation to the natural environment. They then use that standard to judge others as being impure, as being the cause of the problem. And thus, you see that even though most people in the environmental movement do not condone violence, there are indeed some who have crossed the line and have started using violence to suppress the people that they have now labeled as the problem. And even most people in the environmental movement are indeed willing to use certain non-violent types of force in order to force other people to stop doing what they have labeled as the cause, the material cause, of environmental problems.

For example, many environmentally aware people are quite willing to use governmental power to force corporations and businesses, or even farmers, to alter the way they do business or grow crops. I am not saying that this is completely inappropriate, but what I am saying is that this is still attempting to solve a problem created from the lower state of consciousness by using another aspect of the lower state of consciousness—and thus it cannot lead to an ultimate solution.

***

What, then, is the higher approach to environmental problems? Well it must begin by realizing one underlying truth, that both Mother Mary and the foregoing three chohans have attempted to make clear to you. This truth is that the entire purpose for the existence of the earth is to serve as a kind of cosmic schoolroom, a platform for the growth in the self-awareness of the self-aware beings who inhabit planet earth.

When you do begin to lock in to this truth, you begin to see that you cannot allow yourself to become blinded by the foremost characteristic of the consciousness of separation. This characteristic is the age-old axiom that the ends do justify the means.

Accelerating yourself to a higher view of environmental issues   189

You might, for example, see that even though Christians claim to believe in the teachings of Christ – who told people to not resist evil but to turn the other cheek – there have been times in the history of the Christian religion, where church leaders have argued that it was justifiable that Christians attempted to kill non-Christians in order to prevent some greater calamity. Likewise, there are people in the current environmental movement who think that the urgent need to stop pollution and prevent a global catastrophe justifies the use of force towards certain groups of people in society.

Yet what I have attempted to explain here is that the real cause of environmental problems is precisely the use of force against nature. And thus, how can using more force to suppress other people help heal the body of the Earth Mother? Can you perhaps begin to see, that the way forward is to overcome the very consciousness that causes people to feel that they are separated from the planet upon which they live?

You may be aware that many native peoples around the world have or have had a much greater sense of oneness with the natural environment than do most people in the modern industrialized world. You may have sensed that part of the solution to environmental problems is to strive back to some edenic state represented by these native cultures. I am not hereby saying that this is the solution that we of the Ascended Host advocate. We actually advocate a higher approach, where you do not abandon the progress made in Western civilization, but where you transcend the fascination with the force-based approach and force-based technology that has taken over Western civilization.

The stark reality is that if you were to turn the clock back, so that all people lived in native cultures, then you would have to use force to eliminate the majority of the people who currently live on earth. And when you begin to realize that the entire purpose of the earth is to provide a learning experience for a certain number of lifestreams, then you see, that it would not be congruent with the Creator's and the Elohims' vision for earth if only a few hundred thousand people lived as hunter-gatherers. It is indeed perfectly in accord with the vision of the Elohim that there are more people on earth than can be sustained by a hunter-gatherer society. And thus, it is absolutely necessary to find a way to sustain a larger number of people, without using so much force that it destroys the ability of the Earth Mother to feed that number of people through so-called natural processes.

In other words, people do not need to abandon technology and science; they need to accelerate technology and science beyond the level of consciousness where technology can only be seen as using force to manifest what you need. Instead, it is necessary to transcend that level and find a new approach, where you can use technology in a way that is in harmony with the very principles that the Elohim used to design planet earth. And when humankind begins to know and follow those principles, it will indeed be seen as perfectly possible that the earth can sustain a very large number of people without disturbing the natural processes. In fact, planet earth is designed by the Elohim to provide a cosmic schoolroom for ten billion people. I know that this will be a shock to many people with environmental awareness, yet have you ever seriously considered the alternative?

There are many people in the environmental movement who look with disdain upon industrialized society, thinking that the only alternative – the only way to avoid a worldwide environmental disaster – is to abandon much of the technology used today. Yet the reality of doing this would be that current problems with starvation, malnutrition and inequality would be accelerated to the point, where two-thirds of the current population of the earth would be eliminated, either through starvation and disease or warfare. In other words, what many people in the environmental movement are envisioning as an ideal solution, would require the elimination of two-thirds of the people on this planet.

Ask yourself, then, whether you really are ready to implement a solution that would lead to the death of two-thirds of the people, realizing that most of those people would be in Third World countries, where they are the most vulnerable. If you do think that environmental problems are so severe that the ends of preventing a worldwide disaster can justify the means of eliminating two-thirds of the current world population, then we of the Ascended Host have nothing further to offer you—although I will offer you one more thing.

***

We have talked about the fact that there is a relatively small group of fallen beings who have attempted to control planet earth and all people upon it. If you are willing to look at history, you will see that there have been many societies in which a small elite had near total control of the

Accelerating yourself to a higher view of environmental issues 191

population. One such society is the feudal societies found in Europe during the Middle Ages.

If you look at the historical facts, what was it that overturned the power elite of the feudal societies? You may have been told various things, but the reality is that the decisive condition was the growth in the population. The feudal societies had such an unequal distribution of wealth, such an unequal use of natural resources, that they simply could only feed a certain number of peasants. When the peasant population grew beyond that critical level, the peasants realized that they could not survive with the present social order. And thus, it became a matter of life and death for them to overthrow the feudal lords, leading to the collapse of the feudal societies.

My point is, therefore, that it has always been the goal of this power elite of fallen beings to keep the human population at the level that they feel they can control, while maintaining their own positions of privilege and power. It has always been the growth of the population that overthrew the power elite in any society. They know this, and therefore they have, since the environmental movement began to gain more widespread acceptance, used various means to induce into the population – especially the more aware members of the population – these subtle beliefs that the real problem is the size of the human population.

My beloved, when you begin to grasp the Christ consciousness, you realize that "he who would be greatest among you, must be the servant of all." Thus, you realize that if you truly are one of the people who want to be forerunners for healing Mother Earth, you cannot allow yourself to be fooled into advocating solutions that would, in all reality, require the elimination of a large number of human beings—and thus subverting the very spiritual purpose for the existence of the earth.

If you allow yourself to be pulled into the schemes created by the power elite, then you will not contribute to the healing of the Earth Mother. You will only allow your own light to be perverted and used to create another kind of force, that will only accelerate the problems created by the force-based state of consciousness in its many varied manifestations.

The current problems seen on earth – be it the problems relating to the environment or problems relating to human interactions, such as war and all kinds of conflicts – are the outpicturings of the force-based state of consciousness. They will not be solved by adding more force; they will be solved only by reducing force and finding balance.

***

This, then, is the essence of the fourth ray. When you have balanced the threefold flame representing the first three rays, you can then use that balance as a platform for accelerating your consciousness to the distinctly higher level, where you go beyond seeking to raise yourself as an individual. You then grasp the vision of the underlying oneness of all life, and you then make a fundamental shift in awareness, where you are no longer seeking to raise yourself.

But more than that, you are no longer seeking to work for some kind of cause based on the vision of yourself as an individual. Instead, you are beginning to grasp the underlying vision of oneness, and now, instead of promoting solutions that seem right from your viewpoint as an individual, you rise up to the greater vision of seeing the All. And thus, you begin to grasp and promote the very solutions that will raise the All in accordance with the original vision of the Elohim, and the greater purpose of the Creator for raising all self-aware beings to the ultimate level of self-awareness.

It is not the goal of the Elohim to create at planet on which there is a static state in nature. It is the goal of the Elohim to create a dynamic planet upon which everything in nature is an expression of the drive for self-transcendence.

Thus, the very attempt to solve environmental problems by returning to some supposedly edenic state in the past – when nature existed undisturbed by man – is simply not in alignment with the reality of life and the purpose of the universe. There never was a static state on earth, and there never can be. This becomes obvious when you begin to understand what Mother Mary has explained about the second law of thermodynamics, that will break down any closed system.

As long as the environmental movement is focused on returning the planet to some closed state, it will only make environmental problems worse by increasing the amount of force in the collective consciousness. It is time for those who are willing to be the true forerunners for healing Mother Earth to see the fallacy of the force-based state of consciousness and to accelerate themselves beyond it.

Accelerating yourself to a higher view of environmental issues   193

I know well, as do all of us who have been in embodiment, how subtle and how tempting it is to believe that if we can only find this new ultimate system or philosophy and force all people to comply with it, then we can solve all of humankind's problems. Yet there is no outer system that will solve all problems, for the only solution to all problems is the acceleration of the individual consciousness, until so many people have accelerated their consciousness that they raise the All of the collective consciousness to a distinctly higher level, where problems are not created.

As long as you focus on solving a problem, you are attempting to solve a problem with the same state of consciousness that created it. The true way to "solve" problems is to transcend the very consciousness that manifested the problems.

***

And thus, as the other chohans have explained, the true way is to look at what is currently manifest on earth and then evaluate it based on a higher standard. Not a standard created on earth through the duality consciousness, but the true standard of the Christ consciousness that sees the underlying oneness of all life.

On the fourth ray, the challenge is to accelerate yourself beyond your sense of being an individual, so that you see the vision of the All. And then, you compare everything you see on earth to that vision. And when you begin to grasp the underlying vision of oneness, you will gain an entirely new perspective on the real cause of the problems on earth—and therefore the real way to transcend the consciousness that manifested the problems.

This is a real approach to healing Mother Earth. I, Serapis Bey, have now given you the impetus to accelerate yourself beyond your current mental box. I offer you my rather considerable momentum on self-transcendence and self-acceleration—if you will apply to me.

You may even have heard that it is possible for a part of your being, namely the Conscious You, to leave the physical body at night and travel to the etheric retreats that we of the Ascended Host have in the etheric realm over various locations. As I said, I have such a retreat located over Luxor, Egypt. I thus offer you that if you are willing, you may make a simple prayer to me before going to sleep at night, that I will send my assistants, my angels, to guide you to my retreat, so that you may receive not only instructions but also an acceleration of your being.

For truly, the fourth ray is the ray of acceleration, and I am willing to help you accelerate your being, according to your own willingness to multiply the talents that you already have.

Try me; test me.

But realize that it is not me who is being tried or tested; it is yourself and your willingness to transcend what you have so far seen as the limitations for yourself—and therefore have also seen as the limitations for how it is possible to solve environmental problems on earth.

With men, this is impossible, but not with God, for with God all things are possible. I am perfectly aware that when you look at environmental problems from the level of the force-based consciousness, many of them will seem impossible to solve. But I tell you, this is an illusion.

And when you do accelerate your own consciousness to the level of the Christ consciousness, you begin to see that it is indeed possible to accelerate the earth beyond all current environmental problems, so that you can have a planet that can feed and give the abundant life to 10 billion lifestreams and still have the perfect balance of nature. This is a balance that most people cannot currently envision, but which is indeed envisioned in the minds of the Elohim, who have untiringly held the blueprint and the immaculate vision for the earth while humankind has taken a sojourn into the lower levels of the duality consciousness.

Will you be one of those who accelerate the earth? Or will you remain as one of those who continue the deceleration spiral? This is the choice I put before you, and thus I say: "Choose life! That you and the planet upon which you exist may indeed find a higher state of life!"

Key 12
Bringing a higher truth into the environmental debate

Hilarion is the name of the Chohan of the fifth ray, and indeed, Hilarion I AM. The fifth ray has traditionally been called the ray of truth and healing. Yet it would be more constructive to call it the ray of vision, particularly the ray of a higher vision, of a purer vision, of an immaculate vision.

It is the ray that enables you to see beyond the current conditions manifest on earth or in your own state of consciousness, and see that immaculate vision—and then hold the immaculate concept that the earth can be transformed into manifesting the purity of the vision. It is also, on the individual level, the ray that empowers you to hold the immaculate concept for yourself and the manifestation of your own Christhood.

You may recall – whether you grew up in a Christian culture or not – that the Christian religion claims that Jesus was not conceived in the traditional or natural way, but that he was conceived by the Holy Spirit in an immaculate conception. This is, of course, simply one example of how people seek to use actual conditions on earth to set themselves or their religion apart from others. The entire idea that Jesus was conceived without natural means was an attempt to set him apart from all other children, and thus support the claim that Jesus was God's only son come into a physical body. This was not something claimed by Jesus himself, nor by his mother, Mary, or his father, Joseph. It was indeed a later addition to the Christian faith, but there is a validity here in the immaculate concept, and I would like to give you the deeper understanding.

***

What is, in a sense, the entire underlying message behind the mission of Christ? As Serapis Bey has explained, Christ is a universal state of consciousness that allows you to divide the real from the unreal, the pure from the impure, the true from the untrue. It allows you to see the underlying oneness of all life and to see that all of the many diverse forms in the world of form are not separate but did indeed spring from the same source.

Even though the many different forms may appear to be separate, they are nevertheless created in the same way, namely by self-aware beings projecting images upon the one, universal substance of the Ma-ter light. And thus, it is only because the Creator has manifested itself as the Ma-ter light and as self-aware extensions of itself that any form can be created and upheld.

And this very fact, then, proves the potential that any form, no matter how imperfect or impure, can be accelerated and transcended until it now outpictures a higher vision. This is the true message behind the mission of Christ, namely that no matter how far an individual may have descended below the level of the Christ consciousness, that individual could never lose the potential for being redeemed, for being reborn, for accelerating itself beyond the lower consciousness and manifesting the Christ consciousness.

Likewise, no matter how far a planet has descended below the level of the original purity created by the Elohim, the planet could never lose the potential for again being accelerated back to the pure vision, to the immaculate concept that is still held in the mind of Elohim. That vision has not been destroyed or distorted by anything human beings have done, as they have exercised their free will in the cosmic schoolroom on earth.

When you begin, after having passed the initiations of the fourth ray, to see this underlying reality, you gain a new perspective on everything on earth. This does not mean that you instantly become the Christ and have the full vision of the Christ, but you do begin to understand that there is a higher way of looking at everything on earth. And when you do, then, begin to have this Christ vision, you can do what Mother Mary did, as he watched Jesus grow up and eventually mature to the point, where he could begin to fulfill his spiritual mission. You can hold the immaculate concept, both for yourself and your own acceleration towards Christhood, and for the planet and its growth towards a higher state of life.

Can you perhaps see that although there are many people today who have become more aware of environmental problems, there is a con-

Bringing a higher truth into the environmental debate 197

siderable percentage of them who have not actually grasped what the fifth ray is all about? Instead of holding the immaculate concept that the earth might transcend environmental problems, they are pulled into following this or that doomsday scenario.

Can you perhaps sense that if everything is consciousness and if everything on earth is affected by the consciousness of humankind, then focusing your attention on a doomsday scenario – or on some theory that presents environmental problems as having no solution – will not help heal the Earth Mother? On the contrary, when you focus on a doomsday scenario – or when you see some physical condition as setting an absolute limit for the changes that could potentially occur – then you are actually allowing your mind to become a tool for either upholding current environmental problems or even making them worse.

***

As we have said, the real underlying cause of all problems on earth is the force-based state of consciousness. Why is there a need to use force? Well, in reality there is no need to use force, for as Jesus said, "Fear not little flock, for it is your father's good pleasure to give you the kingdom." The reality of life on earth is that the Elohim designed this planet in such a way that it can provide, not only sustenance but an abundant sustenance to 10 billion people. It is perfectly within the design of the Elohim that 10 billion people can live on earth and that they can do so in such a state of balance, that there is plenty of food for them but also a perfect balance in the natural environment. If there is balance in the collective consciousness, there will be balance in nature.

Thus, if human beings were aware of and were willing to follow the very design principles that the Elohim used to design planet earth, there would be no need to use force in order to get what you need from nature. It would be perfectly possible for 10 billion people to live the abundant life on earth without using force, but simply using the natural processes designed by the Elohim—and thus receiving their sustenance from nature in a way that most people on earth can scarcely imagine today.

The need to use force, therefore, comes about when people go below the 48th level of consciousness at which new co-creators start. When people go into the realm of separation and duality, they inevitably begin to see themselves as separated from other people and from the planet upon which they live. The more you sink into this illusion of separation, the more you begin to see yourself as disconnected from everything else. And the more disconnected you think you are, well you obviously will then begin to see yourself as being in opposition to the planet upon which you live. You will begin to see nature as a limitation or even as an enemy. And thus, you will see why, for thousands of years now in recorded history, human beings have tended to see nature as something to either be feared or as something to be fought and conquered.

It could be said, indeed, that all environmental problems currently seen on earth are a product of the very fact that Western civilization has seen itself as being in opposition to the natural environment. And this civilization has believed that rather than accepting the kingdom that it is the father's good pleasure to give them, they have to use force to wrestle a living from the stubborn forces of nature that seem to oppose them.

Truly, the entire belief that you need to use force to get what you need for your sustenance on earth is an expression of the force-based consciousness. This, I trust, you can begin to see. And thus, it should be clear that it is indeed this attempt to take nature by force that is the cause of environmental problems on earth. It is, of course, also the cause of all conflicts between human beings, where one person uses force to take from another.

So can you now begin to see why it is extremely important that those who want to be forerunners for healing Mother Earth begin to attain a higher vision, begin to see that vision, so that they can use it to no longer focus on the doomsday scenarios or the "absolute" limitations but instead hold the immaculate concept for what is indeed possible on earth? Namely that society can be accelerated to the point, where there is such an equal distribution of wealth and resources that all people on earth can live in a reasonable state of abundance without destroying the natural environment. To this end, then, I, Hilarion, will give you some thoughts.

***

Let me first comment on the teaching that the fifth ray is the ray of truth. If you have some familiarity with the New Testament of the Christian Bible, you will know that there is a situation where Jesus is brought to trial in front of the Roman governor, Pontius Pilate. Jesus states that he came into the world to bear witness to the truth, and Pontius Pilate then

Bringing a higher truth into the environmental debate

asks him the pivotal question, "What is truth?" This, then, is a topic that you need to understand, when you accelerate yourself beyond the initiations of the fourth ray and aspire to the initiations of the fifth ray.

What has my beloved brother, Serapis Bey, told you about the initiations you must go through on the fourth ray? Has he not explained that after having gone through the initiations of the first three rays, you have been focused on raising yourself as an individual being? Yet even though this has been a necessary phase in your growth – and even though it has therefore been perfectly in order that you developed a certain momentum of power, wisdom and love as an individual being – you have now come to a point, where that which brought you to that point cannot bring you further.

Suddenly, what you have come to see as your greatest asset, has now become your greatest liability. If you insist on raising yourself as an individual being, you cannot go beyond the kindergarten at the retreat of Serapis Bey. You will continue to stand at that level, perhaps for lifetimes, before you begin to develop the willingness to let that individual self die and be reborn into a self that sees itself as one with the All. Yet what exactly does that mean? Well, it means that you begin to grasp the vision of the Christ mind, the vision of the Christ reality.

When you look at planet earth today, you will see many religions, many political ideologies, many philosophies, even the philosophy of materialistic science, which all claim that they have the truth—perhaps even the highest truth, perhaps even an absolute truth, perhaps even the only truth. Anyone willing to use logic can see that they cannot all be right, for their "truths" are very different and often mutually exclusive. This has caused many people to go through a period, where they have started to doubt what they were presented in childhood as the absolute truth.

This is a healthy stage to go through, for you cannot grasp a higher truth until you are willing to doubt what has been defined on earth as the highest possible truth. If you have been brought up to believe that there is one thought system on earth that presents the highest possible truth, then you will obviously never go beyond that level until you begin to doubt the validity of this claim.

Unfortunately, the danger of going through this process is that you begin to doubt everything and begin to doubt that there is a higher truth. And thus, you might sink into agnosticism or simply depression, for you no longer have anything in which you believe. Yet on the fifth ray, it is not a matter of believing that a certain thought system on earth is the truth. It is a matter of going beyond belief and truly experiencing what Jesus talked about when he said, "God is a Spirit and they that worship him must worship him in spirit and in truth." Truly, it is in the Spirit of Truth that you must "worship" God, and you do this by opening your mind and heart to a direct experience of the Spirit of Truth.

***

Can you begin to draw a parallel between what I have said here and what has been said by Mother Mary and the other chohans? I have said that there are many systems on earth who each claims to have the absolute truth, and the other chohans and Mother Mary have explained that the underlying reality is consciousness. Can you see that what quantum physics has proven is, that even when a scientist conducts an experiment, then the outcome of that experiment, the observation made by the scientist, will be – in a fundamental way – affected by the consciousness of the scientist?

You probably do know that there was a point, when the medieval Catholic Church persecuted the early scientists. You probably also know that there was a point where science attempted to distance itself as far as possible from religion. You may be aware that in this process, science determined that the consciousness of human beings can only be subjective. Thus, scientists claimed that all religions, all religious beliefs, were a product of the subjectivity of the human mind. Therefore, they attempted to create scientific instruments and scientific processes that would give the same results by anyone performing them, regardless of that person's individual beliefs. Scientists therefore claimed that if an experiment was repeatable by many different kinds of people, then the results of that experiment could be considered objective.

My beloved, it is not my intention here to cast doubt upon the validity of science or the scientific method, for it was indeed sponsored by the Ascended Host. What I would like is for you to consider that if truly any experiment performed at the quantum level is affected by the consciousness of the scientist, and if all matter is made from subatomic particles, then is it not possible that the consciousness of human beings will have

Bringing a higher truth into the environmental debate

a fundamental effect on all observations made, including those made through scientific instruments and the scientific method?

What is it that quantum physics has really proven? It has proven that everything in the entire universe, every form you see in the world of form, has a corresponding quantum waveform. As we have explained, this quantum waveform is truly a mental image, a matrix, formulated in the minds of self-aware beings and then projected onto the Ma-ter light. We have explained that there are different levels of vibration and that the entire material universe vibrates within a certain level of frequencies. Is it not therefore possible, my beloved, that the human mind has an ability to go beyond the level of subjectivity?

Do you see that when science made the observation that many religious beliefs sprang from the subjectivity of the human mind, they made an error of judgment? They assumed that because it was readily observable that the human mind has a subjective aspect, this proved that the mind could only be subjective. In other words, they assumed that it was not possible for the mind to have an objective aspect.

Yet we have attempted to explain to you that everything in the entire world of form has an Alpha and an Omega aspect. Is it not possible that what scientists have seen as the subjective aspect of the mind is only one side of the coin? Thus, the mind has another side; it has the potential to have experiences that are not subjective. The mind has an Alpha aspect that allows you to tune in to a reality that is beyond the level of subjectivity.

***

Let me attempt to illustrate this in a simple way. When a scientist is studying a faraway galaxy through a powerful telescope, you know very well that that telescope is only transmitting light rays. Or should we perhaps say that what the scientist can see with the physical eyes is only the light rays that enter the telescope? Thus, what the scientist sees through the telescope is only the visible aspect of what is happening in that distant galaxy.

Let us say, for example, that a scientist is studying a galaxy in which there is the formation of new suns with what appears to be giant explosions. Do you suppose that these giant explosions in this faraway galaxy are only visible phenomena, or do you think they also produce a sound?

Certainly, logic will tell you that there is indeed a sound produced, yet logic and science will also tell you that these sound rays do not have the ability to travel through empty space and thus cannot reach you. My point then is simply this. If the scientist is looking at a phenomenon through an instrument that only gives a visual impression of that phenomenon, well then the scientist cannot be said to have the full impression of the phenomenon.

So how does this relate to the attempts of scientists to distance themselves from being influenced by the subjectivity of the mind? Well, if scientists have reasoned that in order to gain an objective understanding, they have to shut out the mind – and then they had used that reasoning to create scientific instruments and processes that do not include the mind – then what exactly have they done?

Well, what they have done so far is that they have attempted to develop scientific instruments that are made only of matter. A telescope is an instrument made of physical matter, and it can detect visible light. There are radio telescopes and other instruments that can detect energy waves that are not within the spectrum of visible light. Yet if there is indeed a realm of reality made of vibrations that are beyond those found in the entire material universe, is it not plausible that no instrument made of matter could possibly detect those energy waves?

Do you see my point? It may well be that scientists have come up with experiments that can be repeated and that will give consistent results for any person who conducts them. It may well be that these processes and instruments have never proven the existence of anything beyond the material universe, such as a God or a higher realm. But does this necessarily mean that these processes have proven that there could be nothing beyond the material realm? Does the fact that you hear no sound from a distant galaxy through a telescope prove that there is no sound produced? Nay, it only proves the limitations of the telescope.

Thus, my point is that seeking to completely eliminate consciousness is not the way to true objectivity. Can you see, that there are certain scientists who have a very strong opposition to anything related to religion? Can you see, that there are certain scientists who have a very strong attachment to the materialistic paradigm and who will do almost anything possible to prove, so to speak, that there is no validity to anything that points beyond the material universe?

Bringing a higher truth into the environmental debate   203

These scientists will readily say that any experience you could possibly have of the spiritual realm is a subjective experience and thus not valid. Yet can you begin to see the flaw in their reasoning? When they use their scientific instruments and processes to study the world – and when they fail to see that there is anything beyond the material universe – they are simply making an observation. But when they then begin to say, that the fact that they have not found anything beyond the material universe proves that there is not and never could be anything beyond the material universe, then they are no longer making an observation. They are making an interpretation, and that interpretation will inevitably and undeniably – for those who are willing to look at reality – be affected by the consciousness of the interpreter.

In other words, when scientists say that anyone who has any form of spiritual or religious experience has had a subjective experience, they must – if they are willing to be consistent – also say that anyone who uses the findings of science to claim this has proven there is nothing beyond matter is also having a subjective experience. If one is subjective, then the other must be subjective as well. You cannot have it both ways, you cannot have your cake and eat it too.

Thus, what you see currently on planet earth is what might be considered a battle between those who still hold on to traditional religions, especially traditional Christianity, and those who espouse a materialistic paradigm and the materialistic approach to life as the absolute truth. Can you begin to see that if you enter this battle on either side, then you will not truly contribute to the healing of Mother Earth?

There is no doubt that the approach taken by traditional religion, and especially traditional Christianity, is indeed a force-based approach. Yet the approach taken by materialistic scientists is likewise a force-based approach. Each side claims that they have the only truth and that that truth has been expressed by their thought system. They claim they have defined truth, and in making this claim, they are proving that neither side has made use of the mind's ability to go beyond the level of subjective experience and interpretation. Neither side has been willing to look beyond the mental boxes defined by their thought system and have a direct experience of the Spirit of Truth.

***

What, then, is truth? We have talked about the River of Life as a process of self-transcendence—eternal, ongoing and never-ending self-transcendence. The Spirit of Truth is indeed a process of self-transcendence. When human beings consider the concept of truth, they want to believe that it is a fixed entity, a fixed quantity.

Religious people want to believe that "up there" in heaven is a God who has an exact formulation of what truth is. Many of them even want to believe that God has given this formulation of truth to them in the form of their own religious scripture. Scientists on the other hand like to believe that somewhere "out there" in nature, built into the universe, is a set of principles or laws that are absolute and invariable and thus represent the highest truth. And they believe that by studying the universe through their scientific instruments, they will eventually uncover the fullness of that truth.

Yet what is it that drives people to want a truth that is never changing? It is indeed the very consciousness of separation. As we have explained abundantly in other books and on the askrealjesus website, once you go into the illusion of separation, you must create a new kind of self, which is known in many spiritual teachings, and even the science of psychology, as the human ego. This ego is a self that is born from the illusion of separation. It is not the individual sense of self that Serapis Bey explained you have, when you go up from the 48th level and go through the first three rays. This is a self that is created as you go below the 48th level and go into the levels of separation and duality.

In the Gospel of John, Jesus makes an interesting statement to a Jewish man, named Nicodemus. Jesus explains that the only person that can ascend back to heaven is the being that descended from heaven. The being that descended from heaven, from the spiritual realm, is, as we have now explained, the Conscious You.

When the Conscious You decides to focus its attention below the 48th level and go into the lower levels of consciousness, then it can do so only by creating a separate self, namely the ego. That ego can only see itself as a separate, disconnected being. It is disconnected from any God that it can envision, and thus it can only envision God as the remote being in the sky. It is disconnected from other beings around it, and thus it can only see itself as being in competition with or in opposition to other human beings. And it is, of course, disconnected from the planet

Bringing a higher truth into the environmental debate 205

upon which it lives, and that is why it can only see that it must use force to subdue nature and get what it wants from nature through force.

This ego is the real cause of all human conflict. This is not to say that the ego alone is what we might call the subjective or the Omega aspect of the mind. As we have explained, the Conscious You is an individual extension of your I Will Be Presence. The Conscious You is like a clear pane of glass, because the Conscious You can project itself anywhere it can imagine.

It is precisely this ability, this characteristic as a clear pane of glass, that allows the Conscious You to project itself into a physical body on earth, so that it can experience the earth from the inside and act in this world. Yet the Conscious You also has the ability to project itself in the other direction and project itself up into the Presence. When the Conscious You projects itself into a physical body on earth, then it will of necessity look at the material world from a localized vantage point.

***

If you are sitting in a chair opposite another person, then you are obviously looking at the room in which you are sitting from a localized viewpoint. You can see what is behind the other person, yet you cannot see what is behind yourself. The other person can see what is behind you but cannot see what is behind himself or herself. As long as the Conscious You is looking at the world through a physical body, it will have a localized – and therefore a subjective – view of the world.

This means that as long as the Conscious You is looking at the world from inside the world, it can only have a subjective experience of the world. The question is how subjective that experience is, and that is, indeed, determined by how sophisticated an ego the Conscious You has created and how identified the Conscious You is with that ego.

You see, the ego can only look at the world from a relative viewpoint, meaning that the ego has a dualistic scale with right at one end and wrong at the other end. And the ego then applies a value judgment upon right and wrong.

Do you see, here, that there is a subtle but all-important difference between the subjective viewpoint and the ego-based or dualistic viewpoint? When you are sitting opposite another person, you are looking at the room from a particular angle. If you are aware of this, you realize that your particular perspective cannot give you the full view of the room. And thus, you will not necessarily believe that what you see is all there is to see or that your view of the room is superior to the view of the other person. You can have an awareness that you have a localized perspective without implying that this perspective is absolute or is superior to any other perspective. In other words, you can realize that this is simply your viewpoint and you have no need to apply a value judgment to it.

Yet when the ego comes into the situation, the ego will want to believe that its viewpoint is, while not necessarily the only possible one, certainly the only right one. And it will want to apply the value judgment that its view is superior to the view of the other person. The ego will say that looking at the room from your perspective is fundamentally superior to the other person's perspective of the same room. This particular mechanism is what gives rise to all human conflict.

Now, as you go through the initiations of the first three rays of power, wisdom and love, it is possible for you to have remnants of ego with you. There are few people who can go through the process of raising their individual self through the first three rays without being affected by the relativity and the value judgments of the dualistic state of consciousness.

This is precisely why Serapis Bey puts them in a kindergarten situation with other people, who also have their strong belief in the superiority of their viewpoints. And they then have to go through perpetual conflicts with each other, until they finally decide to go beyond the kindergarten level and let go of the desire to prove the superiority of what is, after all, only their localized, subjective view of the world.

So when you come to the initiations of the fifth ray, you must begin to understand the limitations of the dualistic worldview, the value-based view of the ego. You must realize that the only way to truly know truth is to go beyond any desire to prove the superiority of your personal, localized view.

In a sense, this is precisely what scientists have attempted to obtain through the scientific method. Many scientists have indeed attained a state of consciousness, where they are completely neutral when performing an experiment. They have no preconceived value-laden judgments about what should or should not be the outcome of the experiment. They are open to whatever the outcome may be, and they are willing to change their theories based on the outcome. Unfortunately, that is not true for all people who are part of the scientific community, as some people are indeed as attached to the superiority of the materialistic paradigm as the Pope and his Cardinals are attached to the superiority of the Catholic paradigm.

***

Yet what you need to be aware of is, that if you want to be one of the forerunners for healing Mother Earth, you need to come to the point, where you fully and finally realize the fallacy of trying to prove the superiority of any particular thought system on earth. As I have said, the ego has a desire to elevate one thought system as the superior one. What is the psychological mechanism that drives the ego to do this? It is, as I said, the very fact that the only being that can ascend back to heaven is the being that descended from heaven, namely the Conscious You.

The ego did not descend from heaven but was created in the lower realm, and thus it can never have any permanency, meaning it cannot achieve immortality. At the moment the Conscious You begins to see the limitations of the ego and begins to dis-identify itself from it, the ego will indeed begin to die. And when the Conscious You finally surrenders all identification with the ego, the ego will die.

The ego does not want to die, for as all other lifeforms it has a survival instinct. And thus, the ego is constantly attempting the impossible of securing its own immortality. And this is what drives the ego to seek to define a thought system on earth as the superior and infallible one. The ego believes that if it is a member of this particular thought system or religion, then its salvation – survival – is guaranteed.

When you look honestly at humankind, you will see that the vast majority of people believe in this illusion. And they even believe, many of them, that by being a member of this particular religion and following all its outer beliefs and practices, they are guaranteed to be saved. Even materialists have a similar belief, even though not clothed in religious lingo.

The reality is, of course, that truth, the Spirit of Truth, is the River of Life. The ego wants to believe that somewhere there exists this absolute definition of truth that can never change. The reality is that there is no such definition of truth, because the entire world of form is constantly transcending itself. And as the world transcends itself, especially as it makes a quantum leap to an entirely new level, then the definition of truth changes accordingly.

We might say that there is an absolute truth, but that truth is the consciousness of the Creator itself. In the mind of the Creator is the absolute truth for what is possible in the world of form created by the Creator. That absolute truth is, of course, that every individual extension of the Creator's Being has the potential to reach the same level of self-awareness as the Creator. And when an individual extension reaches the level of the Creator, then the individual will know the absolute truth held in the mind of the Creator, because the individual being will now experience the world as the Creator experiences it.

***

Do you see the subtle point I am seeking to convey? As long as you see yourself as a being who is not in complete oneness with your source, with your Creator, you are seeing a distance between your individual self and the Self of the Creator. This means that you are looking at the Creator from a distance, and you are seeking to know the Creator from a distance. Yet it is not possible to know the fullness of the Creator from a distance. It is, for that matter, not possible to know the fullness of anything from a distance.

Take note of what we have said: the underlying reality is consciousness. What scientists call a quantum waveform is a matrix held in consciousness. The entire planet earth was originally created as the manifestation of a thoughtform held in the consciousness of the Elohim.

I can tell you this, and when I tell you, your mind will instantly formulate an image that somewhere up there in a higher realm is a group of beings, and in the minds of those beings there is a – shall we call it a "blueprint" – for the earth. Thus, your mind will believe that it should be possible for the Elohim to transmit that blueprint to your mind, so that you could see that blueprint with your present state of consciousness. Yet what I am seeking to explain is that this simply is not possible; it is an illusion created by the fact that you view the universe from a localized vantage point.

As long as the Conscious You is looking at the universe from the localized vantage point of a physical body on earth, you will think that somewhere outside of this body is the knowledge of a particular object and that knowledge can be transmitted to your mind—and then your mind will know the object. This is an illusion that is very much tied to the physical senses and the outer mind.

You know very well that you can study a topic, such as the backside of the moon. You can look at photographs taken by spacecraft, and therefore you can gain a knowledge in the outer mind of what are the conditions found on the backside of the moon. In other words, most people believe that they can know what it is like on the backside of the moon without ever entering a spacecraft. There is, of course, some validity to this, but I think you will also realize that a person who has indeed entered a spacecraft and has traveled to the backside of the moon will have a completely different perspective than a person who has only studied the backside of the moon from earth and thus has never actually seen it.

My point, therefore, is this. The consciousness of the Elohim is many degrees beyond the 144th level of what is possible on earth. The blueprint for the earth that is held in the minds of the Elohim is of such a nature, that it simply cannot be fathomed through the outer consciousness of a human being on earth. It is not possible for I or the Elohim themselves to convey to you the fullness of the blueprint for the earth that they have created in their minds. In fact, this blueprint cannot be described in its fullness through words or even through religious or scientific concepts.

Yet this does not mean that you cannot know this blueprint. For as I have said, the Conscious You has the ability to project itself both down into the material realm and up into the spiritual realm. How then can you know the concept for the earth held in the minds of the Elohim? You can know so only if the Conscious You projects itself into the mind of the Elohim. And when you see the world from the vantage point of the Elohim, then you can know the fullness of the blueprint held in the minds of the Elohim.

Likewise, you can project yourself into the consciousness of the Creator and actually attain an experience of what the universe looks like from the viewpoint of the Creator, the omnipresent viewpoint of the Creator, as opposed to the localized viewpoint that you are so used to experiencing. Of course, seeing the universe from the viewpoint of the

Creator is not possible as long as you see yourself as a typical human being, as a disconnected, separate being.

The Bible has a sentence in which it says, "No man can see God and live," but the deeper meaning is that no man can see God and live as a man. For once you see even a glimpse of the Creator's Being, you can no longer believe in the illusion that you are confined to a physical body on earth. And thus, you cannot maintain the sense of self, the sense of identity, as a human being on earth. Therefore, for you to experience the fullness of the Creator, you must transcend the earth. For the earth is still in such a low state, that you cannot be in embodiment and at the same time experience the fullness of the Creator.

Nevertheless, my point is that even while you are in embodiment, you can project yourself up into the I Will Be Presence and even into the I AM Presence. And through that, you can experience what the universe looks like from that level of awareness. And when you do this, when you use the mind's ability to project itself outside of the physical body and the separate self, then you will know a higher truth than you could ever know through the means of the physical body and the outer mind, including any religious doctrine or scientific experiment.

***

There is a concept that was known by many in the early Christian movement, but it was suppressed when the Catholic Church began to set itself up as the only and absolute source of truth. It was the concept of gnosis.

What I have described is that when you are looking at the world through the physical body and the outer mind, you have a duality between the subject, namely you, and the object you are studying. Gnosis is the process of bridging the gap between subject and object.

How is this possible? Well, as I have said, everything in the world of form is the manifestation of a matrix held in consciousness. Thus, if you pick up a rock, there is a matrix of consciousness that exists in the etheric realm, the mental realm and the emotional realm. In order to truly know a rock, you cannot simply study it with the outer mind and scientific instruments, for this is studying at a distance, where there is still at gap between subject and object.

In fact, studying a rock with scientific instruments can for many people reinforce the subject-object duality. In order to truly know the rock, you must use the Conscious You's ability to project itself beyond the physical body and the outer mind. You must experience the emotional blueprint for the rock, the mental blueprint for the rock and the etheric blueprint for the rock. When the Conscious You projects itself into those blueprints, then you will know a rock. You will know the consciousness that precipitated the rock.

This, then, is what Serapis Bey explained about the need to go beyond seeing only the material – so-called – causes of environmental problems. Every problem found on earth has more than a physical cause. It has an emotional, a mental and an etheric cause. In other words, for every problem that you see physically manifest, there is a blueprint in the emotional, in the mental and in the etheric realm. And only when you use the mind's ability to project yourself into experiencing those blueprints, will you know the fullness of the cause behind a specific material problem. And of course, only when you know the cause, can you then be an instrument for bringing about a real solution—which is, truly, the transcendence of the very consciousness that manifested the problem.

When you take the approach that a thought system on earth can define an absolute truth, then you become seduced into thinking that the solution to all problems can be defined by your thought system. And then it becomes, so to speak, "obvious" to you that the way to solve all human problems is to force all other people to adhere to your thought system.

And then, you easily become seduced by the further illusion of the fallen beings, namely that the ends justify the means. For after all, if it seems that unless all people comply with our view, then the earth will be destroyed by some environmental catastrophe, it will seem imperative that all people be forced to comply with our view—NOW! And then, it is only a matter of how far people are willing to go in forcing other people to comply with their thought system.

***

Can you see my deeper point here? Environmental problems on earth will not be solved through a particular thought system that defines solutions in the material realm. There is no thought system that will guarantee the solution of environmental problems. Those who are willing to be the forerunners for healing Mother Earth, must realize that environmental problems actually point to a much deeper problem, which is the entire relationship between human beings and their source, between human beings and other human beings and between human beings and the planet upon which they live.

That problem springs from the fact that the majority of human beings on earth have descended below the 48th level of consciousness and have been blinded and seduced by the viewpoint that they are separate beings, that there is an external standard with right at one end and wrong at the other, that there is a value judgment associated with that standard and that it is therefore justified to force that standard upon others.

The entire desire to force your standard upon others is the real cause of not only environmental problems but also the conflicts between human beings that already have, and could in the future produce even worse, consequences for the environment. For how can you look at the environmental issue and only consider what human beings are doing to nature?

What would be the greatest potential environmental disaster that could be produced by human beings? Would it not be an all-out nuclear war? So if you truly are concerned for the environment, would you not say that you cannot only look at pollution or global warming? You need to look at the potential for nuclear war and take steps to reduce that potential to zero. If the nuclear superpowers decided to push the buttons, then within 15 minutes the earth would be propelled into an environmental catastrophe worse than anything that could be produced by global warming or industrial waste.

It is therefore imperative that those who want to be forerunners for healing Mother Earth accelerate their view of the earth beyond the duality consciousness, with its relative scale and its value judgments.

This, my beloved, is truth.

There is a truth that is beyond the subjectivity and the value judgments of human beings. Your mind has the ability to know that truth, but you cannot know it from a distance. You cannot know the truth from within your current mental box, for the truth – the Spirit of Truth – will never fit in any mental box, in any thought system, that can ever be defined on earth.

If you want to know the Spirit of Truth, you must become aware that you are – the core of your being is – the Conscious You, which is a clear pane of glass. And you must use the ability to project yourself beyond the physical body, beyond the mental box of the outer mind, beyond the material universe itself.

You must project yourself up into your I Will Be Presence, so that you may gain a perspective on the material world that you could never gain from within the material world. Only then will you be able to know the truth that will set you free from the very consciousness that has created all environmental problems. And only when you, your sense of self, is set free from that consciousness – so that you no longer see yourself as a being who is in opposition to others or in opposition to Mother Earth – well, only then can you become part of the solution instead of being part of the problem.

***

The fifth ray has been seen as the ray of healing, but what is healing? Healing is wholeness. Healing comes about only, when you see beyond the illusion of separation and see the underlying wholeness of all life.

When you align your own consciousness with that underlying wholeness and oneness, then you will manifest wholeness in your physical body. When a critical mass of individuals align their individual states of consciousness with that underlying wholeness, they will pull up the collective consciousness, so that wholeness will begin to manifest in human relationships and in the relationship between humankind and Mother Earth. And then, you will begin to see wholeness in human society and wholeness in the planetary body. You will begin to see a wholeness in nature, whereby people will begin to see, that they do not have to fight nature in order to get what they need for their sustenance.

Yet, of course, for this to occur, a critical mass of people must free themselves from the very consciousness that creates conflict, the consciousness of the power elite of the fallen beings, who are not seeking to bring about wholeness. These are the beings who have created the environmental problems in the first place, in their never-ending quest to attain power and privileges beyond that of the population.

When you see truth, you see that it is not in the design of the Elohim that two-thirds of the world population should live beneath the poverty level, while a small elite in the so-called rich countries have become so rich that no individual could even spend the money in the rest of a lifetime. This is clearly an elitist condition, brought about by people who have no sense of wholeness with all life. They see themselves as separate beings and they want to raise themselves up to the highest possible status as separate beings on earth. They will do absolutely anything in order to attain that status, and they will continue – until enough people see through it – to use the environmental issue in order to further their quest for power and privilege.

These are the beings who in their quest for power and privilege created the industrial revolution and the pollution you see. These are the beings who in their quest for power created the arms race and the potential for a nuclear war. They are now attempting to use the environmental issue to set themselves up as the very people who can solve the environmental problems that they have created.

This is the typical consequence of the presence of the fallen beings and the fallen consciousness on earth. These beings are trapped in the consciousness of separation. The consciousness of separation, as we have explained, is a closed system, and thus it will be subject to the second law of thermodynamics.

As a result, the closed system of the fallen beings will inevitably create problems, and current environmental problems are a typical example of how the second law of thermodynamics seeks to break down the closed systems created by the fallen beings on earth—the very closed systems that allow them to have special powers and special privileges. So what the fallen beings attempt to do is to, then, use the inevitable problems they have created in order to set themselves up as the saviors, who can save humankind from the very problems they have created.

This is not truth; this is not vision. And thus, for current conditions to fundamentally change, it is necessary that a critical mass among the forerunners will raise themselves to the higher vision. This is where they not only see the immaculate concept for earth, but precisely because they do see that immaculate concept, they also gain the sense of co-measurement, a frame of reference, to see just how far below that immaculate concept things have gone on earth.

***

Most of the people who have loving hearts and good intentions – and who have used these to become engaged in the environmental issue –

Bringing a higher truth into the environmental debate   215

have not even begun to realize the deeper causes behind environmental problems. Thus, they are vulnerable to being pulled into the half solutions suggested by the very fallen beings, by the very power elite, that have created the problems in the first place. They go for feel-good "solutions" that have no objective possibility of ever being a real solution.

If there is to be a fundamental shift, then a critical mass among the well-meaning people must awaken to the higher reality, that there is much more to understand about environmental problems than what is currently being brought out in the public debate. They must come to see the deeper spiritual causes, and then they must use their minds' ability to project themselves beyond the mental boxes of earth and encounter the Spirit of Truth. They must then use that frame of reference to develop and communicate a higher view of the problems.

This is not necessarily an easy task, for the higher vision you see is beyond words—yet you must, of course, seek to communicate through words. And when you begin to see this, you begin to see the essential problem that the Ascended Host face, when we attempt to enlighten our unascended brothers and sisters, such as we are doing through this messenger and this book.

We have a vision that is beyond words, but we must communicate that vision through words. Thus, when you begin to realize this, you will see that it is not enough for you to take our words. You will not fulfill your highest potential for having an impact on the environmental debate by taking the words we have given in this book and then going out and arguing based on them. You will fulfill your highest potential only when you are willing to project the Conscious You beyond your current mental box and experience the Spirit of Truth, so that you experience our consciousness from within instead of from a distance.

We are not seeking here, with this book, to only give a teaching. We know that there are some people who are only ready for an outer teaching and who can benefit from this book. But we are also seeking those who are willing to go beyond the outer teaching and come into gnosis with ourselves, so that you can be the open door for ourselves. And so that you can speak the word of truth, the WORD, the LOGOS, in the environmental debate.

It is not our desire whatsoever, nor is it the desire of this messenger, to set up one person as the only or ultimate source of truth. We want many people to become the open doors for the word of truth to be spoken in various contexts, not necessarily claiming that this comes from an ascended master but simply speaking the word and allowing the word to speak for itself. So that those who are willing can sense that you have an understanding, a perspective, that they do not have. And thus, they might look, not at your words, but look at you as an example and say, "When that person can gain a wider perspective, then I must be able to do the same."

And thus, we again have the old axiom: "What one has done, all can do." All have the ability to project themselves beyond their current mental box and to attain that wider perspective that comes from oneness, from gnosis, with the Spirit of Truth.

I am Hilarion, the Chohan of the fifth ray. I am one with the Spirit of Truth, and thus I say to you from that oneness: "Be one with me, be one with the Spirit of Truth of the Ascended Host and be the open door for that Spirit to express itself and change – fundamentally – the public debate on earth."

It is possible. The immaculate concept is a reality in the etheric realm. It can become a reality in the physical realm, but only through you and people like you.

Dare to be the open door for the Spirit of Truth to flow through you.

Dare to be the clear pane of glass, through which the Spirit of Truth can express itself in the purest possible form, and thus awaken those who cannot be awakened through ordinary words and arguments. For they need to sense the resonance between what is said and what they know deep within their beings.

The desire to be MORE is within all life. When you become the open door for that River of Life, that Spirit of Truth, you will rekindle the desire to be MORE in others, and that is what will awaken them. No amount of arguments will solve the environmental debate. Not to say that arguments are not needed, but the arguments alone will not achieve the ultimate result. That result will be achieved only when the words become chalices for the higher vibration of the Spirit of Truth to shine through the lens of the Conscious You.

Be that open door.

Be that open door—and then be MORE!

Key 13
Overcoming duality in order to give true service

Lady Master Nada is my name. I am the Chohan of the sixth ray. The sixth ray has traditionally been seen as the ray of ministration and service but also as the ray of peace. Let me thus give you a teaching on how service and peace are inextricably linked together, so that you cannot understand one without the other.

You have no doubt heard the saying that the road to hell is paved with good intentions. It is a readily observable fact that some of the people who have committed the greatest atrocities of history have done so out of a misguided belief that they were serving some ultimate cause. If you have a sincere desire to be one of the forerunners for healing Mother Earth and transcending current environmental problems – or even the potential environmental problem caused by a large-scale war – well, then you need to understand how it is possible that over the course of history so many well-meaning people have been trapped into activities that did not serve life, that did not promote peace.

As Mother Mary and the other chohans have explained, there was indeed a group of beings who rebelled against God's purpose in a higher sphere, and they have kept falling until they ended up in this sphere, some of them embodying on planet earth, others being attached to planet earth outside of a physical body. These beings, then, form what we have called a power elite, where they seek to control humankind for two main purposes.

***

One is, of course, their own survival. For the reality is that even though all beings have free will, when you start violating the free will of others, the light you receive from the spiritual realm – from your own I Will Be

Presence – is reduced in quantity. Those who have systematically misused or violated the free will of others, will eventually have the flow of light from the spiritual realm reduced to a point, where they can barely sustain a physical body. Some of them have even had it reduced further, which is why they are not in physical embodiment but are attached to the earth in what we have sometimes called the astral realm, which is part of the emotional realm.

So then, what happens when a being has reduced the flow of light from the spiritual realm to the point, where it can barely stay alive? Well, what happens is that this being – if it is not willing to change its state of consciousness – must then seek to steal spiritual light from other human beings. This is done by in various ways manipulating them into giving their light.

This can be done through direct force, as you see in violence, rape and war. When emotions are forcefully stirred up or when blood is spilled, spiritual light is released. But the spiritual light will not be in its true form, it will be qualified by the emotions that the person had at the time. This misqualified light can thus be absorbed by the beings who have, no longer, the flow or the sufficient flow from the spiritual realm.

These beings cannot absorb pure spiritual light, and if they are exposed to it, it makes them extremely uncomfortable—which is why you will indeed see some people who can become angry and hateful towards others. Why, for example, do you think the angry mob – that suddenly turned on Jesus 2,000 years ago at his trial, crying "Barabbas, Barabbas," – was so agitated? It was indeed because Jesus carried great spiritual light, and the effect of the light is that it flushes out the darkness in those whose personal forcefields are filled with darkness.

Normally, these people can cover over the darkness, for in their minds they have made it seem like something that is benign. Yet when they are exposed to spiritual light, it suddenly comes up to the surface, and they can no longer deny it. And if they are not willing to change, well then they must take their anger out on the person who is the cause of the stirring up of what they themselves refuse to see.

So then, you see many times throughout history, where this has taken place. For example you will see in the entire process of the Inquisition and witch hunts, how those who were leaders of the Catholic religion had indeed an anger and hatred towards those who dared to take a stand

Overcoming duality in order to give true service

against doctrine, or against those women who had studied life and had developed certain abilities for healing.

Many of the witches that were burned at the stake were indeed the forerunners for a shift in consciousness. They were more advanced than the people who persecuted them, either the people who reported them to the authorities or the authorities themselves. And thus, what you saw during the Middle Ages and the witch hunt processes was indeed an attempt by those who have less light to eradicate those who have more light, so that there could not be a shift in the collective consciousness.

***

This is and has always been one of the great motivations behind not only war but any attempt to limit the size of the human population. If you look at a society, such as the feudal societies of Europe in the Middle Ages, you will see, that there was only a certain amount of land. And due to the inefficiency of the farming methods at the time, there was very strict limits to how much crop could be grown on that land. And thus, there was also a very strict limit to how many people could be fed on a given area of land.

Which means that once the population grew beyond a certain level, people of the peasant class – who were virtually the slaves of the noblemen – began to die from starvation. And faced with dying from starvation or rebelling against their overlords, well then the choice was somewhat easier than when they were well fed. And thus, if you look at the historical reality, you see that, indeed, it was the growth in the population that caused the overturning of the feudal societies.

I can assure you that those who were the overlords in the feudal societies would gladly have seen that kind of society continue indefinitely, where they could form a small elite with special powers and privileges that no one among the population could threaten. Of course, this small elite – as you might see if you take an honest look at history – has still managed to reinvent itself as society has changed.

When the Industrial Revolution began, some among the elite managed to set themselves up as the first industrialists. And thus, they became as rich and as privileged as the noble class had been during the feudal societies. Even today you see the same, with people who are rich or who are in other ways in special positions to exercise power. You even see in democratic nations a small elite that manages to exercise power without ever being held accountable for doing so—partly because they do not run for any public position, partly because they are not known. As they either own the media or influence the media so that they, so to speak, fly beneath the radar of public awareness.

***

So you see, indeed, that there has always been a movement from the power elite to force people to release their light, so that these beings could absorb it and use it to not only survive but even to extend and multiply their power. For once they have absorbed the misqualified light, they can indeed turn it into an aggressive force that then forces people to release more light, and so on and so forth.

What has changed society from one that was entirely dominated by raw force to at least some societies in the world, where raw force is no longer a determining factor? Well, it is indeed that many among the people, especially those who have light, have realized the need to become more peaceful, to become non-violent. And thus, they have been less and less willing to fight the wars precipitated by the power elite. You saw, for example, in Europe during the Middle Ages how one king more insane than the next king started war after war, causing the loss of the lives of tens of thousands of people over something that was barely worth mentioning, such as a personal insult of some kind.

Over the centuries, many people who have reembodied again and again, and have had their lives cut short in these meaningless wars, eventually learned that this was not the way that they wanted to continue to spend lifetime after lifetime. And so, they manifested a lesser willingness to engage in these war-games of the fallen beings. They were less willing to give their light and their lifeblood on the bloodstained altars of the fallen beings.

Yet as the population has become less willing to engage in violence and warfare, the fallen beings have not given up. They have started using the second method for getting people to give them their light, namely to get people to give their light voluntarily because they have been misled into believing that doing so serves some greater cause, perhaps even an ultimate cause.

Overcoming duality in order to give true service

If you look back at the Middle Ages and the warring of the kings, you can clearly see that this was a dualistic struggle. You had two opponents, one king and another king, such as the King of England and the King of France. They went to war over some insignificant incident, and then they demanded that their people not only pay for the war but also give their lives to fight the war.

Clearly, you can see – from today's viewpoint – that neither the king of one country nor the king of the other had some ultimate cause. In fact, in many cases, you can see that none of them had even a just cause—for can there ever be a truly just cause for killing other human beings?

***

Well, there certainly can be according to the fallen beings, for you may – if you are willing to take an honest look at history – realize that one of the most amazing questions about human history is indeed how it has been possible – over and over and over again – to seduce people into thinking that killing other human beings is justified by some greater cause.

Consider, my beloved, if you go back to Old Testament times, and look at the fact that one of the defining moments in the Old Testament is indeed Moses descending from the mountain with the Ten Commandments. What is one of these commandments? It is a very simple statement: "Thou shalt not kill." Can you see that there is no qualification in this commandment? No conditions are defined according to which it is acceptable to kill in some instances while not in others. The statement is unqualified; it is unconditional: "Thou shalt not kill." Could it be any more simple?

Nevertheless, you will also see that beginning from Moses and forward many people in Israel found it easy to still kill. They claimed to be honoring the Law of Moses, yet they were still killing their fellow man. And not only that, they felt that killing their fellow men was perfectly justified by the God of Moses, the very same God who gave the unconditional command "Thou shalt not kill."

Now go forward to the time of Jesus, when he gave his timeless universal teachings. Resist not evil but turn the other cheek. Do unto others what you want them to do unto you. Yet then go forward and see how, after the establishment of the Roman Catholic Church, there was a shift.

Before Christianity became the official religion of the Roman Empire, Christians were persecuted by the Romans. They were pulled into the arena and executed by the thousands.

Did the Christians seek to fight the Romans by force? Nay, they submitted to this public slaughter, and in doing so with peace and serenity, they actually caused many among the Roman people to become interested in or converted to Christianity. For the Romans could not understand how anyone could meet their death with such peace.

Yet no sooner had the Christian religion become the official state religion of the Roman Empire, than the shift began to occur. And it was not long before there was now this subtle sense that in order to spread Christianity, in order to further the cause of saving the world, it was justified to kill other human beings in the name of Christ.

This eventually led to the Crusades, it led to the persecution of scientists, to the witch hunts, to the Inquisition. My beloved, how is it even possible that a multitude of knights can raze a Muslim city and – blinded by bloodlust – indiscriminately kill men, women and children— and then claim that they have done the work of Christ, that they have served Christ in brutally murdering their fellow men? How is it possible that someone holding a high position in the Catholic Church can torture other human beings mercilessly – which by the way also releases their light – and then commit them to being burned by the stake? And after having done this to any number of his fellow men, he now goes to pray in front of the crucified Jesus and feels that he has served his Lord?

How, my beloved, is this possible? Well, it is possible because all of the people who started this process were the fallen beings in embodiment. They already believed in the illusion that makes it possible to justify virtually anything on earth. That illusion is, of course, the illusion of separation, but it is more than that.

The underlying reality – that can be seen only from the perspective of the Christ mind – is that all life is one. As the Gospel of John says, without him was not anything made that was made. The Christ mind is the unifying principle that allows all self-aware beings to know that underneath the confusing array of seemingly separate forms, there is an underlying oneness, an underlying unity.

And this means that everything is created out of the Creator's being, and thus nothing in this material universe is separated from its source. The material universe is not separated from God's kingdom, and it is

Overcoming duality in order to give true service

not a separate, independently existing unit. It is part of God's own Being, and therefore God is everywhere. God is all and in all, and thus the concept that you could be separated from God is simply an illusion.

What you do to any other human being, you are doing to God. This is what Jesus knew, when he told you to do unto others as you want them to do unto you. Yet once you go into the consciousness of separation, you must leave oneness. And how do you leave oneness? Well, you do so by dividing it into at least two.

***

And so, now you have two opposing polarities, which is what gives rise to a dualistic belief system. But what makes this a belief system is that you think these polarities are absolutely real and that there is nothing beyond them. One of these polarities then becomes God, the other becomes the devil.

But my beloved, can you begin to see, based on everything we have told you, that the God who can be fit into such a dualistic worldview cannot be the true God of the Creator? For in the Creator, there can be no division. This is what you see, when you attain the Christ perspective.

And thus, you begin to realize that any division is not of God, and therefore the division into a dualistic system – with God as one extreme and the devil as the opposite extreme – is simply an illusion that springs from the mind of anti-christ. It has no reality in God; it has no reality in the Christ mind.

Yet once you go into this dualistic view of the world, it is inevitable that you will also apply a value judgment. One extreme has to be good; the other extreme has to be bad or evil. And this is what the fallen ones did in order to separate themselves from God and justify that they would not ascend with the rest of their sphere. They went into the dualistic belief system of thinking that God had made a mistake, and that they were here to correct the mistake. And therefore, it was justified that they did not ascend but instead stayed in an unascended sphere and attempted to correct God's mistake.

Thus, can you see that, from the very beginning, the fallen ones created this epic, dualistic struggle between two extremes? Of course, God does not see anyone as opposing it. In the view of God, there is no opposition, there is no division. There is only reality and unreality. It is only in the realm of unreality, that there can be a dualistic system with two opposites. And thus, the fallen beings were not opposing the real Creator; they were opposing a God of their own making and they were then setting themselves up in opposition to that unreal, artificially created God.

However, once you divide, you cannot stand still—you must keep dividing. And so, as the fallen beings separated themselves from the ascending sphere, and fell into the next, they themselves were divided into two polarities. What you have now is that you have one group of fallen beings who set themselves up as being the "good" polarity, and you have another group of fallen beings who set themselves up as being the bad or the "evil" polarity.

Those fallen beings who formed the evil polarity became the ones who used direct force to either enslave people or to get them to release their light. Yet the opposite polarity were those who appeared to be good or benign, those who appeared to be serving God or serving the people. These fallen beings were the deceitful ones, as opposed to the forceful. And what the deceitful ones have done over the course of history is that they have attempted to define the ultimate cause. And to them, the ultimate cause is that they win over the other group of fallen beings. And this has caused a to-the-death struggle between the so-called "good" fallen beings and the so-called "evil" fallen beings, each of them seeing it as the ultimate cause that they eradicate the other.

The so-called evil fallen beings are not as skilled at deception, and therefore they use what they are better at, namely force, direct force. Yet the so-called good fallen beings are the ones who are very skilled at deceiving people with their serpentine logic. And they are the ones who have created any number of these ultimate causes, where it seems that if we can only defeat this other group of people, then we will have done some ultimate good, we will have furthered some ultimate cause.

If you look at the Old Testament, you will see how this was indeed what caused the Israelites to feel that they were God's chosen people and that they were doing God's work by eradicating other tribes. This was simply tribal warfare with a twist, the twist of some ultimate cause. "We are not doing this because we want the land of the other tribe, nay we are doing this because we are doing God's work because we are God's chosen people."

Overcoming duality in order to give true service

You can see the same in the Crusades, where both Muslims and Christians felt that they had the ultimate religion, and thus they were the ultimate servants of God. And therefore, both felt that it was justified to go out and kill the other side in order to further God's cause. The irony, of course, being that Muslims and Christians were serving the same God, or at least claiming to do so. And they both honored the Old Testament which says, "Thou shalt not kill."

***

If you are serious about being one of the forerunners for healing Mother Earth, it is absolutely essential that you learn this lesson from history, so that you do not allow yourself to be pulled into another epic struggle created by the deceitful fallen beings. For if you allow yourself to be deceived, then you will not be helping to heal Mother Earth. You will only help to further the dualistic struggle, to keep it alive—and this is the very dualistic struggle that has caused all environmental problems.

Can you see, perhaps, that in the beginning of the industrial revolution, the most forceful of the fallen beings were the ones who set themselves up as industrialists? They were willing to use any amount of force on nature in order to wrest resources and raw materials from her, and they were willing to use any amount of force on their own laborers or in order to destroy the competition. They were the ones seeking a monopoly.

Can you then see that as time has passed on, another group of fallen beings have attempted to set themselves up in opposition to these forceful industrialists? They have attempted to appear as the benign ones, using science and other means to curb the activities of the forceful beings by saying that they are creating environmental problems which must be stopped.

I am not hereby denying that the forceful fallen beings have created environmental problems. I am not hereby saying that they should not be stopped, or at least restricted. What I am saying is this: much of the current environmentalist movement is indeed influenced by the deceptive fallen beings, and thus the very goal of much of this movement is simply to perpetuate the dualistic struggle and take it to a different level.

For the deceitful fallen beings – and even to a large degree many among the forceful fallen beings – have realized that it has become more difficult to motivate people, especially in the Western world, into going to war. And so, they seek to create a different kind of warfare, warfare that is fought with ideas but is nevertheless still efficient in deceiving people into giving their light to the fallen beings and the causes they have defined.

***

I know this can be a somber and sobering message. I know that many of the people who are potential readers of this book will have the best of intentions of helping nature, of helping Mother Earth. Thus, it can be a very difficult task, a very difficult challenge, to have to admit that your best intentions have been misused and channeled into serving causes that do not actually help nature, that do not help the Earth Mother.

Yet my beloved, consider what is ultimate service? Can you see that the entire epic struggle between the two dualistic extremes has created the illusion that you can give an ultimate service by engaging in the dualistic struggle and fighting against those who have been labeled as the evil polarity? Can you also begin to see that this is not true service; it is false service. It is a form of service that has no possibility of actually attaining the goal that has been defined. For do you see, that destroying evil simply is not possible?

When you consider that duality is a division into two polarities, you realize that these two polarities cannot exist without each other. You have seen the symbol from the Taoist religion of the Yin and the Yang. Well, the Yin and the Yang are the two basic forces of creation, expanding and contracting. But what you have in the dualistic thought system is a perversion of these two forces, a polarity of two opposites that will annihilate each other.

The original polarities of the Yin and Yang do not annihilate each other. On the contrary, they complement each other and thus they create new life. But the perverted polarities of the dualistic thought system are indeed opposites and will seemingly annihilate each other. However the reality is that they will not actually annihilate each other, for they cannot exist without each other.

In the dualistic thought system, good is defined only in opposition to evil, and evil is defined only in opposition to good. Good cannot exist without evil, for even if some representative of evil was destroyed, then

Overcoming duality in order to give true service

what would happen? What would happen is, indeed, that the so-called good fallen beings would now have no justification for their existence. For can you see, that even those who appear to be the good fallen beings can justify their existence only as long as they are fighting the so-called evil beings? And if ever good managed to eradicate those it has defined as evil, then what would be the justification for continuing the struggle? And without the struggle, how would you force people, how would you seduce people, into giving their light to the fallen beings?

Good cannot annihilate evil, but what you need to realize is that the more sophisticated among the fallen beings do indeed know this. And therefore, they are not actually seeking to annihilate evil. This is only a smokescreen. Their goal is to simply keep the struggle going, so that they keep themselves in power and keep themselves alive by getting people to voluntarily give them their energy.

I am not hereby trying to say that the environmentalist movement in its entirety is driven by this. But I am indeed saying that the environmentalist movement has been pulled into this dualistic struggle, and much of what is going on in the environmentalist movement has no chance of solving environmental problems. It will only perpetuate the struggle between different groups of people, between different groupings of the power elites that seek to rule this planet.

***

So when you realize that there is a false form of service, then you might begin to consider: "Well, what is then a true form of service?" And indeed, this we shall consider more closely.

As we have attempted to show you throughout this book, you have been brought up in a society, where everything is enveloped in a fog of illusion. It is almost as if you have been brought up inside a dense cloud, where you cannot see very far, where you cannot see exactly what is going on. This is the veil of illusion created by the fallen beings, and the illusion of the dualistic struggle between two opposing polarities.

What is it that has brought humankind forward, towards societies that are not entirely dominated by a power elite? Why did the feudal societies give way to modern democracies that have greater freedoms and rights for the common people than did the feudal societies? Well, it is indeed because there is a force that is seeking to raise the consciousness of humankind. And as a result, the consciousness has indeed been raised.

We might say that what has been happening for a long time is, that this veil of illusion has gradually been thinned or lifted, so that more and more people are beginning to see more clearly what is happening on the earth. We are therefore approaching a point, where many among humankind are prepared to take a quantum leap forward in their understanding of life. They are ready to begin to see the great underlying illusion, namely the dualistic struggle itself and the presence of those beings who are completely committed to it.

Many people are ready to take their understanding of the dynamics of life to a new level, where they can indeed begin to see more clearly what is the real cause – and therefore what is the real solution – of many of the problems present on earth. And the last big leap that needs to be made is, of course, that people begin to understand the epic struggle between the dualistic polarities. Yet how can this understanding come about? It can come about only through the Christ mind, for only the Christ mind can give you the vision that beyond the two polarities there is unity, there is oneness.

As Hilarion explained in the previous discourse, there is a certain level of consciousness, where you only see a so-called subjective truth. Yet it is possible to go beyond this level of subjectivity and attain an objective view of reality. This objective view can be attained only through the Christ mind. You might call it by other names, yet as we have explained before, we have chosen to use the word "Christ" as that is the universal term used in the spiritual realm. And so we hope that those on earth who are open to these ideas will be willing to also realize, that no matter what has happened with the Christian religion on earth, Christ and the Christ consciousness are still universal terms that apply to all people.

When Jesus said: "Go ye into all the world and make all people my disciples," he did not mean that you should go into the world and forcefully, or deceitfully, or by fear get people to join the Christian religion. He meant that you should go into the world and help people attain the Christ perspective, that is beyond the dualistic struggle and the subjective level of awareness.

So then, if you are serious about being one of the forerunners for healing Mother Earth, what is the greatest service you could possibly

Overcoming duality in order to give true service

render? Well, it is indeed that you first lock in to the reality I have explained – and that all of us have explained in this book – and that you realize that the greatest service is to help humankind begin to see the dualistic struggle and see the difference between the subjective dualistic state of consciousness and the objective universal state of consciousness that is the Christ mind.

This is not to say that you cannot be engaged in the environmental issue and in the environmentalist movement. On the contrary, we are not here talking about you withdrawing from society and sitting in a cave and meditating on God 24 hours a day. We are talking about people engaging themselves actively in society, but doing so in a way, so that they bring the Christ perspective into every activity. This is indeed the ultimate form of service that could be rendered at this particular time in Earth's history.

***

It is absolutely imperative that this shift in awareness begins to happen. You may notice, that I used the word "imperative," which is a word that has often been used by the deceitful fallen beings in order to get people to engage in some dualistic struggle, in some ultimate cause. Let me attempt to help you understand that it is not our intention whatsoever to get you to engage in a battle against the fallen beings or the power elite. We are not here talking about fighting against other people, we are talking about exposing reality and unreality, so that the population has a choice that they do not have today, where they do not understand the dualistic struggle.

Can you begin to see that the entire idea behind the dualistic struggle is the division between good and evil? Can you then see how, throughout history, this basic dynamic has been applied to many different situations on earth? It has therefore been defined that "our" group of people represent good and this "other" group of people – that we are against or that are against us – represent evil. The ancient Israelites applied this in their fight against other tribes, the Nazis applied it in their attempt to exterminate the Jews. Yet it has been applied many times in many different contexts.

Can you begin to see that even the modern environmentalist movement is affected by this mindset? It has attempted to magnify or even create a division in Western societies between the people who are engaged in the environmentalist movement and those that are labeled as the ones who cause pollution. I know very well that I have stated myself that environmental problems are caused by a certain group, a certain power elite group. Yet can you see that if you allow yourself to be pulled into a dualistic struggle against this group, then you are not serving the ultimate cause of awakening humankind? You are serving the so-called "ultimate cause" of simply perpetuating the dualistic struggle.

In the dualistic struggle, it seems as if there is an ultimate cause to defeat evil, and therefore whichever group of people is labeled as evil, well they are the ones we must defeat. Yet in the real cause – the cause of Christ versus the cause of anti-christ – the ultimate cause is to raise up all life, or at least raise up those who are willing, until a planet reaches the ascension point.

When a planet reaches that ascension point, it will jump to a different level. This is not unlike the image that many have been given in elementary school of a nucleus of the atom with a number of electrons orbiting around it, almost like planets orbiting around the sun. One of these electrons has a certain energy level, but it can make a jump to a higher energy level, and thereby it makes a jump to an orbit that is further away from the nucleus. A very similar process can happen for an entire planet, and when such a jump is made, there is a dividing line, there is a choice that must be made.

Those beings on the planet, who are willing to also make a leap in their own consciousness, will be able to stay with the planet. Whereas those who are not willing to make that leap, will be removed from the planet—and will thus go to some other realm that resonates with their level of consciousness.

Thus, can you see that the ultimate service that you could render for healing Mother Earth is not to fight against another group of people? It is to seek to raise the awareness of a critical mass among humankind to the point, where the planet can make a quantum leap and ascend to a higher level. When this leap is made, the lifestreams who are not willing to raise their consciousness, will no longer be on earth. And thus, the power elite groups that have created the environmental problems will be gone.

At the same time, the general level of consciousness will have been raised. And therefore, there will be a very dramatic shift in the collec-

Overcoming duality in order to give true service

tive awareness. To illustrate this, let me ask you to take a look back at the time, when most societies on earth either had slaves or looked upon slavery as something that was inevitable. Yet gradually an awareness began to build, that it was not right for people to be treated as property and that it was not right for one person to own another.

If you take a step back and look at where the concept of slavery came from, you will see that it came precisely from the forceful fallen beings, who were quite willing to subdue everyone on earth and make them their slaves. So that they could reap the fruit of other people's labor and live a life of leisure, luxury and privilege. For millennia, this consciousness had permeated the collective consciousness and most societies had slaves. Most people thought that slavery was just a natural, or at least an inevitable, part of life. Yet during the 1700s and 1800s a shift gradually occurred, and at least in the Western nations, it suddenly became obvious to the majority of the people that slavery simply was not right—and thus, they were no longer willing to accept it. Therefore, without a shot being fired, so to speak, slavery was abolished.

***

Can you see, then, that this points to a potential that has not been well understood, but needs to be understood? There is what we might call a forward progression in human society, but there is a false progression and a true progression.

The deceitful fallen beings have attempted to create an understanding of history that has a very specific purpose. That purpose is to portray themselves as the saviors of the people, the very people who have brought society forward, often by fighting and destroying the so-called forceful fallen beings. What the fallen beings attempt to do, is to set themselves up as the saviors, who can save humankind from the very problems created by the fallen beings, as we have already explained. But what this has led to is the creation of a very subtle concept. And the concept says that progress on a world scale has often been brought through force, and therefore it has been necessary, so to speak, to "fight for peace."

The 1900s saw two wars that were considered as world wars. For each war there were some people who thought that this would be the last great war, the "war to end all wars." Yet can you begin to see that this is entirely the dualistic struggle and the epic consciousness?

How can you, my beloved, possibly end war through war? How can more war bring peace? It is a complete illusion that it would be possible to have a final war or a final battle, that would bring true and permanent peace to earth. It cannot be done. It never has been possible; it is not possible today; and it never will be possible in the future.

The greatest service that could be rendered to planet earth at this particular time, is the spreading of this awareness, the awareness of the dualistic struggle and its causes, the awareness that it simply is not possible to solve humankind's problems by fighting some final battle in the epic struggle.

There never will be a final battle that will end the dualistic struggle. Any battle will only perpetuate the struggle. If a critical mass among human beings could be awakened to see this, as is already close to happening, then a dramatic shift could occur. People will wake up and realize that instead of continuing the struggle, instead of fighting this last epic battle, there is only one way forward. And that is to simply walk away from the struggle.

It is not by using your swords to kill the ultimate enemy, that you would bring peace. It is when you decide to simply walk away from the battlefield and turn your swords into plowshares, that you will bring peace. It is not our intention with this book to cause the most spiritually aware people to awaken to the dualistic struggle, only then to see themselves in opposition to the fallen beings who have created the dualistic struggle. Our intention is to awaken you fully, so that you see the need to simply walk away from the struggle.

Yet as I said, walking away from the struggle does not mean that we want you to withdraw from society and sit in a cave and meditate. We want you to engage in society, but to do so from the middle way of the Buddha and the non-dualistic view of the Christ. We want you to engage in society in such a way that you help expose the dualistic struggle— and therefore help bring an awareness that can lead to true and lasting peace. This is our aim, this is our desire, this is our vision. May it be your vision also!

***

Overcoming duality in order to give true service

That is my fondest hope for the future of planet earth. Nada I am, the Chohan of the sixth ray of service and peace. If you want to give ultimate service, then you must give that service from a consciousness of ultimate peace. And the only consciousness that can bring ultimate peace is the one that is raised beyond the dualistic struggle.

The only way to escape the struggle is to first go into the consciousness of Christ, and then continue to the higher levels of Christhood that were outpictured by the Buddha and the non-attachment to anything on earth.

When you become attached, even become attached to fighting a good cause, then your attachment stirs up your emotions. And then you release energy to the fallen beings, and they will use that energy to keep themselves alive and to perpetuate the dualistic struggle that ultimately is what keeps them alive. Allowing your light to be given for this purpose is not service—it is false service. Thus, strive to have the scales fall from your eyes, so that you will have an awakening experience—and suddenly see the unreality of the dualistic struggle and the reality of the oneness of the Christ mind.

When you have this awakening, you will find a deep inner peace. And as you allow yourself to become more and more anchored in that peace, you will be the open door through which your own I Will Be Presence and the Ascended Host can bring the light and the teachings that will awaken others and thus expose what is real and what is unreal.

You will not heal Mother Earth by fighting an unreal cause. You will heal Mother Earth only by espousing the true cause, the cause that cannot be promoted through force, through fighting or through deception. It is the cause of reality, the cause of awakening all life to the reality of Christ, so that they may freely choose between what is real and what is unreal.

The entire lie of the fallen beings is that free will is a threat to God's plan for raising the universe. Their entire agenda – the ultimate cause that they have defined – is to seek to force people to be saved.

Yet, there is no flaw in God's plan for the universe. When people know better, they will choose better. Therefore, it is a complete illusion, a flawed reasoning, to seek to force people's choices. Instead, simply give them the truth and set them free to choose.

And in so doing, set yourself free to be the open door for giving people the higher reality, while being completely non-attached to how they respond to it. Be not concerned what people do with the truth that streams through you. Allow that truth to flow and continue to flow, regardless of how people respond or do not respond.

"I am the open door, which no man can shut." These are the words of Christ. They can become your words, when you decide to open your mind to become a clear pane of glass, through which the light and the truth of your I Will Be Presence can shine and be expressed on earth. That is your highest potential, that is your highest form of service—and that is the highest way for you to help bring peace on earth and good will among men, and among men and nature.

I greet you in the Flame of Peace that I AM. I greet you in the Flame of Service that I AM. I greet you in the flame of unconditional peace and unconditional service that I AM. For it is only in unconditionality that you find peace, and it is only in expressing unconditionality that you give true service. Nada I AM.

Key 14
What it truly means to be free

Saint Germain I AM, and I come to speak to you on the seventh ray of God Freedom. My beloved, there is scarcely a concept on earth that is more misunderstood than freedom. Freedom, truly, is the essential gift, given by the Creator to each self-aware extension of itself. Freedom is opportunity to transcend the self one has—in any way that the self one has can imagine and conceive of.

It is therefore essential for you to understand that neither the Creator nor any of the representatives of the light and the mind of Christ would ever do anything to limit or restrict your knowledge, your understanding, your vision or your imagination. God has given you a sense of self, and God has given you complete freedom as to what to do with that sense of self here in the material realm.

The purpose for which the sense of self that you are was projected into this realm by your I Will Be Presence is, as we have explained, the expansion of the self-awareness of the Presence. Yet the Conscious You has its own free will, so that it can respond to the conditions it encounters in the material world, based on its current sense of self.

You can therefore, as we have explained, either expand that sense of self beyond the 48th level, or you can constrict it beneath the 48th level of awareness. As you go higher from the 48th level, you will gradually begin to feel more and more free. And as you reach the two-thirds mark towards the 144th level, you come to a distinctive turning point. This is the point, where you now fully embody and understand the seventh ray of freedom. Which means that you are now beyond the point, where you would ever even conceive of restricting the freedom of another human being.

In contrast to this, of course, you see that as you go below the 48th level, you will inevitably feel a compulsory need to restrict the freedom of other people. You will, therefore, be easily ensnared by what Nada has described as the fallen beings who have defined an ultimate cause, a cause that requires the killing of a specific group of human beings.

All of the people who are below the 48th level of awareness are trapped in some form of this epic struggle, feeling that their hatred of another group – even their acts of animosity or hostility towards that group – are justified by God, because of the epic struggle that portrays these other people as the enemies of God. And thus, the epic struggle defines that those who are on the side of God, have it as their sacred duty to oppose or even destroy those who are the enemies of God.

***

Yet even those who rise above the 48th level, can be seduced by a milder version of this philosophy, a more deceptive, a more serpentine, version of this philosophy. Those who are above the 48th level, are not as easily seduced into actual acts of violence. Nevertheless, they can still be seduced into seeing another group of people as the problem or the enemy, and therefore taking non-violent or non-hostile means to restrict the freedom of that group.

We might say, for the sake of an overall perspective, that while you are below the 48th level of awareness, you have no problem using physical violence to restrict the freedom of others. As you go above the 48th level, you become reluctant to use physical violence, but you are still willing to use non-violent means, even psychic means, in order to restrict the freedom of others. You are willing to project certain thought-forms and certain emotional matrixes into the minds of other people, in order to restrict the freedom of their imagination. And you are willing to either restrict their knowledge and understanding or to seek to use psychic force in order to get people to accept and conform to what you still consider to be the superior belief system.

It is only when you begin to approach the 96th level of awareness, that you become able to question this use of force, this use of psychic force. It is only then that you begin to realize, that it is never your sacred duty to restrict the freedom of any other human being. Neither is it ever justified by some ultimate cause to restrict the freedom of any other human being. And certainly, it is never mandated by God that you should use the unconditional freedom that God has given you, in an attempt to restrict the unconditional freedom that God has given to all other self-aware beings.

What it truly means to be free   237

We might therefore say, that as you approach and reach the 96th level of awareness, you finally attain your personal freedom from the entire consciousness that seeks to use force. And as you attain your personal freedom, you become able to also set all other people free.

***

How does this relate to the topic of the environmental debate and the healing of Mother Earth? Well, as Nada has already explained, if you go into the environmental debate with the approach that you need to find a scapegoat – that you can label as being responsible for environmental problems – then you will easily be trapped into thinking that you need to somehow oppose or restrict the freedom of that scapegoat. Yet as long as you see the problem as being outside your self, as long as you project responsibility outside your self, you will not be free personally.

I know well that this is difficult to grasp for those who are still below a certain level of awareness. Yet I will endeavor to explain, for those who are willing to open their minds and hearts to a new vision of freedom, a vision that you cannot find in hardly any philosophy on this planet.

What is the ultimate consequence of the fact that you have a number of self-aware beings on earth and that each and every one of them has been given free will by the Creator? The ultimate consequence is that since all of these beings have free will, yet have been put together in the same environment, there must be a purpose. And that purpose is, of course, the growth in self-awareness, but how does this come about? It comes about when you – as a being with free will – interact with other people who also have free will.

Some of you will know that in a previous lifetime, I was involved with the writing of the Shakespearean plays. In one of these plays, it is said: "All the world's a stage." Well, what exactly does this mean?

It means that this world, this planet, can be conceived of as a giant theater, in which self-aware beings have the opportunity to play a number of different roles. If you look at earth, you will see that the roles that human beings play can be divided into several groups, several archetypes if you will.

There is the role of serf or servant and the role of master or ruler. There is the role of husband and wife, of children and parents and many other roles. Each of these roles cannot exist independently. As has been said: "No man is an island" and the same is, of course, true for any woman. A role is not a solo performance but is part of a play. One role fits into the play, but it only has meaning in how it interacts with others. It is the interaction of a number of different roles that creates the wholeness of the play.

When a self-aware being comes into embodiment for the first time at the 48th level of consciousness, it has some sense that it is just playing a role. If you go below the 48th level, you become gradually more identified with the role, so that you forget that you were ever a spiritual being who simply entered the role in order to have certain experiences. That is why you see people who are so identified with their roles, that they are ready to use force in order to force upon others the philosophy that seems right according to their role.

As you go above the 48th level of consciousness, you become less and less identified with the role. And as you reach the 96th level, you finally come to the realization that all of the roles that you currently see on earth are ultimately unreal. They are simply tools that enable the Conscious You to have particular experiences.

How do you have a particular experience? You do so by projecting the pure awareness of the Conscious You into a particular role, a particular sense of self, so that you now experience – you perceive – the world through the filter of that role. We have often used the analogy that you put on colored glasses, and now everything you see through the glasses is tinted by the color of the glass.

While you are inside a role, you cannot see the world in any other way than through the role—or so it seems. Yet the reality is that the Conscious You is pure awareness. It is precisely because it is pure awareness, that it has the ability to project itself into a particular role on earth.

Yet even though the Conscious You is seeing the world through the filter of that role, the Conscious You has the ability to return to the state of pure awareness. And when you do so, you realize that you are not trapped in the role. You can, in fact, project yourself outside the role, you can protect yourself up into the I Will Be Who I Will Be Presence. And thus, you can gain the perspective on earth and the perspective on your personal role that the Presence has.

You can also project yourself mentally into some sense of oneness with other people, so that you "see" the world from their perspective.

What it truly means to be free

And this is, in fact, one of the ways that human beings have overcome the consciousness that causes them to seek to destroy others.

***

Truly, there is a certain survival instinct built into the human body and the mind that runs the body. Truly, this survival instinct makes it difficult for one human being to kill another. Only when a human being has been deceived by the dualistic consciousness, can it see other people as enemies.

But this is truly achieved by creating the illusion that because these people are now a threat to some superior cause, they are not actually humans anymore. They have become a kind of non-humans. And therefore, it is no more wrong to kill them, than it would be to kill an animal that threatens you, that threatens your crops.

In other words, one human being cannot kill another human being. In order to kill another human being, you must first come to see that human being as a non-human, as a fundamentally different type of being than yourself. This is what can be believed only beneath the 48th level of consciousness.

Yet even above the 48th level, it is possible to believe that other people are in a different category, not in the sense that they deserve to be physically killed, but certainly in the sense that they deserve God's punishment, or that they deserve to have their freedom restricted in some way.

We might say that beneath the 48th level, you are open to the idea that you could personally kill or restrict the freedom of others through force. Above the 48th level, you are open to the possibility that God or society might kill or at least restrict or punish other human beings.

When you rise towards the 96th level of consciousness, you begin to realize, that what you see through the filter of your role is not reality. It is only a perception that is created by the fact that your role shows you a limited perspective on reality. Thus, you begin to realize that any role, any philosophy, which defines another group of human beings as the enemy – or as fundamentally different from yourself – is simply a lie, an illusion.

It is truly one of the most subtle and one of the most dangerous aspects of the duality consciousness, that it divides human beings into categories and then applies a value judgment to those categories, so that one category is labeled as good and another as bad or evil. This can be found in many subtle forms, even what you see in the Western world, where many Christians believe that they themselves, and all members of their church, are guaranteed to be saved by Jesus and his sacrifice on the cross. Whereas those who do not belong to Christianity, or even to their specific church, are guaranteed to go to hell.

This is truly the dream of the fallen beings. Because, you see, when the previous sphere ascended and the fallen beings were not willing to ascend with it, what truly happened was that the Law of Free Will was simply applied to the fallen beings. The Law of Free Will gives you the right to create any sense of self for yourself that you can imagine. It gives you the right to define any role you can imagine, and then to project the pure awareness of the Conscious You into it.

Yet in order to ascend, you must also free the Conscious You from that sense of self and return to pure awareness. In other words, the determining factor for your ascension is your state of consciousness. If your state of consciousness is below pure awareness, you cannot ascend. It truly is that simple.

In other words the consequence of this law is that there is no external God or external being in heaven who judges you and decides that you cannot go to heaven, whereas these other people can. The being who judges you and determines whether you can ascend or not is yourself—by your own willingness to transcend any self you have created, any role you have defined, and return to the pure awareness with which you descended out of the I Will Be Who I Will Be Presence.

***

What the fallen beings refused to do was to acknowledge the most central aspect of the Law of Free Will. What is that aspect? It is that you are completely and fully responsible for yourself, and you are completely and fully not responsible for any other self-aware being.

The fallen beings did not want to take responsibility for themselves and their own state of consciousness. They did not want to admit that their consciousness was below the level that can ascend, and therefore they needed to let go of the old, to let the limited self die, and transcend all limitations into the pure awareness that can ascend.

What it truly means to be free   241

And so, in this denial of responsibility, they projected out that God was responsible for their fall, that God did not like the fact that they were wiser than God. And therefore, this jealous and angry God cast them out of heaven. And they then created the idea that it was their sacred duty to prove God wrong. And that in seeking to prove God wrong, they had the right to violate and restrict the free will of other beings.

As we have said, you can only separate from oneness by creating at least two dualistic polarities. And therefore, when you refuse to take responsibility for yourself, it is inevitable that you then begin to take responsibility for others. Instead of being willing to look at the beam in your own eye, you now focus all your attention on the splinter in the eyes of your brothers. And then, in order to avoid and ultimately justify why you do not have to look at the beam in your own eye, you create the epic struggle. Which says that it is your sacred duty to force all other people to change, instead of doing what the law free will mandates: change yourself.

So do you begin to see that when you reach the 96th level of awareness, you take full and final responsibility for yourself? You acknowledge the fact that your ascension will be determined exclusively by one factor, namely your state of consciousness. Your ascension will never depend on the state of consciousness or the choices made by other people. And therefore, you have no need to seek to force other people, to limit their knowledge, to limit their imagination or to force their imagination into the same track where you have forced your imagination.

***

When you begin to approach this level, you will also gain a new understanding of the earth. What truly is Mother Earth? Well, the simplest way to explain this is to say that Mother Earth is the ultimate servant of her children, who live upon her material body.

How is Mother Earth serving her children? She is doing so by giving them a framework in which they can exercise their free will. As we have said, the earth was originally created in a far higher state of purity and balance than what you see today. This is the state where it was created by the Elohim. Yet what has happened since? How did the earth ever descend below that level? Why is the body of the Earth Mother now embodying so much imbalance and inharmony?

Well, it is indeed because the Earth Mother has vowed to serve her children in a very special way. She has vowed to serve as a kind of cosmic mirror, that reflects back to the children whatever they are projecting into it.

Do you see, that when you step into a particular role, you are perceiving the world through that role? But now realize that the act of perception is not what you have been conditioned to believe.

Even your physical eyes are not simply passive receptors of light; they work both ways. As you direct your attention at something, you are projecting psychic – mental and emotional – energy upon that something. You will know this from your common experience of looking into the eyes of another human being, where you can feel that they are either directing positive or not so positive energy at you.

So you see, the act of perception is also the act of projection, where you – trough your faculties of perception, included but not limited to your physical senses – are projecting psychic energy out from yourself. This psychic energy will be determined by the role that you have taken on, for the role will give the psychic energy a specific form. This form will then be projected onto the body of the Earth Mother, and the Earth Mother will adapt to whatever the human beings who live on earth are projecting upon it. In other words, the Earth Mother will act as a kind of mirror that shows people their own state of consciousness.

So when you look upon the earth and see, for example, that there seems to be a lack of resources, this is a reflection of the state of consciousness of most people. Likewise, when you look at so-called natural disasters – floods, hurricanes, volcanic eruptions, earthquakes and what have you – these are also reflections of humankind's state of consciousness.

How exactly does this work? Well, as we have said, the underlying reality that can be seen only through the Christ mind is that beneath all separate forms, all life is one. It is only when you approach the 96th level of awareness, that you begin to grasp this reality. And it is only then, you begin to see that the idea that you are a separate being is a complete illusion.

You begin to realize that you are not separate from other human beings, and that is when you can truly begin to follow the call of Christ to do unto others what you want them to do unto you. The reason is that you begin to realize the deeper truth behind Jesus' words, namely that

What it truly means to be free

what you do unto others, you are also doing to yourself because all life is one.

What eventually begins to emerge is that although you are an individual being, you are not existing as an island. You are existing within a unit, namely the collective consciousness of humankind. And thus, whatever you project out into that collective consciousness, will inevitably come back to you multiplied.

That is why the Bible states that if you sow the wind, you will reap the whirlwind. If you project anger out into the collective consciousness, you will receive that anger back, but it will be multiplied. And you will often see how people have created these patterns of action and reaction, of revenge and revenge for revenge, that can go on almost indefinitely. Just look at the Middle East and how people there have been warring with each other for millennia, for as far back as there is recorded history.

Yet as you begin to overcome the illusion that you are separated from others, you also begin to overcome the illusion that you are separated from the planet upon which you live. As you begin to see a connection between your own consciousness and the consciousness of other people, you also realize there is a connection between your consciousness and the consciousness of the planet.

As we have said from the very beginning, the underlying reality is that everything is consciousness. Obviously, any person below the 48th level will outright deny this, but many people beyond the 48th level will also deny it, or at least be reluctant to accept it. It is only as you begin to approach the 96th level, that you become able to grasp the reality that everything truly is consciousness. And therefore, the Earth Mother is not some entity that is separated from you.

The Earth Mother is a state of consciousness. You are a state of consciousness. And since you live within the field of consciousness, the matrix of consciousness, of the Earth Mother, you are part of the Earth Mother. You are a drop within the ocean of the Earth Mother. Thus, you affect the totality, and the totality affects you.

***

This means that you have the potential to have a negative impact on both the collective consciousness and the physical planet. But it also means you have the potential to have a positive impact. The question is though: how might you have a positive impact?

You see, what we have attempted to explain is that the current state that you see on planet earth – including environmental problems and the increasing frequency of natural disasters and erratic weather patterns – is entirely an outpicturing of the collective state of consciousness of humankind. Thus, what we have attempted to explain is, that environmental problems do not have exclusively physical or material causes.

And therefore, it should be beginning to become clear, that if you truly want to solve environmental problems, you cannot focus exclusively on physical or material causes. Restoring a state of balance to the natural environment is not only a matter of stopping physical pollution. It is even more important to also stop the emotional and mental pollution that creates a state of severe imbalance in the body of the Earth Mother.

Even doctors are now beginning to realize that a patient's mental and emotional state has great impact on that person's physical health and on the person's ability to recover from a disease. The deeper explanation, that is now beginning to emerge, is that the disease was caused by the mental and emotional state in the first place. And therefore, healing can never be complete by cutting out an organ or ingesting a pill. For there to be complete healing, there must be a healing in the emotional and mental bodies, even a healing of the sense of identity. And this, of course, applies to the Earth Mother as well.

Take, as an example of this, the very fact that you have a planet upon which two-thirds of the people live beneath the poverty level and upon which millions and millions of people live very close to the starvation level. They are constantly in danger of not having enough food to survive, and they are constantly living in a state of malnutrition.

You have been conditioned to believe that this is because there are simply too many people on the earth. Yet I tell you, this is a complete illusion, spread by the fallen beings who, as Nada explained, have realized that as the population grows beyond a certain level, they cannot maintain an unequal distribution of wealth and resources. And therefore, they cannot maintain their privileged positions as being more rich and more powerful than the general population.

These egomaniacs realize that as the population grows, they cannot continue to dodge the need for a more equal sharing of the available re-

What it truly means to be free

sources. Yet in order to deceive people into voluntarily limiting the size of the population – and thus maintaining status quo for the privileged elite – they are attempting to make people believe in one simple lie.

The lie they attempt to make you believe in is that because the earth has a limited physical size, there is an absolute upper limit to the resources that are available on earth. And given that these resources are being consumed at a ferocious pace – as a result of their own insatiable greed – they have managed to make many people believe that a crisis is approaching, where even the present level of population is not sustainable.

The equation promoted by them is simple. There is a fixed upper limit to the amount of resources available, and therefore there is a fixed upper limit to the size of the human population.

***

Yet what exactly is a natural resource, my beloved? Do you realize that a few centuries ago, the primary resource on earth – the primary resource to determine the size of the population – was the area of land that could be used for agriculture. There was only a certain amount of land that could produce food, given the technology that was available at the time.

Yet since the Middle Ages, various forms of technology have allowed the area of arable land to be expanded greatly. At the same time, other forms of knowledge and technology have made it possible to grow a far greater amount of crops on one unit of land. And thus, you see that what was considered an absolute resource 500 years ago has now been expanded greatly.

In other words, if you had taken the power elite's logic and applied it to society as it was 500 years ago, you might have come up with the idea that the entire continent of Europe could only sustain a few dozen millions of people. Yet today you see that the same continent can sustain hundreds of millions of people, who live in a far greater state of abundance than was the case 500 years ago. Yes I know, my beloved, that you can apply a number of complicated considerations. But I am trying to avoid getting lost in details and giving you the overall picture.

As another example, take the fact that 500 years ago there were places on the earth that were considered useless, because out of the ground was bubbling this black, tarry substance that nobody had any use for. I am, of course, talking about oil, which became the source for the industrial revolution that also allowed for more effective farming methods, and therefore made it possible to grow a greater amount of crops on the same area of land.

You will also notice, for example, that only a few decades ago sand, silicon, was considered relatively useless. Yet today, it is the very basis for one of the most important growth industries of modern society, namely the computer industry. Just look at how computers have revolutionized every area of human society, and then let me tell you that the potential for the use of computers is only in its infancy. There is the potential to revolutionize technology beyond what even the most optimistic futurists can imagine today.

So my point is simply to show you, that it is a complete lie that Mother Earth has a fixed amount of natural resources. Because there is really no such thing as a "natural" resource. A resource that exists out in nature is truly not a resource, until human beings have the knowledge of how to make use of it. And so, if you claim that there is an upper limit to the amount of natural resources found on this planet, you are actually, indirectly, claiming that there must be an upper limit to human knowledge.

This is, of course, the very central weapon used by the fallen beings to control humankind. What the fallen beings are attempting to do is precisely to limit the knowledge and the imagination of the majority of the population.

Yet what is it really they are trying to do? Well, they are truly seeking to limit the access that people have to the Christ mind. The Christ mind is the LOGOS out of which everything is made. The Elohim used the LOGOS of the Christ mind to design planet earth.

The Elohim designed planet earth in such a way, that it could sustain 10 billion people, who all had the abundant life. So yes, there is an upper limit to the size of the human population, and that is the limit defined by the Elohim and not the limit defined by the fallen beings. That limit is 10 billion people, but those 10 billion people have the potential to live in a state of abundance that is beyond what you see in even the richest countries today. For the earth is designed in such a way that it can provide sustenance for 10 billion people without them even having to labour at the sweat of their brow.

What it truly means to be free   247

***

I know very well that this is a concept that can scarcely be fathomed by
most people today. Yet as you grow beyond the 96th level of awareness,
you begin to realize that if everything is consciousness, then it is entirely possible for consciousness, for mind, to have power over matter.

And that is when you begin to realize, that there is a potential for
bringing forth abundance beyond what can be done through technology.
Nevertheless, even technology has two aspects. What you see in most
technology on earth today is what we might call a force-based approach,
a force-based technology. It is a technology that uses great force, great
energy, to produce a result. As an example of this, let me talk about how
energy is currently generated.

When you talk about energy, you can see, for example, how energy
is generated in order to drive your car. You have what is called an internal combustion engine. This is an engine that is made of a very hard
material, called steel or aluminum. This hard material is used to create
an enclosed space. In that space is a piston, and the piston can move
only in certain directions. And what forces the piston to move is the literal explosion that is achieved by injecting a combustible material into
the cylinder.

It should be relatively easy for you to see, that this explosion is indeed the use of force. It is a violent explosion that forces the piston to
move, and thus creates the power that can drive the car. You will also
notice that this is very complex technology. Another example of force-
based technology is nuclear energy. You are literally forcing the atom
apart in another violent explosion.

Let me instead give you an example of a technology that is not force-
based, and it is solar cells. What is it, my beloved, that makes organic
life possible on earth? The very basis for organic life is photosynthesis.
It is a process whereby plants absorb the energy coming from the sun,
and then convert it into another form of energy that can be used to drive
organic lifeforms. What nature provides in such abundance, in every
blade of grass and every leaf on the trees, is non-violent technology. It
is beginning to be emulated in solar cells, but there is an almost infinite
potential for the bringing forth of this kind of non-violent technology.

So the vision I am seeking to give you here, is that planet earth is
on the brink of a major shift. You have seen such shifts within the last

several centuries and even beyond. For example, you saw the shift from the Stone Age to the Bronze Age, from the Bronze Age to the Iron Age. Then you saw a shift into the Enlightenment, into the Industrial Revolution, into the scientific and technological revolutions.

But the shift you are about to see – and which many of you who are open to this book have already begun to sense – is an even greater shift than all the foregoing. It is a shift where humankind will begin to see the limitations of force-based technology, and will begin to open their minds to receiving from the ascended realm the ideas and concepts, that would allow the development of a new form of technology that is not force-based.

Can you begin to grasp the vision that I am seeking to give you? Can you see that virtually all pollution that you have on earth today is caused precisely by force-based technology? Can you see that if such force-based technology was replaced by a form of technology that is not based on force – but is based on working with the laws of nature – well then all pollution could be eliminated?

***

Do you see what I am explaining here? The Elohim designed the earth in such a way, that it can provide the abundant life for 10 billion people. This is literally written into the design principles, that the Elohim used to define the earth. This is what you often call the laws of nature.

Thus, what I am saying here is, that if human beings will learn to know, to respect and to work with the laws of nature, then all environmental problems will be eliminated in a natural way. And thus, the real question for those who are sincere about healing Mother Earth is: How can we move beyond the force-based approach to life and move into an approach to life that is not based on force?

And of course, the other chohans and Mother Mary have already given you the answer. All you need to do is put it together and see the big picture. Because we have told you that what has truly caused people to go into the dualistic struggle is precisely the illusion of separation.

Therefore, it is this illusion – promoted and projected upon you by the fallen beings – that is the real cause of environmental problems. You see yourself as separated from the planet upon which you live. Therefore, you cannot work with the planet and with the laws of nature in

What it truly means to be free

order to provide a living for yourself and others. Instead, you think you have to find a way to misuse the laws of nature into generating a force, and then you seek to use that power to force Mother Earth to give you the very sustenance that she is designed to give you voluntarily—if you will only accept it.

You will know, I am sure, about the story in the Old Testament about the Garden of Eden. Yet have you ever considered that there might be a deeper meaning that has been misunderstood by virtually all of the religions and churches and sects that make use of the Old Testament?

The reality is that the Garden of Eden that is portrayed in the Genesis story is an allegory, a symbol, for the state that the earth was in, when it was first designed by the Elohim. At that point, the self-aware beings who lived on earth lived in complete harmony with the laws of nature. And therefore, they literally lived in a garden with wonderful fruits that were there for their taking.

Yet the fall of Adam and Eve is a symbol for what has happened to all human beings in terms of falling into the duality consciousness. Of falling into the illusion of seeing themselves separated from their divine source and from their material source, from their Divine Father and their Earth Mother—who is truly a manifestation of the Divine Mother.

So the casting out of paradise was not God and his angels casting people out. It was people casting themselves out by going into the duality consciousness. And the story that Adam and Eve now had to make their living "at the sweat of their brow" is a symbol for the fact that when you go into the duality consciousness – when you go below the 48th level of awareness – then you do indeed need to use force to make a living and to wrest your sustenance from the body of the Earth Mother.

As Jesus said: "Fear not little flock, for it is your father's good pleasure to give you the kingdom." Well, so we might also say: "Fear not little flock for is your mother's good pleasure to give you her nurturance."

The earth is truly designed to give you everything you need for your physical, material survival, and to do so without you having to use force. Yet this requires that you align your consciousness with the reality of the Christ mind and the principles defined by the Elohim. If you separate yourself from the Christ mind and rebel against the laws of nature – the laws of the Elohim – well, then you cannot receive what the Earth Mother offers you freely. And then you will have to use force to take from her what you could have received freely in a different state of consciousness.

**

This use of force is, then, what has created all of the imbalances that you see on earth today, both the imbalances in nature and the imbalances in human society—where there is constant use of force by one group of people to subdue another. This use of force, of course, goes back to the fallen beings. But as Nada so eloquently explained, it is not our vision that our students should start using force to fight the fallen beings, or even see themselves as being in opposition to the fallen beings.

Instead, it is our vision that our students will be willing to be awakened, so that they completely transcend the consciousness of the fallen beings, so that they transcend the consciousness of duality and separation and see the deeper oneness of all life. And therefore, they start doing what Jesus himself did: working to raise up all life. This, of course, does not necessarily mean that you are always soft-spoken and gentle. It does mean that you never use force, you never use physical force and you never use psychic force. But it does not mean that you allow those who are using force to intimidate you into silence.

You do what Jesus did, you bear witness to your truth, the non-dualistic truth of the Christ mind. You bring that truth into every area of public debate, so that you seek to enlighten people to the fact, that there is an alternative to the limited perspective they have, when they see life through the duality consciousness. This is your true role; not to oppose anyone, not to force anyone, but to give them the choice between the non-dualistic reality of the Christ mind and the dualistic "truth" and untruth of the separate mind, the mind of anti-christ.

When you have given them that choice, you must give them complete freedom to do with it as they want. Why must you do this? Because this is what the Creator itself has given to all self-aware beings. It has given them complete free will to do with its own Being as they see fit.

The Elohim have done the same; the Elohim did not create planet earth as a separate entity. The earth is a material phenomenon and something cannot come from nothing. So the earth is created out of the very substance and Being, the energy if you will, of the Elohim. The Elohim

What it truly means to be free

embedded their own energy, their own Beings, into the earth, and they have then set the inhabitants of earth free to do with it as they see fit.

Thus, we can say that the Earth Mother – as a creation of consciousness that has taken on a sense of being – has done the same, has allowed the people on earth to do with her body as they see fit. And thus, you must do the same if you will stay aligned with the Christ mind in the hierarchy of Christed beings, reaching all the way back to the Creator. If you do not set others free, well then you will again go into the duality consciousness and seek to force them into compliance. And do you see, that that is a complete misunderstanding of the purpose of creation?

***

The earth is not truly created for the purpose of being a pristine environment that is never affected by man. The earth was created precisely to give a framework for human beings to exercise their free will, and to see the results of their free-will choices, their imagination and their actions outpictured in physical matter. The earth was not created to exist without human beings. Planet earth has no meaning whatsoever without human beings.

You may look at other planets in your solar system, where there is seemingly no life, and you may say, "Well, then what is the purpose of venus?" Yet I tell you, there is indeed intelligent life on venus. There are self-aware beings on the planet venus. Only you have to understand that the self-aware beings on venus have raised their collective consciousness to a higher level than the collective consciousness of humankind. And that is why the self-aware beings on venus do not exist in the same vibratory spectrum that you exist in as human beings on earth. And that is why you cannot – with your physical telescopes and other instruments – see the intelligent life on venus. Venus appears to be a barren planet, but it is barren only when viewed from the perspective of the collective consciousness on earth.

Thus, my beloved, my last task in this discourse is an attempt to pull aside the curtain, that you might gain a broader outlook on the future of this planet. I am Saint Germain and I am, as many of you will know, the hierarch for the coming 2,000-year cycle, that has often been called the Age of Aquarius. My beloved brother, Jesus, was the hierarch for the previous 2,000-year cycle of the Age of Pisces. The Age of Aquarius officially started on March 22, 2010. Thus, I am now the hierarch for the earth. It is my task to continue the work begun by Jesus, of raising the consciousness of humankind.

The ideal outcome of the 2,000-year cycle of the Piscean age was that a critical mass among human beings would have been raised to the 96th level of consciousness. So far, that goal has not been achieved. But there are enough people in embodiment who are close to this level, so that they could relatively quickly come up. It is, then, my role, as the hierarch of the Age of Aquarius, to raise people even further, beyond the 96th level, and therefore bring in what we have called a Golden Age.

A Golden Age is not something that can be easily understood by the level of consciousness of most human beings. Yet it is – to use the terminology I have used here – an age in which human beings begin to go beyond the level of force-based technology. They begin to receive technology that is not based on force. For example, within the foreseeable future, new forms of energy generation will be released, so that you do not have to use fossil fuels. But in the longer term, energy will be freely available to all human beings in unlimited quantities.

Yet even beyond this level of non-force-based technology, there will come a time, when human beings begin to realize that you do not actually need to use material technology. For they have access to the most superior technology that can possibly be imagined. That technology is the mind.

For as we have attempted to explain, everything is consciousness. Which means that every aspect of the material universe is really created from consciousness, by consciousness. It is created from the underlying consciousness that we have called the Ma-ter light, and it is created by self-aware beings projecting matrixes upon that substance, so that it takes on form.

And when you go beyond the 96th level and start approaching the 144th level, you begin to become aware of the potential that – given that all form is created by mind – your mind can also begin to create its own forms. And when a critical mass among human beings reach that level, well then even non-force-based technology will become obsolete and will be replaced by the mind itself. The mind is the ultimate form of technology.

I know that this can be difficult to grasp for many people. Yet as I have attempted to explain, the basis for the exercise of free will is truly

What it truly means to be free

imagination. For you cannot do what you cannot imagine. If you cannot imagine something, then you cannot even see it as an option. And so, my role as the hierarch of the Aquarian age is, indeed, to expand the vision, to free the imagination. For how can you ever be truly free, if your imagination is restricted within a certain framework, within a certain mental box?

What the fallen beings have attempted to do on this planet is to create any number of mental boxes, any number of thought systems, that seek to portray human beings as limited, and seek to set absolute boundaries for what the population can do, can be, can achieve. And when the population at large accepts these boundaries for themselves, well then they will give the elite a privileged position—for they are willing to use force to set themselves above the general population.

And if the general population does not have the imagination to challenge this elitist society, well then how can that unequal society be replaced by the true vision of the Elohim? In which all men are not only created equal, but are truly equal in their freedom to imagine a better life for themselves and a better world in which to manifest that life?

If you are serious about making an effort to heal the Earth Mother, then I, Saint Germain, give you a vision. Make it your main priority to do the Alpha and Omega of first seeing how limited your current vision is, and then freeing your imagination to go beyond the mental boxes currently defined on earth.

Be willing to project the pure awareness of the Conscious You out of your current role and into oneness with your I Will Be Who I Will Be Presence, so that you can see the earth as your Presence sees it. So that you can see the highest potential for your own life and see the highest potential for the earth.

Only when you have this freedom of imagination, will you be able to make the best possible contribution to the environmental debate. And only then, will you be able to promote real solutions to environmental problems. Instead of being seduced into continuing the dualistic struggle of promoting the so-called solutions defined by the fallen beings, to the very problems created by the fallen beings. And thus, no matter what solution is implemented, it only perpetuates the struggle.

Be willing to be free of the consciousness that creates the struggle, and thereby become an open door for bringing forth the vision and the technology that can take human beings beyond the need to force Mother

Nature into giving them what the Divine Father has created her specifically to give them freely.

Be willing to free your imagination, so that you can accept the kingdom that it is your Divine Father's good pleasure to give you, and the nurturance that it is your Divine Mother's good pleasure to give you through her material body, called earth.

PART THREE

Key 15
The illusion that there is something wrong with the earth

Mother Mary:

Now that you have a feeling for the seven spiritual rays, the seven God qualities, that were used by the Elohim to construct the entire world of form, particularly planet earth, we can build upon this foundation. When you look at the rays, you realize that if they are viewed as a linear progression, they lead from the first ray of willpower and the willingness to experiment, to the seventh ray of freedom. This should give you a clue, that you can then apply to the relationship between human beings and Mother Earth—and to the relationship between human beings.

Do you see that the seven rays can be seen as representing a path of initiation, where a lifestream starts out with a strong will to experiment, and even to impose its own mental images upon the Ma-ter light? As a being experiments, it will gain experience. And if it is, indeed, willing to evaluate the results of its experiments, then it can begin to acquire wisdom. As a being grows in wisdom, it can then come to feel the love for something higher than its own perception of life. And as this love is nourished, the being can come to understand the need to accelerate itself into the purity that comes from realizing that you, as a self-aware being, are meant to be the open door for the expression of your I AM Presence, your true individuality anchored in the spiritual realm.

This, then, can help you tune in to the higher vision of your Presence. And as you grasp not only the higher vision of your Presence, but the higher vision of the Creator – and the purpose for the entire world of form – you attain the inner peace that is the foundation for giving true service. And as you grow in service and in peace, you will then begin to grasp that the goal of life is self-transcendence into complete freedom of expression. Yet this freedom is not what many people on earth see as the ability to do anything they want. It is the freedom to express your divine individuality in such a way that it raises up all life, and therefore serves to raise up the sphere in which you live.

***

Can you now begin to see, also, what this truly means? The Creator has created a world of form for the specific purpose of helping the self-aware extensions of itself grow in self-awareness. The underlying purpose of the entire world in which you live is the growth in self-awareness. Everything in the entire world is designed specifically to facilitate the growth in self-awareness, the growth that leads from the willingness to experiment to complete freedom of expression.

Can you see, perhaps, that the path of initiation represented by the seven rays is a long process? As we have explained, a new co-creator starts out at the 48th level of awareness. And if it grows from there, it will reach the 144th level, which is represented by total creative freedom and the mastery of mind over matter. Yet, I can assure you, that there is a very large span between the 48th level of awareness and the 144th level of awareness. This span is much larger than most people can even envision or imagine, for they have never encountered a person who was at the 144th level. And so, they have, really, very little sense of co-measurement about the gap between their present level of awareness and the highest level possible.

Yet my point is to show you, that there is no force – created by the Creator itself or by the representatives of the Creator, such as the Elohim – that seeks in any way to restrict your growth or to force your growth. Everything is guided by the Law of Free Will, for it is only through your free-will decisions that you can actually grow from one level of consciousness to another.

Understand, if you will, the delicate balance I am seeking to explain. Growth does not happen by itself, yet neither can growth the forced. As we have attempted to explain, there is a force built into the material universe, that will seek to reduce any closed system to its lowest possible energy state. So if you are not consciously seeking to accelerate your consciousness and go to a higher level, then you will become subject to

The illusion that there is something wrong with the earth 257

this force. And that is why you cannot simply sit back and expect that you will automatically grow in consciousness. So it is indeed necessary that you make an effort in order to grow in consciousness.

This was illustrated in the parable Jesus gave, about the master who went away and then gave to three of his servants a number of talents. When the master returned after a long absence, he asked the servants to give account of what they had done with the talents. Two had multiplied the talents they were given, whereas one had buried them in the ground. The symbolism in this parable is that in order for you to grow, you must be willing to multiply what you have, to appreciate what you have, to make the best of what you have—instead of burying it in the ground.

Yet there is a deeper symbolism here. For what is it that prevents people from multiplying what they have? It is, indeed, what we have talked about, namely the mindset created by the fallen beings, which says that there is a fundamental flaw in the design of the universe. A flaw that must be corrected by the people on earth adhering to a particular belief system, and seeking to get all other people on earth to adhere to the same system. When you think that there is a fundamental flaw in the design of the universe, you cannot multiply the talents because you cannot appreciate what is there right now.

My beloved, please make an effort to step back from your normal state of consciousness and intuitively sense what I am explaining here. When you believe – perhaps even without realizing this consciously – that there is something wrong with the earth, then there will be – in your mind – a gap between where the earth is today and where it supposedly should be according to the standard that you use to determine that there is something wrong.

Can you see that in order to believe that there is something wrong with the earth, you must have a standard in your mind, that says: "This is what things should be like." And then you look at the earth and see that what is actually outpictured on this planet is not the way things should be. And when there is this gap in your mind – between what is and what supposedly should be – then you cannot appreciate what is. And if you do not appreciate what is, then you cannot multiply the talents by taking what is as an opportunity for growth.

***

This is a very subtle concept, that will require you to think outside the box of how you have experienced life thus far. You need to make a very subtle distinction. You need to realize that what the fallen beings have done on this planet is that they have made use of your built-in desire for growth, combined with your lack of full awareness of how life works.

As we have explained, the driving force behind all life is the desire, the drive, for self-transcendence, for growth in self-awareness—until one reaches the ultimate self-awareness of the Creator level. So the most basic drive that you have as a self-aware being is the drive for self-transcendence. Self-transcendence, of course, implies that you go from one state to a higher state. And so, it also follows that there is a desire, a drive, to see improvement. Yet can you see, that there is a very subtle difference between the true desire for improvement – which is a desire to multiply what is and go beyond to a higher level – and then the perverted desire for "improvement" based on a dualistic, relativistic evaluation, which says that what is is wrong or flawed?

When you step back and realize, that the entire material universe is a giant schoolroom – that is designed to facilitate the growth in self-awareness – then you gain a different perspective on life. The universe is designed to facilitate the growth in self-awareness, and the growth in self-awareness happens through free will. One of the consequences of this reality is that there truly is no standard for what the material universe should outpicture. There is no standard which says, that the earth should be like this—and if the earth currently outpictures something that is below the ideal, then that is wrong. This is not the way God or the Elohim think about the earth.

As we have explained, the earth was originally created by the Elohim at a certain level of purity. The Elohim then sent self-aware extensions of themselves into embodiment on this original earth. Several of these waves – in some spiritual teachings called root races – were sent to earth, and they all ascended to the spiritual realm without going into the duality consciousness. Yet in what is called the fourth life wave, or the fourth root race, there was a descent into duality. And this, then, opened up this planet to the embodiment of certain fallen lifestreams, who then accelerated the downward spiral created by the inhabitants of the earth.

Yet even though this has taken the earth below its original level of purity, we of the Ascended Host are not looking at the earth and saying that this is wrong. This does not mean that we accept, that what is outpictured upon the earth right now is "right" or is permanent or is the highest potential. However, we do accept that what is outpictured on the earth right now represents the greatest possible opportunity for growth for the inhabitants of the earth. And as I have explained, our only concern is precisely the growth in consciousness of the inhabitants of the earth.

We of the Ascended Host do not have an image, which says that planet earth should be in a certain state. And we do not see it as our goal to raise planet earth to a certain state, where it can then exist for an indefinite future in that supposedly edenic or perfect state. We are attuned with the driving force of the universe, the River of Life. There is no perfect or edenic state for the earth, as the entire universe is meant to continue transcending itself. So even though the Elohim created the earth in a certain state, the Elohim did not envision that the earth should stay at that level forever. They envisioned that it would be raised up from there.

There is nothing that is the permanently "right" state for the earth. So do you see that – even though at some point the earth began descending to a lower state than what was created by the Elohim – this is not seen as a flaw? For again, the earth is a schoolroom for the inhabitants on this planet. The earth is made out of the Ma-ter light, which is the Divine Mother that has vowed to take on whatever form self-aware beings project upon it—so that they can see outpictured in matter a reflection of their own state of consciousness. And thereby, they gain the opportunity to learn, to acquire wisdom and to transcend that state of consciousness.

So do you see, that when you look at planet earth today, you realize that the current state of the earth is an outpicturing of the collective consciousness of the self-aware beings that are in embodiment on earth? And precisely because the earth outpictures the consciousness of the beings who embody here – well, precisely because of that – the current conditions on earth represent the perfect opportunity for the inhabitants of earth to learn a lesson and transcend their current state of consciousness.

If you truly accept that the purpose of life is the growth in consciousness, then you can see – can you not – that it is meaningless to say that there is something wrong with the earth as it is today? The current state of the earth is an outpicturing, an outplaying, of the Law of Free Will. And therefore, it is not constructive or necessary to say that something is wrong and something needs to be corrected.

Key 16
A deeper understanding of consciousness

If you are to be one of the forerunners for healing Mother Earth, then it is extremely important that you understand the point I am seeking to make here, namely that using force will never heal the earth. Using more force, seeking to appoint a scapegoat, will only add to the tension that is, in fact, the main cause behind the imbalances you see in the natural environment on earth.

I am fully aware that there is nothing in your upbringing in Western society, or any other society on earth, that has prepared you to understand and accept this point. So in order to explain this to you, I need to ask you to step back and take a deeper look at consciousness. We have attempted to explain to you, that everything is created out of consciousness. But we now need to take a look at what exactly this means.

When I say the word "consciousness," you tend to understand and interpret the word based on your own experience of consciousness. You are a self-aware being, and thus you tend to think that anything that is or has consciousness has the same level of consciousness that you experience. However, this is not the case. When I say that the Ma-ter light is consciousness, it does not mean that the Ma-ter light has self-awareness. When I say that a rock has a form of consciousness, it does not mean that the rock has the kind of consciousness that you have.

In its basic form, consciousness is the ability to respond to an external stimuli. For example, you can take an animal, such as a pet. A dog clearly has a form of consciousness, and this is what makes it possible for you to teach the dog certain tricks. The dog can learn these tricks because its consciousness allows it to respond to the stimuli that you provide.

Yet consciousness also allows whatever entity has consciousness to retain something, so that it not only can respond to external stimuli, but so that it can change itself on a more long-term basis, based on such stimuli. So we can say that the Alpha aspect of consciousness is the ability to respond, and the Omega aspect is the ability to retain, or what we might call memory. In its simplest form, then, we can see that consciousness is the ability to respond to a stimuli in such a way that it changes form, and then the ability to maintain that change, to maintain the new form. Once a dog has learned to go to the bathroom outside of the house, it will retain that ability in the future.

A dog, of course, has a much more developed and sophisticated state of consciousness than you find at lower levels, such as that of what you normally call inert matter. Yet even at the level of so-called inert matter, there is consciousness.

***

How can anything even exist and retain an existence over time? Your scientists have told you that everything is made out of tiny microscopic entities, called subatomic particles. These particles combine in various ways to form atoms, and yet there are 108 – at least according to what science has discovered so far – of these atoms. The same subatomic particles that make up a hydrogen atom can be combined in a different way in order to make up an oxygen atom that is distinctly different.

So can you see, that for a hydrogen atom to exist, there must be something that has the ability to respond to an external stimuli in such a way that it forms a hydrogen atom? And then, once it has responded to that stimuli, it must have the ability to retain that form, so that the hydrogen atom does not suddenly disappear. How could you have a material universe with continuity, unless there was – first – the ability to take on a specific form and – second – the ability to retain that form for a period of time, perhaps even indefinitely?

So can you see, that even at the most fundamental level of what scientists call matter, namely that of subatomic particles, there is this rudimentary form of consciousness, namely the ability to respond, to take on form, and the ability to retain that form? Yet, of course, you can also see that at the basic level of matter, there is no self-awareness. A hydrogen atom does not know that it is a hydrogen atom, it has not consciously chosen to take on that form. The form has been impressed upon it by an external force. This is precisely what scientists have discovered through quantum physics, where they have realized that the conscious-

A deeper understanding of consciousness

ness of the scientist co-creates the subatomic particle that is being observed. And this is, indeed, what proves that the entire material universe could not have come into existence through an entirely mechanical or mindless process.

For there to be a universe, two conditions must be met. There must be a basic substance that has enough consciousness to take on form and to retain a specific form. But there must also be a "force" that can impress a specific form upon the basic substance. And that force, of course, is self-aware beings.

Self-awareness is a form of consciousness, but it is a much higher and much more complex form of consciousness than the consciousness you find at the lower levels. As I have said, a subatomic particle, or even a number of subatomic particles, cannot spontaneously combine themselves into forming a hydrogen atom. There must be a being that can hold the mental image of a hydrogen atom and then superimpose that image upon the subatomic particles, making them combine in such a way as to form the image in physical manifestation.

***

Of course, the ultimate self-aware being is the Creator, but there is an entire hierarchy of self-aware beings extending from the Creator through successively lower levels, until you reach what is currently the lowest level of self-aware beings, namely what you see as human beings on planet earth. Yet what I desire you to understand is that precisely because everything is consciousness, every "thing" is affected by the driving force behind creation, namely the drive for self-transcendence. Even subatomic particles are created out of the Creator's Being, the Creator's consciousness. And the Creator has not vowed to permanently trap its own Being in the form of physical matter. The Creator has, so to speak, extended its own Being as a loan, so that the self-aware extensions of itself can have a world that forms the basis for their growth in self-awareness. Yet in the long run, the Creator wants all extensions of its own Being to return to their source. And this means that everything in the universe is required to grow, to self-transcend—and therefore reach higher and higher levels of consciousness, until it again unites with its source.

You now see that in between the level of the most basic forms of matter and the level of self-aware beings, such as human beings, there is a range of consciousness. This can be difficult to grasp with the linear, logical mind, that you so often seek to apply in order to understand something. So I encourage you to use your intuition. But in order to give you a foundation, I will give you a somewhat linear image. Let us, for the sake of simplicity, say that consciousness can be divided into specific units. Let us say that there is a basic substance, out of which the entire world of form is created. That basic substance is what we have called the Ma-ter light.

Let us say that this substance is made out of something that is even smaller, even more subtle, than subatomic particles. Let us say that this substance can be conceived of as the finest possible particles, much finer than a grain of sand or subatomic particles. They are so small that they are almost like points, they are almost like the singularity that your scientists say existed just before the Big Bang. And then, let us say that each of these points is a basic unit of consciousness. This basic unit has the ability to respond to an external stimuli, so that it places itself into a matrix applied by the outside force. And once it has found its place in that matrix, it retains that place indefinitely.

Yet what you now need to understand is, that consciousness can be divided into these infinitely small points, but once you take two infinitely small points and combine them into a whole, then that whole acquires a state of consciousness that is more than the sum of the parts. This is possible because these infinitely small points of consciousness are extensions of the Creator's infinitely greater consciousness. And so, when this basic unit of consciousness combines with another basic unit, the combination of the two is closer to the whole than the sum of the individual parts.

Take for example what I just explained, that you have a number of subatomic particles that really do not make up anything visible or physical. But when you combine them into a certain matrix, then they form a hydrogen atom. And now you have a basic unit that exists in the physical spectrum and can, therefore, be used to build more complex forms in the physical spectrum. And when you then take a number of atoms and combine them into a matrix, you form a molecule. When you combine a number of molecules, you can form a basic substance that can be used to create more complex visible forms, such as an entire planet.

A deeper understanding of consciousness

You can even combine the basic physical substance in such ways that it forms a living cell that can reproduce. And then, you can combine these living cells into forms that have an increasingly more complex state of consciousness. You might be aware that there are scientists who have conducted experiments on plants that show that plants can feel pain, or that they can respond positively to certain forms of music by growing faster. This shows you that plants have a certain state of consciousness. Yet obviously, when you go to animals, you can see that animals have a more sophisticated state of consciousness than plants. And then you can set up a scale from more primitive animals to the most sophisticated animals, such as monkeys or whales.

And then, of course, you see another jump, where you have the most sophisticated state of consciousness seen on the earth, namely that of human beings. And here, then, is where you again need to make a distinction that you have not been prepared to make, neither by a Christian upbringing or a scientific, materialistic upbringing.

***

What I am explaining here is that there is indeed a process of evolution happening in the material universe. This process is, however, not the mechanical, mindless process envisioned by scientists. It is a highly intelligent and directed process, and it is a process that leads from less sophisticated towards more and more sophisticated lifeforms—meaning lifeforms that have an increasing level of consciousness.

And of course, the highest level of lifeforms that you see on earth is that of a human being, which has a sophisticated enough state of consciousness to actually have self-awareness. Self-awareness means that a being is not simply responding to external stimuli and retaining the changed behavior, but it is actually now able to generate its own internal stimuli and change its behavior without being forced to do so by external stimuli.

Now, here is where you need to make a subtle distinction. Because of the inherent driving force behind all of creation – the force that compels all of creation to transcend and come closer to union with the source – then there is, indeed, an evolutionary process that raises up everything in the matter world towards higher and higher levels of consciousness. Yet there is another force that is working in the material universe, and that force is what we might call a revolutionary force, which is that self-aware beings in a higher realm have extended themselves – as self-aware extensions – that have been sent into the material universe, having already a state of self-awareness before they entered.

What I am explaining here is that the evolutionary force starts at the basic level of consciousness, namely that of the Ma-ter light, and then raises up that level by creating more and more complex forms that – through the combination of the individual units of consciousness – acquire a more sophisticated consciousness as a whole. This will eventually cause the entire material universe to reach a level, where the universe now sees itself and acts as one unified whole. And at that point, the material universe will then be raised up in the process of the ascension, whereby the sphere in which you live becomes now the latest addition to the spiritual realm—where all life is one.

We might say that the individual points of consciousness that make up the Ma-ter light will first be combined to create forms that are clearly separate and distinct. But as they create more and more sophisticated forms, these forms will eventually combine into one coherent whole, where there are still distinct forms but where the forms are not separate, are not set apart, and cannot be in opposition to each other.

Yet, as I have explained, even this process is not the purpose of creation. For the evolutionary process that raises up an entire sphere does not happen automatically or on its own. Its purpose is, indeed, to facilitate the growth in self-awareness of the extensions of spiritual beings that are sent into this sphere. And that is why the evolutionary process responds to the higher level of consciousness of the beings who are sent into incarnation from a higher realm.

Do you see what I am seeking to explain here? The entire planet earth, the physical planet upon which you live, is made up of unbelievably large numbers of these basic points of consciousness, that I have called the Ma-ter light. And precisely because there are such huge numbers combined to form a single matrix, then the earth has a specific state of consciousness as a coherent whole. This whole – which we might call "Mother Earth" – can be seen as a conscious being. Yet it is not the same as a self-aware being, descending from above. It is a being created through the evolutionary process, and as such it has only one purpose and that is to serve self-aware beings as they grow in self-awareness.

A deeper understanding of consciousness

And that is, indeed, why the being that is Mother Earth responds to the consciousness of the self-aware beings that live upon its body. The earth truly has no purpose on its own. If there was no self-aware life-forms on earth, then the earth would have no purpose for its existence. Mother Earth – as a being – would feel empty, would feel deserted, abandoned, left alone. It gains its sense of purpose by being the home to self-aware beings, who can grow in self-awareness towards the point where they ascend. And therefore, they provide the driving force – that the earth cannot provide by itself – so that the earth can ascend.

***

This is another subtle distinction. I have talked about an evolutionary force that raises all life towards greater and greater complexity. But this evolutionary force cannot drive matter to go beyond a certain level. As Lord Maitreya has explained in greater detail in his book,[1] the evolutionary force can start at a certain level and can then raise up the forms that exist at that level towards greater complexity. But this evolutionary force can only go so far, and then for life to progress further, there must be a leap, a quantum leap, whereby life suddenly rises to a distinctly higher level. And this leap cannot be driven by the evolutionary force; it can be driven only by the revolutionary force.

So for example, the driving force, the original impetus of creation, came from the Elohim, who projected the original force that your scientists currently describe as the Big Bang. Yet your scientists also know that there were certain phases that lead from the original singularity to what you see today. Yet what your scientists have not yet acknowledged is that these revolutionary jumps were driven by an external force, namely self-aware beings. So for example, what caused the formation of the first atoms was a revolutionary leap, driven by the Elohim. What caused the formation of molecules was another leap. What caused the formation of planets, suns and galaxies was another leap. What caused the appearance of the first organic molecule on a planet like earth was another revolutionary leap—and so forth and so on, until you now have the sophisticated lifeforms that can form the basis for the descent of self-aware beings.

---

1   Master Keys to Spiritual Freedom.

And thus, you have now reached the ultimate revolutionary leap, where the Elohim are not providing a creative force from the outside, but where the self-aware extensions of spiritual beings are meant to provide the revolutionary force from inside the material universe.

Do you see what I am saying here? The Creator does not want to be – forever – the external force that provides stimuli from the outside. The reason is that the purpose of the world of form is the growth in self-awareness of individual extensions.

The representatives of the Creator – the Elohim – do not want to indefinitely provide the revolutionary force for planet earth. Their goal was to bring the earth to a level, where it could provide a sophisticated enough physical body that extensions of the Elohim and other spiritual beings could embody on earth. And then – when that incarnation took place – you are the ones who are meant to now provide, or rather be the open doors for, the revolutionary force that takes the earth to another level of sophistication.

**

Of course, because you have free will and the real purpose of the earth is your growth in self-awareness, you also have the ability to provide a revolutionary force that takes the earth to a lower level. And this is what happens, when the majority of the inhabitants on the earth go below the 48th level of consciousness. Yet as I have explained, this is also a legitimate outplaying of the Law of Free Will. Because no matter how low the earth has been taken below the original vision of the Elohim, then even this level is still the perfect foundation for the growth in self-awareness of the beings who inhabit the earth.

And that is, indeed, why we now come full circle, and you see that even though the earth is currently at a far more primitive level than what was created by the Elohim, this still does not mean that something has gone wrong. It only means that the evolution of the earth took a different track than was originally envisioned by the Elohim. Yet even this track is still the perfect opportunity for the growth in self-awareness—that is, it has the potential to provide the growth in self-awareness, whereby the inhabitants of the earth learn from seeing what the Earth Mother is currently outpicturing in physical form. They can learn when they are willing to acknowledge that this is an outpicturing of their own state of

A deeper understanding of consciousness 269

consciousness, and when they then decide to consciously raise up their level of consciousness and follow the path that leads from wherever they are at right now towards the 144th level, where they are ready to ascend.

This, then, is the basic outlook on planet earth that you need to have, if you want to be one of the forerunners for healing Mother Earth. If you do not adopt this positive outlook, then you will simply be pulled into the age-old dualistic struggle. And thus, you will only add to the tension that will further burden the body of the Earth Mother. And exactly how this tension burdens the body of the Earth Mother, and becomes outpictured in various forms of imbalances, will be the topic of the next key.

Key 17
Understanding the elemental beings

As our next step, we need to build on to the understanding that everything is consciousness. As we have explained, the purpose of life is that the entire material universe will eventually be raised up and become part of the spiritual realm. This will happen only when matter attains a higher state of consciousness, where what has started out as separate forms become conscious and become conscious of being expressions of a whole.

So what will it take for this process to be completed? Well, it will take the interaction of the evolutionary and revolutionary forces. The purpose of the descent of self-aware beings, sent from the spiritual realm, is twofold. One is their own growth in self-awareness, but how do they grow in self-awareness? They grow by helping the unascended sphere come to the ascension point. And they do this by, so to speak, passing on their awareness to matter, the matter realm, and the beings who are the expressions of the evolutionary process.

So far, we have only talked about beings that descended from the spiritual realm and who have what we call self-awareness, because they have been endowed with self-awareness from the Beings above them, from the Beings out of which they came. Yet what you realize – when you think about this – is that you, as a human being, have been endowed with self-awareness by a Being who is above you in what we might call the spiritual hierarchy. And that Being originally was an extension of an even higher Being, and was endowed with self-awareness from that Being. And so, as you keep following this Chain of Being, you end up with the ultimate self-aware Being, namely the Creator itself.

You see, now, that when you look at this process going in the other direction, you see that you have been endowed with self-awareness from a Being who is above you in the Chain of Being. And you are meant to descend into the material universe and then endow everything you do with your self-awareness. And therefore, you, so to speak, pass on your self-awareness to the beings who are below you in the Chain of Being, namely the beings who are the products of the evolutionary force.

***

In the last key I mentioned the existence of what we might call a basic unit of consciousness. And when you take several of these point-like units and organize them into a matrix, they form a whole which attains a consciousness as a whole. So we might say that when the Elohim started creating the material universe, they were the ones who impressed this matrix upon the basic units of consciousness. And as they created more and more complex forms, they created matrixes that had a higher and higher level of consciousness. For the more complex the matrix, the higher the level of consciousness.

What you now need to realize is, that there are four distinct levels created by the Elohim. And these four levels all play a role in what we might call manifestation or materialization.

So the image I would like to give you here – again in order to ac-commodate your linear mind – is that we have the spiritual realm. The spiritual realm is made up of energies that vibrate above a certain level of vibration. The Elohim exist in the spiritual realm. They are now look-ing to create the material universe, yet the ultimate goal they have is to create the physical universe that you right now see with your physical senses. This universe is, however, at a much lower vibration – or a much higher density – than the spiritual realm. So because of certain mechan-ics that I will not here describe in detail – as they are not important for the point I am seeking to make – they cannot simply create the material universe directly at a vibration that is so much lower than the spiritual.

Therefore, they first create a realm which we might call the etheric realm, or the identity realm. This is a level of vibration that is lower than the spiritual realm, but not so much lower that it becomes so dense that it loses the transparency that you find in the spiritual realm. In other words, in the physical realm, where you are currently focusing your awareness, matter is so dense that you cannot see that it is an expression of Spirit. Yet in the etheric realm the, so to speak, "matter" of that realm is so transparent that you can indeed see that it is an expression of finer energies.

Understanding the elemental beings

From a purely visual perspective, you might say that the forms in the etheric realm are so transparent that light can shine through them. Instead of a solid wall with a picture painted on it, you could look at it as a stained-glass window, where you still have a picture but you can see light shining through it. So you know that there is something behind the image, whereas with a wall, you might think that it is completely solid and there is nothing on the other side.

In the etheric realm, you find what we might call the cosmic blueprint for the material universe. This is comparable to what an architect creates before anyone starts building an actual building. An architect might start with a sketch that puts forth the basic design of the building. This is what you find in the etheric realm. You find the basic design for the material universe. Yet what you see in the etheric is still somewhat fluid, and it is not designed in every detail.

Now, the next level down is what I would like to call the mental level. This is the level where the Elohim created more detailed plans for the universe. You might consider it as an actual engineering plan for a house, that details all the practical aspects, such as the wiring or the plumbing.

And then, the Elohim stepped down the energies to an even lower level, which I would like to call the emotional realm. This is where things become more concrete, and where the blueprint is, so to speak, set in motion. This is comparable to the architect and the engineers giving the detailed drawings to the actual builders, who then make a plan for how to build the actual house and get all the materials to the location and line up the workers and the machinery that need to come in at a certain time. And then, finally, we have the actual physical or material realm, which is where the actual building of the house takes place.

***

So you now need to understand that these four levels of the material universe correspond to four levels of your own mind. The etheric level corresponds to the highest level of your mind, which is the level where your identity is stored. This is your basic sense of who you are. Then, the mental level, of course, corresponds to the level of your thoughts, where you think in more concrete terms about what you can do and how to do it.

The emotional level, of course, corresponds to your feelings, and the level of the feelings is actually where you set energy in motion, in the form of emotions. This is where you take the many opportunities you can envision at the mental level and crystallize a decision to set one of them in motion, and actually carry it out in the physical. And so, of course, the material or physical level corresponds to the outer mind, where you actually make conscious decisions, perform conscious actions and consciously evaluate the circumstances you encounter on earth.

What you now need to realize is, that this shows the progression of how something is brought into materialization. It is a progression that you need to learn to use more consciously in order to fulfill your reason for being in embodiment. But we will begin by looking at how the Elohim used this process. The Elohim started in the spiritual realm with the desire, the will to create. Let us, as an example, take the creation of planet earth. The seven Elohim and their counterparts met in the spiritual realm. They formed an intent to create planet earth. They then projected that intent into the etheric realm and began to create a more concrete blueprint for what kind of planet it would be, and what kind of lifeforms it was meant to support.

Then, they pushed this blueprint into the mental realm and made more concrete plans and designs for the planet, for how it would evolve over time and what kind of lifeforms it would eventually bring forth. Then, when the mental plans were completed, they pushed further into the emotional realm and now started actually setting in motion the process that would cause the basic units of consciousness to begin organizing according to the plans. And then, as this process became more advanced, they finally pushed the blueprint into the physical realm, where the basic units of consciousness – now organized into subatomic particles and atoms – started forming the physical planet.

***

So far, I have given you a simplified image of this process, in order to give you a gradual awareness of it. We now need to take this to another level. As I have explained, the purpose of life is the raising up of the material realm, the lowest level of vibration, to the level of the spiritual realm. And as part of this process, matter, so to speak, becomes more

Understanding the elemental beings

conscious. And so, as part of the process of raising consciousness, the Elohim actually created specific beings at each of the four levels of the material universe.

There are specific beings in the etheric realm that are created to serve as the extensions of the Elohim, in the sense that they take the basic blueprint and design of the Elohim and they begin to organize the basic units of consciousness around that design in the etheric realm. Then, there are other beings in the mental realm who can take what is being passed on by the beings in the etheric realm and organize it and build on to it at that level of vibration. When they have completed their process, then there are beings in the emotional realm who continue the process, until finally there are beings in the physical realm who take over and who actually create what you see as physical matter.

These beings have been known in various spiritual, esoteric or even alchemical teachings for quite some time. The medieval philosopher Paracelsus was one of the first to write about these beings and give them names. They have been called elemental beings or elemental builders of form, and they can be classified according to the alchemical worldview, in which the world is made out of four distinct elements, called fire, air, water and earth. Thus, there are four distinct groups of elemental beings, the fire elementals, the air elementals, the water elementals and the earth elementals. They have also been given various names, but for this particular release, I would like us to simply call them fire elementals, air elementals, water elementals and earth elementals.

***

It is important for you to understand, that even though the elementals were created by the Elohim, they were not endowed with self-awareness. They were actually created by organizing the basic points of consciousness into complex matrixes. This actually means something that can be difficult to envision for a human being.

Because you have self-awareness, you are aware that you are a self, a being that can do something. Most people who are open to any kind of spiritual teaching are aware that they are not their physical bodies; they are beings who inhabit their physical bodies. Elementals do not have this awareness. They do not, they cannot, see themselves as beings who are inhabiting, for example, etheric bodies or mental bodies. They do not see themselves as beings who are separate from the vibrational realm in which they live.

This means that elemental beings are not actually beings who are separate from matter. They *are* matter.

In order to fully understand this, you need to be willing to look beyond some of the images of elementals that have been created and have found their way into some aspects of popular culture, even some spiritual teachings. A very popular image, for example, is the image of gnomes, which are often depicted as small troll-like or nisse-like beings, who run around almost like miniature humans with a distinct form. And many spiritual people have read or heard about these beings, and they somehow envision that these gnomes are the ones who run around with little tools and who build the earth. This, of course, is not an accurate image, but a very simplified image of elementals and how they work.

The reality is that elementals are not beings who run around and do something with matter. They are not beings who are doing something with the external matter. They *are* matter.

An elemental does not create a form by being a separate being that is working on that form, as you as a human being would create a sculpture out of a block of stone. The elemental creates a form by taking on that form, by becoming that form. Therefore, the elemental is fully identified with the form. This is extremely important for you to keep in mind, for it is the only way that you can fully understand your role and your relationship with Mother Earth.

***

There are fire elementals who represent the fire element on earth. This does not actually mean that every instance of fire is created by fire elementals, but it does mean that there are certain phenomena of fire that are produced by fire elementals. There is, for example, a large concentration of fire elementals in the center of the earth, where as you know conditions are very hot, almost as if there was a sun glowing inside the earth. The air elementals are, of course, associated with the air element. And so many of the phenomena that take place in the atmosphere are performed by these air elementals. Likewise, many of the phenomena that are associated with water are, of course, performed by the water

Understanding the elemental beings

elementals. And the physical earth is also associated with the earth elementals.

Yet it is important for you to realize that even though I am giving you a linear image, you cannot fully understand the function of elementals or the process of materialization through the linear mind. If you are to fully understand the process of materialization, you need to expand your conscious awareness, so that you become conscious of the full extent of your mind, meaning the four levels of your mind.

I have said that the Elohim started in the spiritual realm, pushed certain ideas into the etheric, then the mental, then the emotional and then the physical. Yet the reality is that even though this was the direction and the flow, it took place simultaneously. And the process of materialization was not something that happened just once; it is a continuous process that is taking place constantly in all four levels. The Elohim did not simply release an initial creative intent and then sit back and watch as everything unfolded. They are, indeed, still involved, because it is precisely the spiritual energies passing through the minds of the Elohim that are allowing the material universe to continue to exist.

Yet this does not mean that the Elohim are intimately involved with every detail of what happens in the material universe. The Elohim have created the fire elementals precisely to take care of many of the details, much of the practical work, that takes place in the etheric realm—and so on of course with the other levels of elementals. And so, once a certain blueprint or matrix has been impressed upon, for example the air elementals, then the role of the air elementals is to bring that matrix down in vibration, until it is ready to enter the emotional realm. But it is also the role of air elementals to uphold that matrix, so that the light from the spiritual realm can stream through it.

We might say, that the role of elementals is to respond to the outside stimuli coming from the spiritual realm, and then to maintain the form impressed upon them. They are, so to speak, the memory aspect of creation. And as I expounded upon before, the basic aspects of consciousness is the ability to respond to external stimuli and the ability to retain a certain matrix or form. So this is what the elementals can do.

***

Now, the other function of the elementals is to serve human beings, or rather the spiritual beings who take embodiment in human bodies. As we have said, the purpose of Mother Earth is to serve as a schoolroom for the self-aware beings who embody here. And the earth serves as a schoolroom by outpicturing in matter the matrices that are projected upon the Ma-ter light through the consciousness of human beings. And how this actually happens is, of course, that the four classes of elementals take on the forms impressed upon them through the minds of human beings.

This means that even though the elementals were originally created according to the thoughtforms impressed upon them by the Elohim, the elementals have, over time, become changed – in some cases dramatically – by the thoughtforms impressed upon them through human beings. And so, what you see right now is that the earth no longer outpictures the original vision and blueprint of the Elohim, although this blueprint still exists in its original form in the higher etheric realm. Nevertheless, in the lower etheric realm, in the mental realm, in the emotional realm and in the physical realm that blueprint has been overlaid by the images impressed upon elemental beings by human beings.

Now again, even though this current image is much lower than the original vision of the Elohim, this still does not mean that something has gone wrong with the original plan. For even though the elementals have taken on these lower images – and have in many ways been burdened by them – this is still also an opportunity for the elementals to grow in awareness. For as the elementals take on the thoughtforms impressed upon them by human beings, they still grow in awareness. And when elementals reach a certain level of awareness, they actually acquire the ability to know that what they are currently outpicturing is not the highest possible form. And this, then, can help them grow even further in awareness, until they actually come to the point, where they have the potential – they have the capacity of awareness – to be endowed with self-awareness by the beings who are above them in the chain of hierarchy, namely human beings.

This, of course, can only happen when a human being has expanded its self-awareness to its highest potential, and therefore has attained the higher state of consciousness that we would like to call Christhood, and that has been exemplified by a number of people who have reached beyond the normal level of human consciousness. Such Christed beings

Understanding the elemental beings

can indeed endow upon the more developed elementals a state of self-awareness, which then allows such an elemental being to actually take on a human body and then grow through the levels of the 144 human levels of consciousness, until it reaches the highest level and can then actually ascend to the spiritual realm.

There are indeed beings who have gone through this process over the history of the earth. There are not many, but they are there. And it is important for you, if you want to be one of the forerunners for healing Mother Earth, that you are aware that elemental life can actually be endowed with self-awareness and therefore rise up through the chain of hierarchy, the Chain of Being.

And of course, it is indeed your highest potential as a human being to reach a level of consciousness, where you can do this, where you can be the instrument for the beings above you flowing through you and therefore endowing the beings below you in the Chain of Being with self-awareness—as you have been endowed with it.

Now then, I will end this release, for I have given you much to ponder. There may be those who will find that this key has been so challenging to their previous worldview or to their linear way of thinking, that they will either reject it outright or find it very difficult to grasp. So perhaps it would be appropriate for you to take a little bit of time to reread this and previous keys about consciousness, before you move on with the next key. For in the next key, we will go even further in helping you understand how materialization takes place and how you can find your rightful place in the process of materialization—of matter being realized as Spirit.

Key 18
A deeper understanding of the four elements

When you take a look at elemental beings, you see that they are organized into a hierarchy. Even though I have said that the fire elementals are associated with certain phenomena that relate to physical fire, you need to be careful not to form too linear of an image. What you actually see – when you take a closer look and think about this more deeply – is that fire is not only a matter of the physical, visible fire. It is also the very basic process of energy becoming matter, or rather taking on the form of matter.

You will see, for example, that the most powerful form of fire known to science is that of nuclear processes, such as what takes place in a nuclear reactor or in the sun. The sun, as we have said, is truly the open door for bringing energies from the spiritual realm into the physical vibrational spectrum for this solar system. Therefore, you also see that fire represents the first step in the process, whereby spiritual energy is lowered into the vibrational spectrum of matter.

Fire, if you look at the physical fire, represents something that etherializes physical matter. For example, if you burn a piece of wood in your fireplace, you will see that the flame, so to speak, disintegrates the physical matter of the wood, until there is only a small amount of ashes left. We might, however, also say that fire actually accelerates the vibration of the physical matter, whereby the molecules and atoms that make up the wood are actually freed from the matrix that has kept them trapped in manifesting a block of wood. They are now set free, and the fact that they become invisible actually indicates that they are accelerated into a higher state of vibration, where they are not visible to your physical eyes. Thus, the basic substance of matter that made up the wood is now set free to be organized into another matrix and bring forth a different form.

So by the very fact that fire accelerates what is already physical matter to a higher state, you can see that the reverse is also true; that the fire element brings energies from a higher level closer to the physical vibrational spectrum. And thus, the fire element and the fire elementals represent the first step in materialization.

Thus, it becomes clear that the fire elementals are at the top of the hierarchy formed by elemental beings. After they bring the spiritual energies into the material vibrational spectrum, these energies can then be passed on to the air elementals. And again, of course, you see that air is also a very fluid substance, although not as fluid as fire. Fire does disintegrate matter, air does not, but air can indeed fuel the fire. And thereby, you again see that air is the element that is closest in vibration to the element of fire.

So the air elementals then take the energies and step them down even further, until they can be passed into the element of the emotions, or the water element. Again, you see that water is denser than air, although still quite fluid. And so, it becomes obvious that the final step is where the water elementals, the elementals of the water element, take the energies and step them down into the physical vibrational spectrum, where they can form what you normally call solid matter—but which, of course, is solid only to your senses. The elemental beings, the earth elementals, do not see matter as solid at all. For they do indeed know that it is a manifestation of consciousness, namely their own consciousness that has taken on the form of matter.

***

Why is it important for you to understand this process? Well, for one thing, it is important, if you are to be one of the forerunners for healing Mother Earth. For as we have explained, the key to healing Mother Earth is to change the way that human beings look at Mother Earth and their own relationship to the planet. We have talked about the fact that the illusion of separation has caused people to look at the planet as a separate entity – or even as a mechanical kind of device – upon which they live. And for there to be a real change, it is absolutely necessary that human beings begin to see a connection between themselves and Mother Earth. How can this change in awareness take place? Well, you clearly experience yourself as a self-aware being that has conscious-

A deeper understanding of the four elements   283

ness. So if you conceive of the earth as a dead, almost mechanical, device that has no consciousness, how can you possibly see a connection between yourself and the earth?

So the only way out is that you expand your awareness, so you realize that everything is an expression of consciousness. And therefore, Mother Earth is also—not only an expression of consciousness but is in fact such a sophisticated and complex matrix that it has a consciousness as a unified whole. You can then begin to see that if Mother Earth has a consciousness, then you as a conscious being can possibly relate to Mother Earth by raising your consciousness and tuning it in to the consciousness of the earth as a whole.

You can even, then, take the next step of realizing that you are not a separate being with consciousness living on the greater being of Mother Earth with consciousness. In fact, you are living within the consciousness of Mother Earth. Your individual consciousness exists within the greater whole of the consciousness of the earth.

You are, of course, a self-aware being, which means that you are not an unaware part of the whole, as for example the elemental beings who do not have self-awareness. You clearly have an awareness of yourself as an individual being, but as you are willing to raise your awareness – and realize that you are not a separate being but an expression of a larger whole, namely your I AM Presence – then you can also come to experience a direct connection between your own individual awareness and the awareness of the Earth Mother.

There are already millions of people on the planet who have started to see beyond their individual awareness as a separate being and have attained some greater connection with the earth or with nature. Many people, for example, have a strong sense of connection with a pet, such as a dog, or a cat or a horse. This is just one example of how people can begin to attune their consciousness to elements within the larger consciousness of the Earth Mother.

There are also many people who have an inherent sense for how to grow plants or even crops on a farm. They have an intuitive sense for the cycles of nature, of weather patterns, of how their plants are doing and what they need in order to grow better. The same, of course, with raising animals on a larger scale than your individual pets, where many people again have a deep intuitive sense of how to do this. There are also other people who have a connection to nature in a larger sense, so that they understand how to be fishermen or hunters or how to predict weather patterns. All of these things show how many, many people have already developed a connection to the physical planet.

And what I am saying here is that if these people could take that connection and build upon it, they could very quickly develop a much stronger sense of connection to the earth and the Earth Mother. In fact, for anyone who has a sense of connection with nature or with animals, it will not be that difficult to raise their awareness until they start having a sense of connection with elemental beings. And once you begin to have a sense of connection to the nature spirits, then you will really be able to break down this fundamental barrier between human beings and Mother Earth, between man and nature.

***

As we have said, one of the more subtle outcomes of the consciousness of separation is indeed that human beings have seen themselves as these separate beings, who are threatened by the planet upon which they live. Therefore, Western civilization in particular has come to see nature as something that needs to be conquered and subdued by force. This is precisely what has prevented Western civilization from stepping up to the higher level of being able to work with nature, instead of working against it through force. And it is, of course – as I am sure you can see – absolutely essential that this consciousness begins to be broken down.

Yet how can you break down the sense that nature is threatening human beings, when you – especially in these later years – have seen so many examples of devastating natural disasters? Think about the many disasters that have happened since the year 2,000. You have had very violent hurricanes that have hit the United States or Central America or the islands in the Caribbean. You have had very violent typhoons that have hit countries and islands in Southeast Asia. You have had devastating floods in several countries, major earthquakes that have literally brought entire nations to their knees. You also seem to have more and more erratic weather patterns. And then, of course, you have in the last decade or so been indoctrinated with the belief that there is this major threat of global warming, that hangs as a Sword of Damocles over the heads of humankind, threatening to completely upset their way of life.

A deeper understanding of the four elements

Can you see what I am saying here? We have said that it is absolutely necessary that human beings overcome the sense of separation from Mother Earth. And yet in order to overcome the sense of separation, they must overcome the sense that nature is a threat to their way of life. And as long as they see these enormous natural disasters – such as a tsunami that kills over 100,000 people within a matter of hours – well, as long as they see this happening in nature, how can they overcome the sense that nature is a threat?

Yet if you step back and look at this from a different perspective, you will see an interesting possibility that begins to open up. For can you see that the real issue that separates human beings from Mother Earth – in the minds of human beings, of course – is precisely the sense that nature is the enemy that needs to be suppressed through force? So can you see what is beginning to happen in the awareness of humankind?

For several decades, technological progress has given many people the sense, that there is nothing human beings cannot conquer through science and technology. Huge rivers have been damned, bridges have been built to connect continents, and it seems as if there is no challenge that science or technology cannot master.

Yet within the last decade, natural disasters have taken on a much more prominent place in people's consciousness. And people are beginning to realize that when a hurricane is coming towards their city, there is no technological power that can turn back that hurricane. Likewise, when the earth starts shaking underneath their feet, there is no technological solution. There is no way to prevent or even predict when an undersea earthquake will release a tsunami that will spread, within a matter of hours, to vast areas of various countries. And of course, there does not seem to be a technological solution that will adequately reverse the process that has become known as global warming.

So can you see that the science that has given human beings the impression that they can conquer everything with technology, is now beginning to open up the awareness that perhaps this is not so? Perhaps, there really are processes on the earth that cannot be controlled through force, through any force that can be generated by human beings. At least, this is an awareness that is beginning to emerge in the collective consciousness.

***

Now, the deeper reality is, of course, as we are attempting to explain in this book, that there is indeed a force – that can be generated by human beings – that can protect and defend society from these natural disasters. Yet that force is not a physical force that can be generated through technological and mechanical devices. The force that can truly avert natural disasters, so-called, is the force of the human mind. For it is, indeed, the wrongful use of the human mind that has generated the natural, so-called, disasters in the first place.

Of course, most people in the Western world have been brought up with a materialistic mindset, that predisposes them to immediately reject the possibility that natural disasters are not natural but man-made. And so, the only way to break through this barrier is indeed that those, who see themselves as the forerunners for healing Mother Earth, begin to realize the full consequences of the fact that everything is consciousness.

And the missing link, so to speak, between consciousness and matter is precisely the awareness of elemental beings. Do you see why this is so? I have attempted to explain that elemental beings are not separate little "humans" that are running around in wooden shoes and doing something to matter. Elemental beings are conscious beings, yet not self-aware beings. So they do not do something to a separate substance of matter. They, in fact, take on a form that manifests matter.

The elemental beings are conscious beings who take on the form of matter, and this is what makes matter conscious. This is what gives matter a state of consciousness that allows matter to respond to the higher and more sophisticated state of consciousness of human beings.

There is a debate that has been going on for a long time between those who espouse a purely materialistic, mechanical worldview and those who espouse a more spiritual worldview. It is the debate over whether mind can have any direct influence upon matter. There is, for example, the topic of telekinesis. Can a person, by using the powers of the mind, move an actual object?

The reality here is that if you are sitting as a human being and trying to use your thoughts to move a physical object, then you will not have the power to do so. As long as you see yourself as a separate being, you cannot generate enough psychic force to move a physical object.

However, if you attain a higher state of awareness, where you approach the 144th level of awareness, then you can take a different ap-

A deeper understanding of the four elements 287

proach. Instead of seeing yourself as a separate being who is projecting a force at a physical object in order to move it, you can now tune in to the elemental being that is outpicturing the physical object. And by attaining a sense of oneness with that physical object, you can – because your state of consciousness is higher than the consciousness of the elemental being – move or in other ways influence the object. This is how Jesus was able to perform the so-called miracles that are attributed to him in the Scriptures.

In reality, Jesus performed many more feats than are described in the official Scriptures. Yet Jesus performed these feats very selectively, and he did so only for the purpose of demonstrating that the mind actually has power over matter. The unfortunate fact is that official Christianity – influenced by the fallen beings – have elevated Jesus to an exception, so that they claimed he was the only one who had these exceptional, miraculous powers to influence matter with the mind. Yet, the reality is, as we have attempted to explain, that every human being has the potential to expand his or her awareness and gain the mastery of mind over matter.

Yet, you do not attain this mastery by maintaining the self-image that you are a separate being, who is attaining power over a separate object. You attain this mastery only by raising your self-awareness, until you attain that sense of oneness—first of all oneness with your own I AM Presence, but then oneness with all life, with all awareness, all consciousness. And when you see that matter is consciousness, you can merge your own consciousness with the elemental being that is the consciousness behind matter. And then you can work with that elemental being to produce specific changes, that will seem miraculous to those who are still at a lower level of consciousness.

For indeed, those who descend below the 48th level of consciousness cannot even fathom the possibility that you could attain a sense of oneness with matter. They will only be able to see matter and Mother Earth as a separate entity, that they must conquer through physical force.

When you have the awareness of elemental life, you can see that when the earth was first created, elemental life took on the thought-forms, the matrixes, projected upon it through the minds of the Elohim. And therefore, planet earth in its original state – we might say its edenic state – did indeed have complete balance of nature.

There were no volcanic eruptions, no earthquakes, no violent storms, no floods. There was no erratic or destructive weather patterns. And people did not even have to work to bring forth the physical sustenance that they needed, as it was abundantly provided by the plants growing in nature. For these plants grew according to the matrixes produced and projected by the Elohim and the elemental beings at the four levels of the material universe. It was only after humankind descended into the duality consciousness and started going below the 48th level of awareness, that you started seeing various forms of imbalances in nature.

***

I know that for people with a traditional Western upbringing, what I will say next will seem difficult to accept. But of course, if you had not been willing to look beyond your traditional Western upbringing, you would not even be reading this.

The reality is that the earth was meant to start at a certain level and then grow from there. This means that the earth would have followed along with the force that drives growth in the entire material universe. As we have said, there are numerous planets in the material universe that support intelligent forms of life. The vast majority of these self-aware beings are engaged in the path of self-transcendence, whereby they are continually raising their state of consciousness. This has created a giant force, the life-force of the entire universe. This is the combined mental or psychic force of all the self-aware beings that are growing in self-awareness. This force has in a Christian context been called the Holy Spirit, yet I prefer to call it the River of Life. For it can indeed be seen as a giant stream of consciousness that is the driving force behind the fact that the entire universe is expanding at an ever-accelerating rate.

So the point is that the earth was meant to be part of this flow of the River of Life, and therefore constantly be raised towards higher and higher levels that made the earth come closer and closer in vibration to the spiritual realm. If this process had continued unhindered, then the earth would actually gradually have become less and less dense, meaning that the matter on the earth would have become less and less dense, more and more transparent. And this would, indeed, have expanded the size of the earth. You will know that there are other planets in your solar system that are considered as gaseous planets, because they are made out of matter that is less dense than what you see on earth. This is not to say that the earth would have looked exactly as one of these planets, but

A deeper understanding of the four elements

it is to give you the image that matter would indeed become less and less dense as the entire planet is raised to higher and higher levels.

When you see this, you also see that after humankind went into the duality consciousness, then the earth could no longer follow along with what we might call the background growth rate of the entire universe. And the only way that the earth could avoid being pulled along with this background growth rate was that the elemental beings on earth took on a denser form of consciousness, and thereby made the very matter that makes up the earth more and more dense. Yes, I know, my beloved, that this will require a stretch of the mind, especially for those who have never really questioned the view of matter that they were given in elementary school or even at universities.

For you see, you have been brought up to think that matter is an immutable substance that exists according to certain invariable laws of physics. Yet I tell you that matter is, indeed, a product of the consciousness of elemental beings. And because elemental beings react to the consciousness of human beings, it is indeed possible that the consciousness of humankind – over a very long time span – can have caused the elementals to densify matter.

This, of course, will require you to challenge another doctrine that you have been given by the religion of materialism—which has been as limiting to human thought as the Catholic doctrines of the Middle Ages. This is the concept that evolution can go in only one direction. As I have explained, we of the Ascended Host are in no way rejecting the concept that there is an evolutionary process on this planet. Yet we are indeed seeing that the current version of an entirely materialistic process of evolution is severely limited.

One of the problems with the current theory of evolution is that it must go in only one direction, from more primitive to more complex forms of life. And this is what has given rise to the popular belief that the history of humankind on planet earth is indeed very short, even only a few thousand years of what you would call a sophisticated civilization. As we have mentioned before, this is, of course, not correct. And when you are willing to let go of this doctrine and see that the earth is not flat – and that the history of this planet is not as short as science or even biblical literalists would have it – then a new worldview opens up to you.

***

You can therefore begin to realize that as human beings took on the lower consciousness in the realm of duality, they projected that consciousness onto elemental life. This started in the etheric realm with the fire elementals lowering their consciousness, so that the very fire element – that brings spiritual energy into the material spectrum – became more dense. This means that already at the etheric level, there was a densification of the energies. This densification became more intense or solid in the air element, even more so in the water element. And so, when the energy reached the physical or earth element, then it could solidify even more.

Now, if you look at the earth today, you will see that there are immense processes going on in the crust of the earth. These are the processes that bring about volcanic eruptions or earthquakes. And you know, of course, the many doomsday scenarios of a super volcano spewing so much ash into the atmosphere that it would cause the climate to become so much colder that life could not be sustained. And it is, of course, not my intention here to frighten you with any doomsday scenario. But what I do want you to realize is that volcanoes and earthquakes are a product of the fact that matter has been densified.

We might, to give you a primitive illustration, say that you can imagine that you took the current earth and you shrunk it to about 80% of its current size. Can you see that if you shrunk the earth, so that the same amount of matter would take up a smaller amount of space, then the only way to accomplish this would be that matter – the molecules and atoms of the matter – would have to be compressed, so that they became more dense. Yet can you also see that if you compress matter, you will make it hotter? And this is precisely what explains the fact that there is a very warm core of the earth. If matter had not been densified, then the core of the earth would not be nearly as hot as it is right now. And therefore, I am sure you can see that there would not be the same violent processes in the crust of the earth.

For can you not see that the melting magma in the center of the earth must expand? And as it expands, it hits up against the solidified crust of the earth, and you now have a tension between the expanding hot core and the solidified crust. And when that tension reaches a critical level, something in the crust must give. And so, you either have the emergence of a volcano that spews out hot magma or gas, or you have a movement in the plates that make up the crust, which results in an earthquake.

A deeper understanding of the four elements

So can you begin to see here, that – over a very long time span – the consciousness of humankind has caused elemental beings to take on a more dense state of consciousness that has – through a perfectly natural and even somewhat mechanical process – caused the matter that makes up the earth to take on a certain density? And this higher density of matter has created a certain tension, which then brings forth various so-called natural disasters—that are not truly natural, in the sense that they are an unavoidable consequence of the design of nature. There are no immutable natural laws that are bringing forth or guaranteeing natural disasters.

The one immutable natural law that brings forth natural disasters is the combination of the Law of Free Will and the Law of Action and Reaction. Human beings are the self-aware beings that are, so to speak, at the top of the spiritual food chain on earth. You might even recall that the Old Testament, in the book of Genesis, contains the teaching that God said: "Let us make man in our own image and after our own likeness, and let him have dominion over the earth." The Law of Free Will gives human beings dominion over the earth, in the sense that they have a right to go into and outpicture whatever state of consciousness they desire. Yet because the purpose of the entire universe is the growth in self-awareness, the Law of Action and Reaction also ensures that whatever action you take – in the form of projecting a certain mental image upon the Ma-ter light – you will indeed have to experience the consequences of that action by having the Ma-ter light take on the form of the mental image you are projecting.

***

I am not thereby saying that human beings have deliberately projected the image that they want the planet to bring forth earthquakes or volcanoes or violent storms. But human beings have descended below the 48th level, where they become deceived by the duality consciousness. And the duality consciousness always contains two opposite polarities that can only be in conflict with each other. And can you see, that when human beings take on this state of consciousness, they will inevitably project mental images upon the Ma-ter light that are based on this epic mindset—that there are two opposite polarities who are locked in a to-the-death struggle? And this struggle will naturally create a tension, and when this tension is projected upon the elemental beings, well then they will take on a density that will indeed create what you see as natural disasters.

Yet this is not the workings out of a natural law that *must* bring forth natural disasters. It is not the result of the elemental beings wanting to bring forth natural disasters. It is a result of the fact that the elemental beings over time become so burdened by the energies projected by humankind that there comes a point, where they can no longer handle these energies in a harmonious manner. And therefore, they will do what even human beings do. For as human beings can be put under stress to the point, where they either blow up or break down, well the same thing can happen to the elemental beings.

And my beloved, be honest now and step back and look at the history of humankind, as you know it even for these last few thousand years. Can you see how much conflict, how much warfare, has taken place on this planet, just in the very short time span of known history? Can you see that all of this conflict – all of this warfare, all of these atrocities, of man's inhumanity to man – has generated enormous tension, has generated enormous amounts of emotional and mental energy?

Can you see that this energy cannot simply be destroyed, for as science has told you, energy cannot be created or destroyed. This, of course, is a truth with some modifications. For as I have said, energy can be created, in the sense that energy from the spiritual realm can be brought into the material frequency spectrum. Nevertheless, the truth outpictured in the first law of thermodynamics is, indeed, that when you are below the 48th level of consciousness, you cannot be the open door for bringing spiritual energy into the material spectrum. And therefore, from that level of consciousness, it will seem that energy can neither be created nor destroyed.

And what does this mean? It means that when you generate dense or low-frequency mental and emotional energy, then you cannot destroy or get rid of that energy—when you are still below the 48th level of awareness. And that means, that the energies generated by those who have descended below the 48th level have no place to go. They can only be projected upon elemental life, and therefore elemental life will gradually accumulate these energies.

So my beloved, is it any wonder that there comes times, when elemental life can no longer handle this burden? And therefore, the el-

A deeper understanding of the four elements

emental beings must pass on the energy that is burdening them by acting out? And when these very large elemental beings act out, well then you see a volcanic eruption, an earthquake, a tsunami, a violent storm or completely erratic weather patterns—that suddenly bring drought and immense heat or floods that cannot be controlled.

When you begin to realize that the earth is a living, breathing entity, you can see that the earth must respond to the mental and emotional energies generated by humankind. And when these mental and emotional energies take such a low form – as you can see from just looking at the headlines of any given day – well, then can you really wonder that there seems to be an increase in natural disasters? Can you really wonder that the planet can no longer handle the energies projected upon it by humankind?

Then you can begin to see, that if you are willing to be one of the forerunners for healing Mother Earth, then you need to not only understand the effect of humankind's consciousness. You also need to begin to see, how you can make a contribution to counteracting the negative effects produced by the majority of human beings on this planet.

If you are to be one of the forerunners for healing Mother Earth, then you must understand how energy works. And you must understand how you can become the open door for a stream of high-frequency energy that cannot only counteract – but can indeed transform – the low-frequency energy generated by humankind over a very long time span. And this, of course, is precisely the understanding that I and the seven chohans will give you for the remainder of this book.

Key 19
The relationship between humans and elementals

Before I let the seven chohans give you more specific advice about how you can help bring about the changes that will heal Mother Earth – depending on which of the seven rays you feel resonates most with your current level of consciousness – I wish to make sure that you have the full understanding of how consciousness actually works and what is the role of human beings in relation to elemental beings. As I have said, elemental beings have a form of consciousness, but they do not have self-awareness—although this also is a statement that needs to be understood more deeply.

Elemental beings start out as very simple, we might say, beings. An elemental being in its simplest form is designed to perform one specific task. For example, there are certain elemental beings who are designed to bring forth one particular kind of flower. And so, these very small elemental beings perform only one task, namely to bring forth one particular plant.

You may think that this task requires no intercession from a being with consciousness. You may think it is simply a matter of putting a seed in the ground and watering that seed, and then the seed automatically – according to some mechanical law of nature – grows into a flower. This, however, is not the case.

The reality of materialization is that there are two elements involved with this process. First of all, there is nothing that can exist, there is nothing that has ever existed, unless there first was a mental image, or a thoughtform, or a matrix for how that thing should look. So in order for a simple flower to become manifest, there must be a thoughtform. This thoughtform is, of course, either created in a higher realm by the Elohim—or even by human beings. And so, the thoughtform is then impressed upon elemental life, meaning that a tiny elemental does not come up with the thoughtform on its own.

However, if you consider a seed that is put in the ground, it is not correct – as science would have you believe – that all of the information needed to produce the final plant is encoded in the DNA within the seed. If you have a deeper understanding of DNA, you will realize that DNA contains only one kind of instructions, namely the instructions that tell a cell how to produce protein. Protein is, of course, the building blocks of all living organisms, but the fact is that proteins – as atoms and molecules – can be combined in many ways to produce many different forms of living organisms. So the proteins that are produced by plants can produce the vast variety of plant life that you see on this planet. In other words, the essential question that materialistic scientists cannot fully explain is what allows the seed of a marigold to produce a marigold and not a tulip.

Well, the simple fact is that what allows the seed of a marigold to grow into a marigold is that there is an elemental, which has enough consciousness to receive the matrix or thoughtform for a marigold, and which then works with the material, mechanical aspects of the matter realm in order to have the seed grow into the finished plant. In order to do this, however, that tiny elemental is not a self-contained unit. The tiny elemental that brings forth a flower works within the context of a hierarchy of elemental beings. An elemental bringing forth a flower is clearly an earth elemental, and there is a hierarchy of earth elementals.

Even the smallest elemental works with the more complex or larger elementals above it in hierarchy. Yet the earth elementals, of course, fit into the larger hierarchy of all of the four types of elementals, and so, again, there is a progression and a procession. My point is to show you that even the simplest processes in nature are not completely mechanical, but simply could not take place without the work of elemental life.

***

Now, as I have said, the elemental beings respond to external stimuli. You might recall that my basic explanation of consciousness is that it can respond to external stimuli and it can retain what it receives. So what you see is that elemental life responds to external stimuli coming from higher up in the hierarchy of elemental beings, but they also respond to stimuli coming from human beings—because human beings are higher up in the spiritual hierarchy of the earth. And so, once ele-

The relationship between humans and elementals

mental beings have received either energy or thoughtforms from human beings, they will retain this, they will retain these thoughtforms and energies for a time.

Now, as you go up in the hierarchy of elemental beings, for example the earth elementals, you will see that over time an elemental being can grow in awareness, can expand its consciousness. So for example, an elemental being may start out producing simply one kind of flower. But as it grows in awareness, it may graduate to producing larger plants, such as an entire tree. Then, the elemental may go to an even higher level of producing animal forms, animal bodies, eventually growing to producing the most complex form of living bodies on the earth, namely that of a human being.

Your physical body has an elemental, which is often called the body elemental. It is, in fact, this elemental that is responsible for receiving the thoughtform or blueprint for your physical body. And when your mother's egg is fertilized by your father's sperm, the body elemental is assigned to bring forth your physical body precisely according to the blueprint for that body.

That blueprint is, of course, a very complex blueprint, because it is not simply a combination of the DNA of your father and the DNA of your mother. The blueprint for your physical body is very deeply affected by your own state of consciousness, the consciousness that is a combination of the individuality stored in your I AM Presence and the separate self that you have built over many lifetimes, many embodiments, on earth. So bringing forth a human body is indeed a very complex task, that requires an elemental with a very sophisticated state of consciousness.

Yet even beyond this, there are elemental beings of the earth element that have a wider state of consciousness and are therefore involved with bringing forth some of the larger phenomena you see in nature. This can be anything from particular systems in nature – what has somewhat mistakenly been called ecosystems, such an entire forest or the life in a particular ocean – or even larger processes, such as weather patterns or the planet as a whole. There are, in fact, elemental beings who have such a broad and expanded state of consciousness, that they have an awareness of all of the processes that are involved at the physical level of the entire earth, or at the emotional level, the mental level or the etheric level.

I have earlier mentioned the fact that it is possible for elementals to expand their consciousness to the point, where they can be endowed with self-awareness. This will then allow an elemental being to make an evolutionary jump, a quantum leap, and actually embody in a human body instead of producing – becoming – that human body or another phenomenon. The elementals that can make this jump are not actually at the level of the body elemental. Yet those elementals that are at the level of the body elemental can absorb some of the consciousness of the lifestream that embodies the physical body. And this can then accelerate them to the point, where they can begin to look beyond this one body and gain a wider awareness of some of the larger systems in nature. And when elementals rise up to this level, they can gradually, then, acquire the more sophisticated level of consciousness that allows them to be endowed with self-awareness.

So you do indeed have the potential – by raising your own state of consciousness – to endow your body elemental, the elemental that brings forth your current physical body, with a higher state of awareness that can set it on the path towards self-awareness. This is, of course, one of the ways in which you can serve elemental life. But what we especially wish to teach you in this book is the ways that you can serve elemental life on a broader scale than working with just one elemental being. We are in this book, of course, concerned with the healing of Mother Earth, and this requires you to work with the elementals on a much broader, even on a planetary, scale.

***

Now, in order to fulfill your highest potential for working with the elementals, you need to again understand the role of human beings in relation to elemental beings. This role is twofold. I have so far talked about the process of materialization in the form of two elements. There is a thoughtform – a mental image, or a blueprint – that is created at the etheric level and then gradually passed down to the mental, the emotional and finally the physical level. Yet as I have explained, the process of taking the thoughtform down through the levels, is done by impressing the thoughtform upon the basic flow of energy that comes from the spiritual realm and enters the material frequency spectrum through various open doors.

The relationship between humans and elementals

You see, that there are two elements involved, or two sides to this process, namely the thoughtform and the energy that, so to speak, carries the thoughtform into manifestation by taking on the thoughtform as physical matter. So what you do as a human being is that you pass on both the thoughtform and a particular form of energy to elemental life. The energy is what sets things in motion, so that elemental life has something with which to act, something to act upon. It, so to speak, fuels their activity. And of course, the thoughtform will determine what kind of matter phenomenon that the elementals produce with the energy.

You now see, that for you to serve in healing Mother Earth, you must become more aware of this process, so that you can do two things for elemental life. You can, first of all, help to free them from the immense amounts of negative energy put upon them through the struggle that I just described in the last key. And you can also serve in grasping and formulating a higher thoughtform for the potential of planet earth and the potential of human society—and then impressing that thoughtform upon elemental life to replace the imperfect thoughtforms that are currently influencing elemental life.

Now, in order to fully understand this, you need to understand here that there is a difference between thoughtform and energy. A thoughtform is, as you can see, more fluid than an actual physical form. But it is also more fluid than the mental or emotional energy, the psychic energy, that human beings can project upon elemental life. So what you need to understand is that when elemental life has taken on a particular form of energy from human beings – say the energy of anger – then that energy can neither be created nor destroyed at the level of elemental life—or at the level of human beings who are below the 48th level of awareness.

What it will take to free elemental life from this intense energy of anger – or fear, or any other negative emotion – is that a person who is above the 48th level of awareness will become an open door for bringing a higher-vibrating energy into the material spectrum or into the emotional, mental or etheric spectrum. When you become the open door for bringing a higher frequency of energy into a particular level, you can then direct this high-frequency energy at the low-frequency energy that is burdening elemental life.

If you have ever studied the form of physics called wave mechanics, you will see that if two waves meet, they can interact in various ways. One is that a high-frequency wave can actually raise the frequency of a low-frequency wave. What I am talking about here is that a higher vibration of mental and emotional energy, such as the higher vibration of love, can indeed raise the vibration of lower frequency energy, such as the energy of anger or fear. You might even recall from the Bible, that there is a statement which says that perfect love casts out fear. This is because the higher frequency energy of love will completely transform, will completely raise the vibration of, the lower frequency energy of fear.

Elemental life itself cannot be the open door for the bringing forth of energy from a higher realm, for they do not have self-awareness. So when elemental life in one area of the planet becomes overly burdened by the energy, their only option is to try to spread out this energy by throwing it off themselves. And this is then what creates what we have seen as natural disasters or erratic weather patterns or other phenomena.

What you can do as a human being is to use appropriate spiritual techniques for invoking spiritual light. And then you can – again through the right techniques and through your visualization – direct that energy to specifically transform the negative energy burdening elemental life. You can do this on a local scale, or you can do it on a planetary scale. I have, for several years now, brought forth a number of rosaries and invocations and even decrees through this messenger that are suited for this purpose. We of the Ascended Host have, however, brought forth other techniques through other messengers that are also suited for this purpose. So it is not here our intention to say that there is only one way for you to do this. In fact, even engaging in a positive activity will generate positive energy.

For example, even when people come together in a family and have a positive encounter, they will generate positive energy that will actually ease the burden of elemental life. And if many people come together in a positive endeavor, then that will, of course, have an even greater effect. Yet if you want to have the maximum impact on easing the burden of elemental life, then I do indeed suggest that you look into using various tools for invoking and directing spiritual light.

***

So beyond doing a direct invocation, there is, of course, a more long-term process. Using an invocation to invoke spiritual light is something

The relationship between humans and elementals 301

you can do right now at your current level of awareness. Yet over the long term, as you raise your level of awareness, you will begin to become more aware of the higher levels of your own mind. And this will eventually allow you to become more of an open door, whereby the energies from your I AM Presence and your I Will Be Presence can stream through you in greater quantity and intensity. So what I am saying is that at the lower levels of awareness, you can make a great service, and also enhance your own personal growth, by directly invoking spiritual energy.

But as you rise beyond the 96th level of awareness, you no longer have the same need to invoke spiritual energy. For now your consciousness has become so transparent, that you begin to become the open door for a constant flow of high-frequency spiritual energy. This is indeed what you saw with Jesus, and what you have seen with many other people who have attained some degree of spiritual mastery. Jesus was the open door for more spiritual energy in one second than most people at lower levels of consciousness could invoke by giving invocations for a long time.

Of course, in order to raise your level of awareness, you will have to make a determined effort to follow the spiritual path. We have given several other books and numerous very extensive teachings on our website [www.askrealjesus.com] through this messenger, and these teachings are directly aimed at helping you raise your consciousness. Of course, in order to raise your consciousness, you also have to be aware of how consciousness actually works at your level as a human being.

***

I have said that the basic qualities of consciousness is the ability to respond to stimuli and the ability to retain. Well, you, of course, have that ability. But in your case, you have a much more sophisticated ability than elemental life. Elemental life will literally respond to any impulse directed at them from without, and they will retain whatever has been impressed upon them, both the energy and the thoughtform. You have self-awareness, which means that you have the potential – mind you, that I say "potential," for most human beings are not aware of it and therefore are not exercising it – to choose what you take on and what you retain.

Your highest potential is that you attune your consciousness, your conscious awareness, to your I Will Be Presence, so that you can act upon any impulse you receive, any impulse that comes from your Presence. And you are the open door for that impulse being impressed upon elemental life, and therefore taking on physical form. However, you are, of course, also open to impulses that come to you from the world in which you have embodied, so you can receive impulses from without. However, when you have raised your awareness, you will not simply act on those impulses. You will refer them to your I Will Be Presence, and then you will allow the return current from your Presence to determine your response to the external stimuli.

In other words, what you see in most human beings today is that they do not have enough self-awareness, enough self-mastery, to choose their response to outer situations. Take for example the admonishment given by Jesus 2,000 years ago, to not resist evil but to turn the other cheek. Can you see that most human beings today, if someone slaps them on one cheek, they are likely to respond in a very negative way, by either hitting back or by responding with fear or submission to the abuse? Both of these reactions is not what Jesus talked about.

What Jesus talked about requires you to have complete mastery over your state of mind, so that you do not allow other people to project at you either a thoughtform or an energy that is below the level of love. And when people do project at you lower thoughtforms and energies, you can, as your highest potential, allow them to pass right through you, without creating any emotional reaction in you. And by thus being in a neutral state of consciousness here below, you become the open door for the Presence to respond through you and mirror back to the other people what they are projecting at you.

This is a degree of self-mastery that allows you to be open door for the Presence to bring forth thoughtforms and energy impulses that can transform other people, and on a larger scale even human society. Yet in order for you to attain this mastery, you need to first of all attune to your Presence. But then, you also need to become more conscious of the four levels of the mind, what has sometimes been called the four lower bodies, namely the identity body, the mental body, the emotional body and the level of the physical body, the physical mind. And then, you need to look at both the thoughtforms and the energies that have accumulated at these four levels, not only in this lifetime but in other lifetimes as well.

The relationship between humans and elementals

And by becoming more aware of what you have attained, you can begin to exercise your power to choose what you will allow to remain in your four lower bodies. And then, you can begin to do some housecleaning and clean out both the accumulated energies and the thoughtforms that spring from the duality consciousness and the consciousness of separation. For right now you are likely to have many of the thoughtforms that have been projected upon humankind by the fallen beings, the false teachers. And you are also likely to have a certain accumulation of low-frequency energy, such as fear, anger, resentment, the tendency to judge, to be critical or other energies. And these energies will, of course, block the flow of energy from your I Will Be Presence, and the many thoughtforms from duality will also block you from receiving the pure thoughtforms, the non-dualistic thoughtforms, from your Presence.

***

Now again, going through this process is not something you can do overnight. I know very well that there is a delicate balance to be found here, and I wish to make you aware of it. You see, the people who are most likely to be open to this book are the people, who have a great desire to do something for Mother Earth. And this desire naturally makes you want to do something that seems to you to make the most difference, to have the greatest impact. You want to feel that what you are doing is worthwhile.

However, if you step back and take a look at current Western society, you will see that there are a couple of things in the mass consciousness that can very easily derail your efforts to be one of the forerunners for healing Mother Earth. One is what we might call the push-button mentality and the other is what we might call the desire for instant results or a quick-fix. Because you have grown up around technology, you are so used to having devices around you, where you can push a certain button and then the device will mechanically produce a certain result. And this can often make you think that healing Mother Earth should be a matter of finding the right button to push, and then you should be able to see an almost instantaneous result of your efforts.

Of course, this is closely combined with the other state of consciousness that has been projected by the consumer society, namely that of instant gratification. For you have been brought up to think that you should not have to wait for anything. If you want something and if you find the right buttons to push, then the results should be instantaneous. The combination of these two mindsets can very easily derail your efforts to help heal Mother Earth. As I have attempted to explain, the current state of the earth is a product of the collective state of consciousness of humankind. Yet the current state of the earth was not produced by the collective consciousness overnight; it was produced over a very long time span. So it is not realistic that anything you do as one individual can have an instantly visible result on the planetary level.

Now, please take a look at yourself and see what reaction this statement might have produced in your mind. Do you feel discouraged? Do you feel that if you cannot make an instant difference, then it is not worthwhile to make an effort at all? For if you do, I can assure you that this is exactly what the fallen beings, the power elite, want you to feel.

***

I have talked about a path, a true path, towards a higher state of consciousness, called the path of Christhood. Yet the fallen beings, the false teachers, have created a false path, an outer path. And the very goal of this false path is to make sure that no individual will ever raise his or her consciousness to the point, where they become open doors, just as Jesus and the Buddha and other enlightened beings were the open doors.

And one of the very subtle thoughtforms projected by these fallen beings is precisely that the individual cannot make a difference—and therefore, there is no point in even trying. The reality, that we of the Ascended Host have taught for a very long time – and that Jesus embodied 2,000 years ago and that the Buddha embodied 2,500 years ago – is that the individual can indeed make a difference.

You will obviously make the greatest difference by raising your consciousness to the 96th level and beyond. For truly, when you go beyond the 96th level, then even one person can have an instantaneous, visible impact on the planetary level and can produce visible changes and visible phenomena that demonstrate the power of mind over matter. Yet even if you are currently below the 96th level of awareness, there is still no reason to be discouraged.

For, first of all, anything you do will make a greater difference than doing nothing. There is no effort that could ever be wasted, for anything

The relationship between humans and elementals   305

you do – to raise your own consciousness or to invoke spiritual light
to lighten the burden of elemental life – will improve the planet. And
certainly, you can see that if you do nothing, then you will not have any
positive effect. And then, of course, there is the potential that you can
make your personal effort, and many other people will also make a personal effort. And as soon as you have more than one person making the
same kind of effort, then the accumulated effect will be far greater than
the sum of the parts. You might have heard the saying that the whole is
more than the sum of the parts. Well, this is indeed also what Jesus referred to in a veiled form, when he said that "when two or three of you
are gathered in my name, there I am in the midst of them."

This means that for people who are between the 48th and the 96th
level of awareness, they do not have enough self-awareness to be able
to be the open door for the Christ consciousness on an individual basis.
Yet when two or more people join together, with a state of harmony and
synchronicity, then they will collectively be able to be an open door for
the Christ consciousness. And this means that as more and more people
begin to engage in activities that help heal Mother Earth, they will form
an upward momentum that will gradually enable them to bring forth
new thoughtforms and high-frequency spiritual energies that will accelerate the process of healing.

***

In other words, once a momentum has started building, it will gradually become a self-reinforcing process that will take on more and more
momentum, more and more speed and intensity. And certainly, I think
you can see – if you are open to this book – that the process whereby
people have consciously attempted to raise their consciousness has been
going on for a long time on this planet. And especially since the 1960s,
there has also been a process that has raised people's awareness of and
understanding of environmental issues.

So can you see that anything you do as a result of reading this book,
will indeed tie in to this momentum, this collective momentum that has
already been started? And therefore, it is not as if you are sitting here as
an isolated individual, and you have to start your own personal process
from ground zero. There is already a momentum, and you might envision it as if you are standing on the banks of a river, and you can see

that the water is flowing by you. All you really have to do is to dare to jump into the water, and as long as you are no longer standing still on the shore, the water will immediately begin to carry you with it.

And then, as you raise your consciousness and as you invoke spiritual light, you will actually add on to the momentum of the water. And as many people do this, they can – within a surprisingly short period of time – produce a momentum that will build such an upward thrust, that it will begin to have a planetary impact.

This impact will have two distinct forms. One is that you will see an opening in people's awareness to new ideas. Go back to the 1960s and see how most people were not even open to the possibility that chemicals could enter the food chain and therefore have a long-term effect on their health or the health of their children. Yet this is an awareness that most people are open to today, and you will also see that as people begin to raise their awareness, some of the ideas in this book – that most people at the present would reject outright – will gradually find their way into the environmental debate and the broader debate in society. The more you open your mind to these ideas – the more you talk about them, the more you project them into the collective consciousness – well the more people will be open to such ideas.

And then of course, as people begin to invoke and direct positive spiritual energy, you will see that elemental life will become unburdened by its present burdens. And this will, within a matter of years, have a visible effect in reducing the frequency and intensity of natural disasters.

What we are presenting to you in this book is not some far-flung utopian scheme. It is a very practical, realistic – one might say "scientific" – process. If enough people accept the basic premise of this book and engage in the process of raising their consciousness and invoking spiritual energy, then you can build a momentum within just a few years, and you will notice the planetary impact. You will notice that society will become more open to a connection between consciousness and matter, and you will notice that society will begin to become aware of the limitations of force-based solutions and force-based technology.

This will then open society to the receiving of new ideas and new forms of technology that can, as we have mentioned before, produce unlimited amounts of energy in ways that do not pollute at all—and do not even use up the so-called natural resources, as you currently know them. Just imagine what would happen to the environmental problems you currently see, if there was one form of technology that was available to all people and could not be monopolized by a small power elite. And then imagine that this form of technology could produce unlimited amounts of energy, without polluting and without making it necessary to conduct large-scale mining operations in order to extract oil or coal or other forms of minerals from the earth. Can you see how this one form of technology could completely change the environmental issue on planet earth?

My beloved, let me tell you with absolute surety that this form of technology already exists in the spiritual realm. In fact, the technology and the knowledge required to produce it has already been brought into the lower etheric realm and is beginning to be lowered into the mental realm. Yet it is currently being blocked, partially by the dense consciousness of humankind and partially by the dense energies accumulated in the mental and emotional levels of the collective consciousness.

$$***$$

So, what I want you to grasp here is the potential for changes that most people today would consider unrealistic or utopian. Yet my beloved, let me ask you to consider whether there, in your home country, is one of these museums, where they have taken old houses and moved them to a location and rebuilt them, so that they now stand in their original condition with the original furniture and the original technology and tools used 100 years ago, or maybe even 200 years ago? If there is such a museum, I encourage you to visit it and see how – even a little more than 100 years ago – they did not have electricity. They did not have cars, they did not have nuclear power, they did not have airplanes, they did not have computers or the Internet.

My beloved, if you had taken your great grandfather and grandmother and had told them about the technology that you have grown up to take for granted, they would have looked at you with absolute disbelief and thought you were telling them a lie. You were telling them about things that could never come to pass and certainly could never come to pass in such a short time span as a mere century.

Do you not see that within the last century, there has been incredible changes in human society? So when you realize that all of these immense changes have been based on force-based technology and the force-based mindset, then can you not begin to imagine that when humankind transcends the force-based mindset, even more dramatic changes can take place, and they can take place very quickly?

So this is the vision, this is the potential, that I want you to grasp in this key. For we of the Ascended Host are extremely enthusiastic and optimistic about the future of this planet. And if you are to be one of the forerunners for healing Mother Earth, it is essential that you begin to grasp his optimism, this enthusiasm.

You might recall that there are people who will say that they are not being pessimistic, when they paint a negative picture of the future of this planet, especially about environmental conditions. The motto of most pessimists is indeed: "I am not a pessimist; I am a realist!" But my beloved, with everything we have told you in this book so far, can you see that being a pessimist is not being realistic? For the reality is that the potential for growth, for progress, is unlimited.

When a critical mass of people raise their consciousness beyond the 48th level, you will see a major shift in society. As even a small group of people go beyond the 96th level, you will see even greater changes. The fact of the matter is that matter responds to consciousness; and the higher the consciousness, the more dramatic the response.

The current conditions you see on earth are produced by a lower state of consciousness, and when enough people attain a higher state of consciousness, they can very quickly transcend the current condition. They can project thoughtforms and positive energy onto elemental life, that will remove some of the conditions that many people today think could never be overcome.

This is reality—when you understand that matter is a product of consciousness. When you do understand that matter is a product of consciousness, you see why this is reality. And then you see why I, and other ascended masters, are, indeed, the true realists.

For we know the truth behind the words spoken by Jesus 2,000 years ago: "With men this is impossible, but not with God, for with God all things are possible." With people who are below the 48th level of consciousness, many things are indeed impossible. But for those who are above the 48th level, many things become possible. And we are not here talking about miracles, we are talking about the application of the very fundamental laws of how the universe works.

This is the vision and the enthusiasm that I want you to grasp. My beloved, have you grasped it?

Key 20
The process of materialization, of matter realization

Let us now go deeper into the process of materialization, of "matter realization." Let us begin by looking at an ideal or pure scenario. We begin in the spiritual realm with the Elohim formulating a mental image, a blueprint for the manifestation of a particular form. As a simple example, let us just take a flower. This blueprint is then passed on from the Elohim to the etheric realm. The blueprint is passed on in the form of an image, which is charged with a certain energy impulse, a certain creative impulse.

The image and the impulse are received by the fire elementals at the etheric level. The fire elementals at the etheric level are the ones who are in charge of the most subtle level of matter, which is the level that science currently calls subatomic particles.

However, it is important for you to understand that what science has been doing for far too long is holding on to an image of the world that is based on the senses. And the senses, of course, cannot see subatomic so-called particles. And therefore, to take a sensory-based image, namely that of a particle, and project it upon the subatomic world is simply not realistic.

You might know, if you have studied quantum physics, that there is a phenomenon called the wave-particle duality. Which means that a subatomic so-called particle will sometimes behave like a regular particle, namely a small billiard ball zooming around, and will sometimes behave like a wave. In fact scientists are aware that if they are looking for a particle, the subatomic entity will behave as a particle, and if they are looking for a wave, the subatomic entity will behave as a wave.

This clearly shows you that the subatomic world is not made up of hard particles or waves but is made up of a finer substance or element that has the ability to take on any form. The reason why scientists have been confused about this is that they will not actually accept the logical consequence from certain other findings of quantum physics. As we have mentioned before, scientists have realized that until they make an observation, there really is no actual particle or wave. There is nothing there—if you apply a sensory-based perception to the situation.

So the reality here is that at the subatomic level, the etheric realm, there is no "thing." There is neither a particle nor a wave; there is only what I have called the Ma-ter light. But of course the Ma-ter light is the Mother light, and it is also the "substance" that makes up the spiritual realm. So the reality is that at the etheric level, you find a specific form of the Ma-ter light, which vibrates at the basic frequency that is used to create the entire sphere in which you currently abide.

The important point that I want to get across here is, however, that the basic substance that makes up your sphere cannot be detected by current scientific instruments. What scientists can detect is when the basic substance has been stirred into beginning to take on form. In other words, the Ma-ter light is neither a particle nor a wave. So therefore, scientists cannot detect the light directly. They can detect the light only indirectly, when the light begins the process of materialization, by taking on the form of what scientists see as either a particle or a wave.

In the not-too-distant future, scientists will develop an entirely different conceptual language, which will then allow them to finally develop the theories that they have been attempting to develop now for a very long time. Yet I will not go into that here, as it is too far beyond the purpose of this book.

So what I want to focus on here is that at the etheric level, you have a certain basic energy or substance, namely what I call the Ma-ter light. What the fire elementals do is that they are in charge of taking this Ma-ter light and building out of it the phenomena that scientists are currently discovering as subatomic phenomena. This is, as science has correctly realized, the basic building blocks of the material universe.

So when the Elohim project an image into the etheric realm, the fire elementals begin to provide the first step in a process that will bring this image into the material or physical frequency spectrum as an actual flower. This means that the fire elementals in general are providing the basic substance out of which the flower will be built, namely subatomic particles and waves, the very building blocks of atoms.

Then, a particular tiny fire elemental will be assigned to the flower thoughtform. If the thoughtform is more complex, then a fire elemental

The process of materialization, of matter realization

with a more expanded consciousness will be assigned to the thought-form. The fire elemental that takes on the thoughtform of a flower then becomes a sort of messenger, which now brings the thoughtform, and with it the associated energy impulse, into the mental realm.

***

The air elementals are in charge of the level of matter that scientists call atoms. You will notice that at the level of subatomic particles, matter is really not solid at all; it is quite ethereal. And therefore, it has much of the same substance or appearance that you can see, when you are looking at a fire, where a block of wood is etherialized by the fire. At the level of atoms, you see – if you look at the current model developed by science – that the atom can be depicted as a miniature solar system. There is a nucleus or core of the atom, and around it you have a number of smaller particles that are orbiting, much like planets are orbiting around the sun.

This, of course, is, as even scientists are realizing, not an entirely accurate model of the atom. Nevertheless, the reason why I am using it is that it shows you the basic quality of atoms. When you look at the solar system, you realize that even though there is a certain amount of mass in the solar system – in the form of the sun and the planets – most of what you call the solar system is actually empty space. There is a vast distance between the earth and the sun, for example. And so, the point is that at the level of the atoms, the atom is mostly empty space. Which, of course, corresponds to the element of air, that is also largely empty space. And so, even at this level, things are still very fluid.

Again, at the mental level a particular elemental is assigned to the thoughtform and now takes on a form that is, of course, based on the original thoughtform but is a step closer to actual manifestation—meaning that it is more dense than the etheric thoughtform. The air elemental that takes on this thoughtform is, of course – in the ideal scenario – working under the fire elemental. So we now see the beginning of the formation of a hierarchy, where the fire elemental is at the top and the air elemental beneath it. Which means that the air elemental works within the parameters set by the fire elemental.

The air elemental then becomes the messenger that brings the thoughtform and the energy impulse into the emotional realm. The emotional realm corresponds to the level of molecules, where you now have several atoms that combine together to form a larger structure. And therefore, you see that at the level of molecules – even though there is still great fluidity – nevertheless, the molecule is a more dense or manifest entity than the atoms. This corresponds to the fact that the water element is more dense than the air element. And so, at the level of the water element, you see that the elemental that takes on the thoughtform, has the ability to gather together many different atoms and then hold them in a certain matrix.

This is something that is important to keep in mind, for the water element corresponds to the emotional body of an individual or the emotional body of humankind. And it is often precisely disturbing emotions that prevent the manifestation of a harmonious thoughtform and creates many imbalances in the body of the Earth Mother or the body of an individual human being.

This is precisely because it is essential at the emotional level to hold together the atoms in a certain matrix. And if the atoms are not held together in the right matrix, then the manifestation at the physical level will be disharmonious. And of course, what can prevent the atoms from being held together in the ideal matrix is precisely violent or imperfect emotions.

Yet we were talking about the ideal scenario, so let me not get too far ahead of myself. In the ideal scenario, the elemental in the water element takes on the thoughtform and gathers the atoms together into molecules. And then, the water elemental becomes a messenger that brings the thoughtform and the energy impulse into the physical vibrational spectrum, which corresponds to the earth element.

At the physical level, there is again an elemental which takes on the thoughtform and therefore becomes the bottom level of the newly formed hierarchy. And the earth elemental takes on the thoughtform in such a way that it manifests the actual physical form that you can see with the senses. This can be any matter form that is made out of molecules.

***

Now, because my example centered around the production of a flower, we need to add here a special consideration. You know, of course, that

The process of materialization, of matter realization 315

all living organisms are made up of cells. You also know that cells are made up of molecules, which are made up of atoms, which are made up of a finer energy. Yet the difference between so-called inert matter and living cells is that there is a much higher degree of ethereal or spiritual energy – the fire element – in the living cells than you find in inert matter.

And this, of course, is what gives a cell the basis for serving as the foundation for a more active form of consciousness than you find in inert matter, such as for example a rock. There is a very basic form of consciousness in a rock, because again the Ma-ter light has enough consciousness to respond to an external stimuli and to retain the form imposed upon it through that stimuli.

Nevertheless, when you talk about a living cell, you see something that has a higher form of consciousness, because the living cell will not simply retain the form originally impressed upon it. The cell is actually complex enough to have an entire system, whereby it can respond to external stimuli in a self-sufficient manner. There is enough information and awareness at the level of a cell that it can respond to stimuli from its surroundings at the material level, based on the information encoded in the DNA.

And this, of course, is what has caused current scientists, who are so focused on the materialistic viewpoint, to conclude that the cell is a completely self-contained unit. And that the DNA, therefore, must contain all of the information that is needed to build an entire human body.

This is actually a misinterpretation, because the reality is that the cell has enough awareness, so that your body can maintain itself without your conscious awareness. In other words, you, yourself, do not have to consciously tell your cells how to function, you do not have to tell your heart to beat. Yet these functions are carried out in very close cooperation with – and certainly under the tutelage of – your body elemental. And even though your body elemental does not have to consciously tell each cell in your body how to function, the cells nevertheless could not organize themselves into the complex matrix of your body.

So the point about living cells that you need to keep in mind is, that there is a greater portion of the fire element in a living cell than what you find in inert matter. Which means that the cell can stay alive only when the flow of energy from the etheric realm is maintained at a certain level. When this flow is reduced beyond a certain level, then the very life force that, so to speak, breathes fire into the cell, will stop. And then, the living cell will return to the inert matter out of which it is fashioned.

In other words, the living cell now simply becomes dead matter, that has the same level of consciousness as the dust of the earth. Which is the background for the saying you find in Genesis that you have come from dust and shall return to dust. This saying is, of course, not applicable to the core of your being, for you are a spiritual being. It is applicable only to your physical body, which was fashioned out of the "dust," so to speak, of the earth element and will return to it, when the flow of life from the etheric realm, when the flow of the fire element, is reduced beneath a certain level.

***

So what does this mean for you? Well, I have given you the simple thoughtform of how a flower is brought into materialization, beginning with the thoughtform at the level of the Elohim. Nevertheless, you are a self-aware being that has taken embodiment in the material realm. So you are meant to be – in the ideal scenario – the extension of the Elohim. You are meant to be a co-creator with the Elohim. And you actually have the ability to expand your awareness to the point, where you can literally work with elemental life to bring forth a new thoughtform.

You might know, for example, that there have been certain people who have had an unusual ability to bring forth new plant forms or new animal breeds. These are people who have developed their ability to work with elemental life to the point, where they can actually create the mental image of a new plant and then superimpose that image upon the four levels of elemental life, until the new plant is brought forth. Inventors are doing somewhat similar things, in that they are also able to receive a thoughtform from a higher level. And then bring it to the point, where it can actually be turned into a new form of technology or even a new creation, such as a particular device, or a sculpture, or a painting, or a house, or anything else.

***

The process of materialization, of matter realization

Now, if you take the ideal scenario again, then you will see that when a new co-creator starts at the 48th level of awareness, it does not have the ability to actually materialize something new. Nevertheless, as it experiments with its creative abilities, it can gradually expand its awareness and thereby its creative abilities. At the 48th level of awareness, you can still manifest things but you have to do it by working at the level of the earth elementals.

Do you see what this means? At the level of the earth elementals, you have a group of beings who are working in a hierarchy. They are working under the water elementals, the air elementals and the fire elementals. At the level of the earth element, things have, so to speak, already become somewhat set in a particular matrix, based on the thought-forms that have been impressed upon it from above.

So when your consciousness is able to work only with the earth level, the earth element, then there is a limit to what you can bring forth. In other words, your consciousness has the power to impress a thought-form upon the earth elementals, but it has not yet acquired the higher power required to impress a thoughtform on the water elementals. This is why there is a limit to what you can bring forth at that level.

Now, when you go below the 48th level of awareness, you actually even lose the ability to impress a thoughtform on the earth elementals. And that is why the book of Genesis says that after Adam and Eve were, so to speak, "cast" out of paradise, they had to work out a living at the sweat of their brow. This is a symbol for the fact that they now had to work with the physical power of the physical body. In other words, instead of working with the earth elementals and impressing a certain thoughtform upon the earth elementals – for example the bringing forth of an abundant field with crops – then you now had to physically go out and plow the field and plant the seeds and water and tend them, until they grow into a crop.

Do you see what I am saying? At the level of the earth elementals, the elementals are quite capable of bringing forth plant life. When you have the ability to work with the earth elementals, you can, for example, hold the mental image of a wheat field. And then, when you impress that image upon the earth elementals with sufficient intensity, they will actually bring forth the wheat field without you having to do physical work.

This is actually how people gained physical sustenance in previous ages, before the descent into duality. However, when you go beneath the 48th level, you cannot bring forth a wheat field by impressing a thoughtform upon elemental life. And that is why you have to produce the wheat field by doing the physical work of tilling the ground, planting the seed, watering it, keeping it free from pests or diseases or birds or animals, until it is finally ready to harvest.

***

So again, as you increase your awareness from the 48th level and up, you eventually acquire the awareness, where you can now superimpose an image upon the water elementals, the elementals of the water element. And this means that you can now actually bring forth things that are beyond what is already existing at the physical level.

In other words, instead of bringing forth a field of a pre-existing plant, you can now envision a new plant form, and you can then bring that forth. Yet you will still have to do it by working with the natural processes that are already in place at the level of elemental life. In other words, you are not directly manifesting or precipitating a flower; you are working with the elementals to bring it forth based on another flower that you then manage to breed into a different variety.

Now, as you increase your awareness even more, you become, of course, able to impress a thoughtform directly on the air elementals. And then, as you go beyond the 96th level and come closer to the 144th level, you will actually be able to impress a thoughtform directly on the fire elementals.

And it is at that point, that you acquire the creative abilities that you saw demonstrated by Jesus, where he could directly manifest of form in a way that seemed miraculous. Yet if you actually took a closer look at the life of Jesus, which is beyond the scope of this book, you would see that he gradually followed the pattern I have just described. For example, healing a withered hand is showing mastery over the physical element. Walking on water is showing mastery over the emotional or water element. Calming the storm is mastery over the air element, and so forth. Where the highest was waking up a dead body by breathing new life into it, and thereby demonstrating mastery of the fire element.

So the point I want to make here is that when you reach the level, where you have a high degree of Christ consciousness – and therefore have the mastery of mind over matter – you can formulate a mental im-

The process of materialization, of matter realization

age, even while you are still in a physical body. You can then project that image, first on the fire elementals, then on the air elementals, then on the water elementals and then on the earth elementals. And therefore, you can see a manifestation of your image that is very swift and very direct. The higher your level of consciousness, the more direct the manifestation will be.

At the lower levels of being able to work with all four levels of elementals, it will take some time before your thoughtform is manifest. Because it will be up to the elementals to bring the thoughtform down through the four levels at the speed that you were able to generate. If you are at the highest level, you can generate a creative impulse that is so intense, that the manifestation will be almost instantaneous. But of course, the lower the intensity of the creative impulse you generate, the longer it will take for your thoughtform to be manifest in the physical realm.

So now that you have a greater understanding of this process, you can see how this is your highest potential to heal the Earth Mother. It is, of course, also your highest potential to heal your own physical body and to bring forth all of the things you might desire for your physical survival or physical comfort. Now that we have this understanding, we need to take a look at the current conditions as opposed to the ideal conditions.

Key 21
Overcoming the illusion that matter has permanence

We can – theoretically – begin at either end, but let us begin at the lowest level, namely the earth element. What you see at the level of the earth elementals is that there is currently a very high density and a very high degree of imbalance in the natural environment on earth. This is because the earth elementals are greatly burdened by the negative energy put upon elemental life by human beings. Here is how you need to understand this.

The image I want to give you is that the way you have grown up to look at the material world is a complete illusion. Your senses are telling you that matter is solid, but you know from science that matter is not solid; it is made out of smaller building blocks, called molecules, which are again made out of atoms. And as I have just said, when you look at the atom, you see that most of it is empty space.

So even when you take a rock that appears to be quite dense and solid, you know it is mostly empty space. You may hold it in your hand, and it feels solid to your physical sense of touch. But this is because your physical sense of touch is very much tied to the physical body, and therefore it is attuned to the density of the physical body. And because the physical body is made out of the same basic substance as a rock, it is obvious that to the somewhat solid body, a rock will appear even more solid.

***

Yet what you need to do in your mind is that you need to begin to see that physical matter is not solid, and it is not permanent. In order to give you a linear image, imagine that the physical matter you see around you is really just a projection of an image, much like the image you see on a movie screen. When you are looking at a movie, you can become so engrossed in the movie, that you think you are actually looking at something real. If you are watching a movie of a sunset, you might forget you are in a movie theater, and you might think you are actually standing on the beach, looking at the sun set in an actual ocean.

Yet when you step back from this immersion experience, you see that the image on the screen is not the real world; it is an image that is simply projected onto the screen. It is not even painted onto the screen as a permanent image, for every second many individual images are projected onto the screen. And when you think about this, you realize that what you see in the material world is not a permanent world. It is a fluid world that is projected onto the screen of life, the screen of the Ma-ter might, and it is projected many, many times every second.

The mechanism that is projecting the image is elemental life, which can be compared to a movie projector. You know, for example, that a movie projector has several elements. The driving force in the projector is the light bulb, and this compares to the stream of energy that comes from the spiritual realm and starts descending through the etheric, mental, emotional and physical levels. These four levels of the material universe compare to the film strip. So now imagine that you have a movie projector that has four film strips, and so the light from the light bulb has to pass through all of the four film strips before it reaches the screen. So you can now see, that instead of just having one image, then you have four images.

This is not too difficult to understand, if you consider that instead of having one film strip you had four of them. It might be easiest to imagine this if you imagine an animated movie, where, for example, you had certain characters that were walking through a particular landscape. So you might imagine that there was one film strip that contains the background, such as mountains or a forest scene. Then you have another film strip on which is painted the nearest environment, such as a village. On the third film strip you might have painted certain animals that are part of the scene, and on the fourth film strip you have painted the actual characters that are part of this particular scene. So you now see that the image that was projected onto the movie screen, was projected through these four film strips.

This image is fruitful, because it shows you something very important. Imagine that the four film strips suddenly started going out of sync. For example, the characters might be acting as if they are on the

Overcoming the illusion that matter has permanence

beach, and therefore the film strip showing the background should show a beach scene. But now imagine that the background moved on and started showing a city scene, when the film strip showing the characters still showed them in their beach outfits.

In other words, there would be a lack of synchronicity between the four levels, the four film strips. So you can now imagine that if there is a lack of synchronicity between the four levels of elemental life, then it is no wonder that you see certain imbalances or a certain chaos or confusion at the physical level. What are the earth elementals to do, if they are slightly out of sync with the water elementals? And what if the water elementals are slightly out of sync with the air elementals and so on?

Now, the other thing, of course, that is important for the movie screen to show the right image is that there is nothing interfering with the light, as it is passing through the air to the movie screen. So you can imagine, for example, that you could have various phenomena that would interfere with this process. You might release so much smoke in the movie theater, that the light rays could not pass through it and reach the film strip in their pure form, but that they were slightly distorted by the smoke. You could also send actual light rays into the beam coming from the movie projector and thereby interfere with the image on the screen. And so, this is, of course, what you see when elemental life is burdened by the disharmonious energies of humankind.

The earth elementals, for example, can be so burdened that they are not able to bring forth a completely healthy wheat field. And therefore, they might bring forth plants that have various diseases or even that have fewer kernels of grain on them. You will also see, for example, that the water elementals might not be able to bring forth sufficient rain to nourish the wheat field. Or the air elementals might be so burdened that they will bring a violent storm that will damage the crop.

You now see that in the current situation on planet earth, you do not have the ideal scenario, where the Elohim can impress a certain thoughtform upon the fire elementals, and then that thoughtform with its creative impulse will be swiftly carried through all four levels and manifest as a physical flower that is exactly like the Elohim envisioned it. What you have instead is that – at each of the four levels of elemental life – you have what we might call interference or static. Instead of getting the pure radio signals, so you can hear the announcer's voice clearly, you get static so you only hear broken pieces of the message.

This, of course, is repeated both at the level of the earth elementals, at the level of the water elementals, at the level of the air elementals and at the level of the fire element.

***

So let me now make a leap and start looking at the highest level. Your etheric body is the body that holds your basic sense of identity, your basic worldview. What has happened on planet earth is that human beings have been seduced by the duality consciousness and misled by the fallen beings.

This is symbolized in the Genesis story of how Eve was deceived by the serpent in the Garden of Eden. The reality is that all human beings were deceived by the Serpent, namely the serpentine consciousness— which is based on a fundamental division. The most fundamental division is that the matter world is divided from the spirit world, that God's creation is separated from God. This is the basic illusion that the fallen beings accepted in a higher sphere, and they have attempted to carry it with them and impress it upon all human beings on earth. Needless to say, they have been successful for the vast majority of human beings, who are not even questioning this illusion.

What happens at the etheric level is, that when you begin to accept the serpentine illusion, you begin to see yourself as a separate being. The Conscious You now creates a separate self, a separate identity, and it then enters into and begins to look at the world through this separate self. This has, as we have attempted to explain earlier, not changed the fundamental reality of the Conscious You. You are still pure awareness, but you are looking at the world through the filter of the separate self, as if you – as a human being – were looking at the world through colored glasses.

So what happens in your identity body, when you start looking at the world through the filter of a separate self, is that you become subject to the most fundamental feeling possible on earth. And this feeling is the fear of death. The price you pay for experiencing the world through a separate self is that you cannot escape the fear of death.

There are psychologists who say that there are two basic emotions available to human beings, namely fear and love. There is validity to this viewpoint. When you are not looking at the world through the filter of a

Overcoming the illusion that matter has permanence

separate self, you will feel the stream of God's love from your I Will Be Presence flowing through you and being directed at all life here below. You will have no fear, you will experience the perfect love that casts out all fear. And therefore, there will be nothing in your identity body that will distort or block the creative flow from your I Will Be Presence.

Your identity body is the perfectly open door for receiving thought-forms and energy impulses from the Presence, which it will then pass on to your mental body in their pure form and with no diminishing of the creative impulse. So what happens when your identity body is affected by the illusion that you are a separate self, is that now you can no longer receive the thoughtforms from your I Will Be Presence in their purest form. These thoughtforms will be somewhat distorted by the illusion of separation in your identity body.

So instead of actually believing that any thoughtform which the Presence gives you can be manifest as a physical reality, you now have either a doubt or even a fundamental denial of the possibility that a thoughtform could have power over matter and become manifest in matter. And this, of course, is what you see in most human beings to-day—who think they have to work out their living by the sweat of their brow, by their physical, bodily abilities.

What also happens at the level of your identity body, is that your fear of death obviously generates a certain vibration. In other words, the energy impulse that comes to you from your I AM Presence is pure love, which is simply an energy that vibrates above a certain level of vibration. When you have the fear of death in your identity body, then the flow of pure love will be lowered in vibration, so that it manifests as a lower form of energy than the pure love. And the more fear you have – the more you are focusing your attention on death and the potential for death – well, the more of this disharmonious energy you will create.

If we return to my image of the movie projector with four film strips, you see that your identity body is the first film strip that the light from your I Will Be Presence must pass through in your personal mind, your personal movie projector. So now imagine that at this first film strip, there was an interference. You might imagine that there is physical smoke passing up past the film strip or that the film strip is shaking, so that the light cannot easily pass through it. In other words, there was an interference, a static, a disharmonious shaking of your identity body.

So what you see is that when you believe in the illusion that you are a separate being, you will actually limit your creative abilities right at the very highest level of your identity body. There are certain things you simply do not believe that you can accomplish as a human being. And therefore, you are not even allowing the possibility of it to pass into your mental body.

***

In other words, when a thoughtform and an energy impulse pass through your identity body, the thoughtform – the image on the film strip – is distorted and the energy impulse – the creative impulse – is reduced in intensity by the interference from the fear energy stored in your identity body. So when the creative impulse then enters your mental body, it is already distorted and diminished in momentum. Of course, in your mental body, you also have another layer of distortion. At the level of thought, you have many beliefs about yourself and about the world in which you live and how the world works and what is possible and what is not possible.

So what you really have at the level of the identity body is the raw fear of death, but what dominates most people's mental bodies is doubt—the ability to reason back and forth about what is possible and what is not possible. And therefore, you see that the basic characteristic of the mental body is that people who are very mental or intellectual can argue for or against any issue. And they can come up with many good arguments for why this is true, but they can come up with just as many good arguments for why it is not true. And therefore, such people are not able to actually make a decision.

This, of course, also distorts the image of the creative impulse. And the doubt energy, which is another specific vibration, reduces the momentum or intensity of the creative impulse even further. And so, when a creative impulse has passed through your mental body and begins to go into the emotional body, it is even more distorted and further reduced in intensity.

What now happens is, of course, that at the emotional body, you have another layer. You actually have certain beliefs at the emotional body. For example many people have the belief at the emotional level that anger is a beneficial or at least an unavoidable reaction, and that in many cases it is perfectly justified to respond with anger. You do indeed see, that the dominant emotion at the emotional level is anger. Anger is, again, a specific energy, a specific vibration, and it will reduce the momentum of the creative impulse even further. And again, the beliefs will also distort your actions and how you think it is appropriate to react to certain situations in your environment.

Of course, again, then the impulse goes to the physical level, where you have another set of beliefs. And at the physical level, the most distorting belief is that many people have come to accept the illusion created by the fallen beings that the ends can justify the means. In other words, even though the Bible says "Thou shalt not kill," many religious people throughout the ages have accepted the illusion that in certain situations it is acceptable to kill those who are threatening God's plan for the salvation of the world. This, then, is the belief that even further distorts the creative image and reduces the intensity of the impulse. And this belief gives rise to the dominant emotion at the physical level, namely resentment intensifying to outright hatred.

So what you actually see is that people who are below the 48th level of awareness are completely unable to receive a thoughtform from their I Will Be Presences. Because, as the thoughtform is projected into their four lower bodies, it is so distorted that there is nothing of the original thoughtform left, when it reaches the physical level and their conscious awareness—which is completely focused on the physical level and the body.

What you also see is that the energy impulse coming from the Presence is so reduced in momentum, that it is only enough to keep the physical body alive, to keep the cells infused with enough fire element that they can stay alive. Yet they are barely able to stay alive, which is why you see so many people manifesting either diseases or old age, that gradually reduces the vibrancy and the vitality of the cells, until the body finally dies after a lifespan that is far shorter than what the body is actually capable of providing.

***

Now, you need to take this understanding and transfer it to elemental life as well. The reality here is that elemental life is very much tied in to human beings. As we have said, the Elohim have actually given human beings dominion over the earth. What has happened over a long period of time is, that the collective consciousness of humankind has built up a substantial pool of negative energy at the four levels of the identity, mental, emotional and physical bodies, or levels of the mind. This energy, then, has been projected onto elemental life, and it greatly burdens elemental life and their ability to carry out their essential function.

So you actually see, that what happens is that even the thought-forms being projected onto elemental life by the Elohim cannot reach the physical level of manifestation in their original form. Because there is so much distortion in each of the four levels of elemental life, that the images are simply so shaken, that they cannot be carried out by elemental life, they cannot be manifest by elemental life in their pure forms.

Of course, what you also see is that human beings have created many thoughtforms or mental images and have projected them onto elemental life. And so, this is indeed the very explanation for why you see natural disasters, why you see erratic weather patterns, crop failures, diseases in crops or trees or animals. And it is even, at a deeper level, the reason why you see a world, where there is a feature which was never envisioned by the Elohim.

**

Now, if you take a statement made by Jesus, you will gain a perspective on this. Jesus said: "Fear not little flock, for it is your father's good pleasure to give you the kingdom." Jesus also said, "I am come that all might have life and that they might have it more abundantly." It is, indeed, the vision of the Elohim – which represent the father element – that all people on earth should have a material form of life where they lack nothing. They have the abundant life of everything they need for their material nurturance, so that they have the freedom, the freedom of mind, to focus exclusively on their own growth in consciousness and on fulfilling their reason for being, namely to be co-creators with the Elohim.

What you see on earth today, of course, is that very few people have the peace of mind, where they feel they are adequately nurtured and where they can focus on their personal growth or on serving all life. And this is caused by the fact that the fallen beings have induced an illusion,

Overcoming the illusion that matter has permanence

or rather a set of layered illusions, that distort your view of the world at each of the four levels of the mind.

But the illusion really begins at the level of your identity body, by the fallen beings taking advantage of what I just described as the basic raw fear of death. They have used the fear of death to induce the illusion that the fundamental design of the earth is inadequate or incomplete, so that there will inevitably be lack, there will be a lack of resources, a lack of food, a lack of money.

The reason why the fallen beings have inserted this is twofold. First of all, it keeps people focused on the struggle. People think that life is a struggle, and that they have to struggle against the earth, against Mother Earth, and forcefully take from her what they need. Instead of going through the alternative of working with their own creative abilities, working with their I Will Be Presences and working with elemental life to bring forth everything they need, without having to do it at the sweat of their brow.

However, the other reason why the fallen beings want people to believe in the illusion of lack is, indeed, that it is the only way that they can set themselves up as being a privileged elite, who has incredible material abundance whereas the majority of the people have far less. Look at every society known in history, and you will see the tendency for a small elite to set themselves up in a privileged position, where they have far more abundance than the general population. And how is it possible for a small elite to have more? Well, having more than others is a comparative thing, is it not? And this means that for some to have more, others must have less.

There is also the clearly physical component that – at the current level of the collective awareness – abundance has to be brought forth through physical means. So somebody has to sweat in order to produce abundance, and since the elite of the fallen beings do not want to sweat, they have to get other people to sweat for them.

Thus, you see so many societies, where the general population are working as the slaves to produce the abundance for a small privileged elite. And then, this elite sits there and feels that they are in a fundamentally different category, and that they are of infinitely greater worth than the general population—even though the principle of life is that God is no respecter of persons and that no person is above anyone else.

But can you see that the only way the elite can maintain a privileged position is to make the people actually believe, that they are fundamentally limited or fundamentally flawed, and that the world is fundamentally limited? And therefore, it is a necessity that there is a lack of resources, so only a few can have a materially abundant life.

This is the only way that the elite can maintain their position. They have to get the people to voluntarily reduce their creative powers, to even deny their creative powers, so that they see themselves as limited to the abilities and powers of the physical body. And therefore, they can be controlled by the elite.

***

So, the image I hope you will take away from this key is that the material world is simply a projection of a thoughtform, and that this thoughtform is brought into the physical level by passing through all four levels of the material realm. And yet, at each level there is an interference. First of all, as I have explained, by energy that is accumulated at these four levels and that burden elemental life.

As I have explained before, elemental beings are beings who actually take on a certain thoughtform and therefore become the thoughtform. And so, when you imagine that an elemental being is burdened by negative energy, you can imagine this elemental being starting to shake and vibrate.

And as you know that a building can be destroyed by an earthquake – by being shaken until it starts breaking apart – you can imagine what happens to an elemental being, when it begins to shake as a result of being burdened by energy from human beings. The elemental being simply cannot bring forth the pure form that it is meant to bring forth, and therefore it brings forth a somewhat distorted form. And by the time this has been repeated through the four levels, you see that the earth elementals can be so burdened, that they cannot even bring forth matter in its pure form.

Of course, what you see in nature is not just the earth elementals, but all four types of elementals having an effect on creating these natural disasters or other natural phenomena that are not balanced, not at peace, not in harmony. But you also have to be aware that, at each of the four levels, you have certain thoughtforms that are projected by the fallen

Overcoming the illusion that matter has permanence

beings, by all human beings. And therefore, these thoughtforms come in and directly interfere with the ability of elemental life to manifest the thoughtforms coming from the level of the Elohim. And this is why, as we have explained before, that even matter has become more dense. This is why the earth currently is not able to bring forth enough food or enough other substances that all six billion people can live a materially comfortable and abundant life.

Yet it is extremely important for you to realize, that the current conditions on earth are not the highest potential for earth. And they are not the design brought forth by the Elohim.

My beloved, please make an effort to stand back and understand what is happening here. What is happening is that, after human beings descended into duality, they lost touch, they lost the awareness, the knowledge, I have given you here. They lost awareness about the true potential for the Ma-ter light to bring forth absolutely any form impressed upon it through a self-aware mind. They lost the awareness of the original matrix or thoughtform created by the Elohim for the earth.

Instead, they started to believe that the earth is fundamentally a planet with lack. Yet why is planet earth a world where there is lack? It is only because the creative flow has been diminished or interrupted. And why has the creative flow been diminished? Because humankind, human beings, have misused their creative abilities.

***

So do you see what is actually happening here?

The Ma-ter light can bring forth any form impressed upon it; it can bring forth the pure earth envisioned by the Elohim. But what has happened on this planet is that human beings – over a long period of time – have projected lesser thoughtforms that have been superimposed upon the original thoughtform for the earth.

Now, please understand the basic dynamic here. The Elohim are at a much higher level of consciousness than people on earth. So people on earth have a certain ability to project a thoughtform upon the basic design for the earth, but they cannot alter every aspect of the earth. So there are certain basic traits that humankind does not have the power to distort or destroy, and that is why the earth is still existing as a planet that is able to bring forth life.

Nevertheless, what humankind can do is that they can decrease the creative flow, so that the planet brings forth a lesser form of life than it was designed to bring forth. And that is why there is currently a lack of natural resources, or a lack of food, or other imbalances that make it impossible – seemingly – for six billion people to all have the abundant life.

But can you see that what is happening here is that humankind is not living in a limited world? They have created the limited world, but then they have allowed themselves to become further enveloped in the illusion, so that they actually think that the limited world that they have created is not a result of their own state of consciousness. It was somehow created by an external force, be it an angry God in the sky who wants to punish them for their sins or a completely impersonal set of natural laws, that just happened to bring forth a planet with such limited resources. And also happened to bring forth a living species that could multiply to such numbers, that there is not enough resources for them to survive.

So can you see, that what is happening here is that humankind is becoming a self-fulfilling prophecy? Previous generations, going back into the long forgotten past, have created a state of lack on this planet, through their own state of consciousness. The current generation believes that this state of lack is inevitable, and therefore they accept it and even add on to it by their own disharmonious thoughts and feelings.

And this is what can create a giant downward spiral, where each generation accepts conditions for what they are, and therefore in their minds generate the illusion of lack and the negative feelings that flow from this illusion. And they add on to the negative spiral, so that future generations will experience even more physical lack. And then they take the state of lack that they experience, generate even more negative energy, even more limited thoughtforms and progress the downward spiral even further.

***

My beloved, what can break such a downward spiral? Well, it is simply that a critical mass of individuals refuse to accept current conditions as inevitable. And they believe in and act upon the possibility that current conditions could be improved.

Overcoming the illusion that matter has permanence

Now, if you look at world history, going back to the caveman stage, you will see that in every generation there has been people who did not accept current conditions as inevitable. They were willing to act as if things could be improved, and this is why you have seen the tremendous growth from the caveman society to modern civilization. This did not just happen out of nowhere.

Yet what you also will see is that even though the last couple of centuries have brought forth an incredible growth in knowledge and technology, there is a limit to how far this growth can go. For the simple fact is that the world responds to consciousness. The world is a product of the mental images projected upon it, upon the Ma-ter light. And so, you cannot project an image upon the Ma-ter light if you cannot even imagine that image—because you dare not believe that it would be possible.

What you see is, that even though modern society has created immense technological wonders, there is a price to pay. For the simple fact is, as we have explained, that the second law of thermodynamics will break down any closed system. And the current materialistic outlook on life is a closed system. And that is why many of the forms of technology – the force-based forms of technology that people have brought forth – have side effects, such as pollution or an effect on the body or the psyche of human beings.

My point here is, that even though the earth and humankind are in an upward spiral of bringing forth more sophisticated and more abundant societies, this spiral has a limit—there is a limit to how far it can go. Yet there is the potential that the spiral could be taken to an entirely different level, but that potential can be fulfilled in only one way. And that is, that a critical mass of individuals fully accept and act upon the reality that mind has power over matter, because everything is consciousness. So there is a direct connection between the minds of human beings and the physical planet upon which they live.

For the planet is not physical; it is a creation of consciousness. And humankind's consciousness has a profound influence on the so-called material conditions outpictured on the earth. If a critical mass of individuals – hopefully yourself included – will accept this reality and will begin acting upon it in various ways – as the seven chohans will describe – then the growth spiral – that humankind has been in since the caveman society – could be catapulted, could take a quantum leap, to an entirely new level.

My beloved, I assume you know where the term "quantum leap" comes from? You have the planetary model of the atom, where there are electrons orbiting around the nucleus in fixed orbits. Nevertheless, a particular electron can be infused with an energy impulse, so that it makes a jump, a quantum leap, to another orbit.

And this is exactly what can happen to planet earth—if the collective consciousness of humankind can make the quantum leap to a higher understanding of the connection between matter and mind. Because there is no connection—for the deeper reality is that matter IS mind.

Key 22
Uncovering the central dynamic in human society

My beloved heart, let me give you a slightly untraditional view of this book. Most books are, of course, written for the specific purpose of convincing the reader to accept the point made in the book. And while this is certainly true for this book as well, there is, however, another way to look at this book. You can, in fact, look at this book as a filtering process, that has the specific purpose of filtering out those whom we are not actually trying to reach with this book. You see, there are certain people who have the potential to be the forerunners for healing Mother Earth. Yet this does not mean that all people who are interested in the environmental issue have this potential. This is in no way a judgment or a putting down of the people who do not have the potential.

However, the fact is that there are many, many people who are involved with or interested in the environmental issue out of reasons and motives that make them unable to serve in the highest capacity. Simply because they do not have the openness of heart and mind that makes them willing to question their existing views, their existing beliefs, about the environment and environmental problems.

***

As we have attempted to explain, in order for there to be a real change, there must be a fundamental shift in the way human beings view themselves, the earth and the relationship between the two. And this fundamental shift can happen – really – only when human beings start to see themselves as spiritual beings instead of material beings. It can happen only when those who see themselves as spiritual beings become willing to take responsibility for the fact, that their own state of consciousness is the cause, and the physical conditions they encounter on earth are simply the effects of the cause.

You will, of course, see – if you take an honest look at humankind today – that the vast majority of people have these two things confused. They think that the physical conditions they encounter in life are the cause of their state of consciousness, their state of mind. And thus, they are not willing to acknowledge the simple fact, that if the outer conditions are to change, then a critical mass among human beings must begin by changing the inner conditions—regardless of what happens in the outer world.

If you are to be one of the forerunners for healing Mother Earth, you cannot simply focus your attention without, you cannot project that the cause is somewhere "out there." You must be willing to acknowledge, that you need to begin by changing your state of consciousness, rather than seeking to change material conditions or seeking to change the opinions, beliefs or behavior of other people. You must, as Jesus said 2,000 years ago, begin by looking at the beam in your own eye. Instead of being so focused on the splinters in the eyes of your brothers and sisters, that you make them into scapegoats and project that they are responsible for your situation or even your state of mind.

So can you see, that the essential dividing line between those who will be the forerunners for healing the earth and those who will not, is the openness of mind and heart, the willingness to look at oneself?

***

I realize full well that there are many, many people on earth, who have one of the ingredients necessary for them to have a positive impact on the environmental issue. That ingredients is what we might call good will, the motive to help nature, to help animals, to help the earth. There are many, many people who have this good will, this positive motivation for helping the earth and nature. Yet what I am hoping that those of you who are open to this book can begin to see is, that it is extremely important to consider the question of whether this good will can be channeled in the wrong direction?

Is it possible that there are millions of people who have good will towards the environmental issue, but they have unknowingly allowed their good will to be channeled into supporting causes that will not actually benefit the environment at all? They will only serve some hidden motive, that they are not aware of because they are not willing to take a

Uncovering the central dynamic in human society

critical look at the environmental issue and their own involvement with it. So for those who are indeed open to the possibility that the environmental issue can be misused – as any other issue can be misused – then let us look at a couple of possibilities.

Let us begin by considering the personal view, the personal issue. As I said, there are millions of people who have good intentions and good will towards nature. They truly and honestly believe that what they are doing, the way they are engaged in the environmental issue, will truly help Mother Earth. Yet I submit to you that when people are below the 48th level of consciousness, they have a very interesting ability. That ability is to make themselves feel, that they are working for a good cause, while in reality what they are doing has a self-centered motive.

You can see this throughout human history, if you are willing to take an honest and critical look. You can see how people have done something, which they claim to be for a good cause, but in reality it was for a self-centered cause. In other words, there was a disconnect between the surface motive and the deeper motive.

You will see how people have been able to seemingly justify many actions that have later become seen as clearly selfish and self-centered. Take for example the many, many wars that have taken place on this planet. Do you really believe that the true Creator would have condoned the Crusades, where Christian knights – seemingly with the best of intentions and with a very noble sense of honor – nevertheless massacred Muslim men, women and children for what they saw as a greater cause, even the cause of God or the cause of Christ?

Do you seriously believe, that Jesus – who told you not to resist evil but to turn the other cheek – would be in approval of people killing others in his name? I am sure that if you have read this book up until this point, you are quite aware that there has never been a religious war that was justified or justifiable in the eyes of God or in the eyes of Christ. Likewise, I am sure you can see, that many other wars have been fought for clearly selfish purposes, such as the accumulation of power in the hands of the medieval kings or even the accumulation of profit in the hands of certain modern corporations.

So what I am seeking to help you understand here is, that there are many people who engage in an issue – and they sincerely believe that what they are doing is aimed at helping some greater cause – but in reality, it has the purpose of making themselves feel good.

If you take an honest look, you will see that there is a division that can be made between two kinds of selfishness. There is what you would normally call selfishness, or self-centeredness, namely those who are clearly willing to force others with an obvious force. You may see this in the feudal societies of medieval Europe, where the king and the noble class had forcefully suppressed the population. You may see it, for example, in the Vikings who plundered for the purely selfish reasons of enriching themselves or gaining some sense of entertainment or honor from their lives.

If you contrast the Vikings with the Crusaders you will, however, see a subtle distinction. The Crusaders were also murdering and plundering as much as the Vikings were doing, but the Crusaders believed that they were doing this for a greater cause. So in other words, even though the Crusaders were performing actions that were not different from the actions of the Vikings, the Crusaders were not doing it primarily to enrich themselves. They were doing it – in their own minds – in order to make themselves feel better, in order to make themselves feel that they were serving a greater cause.

***

Now, if you will take a look at this honestly, you will see that this very tendency springs from an element of the human psyche, which is generally known as the human ego. I think that for those who are open to this book, I need not go into a deeper description of the ego, for you will surely have some idea of what it is. So what I am saying here is that the human ego gives people the tendency to focus on themselves, but there are two distinct levels. There are those who are clearly driven by the ego to do whatever they want, regardless of the consequences for others. And these are people – such as for example criminals or people like the Vikings – who clearly do what serves their own interest, even if it means killing or in other ways harming or forcing other people.

Yet, there is a more subtle level of people who are also driven by the ego, but who cannot simply do certain actions that force others, because at some level of their beings, they believe that this is wrong according to their worldview, their paradigm. And so, in order to do the actions that they actually want to do, they have to justify the actions in their own minds, by making it seem like they are doing only what is necessary to

Uncovering the central dynamic in human society

serve a greater cause. This is what I earlier described as the problem at the physical level, namely the philosophy that the ends can justify the means.

What you now see is, that there is a higher form of selfishness, a more subtle, a more camouflaged, form of selfishness than what most people normally call selfishness. It is the form of selfishness that throughout history has managed to camouflage itself – many times – as altruism, as selflessness, as working for a greater cause.

Now, the reality is, my beloved, that this particular form of selfishness originates with the fallen beings. They were the ones who originally decided that they wanted to separate themselves from the rest of God's creation, they wanted to separate themselves from the River of Life. They wanted to no longer be part of the River of Life in which all life is one, and therefore every individual serves the whole and serves other individuals.

Instead, they wanted to stand apart, so that they could set themselves above others by making themselves the leaders and making other people the followers. Now, what you need to understand is that when the fallen beings fell in a higher sphere, it was only a very few leaders who had this attitude of wanting to be above others, of wanting to be the leaders. Yet there were many other beings, serving under the leaders, who chose to fall with them.

And these other beings did it, not because they wanted to be the leaders but because they wanted to be the followers of the leaders—and thereby also be above others, although not as the ones who made the decisions and had the responsibility. So what you see is that there was an unholy alliance between those who wanted to make decisions and those who did not want to make decisions—and therefore wanted to follow those who were willing to make decisions and who claimed to have the authority that they were working for a greater cause.

If you transfer this to the environmental debate today, then you can see a pattern beginning to emerge. In fact, you can transfer this knowledge to just about any area of human society and see the same pattern. That pattern is that there are certain people in the environmental debate who are clearly trying to set themselves up as leaders, and then there is a larger number of people who are blindly accepting what these leaders are saying—and who are seeking to support them and therefore, by their numbers, cause democratic societies to follow the few leaders.

***

Now, if you then take another look at history, you will see that these fallen beings – the ones that are the leaders – are not a coherent or undivided group of individuals. How could they possibly be undivided, when they fell precisely because they accepted the illusion of separation, which is based on the consciousness of duality? As we have said, the consciousness of duality must have two fundamental divisions, that can only be in opposition to each other. And thus, you can see that the fallen beings can never form a coherent whole, they can never form what has been called the One Body of God or the River of Life. And by the very fact that they divided themselves from the River of Life, they have also created inevitable divisions amongst themselves.

So what you will see in every historical period is that there has been an established power elite, which has had control over the general population and society. And then there has been certain periods, where you see the emergence of an aspiring power elite, who is seeking to overthrow the established elite and take power over society.

For example, you will see that during the Middle Ages the Catholic clergy, the Kings and the noblemen formed a power elite that had near total control over society. Yet what you actually saw emerging was an aspiring power elite who now attempted to use science to set themselves up as the ones who were in control of society.

I am not hereby saying that the early scientists were power elite people. On the contrary, they were creative people who were the open doors for bringing forth new ideas. But what I am indeed saying is that every time you see the emergence of new ideas – that have the potential to take society higher – there will be those who embrace and promote these ideas, not because they believe in the ideas but because they see that the new ideas can help them overthrow the established power elite—and thereby set themselves up as the new power elite.

You can look, for example, at Jesus's time and see how the Romans and the clergy of the Jewish religion had near total control over the society where Jesus emerged. Jesus clearly was not a power elite person and neither were the early Christians, who for several centuries were severely persecuted by the Roman Empire. Yet then, you see how there was now a person with political motives, who suddenly made the Christian religion into the state religion of the Roman Empire. And he did

Uncovering the central dynamic in human society 341

this precisely in an attempt to overthrow the old order and set himself up as the undisputed leader of that empire. In other words, the Roman Emperor Constantine did not accept and promote Christianity because he truly believed in the ideas taught by Jesus. He did so only because he used Christianity as a political tool in an attempt to consolidate his own power over the empire.

And then, you saw how, later, the emerging Catholic clergy became a new power block that attempted to extend a power through the Christian faith that even the Roman emperors had not possessed. For the Catholic leaders saw that the real way to control people is not through physical force but through ideas. Yet then, when the Catholic monopoly on the thoughts of the people began to be overthrown by science, you immediately saw the emergence of an aspiring power elite, who attempted to use the ideas of science to control the thinking of the people through the materialistic paradigm. And they have attempted to control the thinking of the people to this day.

***

What you also saw was, that when the stranglehold of the Kings and the noble class was overthrown, then society went through a period of economic freedom and growth. Yet what happened was that as soon as free economies – without the many barriers imposed by the feudal societies – began to emerge, then you also saw the emergence of various power elite groups, often called the capitalists, who attempted to gain a monopoly and thereby control the economy.

These, of course, were the industrialists who had no concern whatsoever for the earth or for human beings. They would mercilessly exploit the resources of Mother Earth, regardless of how that raped the landscape. And they would mercilessly produce products that caused pollution without having any regard for how this affected the natural environment or even, in the long-term, the health of human beings. They would also mercilessly exploit their own workers in the factories, regardless of the safety or health of the workers, in order to produce greater profits for themselves. Yet if you take a closer look at many of these industrialists, you would see, that they were not truly driven by the motive of profit; they were truly driven by the motive of power. For they wanted power over society, and they believed that if they were rich enough, they could buy that power.

And thus, you will also see that as the industrialists gained more power, there was the emergence of an aspiring power elite who set themselves up as the polar opposite to the industrialists. And they, then, became known as the socialists or communists, who attempted to promote a different society than capitalism.

Yet when you take a closer look, is there really any difference between capitalism and communism? The logical consequence of a capitalist society is that eventually one company, one corporation, ends up owning all of the means to production. And is it not so, that in a purely communist society, one entity owns all the means to production? In a communist society, that entity is the state. In a capitalist society, that entity is a corporation. Yet when one corporation owns all of the means to production, does it not also follow that that corporation owns the state?

Is it not so, that capitalism and communism are simply two ways of producing the same kind of society? Namely a society in which the economy and the people are under the total control of one centralized institution, controlled, of course, by a small power elite of individuals.

So, when you realize how this pattern has been repeating itself in various forms over and over again throughout history, is it really that difficult to make the leap in consciousness and see, that the environmental issue has also become a victim for this pattern of an aspiring power elite opposing the established power elite? Can you not see that what has caused most pollution in Western society is the large industrial corporations? And therefore, these corporations have formed a force.

And when you are in duality, any force will inevitably create its own counter-force, any action will generate an opposite reaction. So by the very fact that the industrialists have attempted to take control of society, they have generated a counter-force in the form of an aspiring power elite that has attempted to take away the power of the industrialists. And indeed, this aspiring power elite has attempted to do so precisely through the environmental issue.

So when you look at this from a distance, and attempt to look at the forest instead of the trees, you see that this is simply an outplaying of what we have called the second law of thermodynamics. There is one group of individuals who form a power elite. They then generate a force that attempts to take control over society. Yet this force is, of course, un-

Uncovering the central dynamic in human society

balanced, which means that it is made from what we might call a closed mental system.

The power elite group that wants to control society have formed a closed system; their minds have become a closed system. And so, what happens is that when they generate their force to take control of society, the law of action and reaction will inevitably generate a counter-force, a reaction to the action. And this reaction takes the form of an aspiring power elite, who now want to overthrow the established power elite.

***

Yet from an even bigger perspective, what is truly going on here is that the established power elite and the aspiring power elite – the force and the counterforce, the action and the reaction – are simply the inevitable consequences of the dualistic forces that act in any closed system. And it is precisely the tension between these two dualistic forces that will inevitably cause entropy, cause disorder and chaos, to increase in the system. And therefore, the fight, the tension, between the two opposing factions of the power elite will eventually break down order in society. Until that society collapses, as did the Roman empire, as did the feudal societies of the Middle Ages, as did Napoleon's empire, as did the Nazi empire, as did the communist empire—and as the capitalist empire has already shown signs of doing.

Can you see, that the way the second law of thermodynamics works is, that when the system becomes closed, then it will inevitably become subject to two opposing forces that will eventually break down the system? And of course, what makes the system closed is precisely that people have used their free will to set themselves apart from what we have called the River of Life or the Chain of Being.

What has happened is that people have decided, that they do not want to be part of the hierarchy, they do not want to be connected to their I Will Be Presences, so that they act within the greater framework set by the Presence. They do not want to be an extension of the Elohim, so that they act as co-creators with the Elohim. Instead, they want to act as creators of their own right, who can do whatever they want, regardless of what is the vision of the Elohim and regardless of what consequences this has here below for other human beings or for the natural environment.

This is truly the missing link in your understanding of human history. This is truly what can explain all of the warfare, all of man's inhumanity to man, that you have seen and that you have surely wondered about since childhood. This is what explains the presence of so-called evil.

But can you see, that what you call evil cannot exist alone; it can exist only in a dualistic system with what is clearly seen as evil and what is seen as good? And it is precisely those who are portraying themselves as good, that are the real block to humankind making a quantum leap towards a new approach to problems.

It is so easy for people to identify a scapegoat as being the ones who are evil, but it is very difficult for most people to see, that the evil people are not exclusively the problem. For they exist only in a symbiotic relationship with the people who claim to be good and who claim to be working for a higher cause, but are truly doing this out of a camouflaged form of egotism and selfishness.

The point I am seeking to make here is quite simple. If you really are to be one of the forerunners for healing Mother Earth, then it is essential, that you do not allow your efforts to be sucked into this dualistic struggle between the established power elite and the aspiring power elite. It is therefore essential, that you step back from the environmental issue and seriously consider how it has been influenced by selfish and self-centered motives.

***

If you take a look at the history of the modern environmental movement, you will see that it actually has its roots in the United States. Yet what you will also see is that it was very much born, not from an actual awareness or concern for the environment but based on certain clearly economic and political factors. The reality was that in the beginning decades of the United States' history, economic power was clearly concentrated along the East Coast. There was the emergence of an American power elite on the East Coast, especially in the northeastern states. This power elite clearly wanted to control all development in the United States.

The first serious threat to their economic power came from the southern states, who had started to build wealth based on slavery. It

Uncovering the central dynamic in human society

was precisely the attempt of the established power elite to prevent the emergence of an aspiring elite in the South, that led to the Civil War. The claim that the Civil War was caused by the issue of slavery is simply camouflage. Behind it all was economic powers and economic concerns.

Now, towards the end of the 1800s another threat to the power of the northeastern elite started arising in the West. What happened was, that there was such an immense discovery of mineral deposits, especially gold, that it threatened to shift economic power from the East Coast towards the West. And in an attempt to prevent this from happening, the northeastern power elite actually created and financed several environmental organizations, who started arguing for the need to conserve natural resources.

I am not saying that there were not people involved in these early environmental organizations who had a genuine concern for the earth and a genuine desire to conserve the natural environment. What I am saying is that these well-meaning people allowed themselves to be pulled into the eternal power struggle, where one elite is seeking to maintain its power by destroying all threats, and where another aspiring elite is seeking to use whatever ideas that offer an alternative to the established power elite in order to gain power in society.

So can you see, how you need to be much more discerning, much more critical, when you consider your engagement in the environmental issue? And when you begin to think about this, an entirely new world of possibilities opens up.

My beloved, I fully understand that if you have so far been engaged in the environmental issue out of a genuine desire to do good, then what I am saying here can be highly disturbing. Yet the purpose of this book is to reach those, who are willing to open their hearts and minds to their true potential for serving the Earth Mother, for being the co-creators who will create a new and golden age on earth. And so, if you are to be one of these forerunners, it is indeed necessary that you go through the sometimes difficult and painful process of freeing your mind from the false ideas and beliefs that have been projected there by the fallen beings.

***

Let us now step even further back and realize, what we have already hinted at before, namely that the fallen beings who are seeking to control planet earth do indeed see that the main threat to their control is the growth of the human population.

Can you begin to see, that the current state of lack of resources is brought about entirely because humankind has descended into a lower state of consciousness? As we have explained in the previous keys, human beings are meant to have the powers of mind to work directly with elemental life. And when human beings do work directly with elemental life, then this planet is able to produce the abundant sustenance that is necessary to sustain a population of 10 billion people. Yet after humankind descended below the 48th level of consciousness, descended into the levels of duality, then the natural environment has gradually been burdened by so much emotional, disharmonious energy, that elemental life is no longer able to produce the material abundance necessary to sustain that level of population.

And after humankind started descending into duality, what you have actually seen is, that there have been such tensions between two power elite groups that in past ages this led to wars that are beyond anything you have seen in known history. There were past ages, where wars were fought on such a scale, that it released almost cataclysmic events that eventually caused the sinking of continents and the disappearance of civilizations that were far more advanced than what you have seen today. So what you actually saw in past ages was, that the warring of power elite groups caused such cataclysmic events that it reduced the size of the human population to a mere few millions of individuals.

What you call known history – or the history of humankind, or the history of civilization – is precisely an event that started with a near extinction, caused by the warring of power elite groups. And then, what you see as the emergence of human beings and as the emergence of civilization was actually simply one growth cycle, where the number of human beings has started climbing back towards the intended level of 10 billion.

Yet what you need to understand is, that the power elite groups that are fighting for control of this planet do indeed have some knowledge that this rise of the population is a threat to their control. For the very fact is, that the earth cannot currently sustain 10 billion people. This is, of course, what you have been told for a very long time, and this is what

Uncovering the central dynamic in human society 347

the propaganda of the power elite has put into the collective consciousness.

Yet the deeper reality is that planet earth cannot currently sustain 10 billion people because it is in an unnatural state. Elemental life is currently so burdened by the energies and thoughtforms projected at them by human beings, that they cannot bring forth a natural environment and the kind of foods that can support 10 billion people. Yet there is indeed the potential that if elemental life was freed from this burden, then this planet could easily sustain 10 billion people who all had an abundant material life.

***

And when you realize this, you then need to ask yourself, "Well, why is elemental life so burdened, what is it that has been projected upon elemental life by human beings?" And this is where you realize that the central problem, the central thoughtform or belief, that has been projected upon elemental life by human beings is precisely a specific version of the fear of death.

For the fallen ones have taken the fear of death – that all people experience when they go below the 48th level of awareness – and they have projected a special version, a special philosophy, that takes advantage of the fear of death, while at the same time seemingly offering some relief from it. For you see, what the fallen beings have projected into the collective awareness is that this planet, this material world, has a fundamental state of lack, a fundamental flaw. And therefore, this world can never give them the abundant life. Yet if the people will follow the elite, will follow the religions of the elite, then the people can gain the abundant life in a world that is beyond this one.

Can you see what this actually means? It was the fallen ones who accepted the illusion of separation and who set themselves apart from the River of Life. Precisely because they set themselves apart from the River of Life, they condemned themselves to being in a state of lack. The fallen beings do not have the powers of mind to bring things into materialization. So they have to rely on working at the sweat of their brow to produce material abundance. Yet because the fallen beings do not want to work, they have then created a philosophy that the planet itself, that God's design for the planet, is somehow flawed or at least can only bring forth lack.

And thereby, they have managed to deceive the majority of the people into accepting that they have a certain lot in life, which makes them like the worker bees in a beehive. And if they uncritically accept their lot in life – and work their whole lives to fulfill the natural order, so to speak – then they will be rewarded by a life of abundance in the next world.

Which truly means that what the fallen beings have done is, that they have managed to make people believe that they cannot or are not allowed to be the open doors for the Spirit to transform this world. They have said that no human being has the potential to be one with Spirit in this world, but that you can be one with Spirit only in the next world. Which then effectively means that the fallen beings have managed to cause people to no longer be the open doors, but to be the closed doors who are shutting out Spirit from the material world.

And this is precisely what gives the fallen beings control over the material world on earth. Because, as we have explained, everything is subject to the Law of Free Will. The Elohim and the Ascended Host could very quickly transform this earth into a planet that has the abundant life for all. But we are not allowed to do so, as long as the majority of the people accept a worldview, accept a philosophy or belief system, that makes them close themselves off to their own I Will Be Presences, so that the Presences – and the Ascended Host beyond them – cannot work through people. We cannot bring the abundant life through our own powers; we must bring the abundant life through people who are willing to be the open doors. And if there are not enough people who are willing to be the open doors, then we cannot bring the abundant life.

Therefore, the earth becomes subject to the second law of thermodynamics, which will break down order. And that is precisely why the earth has gone through these cycles of a gradual buildup, and then a major confrontation between power elite groups that trigger the cataclysmic events that cause civilization to decline or disappear. You have seen it on a smaller scale even in known history, with the rise and fall of so many civilizations. But in past ages this has taken place on an even larger scale. And this is, indeed, why most religious and many non-religious myths on this planet contain the idea of cataclysmic events and the disappearance of a civilization. My beloved, this is not simply

Uncovering the central dynamic in human society

fantasy. This indeed has a basis in reality, even though details have often become distorted by the telling and retelling of the stories over and over again.

For indeed, when people have descended to a very low state, such as you saw in the caveman society, how can they even retain an accurate idea of a past civilization that was so advanced that they could barely imagine it? I am sure you can see that if you took a caveman and exposed him to current society, he would not be able to believe what he is seeing, as you have indeed even seen in certain movies.

It should be obvious, that as you have trouble accepting the existence of past civilizations that were far more advanced than your own, then the same is true for any past historical epoch. So how could the people who received the Book of Genesis possibly receive an accurate account of the creation of the universe and the creation of human beings? And thus, is it any wonder that what was given to them back then was a very primitive form, which is why you certainly need, today, to open yourself up to a much more sophisticated understanding—if you want to really understand the dynamics of the earth and how to be a forerunner for healing Mother Earth.

***

So in summary, can you see that what you need to go through in your own mind is the transformation, where you begin to realize that the only way to truly heal Mother Earth is to bring Mother Earth back into alignment with the original vision of the Elohim? That vision is that the Earth Mother is meant to serve as a schoolroom for the growth in self-awareness of the co-creators living upon it.

And this also means that this planet is meant to sustain 10 billion people. It also means that if these 10 billion people are not trapped in the duality consciousness, then the planet is fully capable of producing the abundant life without destroying the natural environment. In fact, there is no actual conflict between the concern of wanting people to live on the planet and the concern of wanting to preserve the natural environment.

For as we have said, this planet was never designed to be a planet without human beings. And thus, human beings are meant to be part of the natural environment. Indeed, the entire purpose of the natural environment is to serve as a laboratory for human beings experimenting with their co-creative abilities.

Even the current imperfect conditions can serve this purpose—if it is understood correctly. And that is why even current conditions can teach people the very important lessons that when they cut themselves off from their own I Will Be Presences and from the Ascended Host, then they will become subject to the fallen beings, who are so trapped in the duality consciousness that they are willing to use force to control others. And it is indeed this willingness to use force that has created the current state of lack.

For can you see, that those who are willing to use force do so for the purpose of setting themselves up as a privileged elite, who has immense material abundance but also has immense power and control over others? And they want to maintain their privileged positions. And the only way to maintain their privileged positions is to maintain an unequal distribution of wealth and control in society.

The only reason why you have a society where there is such immense inequality is precisely because the power elite have managed to make most people believe in the illusion of lack. They want you to stay in this illusion, because they want to maintain their privileged position. They want to feel that they are superior to most other human beings, and in order for them to have that feeling, they must have something to compare with. There must be a contrast between their own state of privilege and abundance and the fact that so many people live below the poverty level, or even live in conditions where they can barely survive physically.

You may look at this and see it as a form of injustice, as something that should not be there. But I assure you that the power elite look at it as something that they very much want to be there and that they will do almost anything to maintain. And so, can you see, that if there is to be true change, then this inequality in the distribution of resources must be overcome?

***

But can you also see an even deeper truth, that the real way to overcome this is not to fight the established power elite? For if you do, you will inevitably become part of the aspiring power elite.

Uncovering the central dynamic in human society

And thus, the real way to bring forth a revolution in society is to bring forth a revolution in higher consciousness, where a critical mass of people raise their consciousness, so that they become the open doors for bringing forth two elements. One is new ideas and a new awareness that suddenly makes it self-evident, that we cannot maintain the current distribution of resources. The other is spiritual light, that will have a profound effect on raising the consciousness of the population, so that they can actually grasp and accept the new ideas.

As an illustration of this, consider what we have already said, that there has been immense progress from the society of the cave man until present civilization. So let us say that the society of the cave man represented a room that was in almost complete darkness. What has happened since then is that, very gradually, a light has started to shine into this room.

Now, of course, in a dark room you cannot see what is actually in the room, which is comparable to the fact that the caveman had very little understanding of how the planet works and how the universe works. So can you see, that what has happened since the caveman society is that there has been a gradual increase in the light? And this has led to a gradual increase in humankind's understanding of not only the earth but the larger universe.

Yet you can also see, that when the sun starts rising in the morning, there is a period of twilight, where the darkness begins to fade but there is still so much darkness left that everything seems to be gray. And so, what has actually happened is that throughout the Middle Ages humankind, at least in the Western world, was in this twilight zone, where there was an increase of understanding but it was being held back by the power elite who had managed to use the Catholic Church to clamp down on new ideas and new thoughts. Yet after that stranglehold was broken, there has been a rapid growth in humankind's understanding.

What has happened is, that the light has increased, and therefore people have now begun to see more and more of what is in the room, the dark room in which they live, the world in which they live. Yet as the light increases even more, can you see that humankind will then be able to see many of the things that they cannot currently see?

Because, again, the current worldview, the materialistic worldview, is also a product of the power elite and their attempt to maintain control. And so, materialism is as restrictive for human thought as was the

Catholic doctrines of the Middle Ages. For as materialism denies the true human potential to be an open door for spiritual ideas and energies, so did the Catholic Church deny that potential—instead having said that it was only Jesus who could be such an open door.

Can you see, that if a critical mass of people open their minds and hearts to the acceptance of their true identity as spiritual beings – and their true potential to be the open doors for ideas and spiritual light – then there can be such an increase in light that, suddenly, more and more people begin to see as self-evident that they have a higher potential, and that the earth has a higher potential? And this is, indeed, the most profound, the most fundamental, shift that could happen on this planet right now. And of course, it all begins with you becoming more aware of the connection between mind and matter, between your consciousness and the planet on which you live.

Having now given you more of the larger picture, I have set the stage for the seven chohans giving you more specific directions on what you can do to bring forth this revolution in higher consciousness, depending on which one of the seven spiritual rays that currently corresponds to your state of consciousness. As you read these descriptions – and probably even as you read the previous discourses by the chohans – you might indeed get a sense for which ray corresponds most closely to your current state of consciousness. And this will, then, give you a clue to the specific contribution you could make to accelerating the environmental debate into a distinctly higher level, that can bring forth true solutions and a true healing of the Earth Mother.

PART FOUR

Key 23
Helping the Earth Mother without doing anything

Master MORE I AM, and it is my intent for this discourse to give you a brief and concentrated awareness of how you can express your will to improve the environment, your will to heal Mother Earth, in a way that will actually accomplish something in terms of healing the earth. Rather than simply perpetuating the dualistic struggle, and thereby adding to the tension that has caused so many imbalances in the body of the Earth Mother.

As I expressed in my first discourse, the first ray is truly the ray of transcendence, the ray of the desire to be more. Yet it has often been seen as the ray of will and the ray of power. This is, of course, not entirely inaccurate, for how do you become more? Well, you must have a will to become more, and you must be able and willing to express power in order to manifest that more.

Nevertheless, it is essential for you to understand, that what you see on earth is an immense perversion of will and power. The reality is that the will of God is that all life will transcend and become more, until all self-aware beings attain the ultimate level of self-awareness, namely that of the Creator itself. In other words, the Creator wants to raise up all life without putting down any form of life.

I am fully aware that if you have grown up in the West – or if you have been affected by any of the three major monotheistic religions – well, then you have been given an image of God that makes it seem like God does not want to raise up all life. For indeed, the image of God that has been portrayed through Judaism, Christianity and Islam is that God is a judgmental and angry God, who actually seems to want to punish some people by sending them to an eternity of suffering in hell. Yet, as I hinted at in my first discourse, this is indeed an injustice projected upon the true Creator by those who have separated themselves from the Creator, namely the fallen beings.

What you see on planet earth, is that the perversion of power, the abuse of power, comes largely from the fallen beings. They are the ones who are perverting power, for they are the ones who are expressing power in a way that seeks to limit or control the free will of the population.

This abuse of power can, of course, only come from a perverted will. And the perversion of the will is that the fallen beings do not want to raise up all life. They want to raise up only themselves, and they want to put down all other forms of life, so that they can seem to have a higher, more powerful, more privileged position in comparison to those who are below them based on external criteria, such as how many material possessions people have.

So can you see, as Mother Mary has explained, how this has been used also in the environmental debate and the environmental issue? The fallen beings are precisely the ones who have no respect for life. Therefore, they also have no respect for the body of the Earth Mother, for the natural processes or for animal or plant species. The fallen beings are the ones who will come in and rape an entire landscape in order to make a profit. They will bring forth chemicals, such as mercury or DDT, that will spread throughout the environment and even get into the food chain. They are the ones who will use nuclear weapons or other forms of weapons that will have long-ranging effects on the natural environment and the natural balance.

***

So can you see, that this all starts with a perversion of the will of God? The will of God is to raise up all life, even to raise up matter itself, so that it eventually transcends and reaches that level, where the material universe can become another sphere added to the spiritual realm. And so, when you pervert this will, you are not willing to raise up all life. Yet, what does this mean?

It means there must be a fundamental division. You must have a way to divide, to distinguish, between what is raised up and what is put

Helping the Earth Mother without doing anything

down. This, then, makes it necessary to have a standard, a dualistic standard with right and wrong. So that those who are right will be raised up and those who are wrong will be put down. And this, of course, is what you see in many areas of society.

Just look at how many people have attempted to enforce such a standard. Look at how many times in history you have seen strong leaders emerge, who are seeking to force a particular standard on society. In many cases such a standard is camouflaged as a particular thought system. It may be a religion, such as the Roman Emperor Constantine who forced Christianity upon the Roman Empire. And the succeeding Christian leaders, who forced Christian dogmas and doctrines upon the minds of all people in medieval European society. It may also be political systems, such as what you saw with Karl Marx, that was taken by Lenin, Trotsky and Stalin and forced upon the Russian people—and then attempted to be forced upon the rest of the world.

Or it may be, of course, scientific materialism, which has been forced upon Western society to the point, where there are people who have attempted to use this philosophy to cause all people in the West to deny their spiritual potential, their potential to be the open doors. For of course, when people are the open doors for the Spirit, well this is indeed the ultimate threat to the fallen beings. And thus, their primary concern is precisely to shut down this threat.

Yet can you also see how there are many subtle ideas, that have been forced upon the collective consciousness through the environmental issue? We have talked about the entire illusion of lack. There was a period some decades ago, when many people were fascinated by a book called "Limits to Growth," which basically promoted the idea that there was a limit to how much society or civilization can grow. There was a limit to the size of the population, there was a limit to natural resources, there was a limit to just about everything.

And while it is true that there is a certain limit, there is only a limit as long as the majority of the population are at a certain level of consciousness. As we have attempted to explain, when people are below the 48th level of consciousness, they will be confined to physical force, physical power. And thus, they will have to work with what most people today call natural resources. They will have to work with force-based technology. And so, yes there is a limit to the growth of the population and the growth of society. Yet can you see, that this entire concept of limits to growth is based on the fundamental illusion that there is nothing beyond this level of force-based technology?

Can you see, how this idea that there are limits to growth has had a profound impact on the environmental debate and on people's thinking? And when you then combine it with the concept of materialism – that denies their spiritual potential – you see how this forms almost a Catch-22, almost a perfect mental box, from which many people in the Western world cannot escape.

***

This, of course, is the very foundation for the current outlook on environmental problems, namely that there is a limit to the growth that is possible. Can you see, then, that this is the ultimate perversion of the first ray? What is the very basic drive, the very basic characteristic of the first ray? It is the drive to be more, the drive to self-transcend.

When you realize what the first ray is all about, you see that there is no limit to growth. For you can always be more, you can always transcend—until you manifest the ultimate state that Jesus called the kingdom of God. Which is the state, where the material universe can make that quantum leap and become part of the spiritual realm.

Can you see, that this is the true potential? Can you also see, that if the earth was indeed to go through this process of transcendence, then what would happen was that, as the earth is raised in vibration, the fallen beings will no longer be able to embody on this planet? For as we have explained, everything is subject to the free will of the majority of the population. If the majority of the population raise their consciousness beyond a certain level, then there are certain fallen beings – who are not willing to raise their consciousness beyond that level – who would not be allowed to re-embody on this planet once their lifespan ran out.

This is, indeed, what you saw happen 2,000 years ago, when Jesus said: "For judgment I am come." The reality is that Jesus came to bring forth – by taking physical embodiment – the judgment of a certain group of fallen beings, some of which were embodied in the Roman Empire, some of which were embodied as the leaders of the Jewish religion. These were, indeed, the people who represented a certain level of consciousness. And by them attacking and eventually killing the living Christ, they received their judgment and were not able to re-embody on earth. Thus, the entire earth was freed from these beings and therefore raised to a higher level, so that no being beneath that level could embody on this planet any longer.

And of course, as this process is continued – as it will continue because there are enough people willing to raise their consciousness – then more and more of these fallen beings will be unable to embody on this planet. They know this, and that is why they will do anything to prevent the collective consciousness from being raised to the level, where they will lose their ability to embody on this planet and thus lose their grip on this planet. For truly, they have attempted to make this planet their own sphere, set apart from the River of Life, where they can set themselves up as the ultimate authority. For truly, the dream of the fallen beings, in their rebellion against God, is to set themselves up as gods in the material universe. They want to be gods on earth by having godlike powers on earth — as you did, indeed, see some leaders attain in various periods of history.

Today, of course, there are those who attempt to attain these godlike powers not through physical force but through ideas. For they feel that if they can determine what people believe in, then they will have the power of a God. And so, there are those who are attempting to make people believe in the materialistic paradigm and thereby deny their own inherent spirituality, and also deny the inherent spirituality of the earth.

***

For truly, what is spirituality in its essence? Well, it is precisely the ability and the willingness to self-transcend, the willingness to look at the beam in your own eye and to transcend your state of consciousness. This is the essence of spirituality — not to be confused with religion. For most religions on earth have become outer religions that present a false path – designed by the fallen beings – where they want you to believe, that if only you are a member of this religion and follow certain precepts, then you are guaranteed to be saved.

The true path is, of course, that there is no guarantee that you will be saved. For your salvation, so to speak, depends on one thing only, namely your level of consciousness. And you will reach the ultimate level of the 144th level of consciousness only by being willing to transcend yourself. Which means you must be willing to look at yourself and your state of consciousness, instead of thinking that your salvation can be secured by fulfilling certain outer requirements. The real path – the real path of becoming more, the real path of self-transcendence – is a creative path. For there is no mechanical way to follow this path; it can be done creatively, only by you looking at yourself and you coming to certain conclusions that will then help you see how you can become more.

There are many people, even those who have been on the spiritual path for decades, who believe that the key to walking the path is to acquire certain knowledge, certain hidden knowledge, so that they reach a state of enlightenment, or whatever they call the ultimate state of consciousness. There is a dream among many people that somewhere out there is this ultimate knowledge, this ultimate book. And once they read that book, they will instantly become enlightened.

Well, with everything we have told you, you should be able to see, that this is a complete illusion, again projected by the fallen beings. For there is no ultimate knowledge, that could ever be given, that would instantly cause you to become enlightened. For enlightenment is a creative process, and even the state of so-called enlightenment is not a static state of consciousness. It is the one where you are constantly flowing with the River of Life and therefore constantly becoming more.

***

So my beloved, if you feel that the first ray resonates with your being, what is the best way to express this? Well, let us first begin by looking at how not to express your first-ray qualities in the environmental issue.

What you see in the environmental debate today is, indeed, that there are many people who are engaged in this debate precisely out of the perverted will and the perverted power that originates with the fallen beings. I am not thereby saying that these people are fallen beings, although there are certainly some fallen beings among the leaders in the environmental debate. But there are many well-meaning people who allowed themselves to become trapped in the mindset of the fallen beings. They have allowed themselves to become trapped in the ultimate illusion that the ends can justify the means.

Thus, they believe that the end is to save or preserve the natural environment from the destructive influence of human beings. And since

Helping the Earth Mother without doing anything 359

human beings have a desire to be destructive or to gain profit, then these people believe that in order to save the environment, it is now justifiable that they limit the activities or the freedoms of certain people. It is even justifiable to limit the size of the human population through various means, such as population control, including abortion.

What you see is, indeed, that there are many people who are engaged in the environmental debate precisely to use force, to use perverted power based on the perverted will that does not seek to raise up all life. But seeks to, again, divide life between those who are right and those who are wrong—and then seeks to put down those who are wrong. Can you begin to see, with everything we have told you, that this will only add to the tension, to the negative emotional energy that will burden elemental life? And thus, it will only add to the imbalances in nature that cause so many of the problems you see in the environment.

Do you realize that pollution is not a natural phenomenon, in the sense that the elementals have a very great ability to purify the natural environment? Have you ever noticed – have you really noticed – that there are examples, where a certain area has been very heavily contaminated by a chemical substance. Yet when nature was left alone, the environment would be purified within a time span that often surprised the experts. So what you see is, that the natural environment has an ability to purify itself, just as the human body has the ability to overcome toxins or viruses through natural processes.

So what you, then, see is, that if elemental life was to become gradually unburdened by the negative energies put upon it by humankind, then the elemental beings would very quickly be able to remove all pollution that is currently burdening the natural environment. In other words, this is not simply a matter of stopping the physical pollution. It is even more important to stop the emotional, mental, and etheric pollution that is burdening elemental life at all levels.

So do you see, that in order for you to be one of the forerunners for healing Mother Earth, the first and most important thing you can do is to stop the pollution at the emotional, mental and etheric level? You can make sure that you are not part of that pollution, because you are not contributing to the age-old power struggle between an aspiring power elite and the established power elite.

The first thing you can do is to make sure, that you are not expressing power in a perverted way. And then, you can begin to purify your will, so that you change your will from wanting to punish the scapegoat to wanting to raise up all life by raising the consciousness of as many human beings as possible.

***

You see, there are too many people – who are well-meaning – who have become focused on the need to change the minds of other people. And thus, they have become willing to use some kind of force to convert others to their belief system. Yet, it is not necessary for you to change the minds of all people on earth. It is only necessary to change the minds of a critical mass of people, first of all what we might call the top 10%. Once you change the consciousness of the top 10%, as we have described earlier, then you will indeed create an upward momentum that will gradually influence the 80% in the middle and thereby shift the collective consciousness.

What has happened to many people is, that they think they have to change the minds, especially of those who are opposing them or opposing their thought system. And so, now they start battling with those who are opposing them, instead of focusing on a positive goal of inspiring those who are open to new ideas.

There will always be people who are closed-minded and who are not open to new ideas. When I say "always" this is, of course, a statement with some modifications. For as the earth comes closer to the ultimate ascension point, well then there will not always be people who are in the dualistic consciousness.

But at least for the foreseeable future, there will be people in the dualistic consciousness. So when you put out any idea, there will be those who will oppose that idea. If you now direct your attention towards battling those who are opposing the idea, then your energies will be directed into this dualistic struggle that has been going on throughout all of known history, but has truly been going on for much longer. This, then, is not the true expression of the power of the first ray.

The true expression of the power of the first ray is that you take an entirely positive approach. You never oppose other people and you never oppose other ideas. This is not to say that you cannot make statements about other ideas, but you do not do it in the way of putting the ideas

Helping the Earth Mother without doing anything 361

down or putting the people down who believe in those ideas. Instead, you are focused on promoting what you see as the better idea.

But you also realize, that what you currently see as the better idea may not be the ultimate idea. For you realize, that as you transcend your state of consciousness, you might have a more nuanced view of the issue. And thus, you are never coming out with this conviction that you see in so many people, that you have the ultimate idea, the ultimate understanding, and that all other people must conform to your thought system—or the earth will go to hell, or humankind will self-destruct due to pollution or war or this or that other calamity.

Do you see, that the whole idea that the earth is about to be destroyed, or the world is about to come to an end, is a perversion of power, that springs from this perversion of will? Where you create some ultimate scenario, some epic scenario, that makes it seem like something must be done now in order to prevent this ultimate disaster that is right around the corner. This, of course, is what you see in the entire debate around global warming. But you saw it also 30 or 40 years ago in the debate around limits to growth.

And you can see the same theme going back throughout history, where even religion has been used to say that any day now Jesus will return and roll up the world as a scroll. And therefore, we need to take these extreme measures in order to make sure that we are ready or that the world is ready. This is a perversion of will that, again, seeks to divide, to create a division between those who are right and those who are wrong—and therefore makes it seem like it is now justifiable to use force against those who are wrong.

So it is extremely important for you to make sure, that you are not engaging your energies – your time, your resources, even your financial resources – in supporting organizations or movements that are simply continuing this age-old power struggle. Based on some epic philosophy of the world coming to an end if we do not immediately reduce carbon emissions by forcing people to stop driving their cars, or whatever the initiative might be. So first of all, pull yourself away from such organizations.

You may think that by doing so, you will no longer be doing something for the environment, but it is not true. Even by withdrawing your energies from such unbalanced organizations, you will be doing something for the environment.

***

You can, of course, do something positive, but the first step towards doing something positive is to stop doing something negative. The first step towards helping heal Mother Earth is to stop activities that are contributing to the disease, to the imbalances in the body of the Earth Mother. And so, once you have, then, "stopped the accident" as they say in First Aid, you can begin to take a pause, to take a break, and see what else you might be able to do that will truly contribute to a positive development in the environmental debate.

So what I am saying here is this. Most of the people who resonate with the first ray will have a very strong will. They will often tend to think that the way they look at things right now is the ultimate or the right way to look at things. And therefore, they have a very strong will to get society to conform to their way of looking at the world. This, then, gives them the desire to exercise power in a very decisive way, so that they really feel they are making a difference.

My beloved, these are positive qualities, but they are only positive if they are expressed in a balanced way. And as I said, if they are expressed in an unbalanced way, then the perversion of the first ray is, in fact, one of the greatest causes of the imbalances you see in the body of the Earth Mother. For most wars are precisely an expression of the perversions of the first ray, where people are willing to use the ultimate form of force, namely that of killing another human being, in order to get their way, so to speak.

Once you begin to see this – and once you begin to balance the first-ray qualities – you can begin to speak out against the abuse of power. You can begin to expose the abuse of power in history and in the current environmental debate. And this can, then, have a positive impact.

You can then – as you go beyond this and go into some of the other rays and begin to also have the qualities of the other rays – you can find a positive expression, where you can now promote an approach to the environmental issue that is not based on the perversions of will and power. It is based on the true will to raise up all life and the true expression of power, that seeks to raise up all life by focusing on the positive instead of battling something else, something that you have labeled as negative according to a dualistic system.

Helping the Earth Mother without doing anything

For the reality is that when I talk about focusing on the positive, I am not talking about positive in a dualistic polarity with something negative. I am talking about the higher positive that does not have an opposite polarity. For the will of God, of course, has no negative polarity. There is an anti-will, which is the will of the fallen beings, but the anti-will of the fallen beings is not in a polarity with the will of God. The fallen beings are not actually opposing the will of God, for the will of God is transcendental. It cannot be put into a dualistic system, and thus it cannot have an opposite.

God has no opposite. The fallen beings think they are in opposition to God, but they are not in opposition to God. They are only in opposition to themselves, to the opposite dualistic polarity that they have created by going into the one dualistic polarity, where they are focused in consciousness.

You see, once you go into duality, you must choose to go into one of two dualistic polarities. And therefore, it is inevitable that the polarity you go into will have an opposite. So the will of the fallen beings is not in opposition to God; it is an anti-will that is in opposition to another form of anti-will. And therefore, the fallen beings are, as we have said, inevitably divided into factions that oppose each other, so that you always have the aspiring and the established power elite battling for control.

It is possible to transcend this and express power and express will in a way that is not dualistic. This is what you saw with Jesus, what you saw with the Buddha, what you saw with Krishna, what you have seen with other people who have attained spiritual mastery and who have focused on raising up all life—in some cases by exposing what is not right in society, in others by simply giving a new idea, a new teaching, that people could then use to transcend their old state of consciousness.

***

Do you realize that the environmental problems on earth will not – my beloved: they will *not* – be solved by someone bringing forth some ultimate idea or philosophy that all people will come to accept? The environmental problems will be solved only when a critical mass of people go beyond the 48th level of consciousness, so that they can begin to find – begin to see, begin to imagine and believe in – solutions that are not force-based. It is not a matter of bringing out a certain philosophy or certain ideas, that everybody will start to believe in. It is about – in many different ways – promoting the transcendence of consciousness, so that a critical mass of people truly rise to a higher level of consciousness. And then, once people are in that higher level of consciousness, they will begin to see ways to begin to interact with Mother Earth, so that they do not create environmental problems.

There are things that seem self-evident to many people today that were not self-evident a hundred years ago. Take for example the issue of slavery. For thousands of years every civilization had slaves, but during the 1800s it became self-evident to a majority of the people in the Western world that slavery simply was incompatible with their approach to life. It was incompatible with democracy and the idea that everyone has certain rights given by a higher power.

You see, that the same has to some degree already happened in the environmental issue. It is self-evident to most people in the Western world that if we indiscriminately pollute with chemicals, then it can affect the food chain and therefore affect our own health and the health of our children. It is self-evident that we cannot allow an indiscriminate raping of natural resources.

And I can assure you that it will gradually become more and more self-evident to people, that there needs to be a new approach to the relationship between man and Mother Nature. This has already started happening, but if you will focus your efforts on bringing forth a higher approach, a new approach based on the ideas in this book, well then this process can be greatly accelerated. So that in a matter of a decade or two, people will indeed begin to accept their spiritual potential. And therefore, they will see the need to start working with elemental life and to stop burdening elemental life with their own negative energy.

And as this awareness begins to spread, at least among the top 10% of the people, you will see a profound difference in how society as a whole begins to relate to Mother Nature in a new way. Suddenly, there will be things that it is self-evident that we cannot allow in an enlightened society. Suddenly, there will be new ideas that will come forth that will become accepted, and there will also be new inventions and new forms of technology that will make it possible to produce energy and many other goods without destroying the natural environment.

Helping the Earth Mother without doing anything

***

The vision I am hoping you can grasp here is that you need to stop being attached to producing specific results. This is indeed a perversion of the first ray, namely that you become very focused on producing a specific visible or physical result, such as for example getting all people to become Christians or getting all people to accept certain limitations that will stop producing greenhouse gases. These specific results are precisely what people become fixated on, when they have the perversion of the first ray. And then, they also become willing to exercise power to force others to comply with their vision.

So what you need to do in order to overcome the perversions of the first ray – and tune in to the true reality of the first ray – is that you need to let go of this fixation on outer results and realize that the real key to producing change on earth is to focus on raising people's consciousness to a higher level. The true purpose of the universe, as we have explained many times, is the growth in self-awareness.

So can you see, that the growth in self-awareness will not be the automatic or guaranteed result of a particular outer change in society, such as a new law? The growth in self-awareness will come about only, when people come to see themselves and the world in a new light, when they develop a new approach, a higher understanding. And thus, those who are truly in tune with the first ray, and have transcended the perversions of the first ray, will indeed focus their efforts and their attention on producing this growth in awareness rather than particular outer results.

This, of course, has many subtle ramifications, that I am sure you can already begin to see. And that you certainly will begin to see, as you study the releases from the other chohans. So what I would like to suggest here, as the conclusion of my addresses, is that if you have been very strongly involved with the environmental issue, or with other issues, in a way that you can now begin to see was a perversion of power and will, then I strongly encourage you to go through a period of cleansing or fasting.

You need to step back from this outer force-based engagement in an issue. And then, you need to be willing to take a rest, to give your mind a rest, so that you can gradually free your mind from the influence of these thoughtforms and ideas promoted by the fallen beings in their abuse of power.

You need to not be tempted into suddenly start fighting the power elite. For as I said, even this will not bring about the desired change. It is only the transcendence of consciousness, where you do not fight the power elite, but you seek to raise the awareness of the top 10%, so that gradually the elite becomes irrelevant to society. And eventually, those who are the lifestreams of the elite will not even be able to embody on this planet.

So in order to give yourself this break and still fulfill your desire to feel that you are doing something actively – which is of course a first-ray quality that I am in no way asking you to suppress – then I have a suggestion. We have, as Mother Mary has mentioned before, released a number of spiritual tools that are directed at invoking spiritual energy from above and directing it into specific conditions, such as lightening the burden of elemental life. We have given a number of decrees, rosaries and invocations through this messenger, but we have also given a number of decrees and other tools through other organizations that we have sponsored over the past century. These are very active tools, very active techniques where you use your voice to invoke spiritual light.

* * *

Now, I am sure that if you are open to this book, you are somewhat aware of certain spiritual concepts. You might be aware that your physical body has an energy field around it, and that in this energy field are certain focal points, that are often called the chakras. Well, there is a chakra located over your throat, and it is obviously called the throat chakra. This is your power center, and it corresponds to the first ray. So if you feel that the first ray resonates with your state of consciousness, I strongly encourage you to start learning how to use your throat chakra, your power center, to invoke spiritual light and direct it into specific conditions. I especially encourage you to use it to direct light into lightening the burden of elemental life.

You will find – if you are a first-ray person – that this will give you a great sense of meaning, a great sense of accomplishment, a great sense of doing something that will indeed make a difference. You might not see a physical result instantly, but if you are open to this book, you will feel intuitively that you are indeed making a difference. And that every time you invoke light, you are doing something that is worthwhile,

Helping the Earth Mother without doing anything

something that will eventually contribute to the upward momentum that will lighten the burden of elemental life and therefore bring about real change.

Your invocations will, of course, also lighten the collective consciousness. And when you contribute to removing the dense energy that is burdening the collective consciousness—well my beloved, is it not obvious that this will make it easier for people to accept new ideas?

Why do you think there are so many people in this world today who are living a very limited life, and who are so closed-minded to any ideas beyond their chosen thought system? Well, it is precisely because the collective consciousness is today so burdened by negative emotional energy, and even mental and etheric energy, that people simply cannot grasp new ideas. It is as if there was a fog or a darkness over their minds, so they simply cannot see anything beyond what they are already familiar with. They cannot grasp, they cannot accept, they cannot believe in ideas that go too far beyond the mental box and the thought system in which they have grown up.

Yet can you not see, that as you lighten this fog, as you lighten the darkness, then all of a sudden people will be able to see ideas that they have never seen before. They will be able to grasp ideas they have never grasped before. They will be able to accept ideas they have never accepted before. It is precisely the analogy given by Mother Mary in the previous key, that when you gradually increase the light in a room, people become able to see more and more. And once they see something, they will accept it—for at a certain level of consciousness it is true that seeing is believing. People will not believe what they cannot see. And they cannot see something if they are too burdened by certain energies. So by lightening the load, you will make it possible for people to see— and then believe. And this will indeed make a huge difference for the future of this planet.

It will also help you, of course, clear your own mind and being from these energies and thoughtforms that spring from the perversion of power. And this will be an immense service to yourself and your own personal growth. For you will find that if you deliberately withdraw yourself from the perverted expression of power and the perverted ideas that give a perverted will, then you will gradually find that your mind will begin to clear. And you will now see things you have never seen before. And when you see them, you will believe things that you might be inclined to reject in your current state of consciousness.

**

If you truly are to be one of the forerunners for healing Mother Earth, I strongly encourage you to make use of the tools and techniques that we have given through various messengers. Explore the different possibilities out there; pick the ones that resonate with your being, and then practice them faithfully and energetically, until you begin to feel a shift in consciousness that might cause you to begin to focus more on one of the other rays. And then, of course, flow with this, as you tune in to your I Will Be Presence and begin to receive these intuitive instructions from your I Will Be Presence.

You will already be familiar with receiving such instructions, for otherwise how could you have found this book? And how could you have read the book and continued to read the book up until this point? There certainly has been certain ideas in this book that will have been contrary to what you have believed before you started reading the book. So in order to continue reading to this point, you would have had to be willing to look beyond these ideas.

And how could you be willing to look beyond your present beliefs, if you had not had an intuitive connection to your I Will Be Presence? For it is only when you are connected to your Presence, that you sense that there is something more to understand about life. And this is the only way you can have the drive to look beyond the ideas that you are familiar with, and that you might be attached to. So congratulate yourself with the fact that you have made immense progress by just reading the book up until this point.

And then realize, that there comes a point, where the time for study has gone as far as it can go without also being supplemented by practice. Therefore, I encourage you to practice. Find these techniques. Go to the website that this messenger has created,[1] use the invocations for world transformation, use the invocations and rosaries for personal transformation, use the decrees. Take this as a starting point. If you feel the need to go beyond and look for techniques from other sources, by all means do so.

1   www.askrealjesus.com

Helping the Earth Mother without doing anything

But do something!

Do something!

For you will accelerate your own personal growth and you will accelerate the growth of the planet beyond what you can even imagine right now. Intellectual understanding will only take you and the planet so far. There comes a time for action, and if you are a first-ray person, you should realize that action is indeed part of the first ray. For those who are of the first ray cannot sit still and just think or talk; they must act.

But what I am telling you is that there is a better way to act than fighting other people or fighting the fallen beings. And that way is to lock in to the true qualities of the first ray. And the way to start locking in to those qualities – the way to transcend the perversions of the first ray – is indeed to invoke spiritual light to purify your own energy field and being, and to purify the energy field and being of the collective consciousness and of elemental life.

Therefore, get started! And then, when you have practiced these techniques, you might come back to this book and study the discourses from the other chohans. Or you might decide to study those discourses while you practice these techniques and therefore get the double effect that you can only get from both study and practice.

Study and practice are the two legs of spiritual progress. How far will you go by hopping on one leg, compared to how far you can go by walking on the two legs that God has provided you? And so, we of the Ascended Host have provided you two legs for your personal and for the planetary progress: Study and practice.

Use both of them!

Key 24
Discerning between dualistic and non-dualistic wisdom

Lanto I am. It is my aim with this discourse to speak to those who sense that their being, their present state of consciousness, resonates with the second ray of God's wisdom. In my previous discourse, I attempted to give you a different view of wisdom, a view that there is something beyond what is called conventional wisdom in this world. There is a transcendental form of wisdom, that goes beyond what has been called wisdom, but which is truly only one polarity in the ongoing dualistic game.

So you will, of course – when you look at world history – see that this planet has been a battleground for ideas. Competing thought systems have been raised up to prominence in various civilizations and societies. But can you take what has been given earlier and transfer this to the world of ideas and philosophies? Can you see how, at any given time in history, there is an established power elite and that power elite is using a particular thought system to uphold or even extend its power. In many cases, it was this thought system that allowed the established elite to gain power.

And then, in many eras of history, there has also been one or even several aspiring power elites who are seeking to bring forth a new thought system that can become an alternative to the old. Yet they are not doing this because they think the new thought system has a higher truth than the old. They are doing it simply because it is different from the old, and therefore they believe it can allow them to overthrow the established power elite and put themselves up in the same position of dominance in society.

Can you see, that there have been a number of instances in the world, where an old established thought system has reached the limit for what it can do in terms of providing a vehicle, a foundation, for progress? Look, for example, at the Middle Ages and the thought system created by the Catholic Church. There was a point, where it became more and more obvious, more and more self-evident, to people that the Catholic doctrines could not give satisfactory explanations to some of the questions they had about life. We might say that the Catholic thought system lost its explanatory power, because people had now become able and willing to ask and consider questions that the Catholic thought system could neither explain nor suppress.

For centuries the Catholic thought system had managed to cause a lot of people to suppress certain questions that could not be explained by doctrine. But there came a point, when more and more people were not willing to do this; they were not willing to ignore, or suppress, or deny their curiosity. They wanted answers, and they became willing to look beyond the Catholic doctrines in order to find such answers.

Yet can you see, that this was not a unique case? The reality is that the same will happen, the same pattern will be repeated, for every thought system. You can go back throughout history and see how a particular thought system, idea or philosophy might have gained prominence in a particular culture or society. And for a time, it was truly dominating the thought world of that society, yet there eventually came a point, when it could no longer answer people's questions. And therefore, people started looking beyond it. And if the thought system could not adapt to this, then it was eventually replaced by another thought system.

You saw this happen with how the Catholic thought system was replaced by a more scientifically based thought system. But can you perhaps begin to see – given that you are a spiritual person open to this book – that the scientifically-based materialistic thought system has now also reached the end of its usefulness? It has reached the limits of its explanatory power. Within the last several decades more and more people have awakened to the reality, to the realization, that the materialistic thought system is not much better at answering their questions than the medieval Catholic thought system. And thus, they have started asking the kind of questions that go beyond both thought systems. And this, of course, is indeed why we have brought forth this book: precisely to give answers that go beyond both thought systems.

Can you see, that if you are to be one of the forerunners for healing Mother Earth, you need to transcend both of the thought systems that have so far dominated the debate in Western society, and have therefore also had an influence on the environmental debate? If you go in and

Discerning between dualistic and non-dualistic wisdom

seek to reinforce or expand the dominance of one of these thought systems, then you will not truly help heal Mother Earth. You will only help perpetuate the dualistic struggle.

***

Yet, while I trust you can begin to see this, I would like to take this to an even deeper level. For you see, when you truly begin to understand the duality consciousness, you realize that the fallen beings have not only distorted the debate by setting up two competing thought systems. For there is, indeed, an even deeper level, where the two competing thought systems are actually expressions of the same underlying approach to life, the same underlying view, the same underlying basic philosophy.

There is a concept that some people are aware of, which is called the privilege of formulating the problem. The idea is that if you can take a particular issue, a particular area that is up for debate, and if you can capture the privilege of formulating what the problem is, then you can control the debate and its outcome. For if you manage to establish the parameters that control the debate, and if you can manage to guide the debate into staying within those parameters, then you will have some degree of control over the outcome of the debate.

And this is, of course, what the fallen beings have attempted to do for a very long time. They have attempted to control the debate in such a way, that there are always two competing thought systems. And thus, it seems like people have to choose one over the other. And this, of course, obscures the deeper reality that both of the competing thought systems are expressions of the duality consciousness and the illusion of separation. And therefore, truth or reality is not found in either thought system, even though both of them claim to have the absolute truth or an infallible authority. As long as people are focused on the debate between these two competing systems, they are not free in their minds to look beyond the systems and transcend the dualistic polarities.

Can you see, of course, how you would not be one of the forerunners for healing Mother Earth unless you do indeed step back and transcend the entire debate between the dualistic opposites of traditional Christianity and materialistic science? You must even go beyond the political philosophies, such as Marxism or capitalism. For truly, neither Marxism or Communism nor capitalism will help the environment. As you can clearly see that the Soviet Union had less regard for environmental issues than the capitalist West, although the capitalist West, of course, also had very little regard for these issues. It was, in fact, as we have explained, political motives that dominated the environmental debate in the West.

So what is the solution, what is the way to transcend? Well, it is to open your mind to the possibility that this world has been dominated for a long time by the very mindset of the fallen beings. You will truly begin to lock in to this reality only after you begin to experience what we have called the Conscious You, that is pure awareness. When you have this experience of pure awareness, of being conscious without being conscious of any particular thoughts, then you will know that there is an alternative to the kind of wisdom, so to speak, that is expressed in thought systems. This is a nonlinear, spherical form of wisdom that is difficult, even in some ways impossible, to express in words. Yet it is something you can experience directly. And when you have this direct experience of what Jesus called the Spirit of Truth, then you will know that you have a frame of reference, whereby you can see, that the dualistic thought systems are out of touch with the deeper reality that all life is one.

***

So, as Master MORE before me encouraged those who have a strong will and a strong sense of power to step back and take a little break, then I will do the same for those who have a strong desire to have and express wisdom. There are many, many people – even many people who have followed a spiritual path or a spiritual teaching for a long time – who think that the world's problems can be solved through intellectual analysis or knowledge. They think that in order to solve, for example, environmental problems, we only need to have the right knowledge, the right philosophy, and then everything will fall into place. Yet what have I just explained about thought systems that might dominate society for a while, and then eventually exhaust the power they have over the minds of the people?

The reason for this is that life is an ongoing process. It simply is not possible to formulate a thought system today, and then that thought system will be valid for all time. And so, what is the way to overcome this

Discerning between dualistic and non-dualistic wisdom

dream of the ultimate thought system, the ultimate philosophy, that has ultimate truth? What is the way to go beyond what you see in the Christian fundamentalists who think that the Bible is the literal word of God and should stand unchanged for all time? Or the scientific materialistic fundamentalists who think that the discoveries of materialistic science carry some ultimate authority and should be interpreted in a strict, literal, materialistic manner?

The way to go beyond is to realize that wisdom is not something that is set in stone. For what have we said is the purpose of life? It is the growth in self-awareness. We have explained that there are 144 levels of consciousness possible on earth. So can you see, that there are certain philosophies or thought systems on this earth that are deliberately designed to appeal to people at a certain level of consciousness? For example, the dualistic thought systems – such as mainstream Christianity, capitalism, communism and materialistic science – are all thought systems that primarily appeal to people who are below the 48th level of consciousness or who have gone not too far beyond it.

What you see is that the purpose for why the fallen beings create these thought systems is, indeed, to keep people trapped at a certain level of consciousness and prevent them from going beyond it. So they formulate a thought system based on their own level of consciousness, and then they project out that this thought system has some ultimate authority. And then, they get people to believe, that they have to continue to adhere to this thought system, without questioning its basic paradigms and premises.

What happens is that there are many, many people on this earth, who have actually grown in self-awareness but who are still held back because in their outer minds they have this loyalty to a particular thought system. And so, they think that they have to not question the basic paradigms of the thought system. They cannot consciously acknowledge, that they have gone beyond the level of consciousness that the thought system was formulated based on—and therefore, they are now ready to ask questions and receive the answers that go far beyond that level of consciousness. And this is why the thought system can no longer answer their questions about life. But if they adhere to the outer authority, they dare not acknowledge this. And thus, they dare not open their minds to a higher teaching.

So can you see, that we of the Ascended Host do not have it as our aim to give forth a philosophy or a thought system that gives you some ultimate truth? This book should not be construed to be the ultimate truth about the environmental issue. It is a book that is carefully adapted to the level of consciousness of the people we hope to reach, namely the ones who have the potential to be among the forerunners for bringing forth a new approach to the environmental issue. Yet of course, as more and more people accept this new approach, it will be possible to give forth a higher teaching and with more concrete knowledge about specific issues. Again, as humankind continues to raise its awareness, we of the Ascended Host – as the teachers of humankind – will obviously be able to bring forth deeper and more detailed teachings.

***

Do you see that wisdom is a living wisdom? If you think that you can take a snapshot of a river, and then you have captured the fullness of the river, then you are sadly mistaken. The uniqueness of a river is that it is constantly moving, and how can you capture this movement on a still photo? You simply cannot. You will experience the fullness of a river not by looking at a still photo, not even by looking at a video, not even by standing next to the river and looking at the river flowing by you. You will experience the fullness of a river only by jumping into it and flowing with it.

If you are to transcend the stationary wisdom that the fallen angels have attempted to make everyone believe in, then you have to be willing to jump into the river of the ever-flowing wisdom that comes from the Ascended Host. This is the true wisdom, the living wisdom, that realizes that as human beings raise their level of consciousness, certain things will become possible that seem impossible today. As we have explained, there are certain individuals who have raised their consciousness to the point, where they have mastery of mind over matter. And then, suddenly, the natural laws that seem completely inviolable to people below the 48th level of consciousness, now become mutable, stretchable, and it is possible to go beyond them. As more and more people raise their consciousness, matter will become less dense. And then, suddenly, there will be possibilities that open up that few people can even envision today.

Discerning between dualistic and non-dualistic wisdom

What can you do, if you want to be one of the forerunners for bringing forth a new form of wisdom? Well, you need to step back from the battle between the dualistic forms of wisdom. If you have a strong desire, a strong resonance with the second ray of wisdom, you probably have a tendency to engage yourself in the debate and seek to get other people to accept the ideas that you see as the highest wisdom.

Yet can you see, that what I encourage you to do here, is to step back from this struggle, to stop seeking to convince others that one idea is right and that all opposing or competing ideas are wrong? For can you see, that this is indeed what the fallen beings have done? They have imposed a standard that something is right and something is wrong, which means that there must be one idea that is right, and then all ideas that are different must be wrong.

But can you see, that at a deeper level, this is based on the assumption that it is possible to bring forth an idea, a thought system, that contains ultimate truth? And so, when you begin to realize that there is no ultimate truth – because truth is not stationary but is the moving river – then you see the futility of this approach. It is not a matter of arguing whether this philosophy or that philosophy is right. It is not even a matter of seeking to find a higher philosophy that will replace the others. It is a matter of truly locking in to wisdom as a living fount, as the flowing river—and then becoming the open door for that wisdom to express itself in various situations.

What is the highest wisdom? It is that everything is an expression of consciousness. And thus, what is manifest right now on earth, what is manifest in the natural environment, is the expression of a certain level of consciousness. But as it is possible to transcend to a higher level of consciousness, then it will also follow that that higher level of consciousness will be expressed as a different outer reality, as a different environment on earth. And thus, when that leap in consciousness has been made, the current environmental problems and the current state of lack of resources will be transcended. And it will now be possible that this planet can give home to 10 billion people, who live an abundant life, materially and spiritually.

***

So can you see, that the purpose of life is the growth in self-awareness? And how do the inhabitants of planet earth grow in self-awareness? They grow by seeing that the natural environment on earth mirrors back to them their own state of consciousness. So that they can then look at the natural environment, look at the imbalances that are found here, and then see that this is an expression of the imbalances in their own state of consciousness. And then, they can make the decision to transcend that state of consciousness. And as they do, they will manifest – precipitate, materialize – a different natural environment.

This, then, is the higher wisdom: that the natural environment is not set in stone, but that the natural environment will evolve, as it has been evolving for billions of years according to science. Yet what is missing from science is the recognition that the development, the evolution, of the natural environment is inextricably linked to the consciousness of humankind. When you begin to realize this, you see that there is not one never-changing truth that must be expressed on earth. For the reality is that what needs to be expressed are ideas that will challenge people in their current state of consciousness and challenge them to transcend that state of consciousness.

For example, the ideas brought fourth by Jesus 2,000 years ago contained much timeless truth. Yet those ideas were then taken and turned into a thought system, namely the Catholic doctrines and dogmas. First of all, by turning any idea into a system, you have already shut off the living flow. Because now the system takes on a life of its own and wants to perpetuate itself instead of flowing with the River of Life. But second of all, what happens is that when you create a system, then you, of course, create a closed box. And according to the second law of thermodynamics, that box will eventually break down.

Do you see, that once a society has been locked into a certain thought system that is limiting people's free flow – their creative consideration of a higher wisdom, their curiosity, their questions – well, then, what is needed are ideas that will challenge the established system and help people look beyond it? If you look at it historically, it was the discoveries of the first scientists that provided the first serious challenge to the Catholic mental box. Yet then you saw how there were people who took the discoveries of science and turned them into a thought system, namely materialism. And then materialism also set limits for the questions people were allowed to ask, and this again hindered the free flow

Discerning between dualistic and non-dualistic wisdom

of thought. And so, today there is a need to question the mental box created by materialism, as there is still a need to question the mental box created by official Christianity.

And yet in 10 or 20 years, there will be a need to ask different questions, for there will always be people who attempt to create a closed mental box out of everything, out of every new idea that comes up. If you were to take an honest look at the spiritual or New Age movement, you would see that there are also people here who have created mental boxes out of various New Age philosophies, even the teachings sponsored by the Ascended Host.

What you realize is, that you have two conflicting forces working in human psychology. One is the ego, which is always grasping for security, and the other is that you are receiving light from your I Will Be Presence that is propelling you forward, to open and expand your mind and therefore transcend your current level of consciousness and expand your self-awareness.

The ego has the effect that it wants to turn any new idea into a system that can give it the security that it craves. And so, what you see in many people is that they will be open to a new idea, but then once they have accepted certain ideas, then the ego will try to take these ideas and turn them into a closed system — and then make people believe that they do not need to ask questions beyond the system, for now they have some ultimate truth.

***

Now, if you transfer this to the environmental debate, you will see how you can begin to question some of the assumptions, some of the fixed ideas, that have dominated this debate for a time. First of all, you need to question the entire philosophy of lack. How can there be a lack of natural resources, when a natural resource is completely dependent on human knowledge? As we have said before, there was a time when oil was not considered a natural resource, because there was not the knowledge of how to make use of it. Yet today you have an entire economy, an entire civilization, that is based on the use of oil as a way to produce energy.

But it is entirely possible to find other ways to produce energy that do not use fossil fuels that have to be taken out of the ground, and that do not produce any form of pollution. The knowledge of how to do this is not currently there, at least not in the public forum. And thus, much of the debate about fossil fuels and the negative effects of fossil fuels could become obsolete by the discovery or public acknowledgment of the knowledge of how to produce energy in other ways. And it would, of course, be much more productive to stimulate the public thinking into bringing forth new sources of energy, than it would be to continue in the current track, where the environmental debate and vast parts of the people engaged in the environmental issue are seeking to limit the production of greenhouse gases or prevent the exploration for new sources of oil, coal or gas.

So do you see, that there is a difference here in approach? What the fallen beings have attempted to do is to capture the privilege of formulating the problem, based on the standard that something is right and something is wrong. Which means that right now the prevailing philosophy that has dominated the environmental debate for a long time, is that there is something that is wrong and this something must be fought, must be stopped, must be destroyed. And of course, since there are people who are promoting or doing what is considered wrong, then those people must be stopped, must be fought or must even be destroyed.

Yet beyond this, there is an even deeper layer, where the fallen beings have managed to make many, many people – many well-meaning people who are truly concerned for the natural environment – believe in the philosophy that what is truly wrong on this planet is human beings. For there is a subtle philosophy underlying the environmental debate, which says that the natural environment would be pristine and perfect without the presence of human beings. And therefore, it would actually be right if human beings were either removed from the earth or at least would withdraw from the natural environment. Or at least would create a sharp division between the areas where human beings can do something with the environment and then these pristine areas that are set aside, where human beings can do nothing.

In other words, this is clearly a dualistic philosophy that seeks to divide the earth into spheres of human influence and spheres with no human influence, and then gradually grow the spheres with no influence more and more. But can you see, that what is really happening here is that human beings are being divided from the planet upon which they live? And thus, can you see how this is in complete opposition to

Discerning between dualistic and non-dualistic wisdom

what we have raised up as the only solution to environmental problems, namely that human beings begin to see a oneness between themselves and the planet upon which they live?

***

Can you see, that once you have this debate – where the problem has been been defined as human beings – then you really have no constructive solution to this debate? For any solution that comes out of this dualistic debate will only continue the age-old struggle, where one group of people seeks to suppress another group of people and the other group of people resist this. And so, you have the ongoing struggle.

And this, of course, is precisely what the fallen beings want to accomplish. They want to keep society trapped in this ongoing struggle between various groups, so that society will not transcend this level of struggle. For it is only when there is struggle, that the fallen beings can form a privileged elite that have power over society. It is the old idea of divide and conquer. Where the elite knows that they must divide the people in order to have any chance of conquering the people and controlling society.

So can you see, that what the fallen beings are doing in the current environmental debate, is that they are keeping people focused on a negative? Where they are always focused on something that is wrong and therefore something that must be fought—which means that there is a group of other people that must be fought? But the different approach, that I am advocating here, is that you step back from the struggle, that you refuse to fight other people or even fight dualistic ideas, by seeking to prove them wrong.

Instead, you plunge yourself into the River of Life that is the flowing fount of wisdom. And then you realize, that the real solution to environmental problems is to bring forth new ideas and new inventions, that go completely beyond the current level of consciousness and therefore can help humankind transcend the current restrictions, the current mental boxes, that dominate the debate.

You bring forth something that is so new, that is so different, that it makes the current debate obsolete. Or it makes the current environmental problems obsolete. There is, as we have said, already technology in the etheric and even in the mental realm that is ready to be released to humankind. And this technology will allow human beings to produce unlimited amounts of energy without any negative environmental consequences whatsoever. Yet this technology cannot be released until a critical mass of people open their minds to the potential for this technology to even exist and to work.

And it also requires, that a critical mass of people realize, that this technology cannot be allowed to be monopolized by a small elite. For my beloved, can you not see that there is indeed various elite groups that have made immense fortunes on certain forms of technology, such as oil, or gas, or coal, or even nuclear power? And they want to keep society trapped in a situation, where people need to use these forms of power to generate energy. So that they can continue to make the profit and exercise the power and control that they have enjoyed so far. And thus, these power elite groups do not want to see the emergence of a new form of technology. Or if a new form of technology cannot be held back, they want to try and control it, so that they can gain a monopoly on it and so that the people are still dependent on these huge conglomerates and corporations for the production of energy.

But the energy production that we are talking about is one that could be entirely decentralized, so that there is no need for huge centralized power plants and huge distribution systems, such as the current power grid that you see. Imagine that every home had a device, a box, that produced electrical power without requiring any fuel and without being hooked up to the grid. Each house would be a completely self-contained unit, which means that you could build a house anywhere, for you were not dependent on being hooked up to a central grid.

Yet can you see how the big corporations would not want such a source of power, because who can control it, who can monopolize it? And therefore, how can one corporation make an inordinate amount of profit on such an invention?

***

These, then, are the kind of ideas that you need to begin to consider and project into the collective consciousness, even insert into the environmental debate. And you can also do a service by challenging the current assumptions. Even if you have no thought system to put in the place of existing systems, you can still have a positive impact by questioning

Discerning between dualistic and non-dualistic wisdom

these systems and pointing out their contradictions and their limitations. Yet for you to be efficient in doing this, you must make an effort to transcend the dualistic mindset, where you always think you have to fight other people or fight certain ideas and label something as wrong.

There are many, many well-meaning people who have taken part in the environmental debate, or have debated in other areas of society, but they have done so based on a negative approach, the approach that requires them to label something as wrong and to therefore fight against other people and the ideas they espouse. It is possible to transcend this and adopt an approach that is entirely positive and that is aimed at challenging existing systems, but not in the sense that they are wrong but in the sense that they are limited and cannot fully answer our questions.

And when we realize that existing systems are limited, then we see the need to look beyond those systems, possibly even to look beyond all systems and lock in to the creative flow that will bring forth new ideas and new inventions. Perhaps even understand that there is an ongoing creative flow that comes from a higher source, and it is precisely this flow that has raised society from the caveman stage to current civilization. And this flow has the potential to raise society much higher, but we are limiting the power of this flow by insisting on holding on to our traditional mental boxes and thought systems.

I can assure you, that there are millions of people in embodiment today, who are ready to actually embrace the awareness of how thought systems limit human progress. These people are willing to experiment and can easily be inspired to experiment by going beyond the traditional thought systems and reaching for an entirely new approach.

***

Now, let us make this a little more concrete. What exactly does this mean for the environmental debate? Well, first of all it means that human beings are not wrong. It is not wrong that human beings are on earth. Human beings are the very purpose for the existence of the earth, human beings have a right to be here and they have a right to exercise their free will as they see fit, regardless of how this affects the natural environment. For the natural environment is not something that existed in a pristine form before human beings appeared on the scene.

The natural environment did exist in a pristine form, as it was created by the Elohim. But the Law of Free Will mandates that humankind has the right to go into the consciousness of duality. And then, the Mater light is content to mirror back, in the form of physical circumstances, what human beings are projecting upon the screen of life through their dualistic state of consciousness.

There is nothing that is wrong with this. It is all a part of the process of the growth in self-awareness. And what humankind needs to do is to acknowledge that current conditions are an expression of their unbalanced state of consciousness, and then transcend that state of consciousness. And so, you see that the consciousness that truly needs to be transcended is the dualistic struggle between different ideas and different groups of people. And when that is transcended, many of the imbalances seen in nature will naturally begin to disappear.

Can you see that, there is a need to challenge the idea that there was a natural environment with certain animal species that existed before humankind entered the stage? This is an idea that has been especially powerful in the United States, because in the recent history of the United States you did have a certain natural environment with certain very prolific animal species, such as the Buffalo, that were only affected by a small number of Native American people. And so, there is this romantic dream in America of the unspoiled and untouched wilderness, that existed before the white man entered the stage and started messing everything up.

Yet can you see, that this dream of an unspoiled wilderness is simply unrealistic? There has not – for many millions of years on this planet – been an unspoiled wilderness. In fact, there has never really been been an unspoiled wilderness in the sense that there has ever been an environment on earth that was not affected by the consciousness of the inhabitants of the earth.

What you see is, that the animal species that existed before the white man entered the stage were not actually brought forth either by God or by a natural process of evolution. Most of the animal species that you see on this planet today are actually expressions of the unbalanced state of consciousness of humankind. That is why you see animal species who compete for resources and certain animal species that outcompete other species that then become extinct. That is why you see carnivores that eat other animals. That is why you see poisonous snakes or insects.

Discerning between dualistic and non-dualistic wisdom

My beloved, it is simply not constructive to argue that humankind should stop being human beings and should return the natural environment to some pristine state that existed in the past. When you know what you know about evolution, even this should make you say – logically – well, what time in the past should we turn the clock back to? When should we choose to stop the clock and say that this was the pristine wilderness? There has never been a pristine state that existed for very long on this planet—if you look at geological time and not human time.

The reality is that most of the animal species you see today are an expression of the unbalanced state of consciousness that people entered into after the fall into duality. Many of the animal species that you see today were actually brought forth in a previous civilization, that had attained the ability to produce genetic mutations and manipulation. This ability was beyond what you have begun to realize now in your civilization. And it was indeed one of the reasons for the collapse of that civilization, because they started even experimenting with human beings and with mixing human and animal DNA.

The reality is that if you really turned the clock back to a truly pristine state that existed before the descent into duality, then there would not be a single one of the current species that you see today that would be in existence. None of these species existed before the fall into the duality. In fact, before the fall into duality, there were very few animal species on this planet.

***

Can you see, that the higher wisdom is to be willing to step back and truly question even the deepest, the most underlying, assumptions that have controlled the environmental debate now for several decades? It is not a matter of looking at the debate in its current form, and then selecting which ideas or which organizations are right in a higher sense—and then going in and fighting for these ideas or organizations to gain dominance.

The higher wisdom is to look at the current environmental debate and realize and acknowledge, that all aspects of it are distorted by the duality consciousness and by the power struggle promoted by the fallen beings. And therefore, it is not a matter of singling out the ideas and organizations that are right. It is a matter of transcending all of them, transcending the entire debate and the foundation for the debate.

I am quite aware that for people who have been engaged in the environmental debate for a long time, this may be a shocking thought. But the reason it is shocking is that you have allowed your egos to create a sense of security out of the belief that you have now figured out the environmental debate. And you have figured out who is right and who is wrong, and therefore you think that by you promoting what you think is right and opposing what you think is wrong, you can feel secure in doing the right thing. But once you let go of this separate self, once you let this separate self die, you will find a new freedom and a new opportunity in espousing a higher approach to the entire environmental issue.

And this is when you will begin to feel, that your mind has attained what you might have glimpsed but never achieved, namely complete freedom to consider new ideas. Look at your life honestly and see how many times a part of your mind has compelled you to limit your curiosity, to not consider ideas that were beyond your existing thought system. And then realize that if you could transcend this mental box, this limitation of your thought process, you would find an immense freedom of mind. For now you are free to flow with new ideas and consider them based on one thing only: do they give you answers that resonate with the inner core of your being?

You do not have to adapt to any outer system in society, any outer philosophy put upon you based on a standard of what is right and wrong. You do not even have to consider an idea based on some ultimate standard of is it right or wrong, is it true or false. You are free to consider any idea based on its explanatory power. Can it answer your questions in a more meaningful way than you have so far found? Does the new idea resonate with the experience you have of the living fount of wisdom that is beyond any thought system in this world?

***

And when you attain this freedom of mind, this freedom of thought, then you can be the open door for bringing forth the ideas that will indeed take the environmental debate to a much higher level. For I trust you can begin to see, that if you are to really solve environmental problems, you cannot look at these problems in an isolated way. You cannot

Discerning between dualistic and non-dualistic wisdom

solve environmental problems by only looking at them as environmental problems, as problems related to the natural environment.

You must see that the environmental debate involves every aspect of human endeavor. Because it goes to the very core of who human beings are, who they see themselves as being. For it is only when human beings follow the old adage, "Human, know thyself" that they can truly develop the right relationship to the planet upon which they live.

It is only when you realize that you are consciousness and the earth is consciousness, that you can begin to feel a sense of oneness that will allow you to transcend the consciousness, where you are an intruder on planet earth. An intruder who can only break down the natural environment, because you are in such a low state of consciousness that you must take what you need through force. And it is only when you transcend that state of consciousness, that you can become what you are meant to be: a co-creator who works with elemental life to bring forth everything you need through the process of manifestation, rather than the process of taking by force.

Again, there are so many ideas that need to be brought out, if the environmental debate is to transcend its current stalemate and be set free to bring forth true and valid solutions. Perhaps you feel overwhelmed, perhaps you feel inspired? But you can overcome the sense of being overwhelmed only by being willing to flow with the river. And you can be ultimately inspired also by flowing with the river.

So allow yourself to step back from your preconceived opinions and thought systems. Perhaps lie down on your bed, when it is quiet. Focus on your heart. Seek to establish a connection to your I Will Be Presence. And then ask your Presence to show you how it looks at specific environmental problems, or at the entire environmental debate, or at the relationship between human beings and the planet upon which they live.

If you can do this with a completely open mind and heart – that does not seek to impose a preconceived opinion upon the answer – then you might find yourself transported outside of your body, looking down at the earth from a great height, and therefore gaining an entirely different perspective on the current problems and issues.

There is a fundamental difference between looking at a problem from inside the consciousness that created the problem, and then looking at the problem from outside that consciousness. Once you begin to experience that difference, you will know true wisdom. And then, you will never again be fully identified with the false wisdom that comes only through the consciousness that sees itself separated from the object—and thus sees a fundamental difference between subject and object.

Once you go beyond this subject-object duality and experience the true gnosis of oneness between subject and object – because you realize that both are consciousness – then you will gain an entirely different perspective. And thus, you will be the open door for the very ideas that can take the environmental debate to an entirely new level.

Dare to flow with the living river of wisdom that I am. For I am Lanto, the Chohan of the second ray of the living fount of wisdom.

Key 25
Selfish love will not
heal Mother Earth

Paul the Venetian is my name. The Chohan of the third ray is my title. Yet beauty is my love.

I come, then, to appeal to those who feel that their being resonates with the third ray of love. I come to appeal that you transcend your concept of love, as explained in my previous discourse. And I come to appeal that you take this higher concept of love and apply it to the environmental issue and the environmental debate.

This will be an opportunity for you to become an open door for bringing a perspective into the environmental debate, that has so far been sorely missing. This perspective can be the distinction between lower love, selfish love, and the higher, unselfish love that is God's love.

What you see in the environmental debate today is that there are many, many people who are engaged in this debate because they have a love for nature, a love for animals, a love for the natural environment, even a love for Mother Earth. Yet the question that needs to be asked – and that needs to be asked openly and honestly – is whether the many people who claim to love Mother Nature truly have a higher form of love, or whether they are motivated by a kind of love that is as yet imperfect, that has not yet reached the highest potential, the highest possible level of love?

***

There are, indeed, many people who will claim that they love nature or love animals. Yet if you look more closely, you do indeed see, that they do not love the object that they claim to love; they love something in themselves. They love an idea, they love a worldview, they love a certain feeling that it gives them to express what they claim to be love, but which is truly possessiveness, the desire to control one's environment.

There are many examples of how this has, indeed, affected the environmental debate, but let us begin at the overall level. As we have said, there are 144 levels of consciousness possible on earth. What is the difference between the very lowest and the very highest? Well, at the highest level of consciousness your love is truly unconditional, which means that you love all life, you love the All, you love life as a whole. You see the oneness of all life, and your entire thoughts, actions and feelings are aimed only at raising up the whole. As you go towards the opposite extreme, you see people who become more and more self-centered, they become more and more centered on the separate self.

Now, my beloved, what is it that makes it possible for the Conscious You to uphold or be trapped in the illusion that it is not an extension of the Presence but a separate self? Well, for each individual that is trapped in this illusion, there is a particular mental image that the individual has created. We might say that each individual has created a personal role that it is playing in the theater of life.

As you go towards the lowest of the 144 levels, you go to people who are completely self-centered. And what does this mean? It means that they love only themselves; they love only the separate self. But what is it they truly love? They love the idea, the mental image, that defines the separate self and defines it as separate from, and in most cases even superior to, all others.

So you now see people who are in love with themselves, who are in love with their separate selves and the image that defines that self. This is why you will see, that there are people – both in the environmental debate and in other forms of debate – that are so in love with a particular idea that they cannot, they will not, look beyond it. They will not see that it is limited or contradictory, and they will not consider that there might be a higher way to look at the issue. This, of course, is the case with the fallen beings, but there are many other beings who have followed them and who still follow them into these deeper levels of selfishness.

Take note, that when you go to the lowest level of the 144 possible states of consciousness, you are not dealing with people who have a very limited state of consciousness. You are dealing with people who have the highest degree of selfishness, and this means that these beings might seem to have very admirable qualities. The reality is that the lower you go towards the lowest level, the more skilled people are at

Selfish love will not heal Mother Earth 391

presenting themselves as not being selfish but as being truly working for a greater cause. The fallen beings who are in embodiment on earth are very skilled at appearing to be truly selfless, truly altruistic, truly capable of promoting a cause, an ultimate cause.

They are great at presenting themselves as being right, and this is why they pull with them many of those who have also gone below the 48th level of consciousness, but who have not yet gone into the extreme levels of selfishness and self-centeredness. And thus, they cannot see that what the fallen beings are presenting is actually a completely self-centered thought system, that really only has the purpose of raising themselves up as being superior to others because they are the leaders.

***

When you look at the environmental debate with this in mind, you can then begin to ask yourself the question: Will a particular idea actually benefit Mother Earth, or will it only, so to speak, benefit certain human beings and their clearly self-centered interests? You see, my beloved, as Lanto has explained, there is a false wisdom of the second ray, a perversion of the second ray.

As we have explained, a co-creator starts out on the first ray by being willing to experiment. And it then moves on to the second ray, where it now begins to evaluate its experiments. But there is, of course, the possibility that the being will go into the level of duality, where it is not evaluating the outcome of its experiments based on the higher wisdom of God. Instead, it is now evaluating the outcome of its experiments based on the dualistic wisdom, where it can set itself up as being "God," in the sense that it defines the parameters, and therefore defines that what it is doing is right—no matter what it is doing and no matter what the consequences are for the whole.

When a being has gone into this false wisdom, there really is no absolute way to determine what is right and wrong, what is true and false, what is real and unreal. For everything is relative, everything is subject to argumentation. So how can a being escape this quagmire of intellectual argumentation back and forth? For you can surely see, can you not, that the most intellectual people are the ones who can argue for or against any issue without finding any higher solution?

The only way to escape, to transcend, this false wisdom, this dualistic wisdom, is indeed true love, a love for something higher than what has been defined by the dualistic wisdom. Yet of course, there is also the possibility that on the third ray people will be deceived into going into the selfish forms of love, where they will now become even more sure that their dualistic wisdom is right. For they are so in love with themselves and their own ability to present sophisticated arguments, that they are not even willing to step back and ask themselves the question of whether there is a higher way to look at the issue than through the dualistic arguments that they have so far seen as the ultimate form of wisdom.

Of course, when you open yourself to love, then the pure love of God is the love for something higher, the love for self-transcendence. And this begins by realizing that what you have right now, what is in existence right now, is not the ultimate potential. Nothing that exists right now – in your personal mind or on the planet upon which you live – represents an ultimate or highest possible potential. There is the potential that you could transcend your current state of consciousness, there is the potential that Mother Earth could transcend her current state, her current physical manifestation. There is nothing in manifestation on earth today that could not be transcended.

Yet what is the condition that must be met, before you can transcend your current state of consciousness? You must be willing to let go of the old state of consciousness, you must be willing to let the old sense of self die. Christ represents the willingness to transcend, the willingness to move closer to oneness. And that is why Jesus said that if you seek to save your life, meaning your old sense of self, you will lose it. But if you are willing to let that old sense of self die, to lose your life in order to follow Christ – the ongoingness – well, then you will find eternal life in that self-transcendence.

But in order to let the old die, there must be something you love more than the old self. And so, can you see that when you begin to feel that love for something more, there is suddenly no belief, no idea, no mental image that you have that you are not willing to question, that you are not willing to look beyond? For you realize that any mental image you have can so easily become a graven image, that stands between you and a direct experience of the pure awareness that connects you to your

Selfish love will not heal Mother Earth

I Will Be Presence, to your I AM Presence, to the spiritual hierarchy, the Chain of Being and ultimately to your Creator.

***

When you have false love, you are so in love with your graven image, the graven image that defines your separate self, that you are not willing to look beyond it. You are literally on your knees day and night worshiping that image, prostrating yourself before it. Even though you may think with the outer mind that you are worshiping either the God defined by your image or some natural law or process of evolution, that you think has brought forth the current conditions on earth.

Only when you acquire the higher love, can you go beyond this perverted love and begin to worship what is beyond your current image—and thus being willing to transcend the image and let the old die. And that, of course, is when you can begin to see the higher reality that is beyond the dualistic wisdom, namely the higher reality that all life is one and that all life has the purpose of coming closer to oneness—oneness between Spirit and matter, but even in the matter realm oneness between all forms. So that human beings no longer see themselves as separate beings, living on a planet that is a dead clump of matter. Instead, they see themselves as spiritual beings, who are one with each other and one with the spiritual being of the planet and one with the spiritual beings who brought forth the planet.

This, then, is higher love. This, then, is true love. This, then, is God's love.

And when you have grasped this love, when you experience this love, then you can look at the current environmental debate and you can clearly begin to identify what is false love, what is self-centered love. And thus, you can begin to sense even the vibration of selfish love, contrasted with unselfish love. You can see through the arguments presented by various groups of people, and you can sense that they vibrate below the level of true love. For even though they claim to be formulated out of concern for the environment or the animals, you know that they are truly formulated based on the absolute desire to uphold the image of the separate self, and to set it up as being superior to other people, using it as a tool to control others—and therefore raise up the separate self of the fallen beings to some ultimate status on earth.

***

My beloved, there are many people who truly think they are well-meaning and who have a great concern for animals. They have created various organizations to promote the cause of animals and to minimize the suffering of animals. Yet there is an important distinction to be made here. It is perfectly true that human beings have no right to cause the suffering of animals. Yet the ultimate way to overcome this suffering is to do what we have already explained. For as long as a human being sees itself as separate from animals, then it will always be possible for that human being to ignore the suffering of animals and to justify why it has to do what it has to do.

You will see this, for example, in medical experiments on animals, where there are people who think it is perfectly justifiable to cause suffering to animals in order to save the lives and minimize the suffering of human beings. And so, you can see that the ultimate way to overcome man's inhumanity to animals is to help man overcome the sense of being a separate being. For when you begin to sense that all life is one, you sense a oneness between yourself and the animals. And thus, you would never do certain things to animals; you would do unto others what you want them to do unto you.

What is actually happening is that many of the animal rights activists are promoting an unbalanced form of love, where these people truly love animals more than they love human beings. Instead of promoting a higher state of consciousness, a higher state of awareness, among human beings, they are promoting a dualistic approach that defines certain actions as right and certain actions as wrong. And thus, they are now seeking to limit or control the people who are doing what they have defined as wrong.

Let us take the issue of medical experimentation on animals. Is it right or is it wrong? Well, you cannot simply answer that question with a yes or no. For you see, given the current state of consciousness of humankind, there are indeed many diseases. And given the current state of consciousness of humankind, there are many diseases that have only what we might call mechanical or force-based solutions. At present, these diseases can only be combated through various forms of medicine. And so, given this state of affairs, it can be seen as a necessary evil to conduct experiments on animals, that although it causes suffering to a

Selfish love will not heal Mother Earth

limited number of animals could eventually alleviate the suffering of a great number of people.

Of course, in order to accept this, you have to overcome the unbalanced love for animals that loves animals more than people. So that you are not caught up in the subtle belief that diseases truly should not be cured, because that would allow the human population to grow and thereby increase the environmental problems overall. When you take a closer look at this, you realize that there are indeed people who are engaged in the environmental debate, and although they on a surface level claim to be engaged because they love nature or love animals, if you go to the deeper levels of the psychology, you see that they actually hate people, they hate themselves.

This is a topic I will talk more about shortly, but let me first finish the topic of diseases. Instead of thinking that the only way to cure diseases is through force-based means, it is indeed possible to take another approach. It is possible to promote a different worldview, a different paradigm, based on what we have given in this book, namely that everything is consciousness. You see, when you recognize that everything is consciousness, you must also recognize that every physical disease is the visible result of a particular state of consciousness, a particular illusion. You could, in fact, map all diseases known to humankind into groups based on the levels of consciousness that are below the 48th level.

So when you realize that everything is a manifestation of consciousness, you realize that when a person has a certain disease, the ultimate way to deal with that disease is not to find some drug or chemical that can mask the symptoms of the disease. The ultimate way is to identify the state of consciousness that has precipitated the disease, and then help the person transcend that state of consciousness—thereby transcending the disease permanently, instead of simply manifesting it again in a future lifetime. You will then see, that if you truly loved animals, you would focus your attention on promoting this shift in consciousness, whereby the current medical testing on animals would simply become obsolete. Because it would then be seen, that there were better ways to combat disease than through chemicals.

And therefore, instead of taking a narrow view of focusing on animal testers, you could also take the wider view of realizing that the current approach to disease is very much driven by the desire for profit.

Because only chemicals can be subject to patents and therefore give corporations an ultimate outcome of profit. And so, when you see the deeper reality of consciousness, and you begin to promote a shift in consciousness, well then you can also help bring society beyond the clutches of the current capitalist system, where so much is driven by the profit of an elite, rather than for the good of all.

***

Let me now return to the concept that there are people who will claim to be engaged in the environmental issue because they love animals. But when you look deeper into the psychology, you see that they actually hate people. And of course, people who hate people ultimately are people, and therefore they hate themselves.

So what you see is that when you go to the highest level of the 144 levels of consciousness, you have people who have no hatred whatsoever, who have only love for the All. But as you go towards the lowest of the 144 levels of consciousness, you see people who on the one hand have an increasing love for the separate self but also must have, at the same time, an increasing hatred for anything that seems to threaten the separate self.

And this is why you will see, that there are people who have displayed this open hatred for other people. Take for example Hitler, who was willing to kill six million Jews – and many more if it had been possible – in order to worship his graven image of what the human race should be like. Take Stalin, take Mao Zedong in China and other dictators who have committed genocide and killed millions and millions of their own people. For they were not their own people; the reality being that when you go towards the lowest level of the 144 levels of consciousness, nobody is your own people. For you are all alone, defining yourself as set apart from the rest of the human race, being superior to all other human beings.

Yet this also means that in order to uphold this illusion, you have to hate anything that threatens the illusion of your superiority. Which also means that you hate God, you hate Christ, which is why the leaders of the Jewish religion wanted Jesus killed. For he threatened their illusion that they were the superior leaders, sitting between the people and God—therefore being gods on earth.

Selfish love will not heal Mother Earth

When you recognize this, you can begin to realize what is the deeper reality. As we have said before, God has no opposite. And likewise, God's love has no opposite. It is not correct to say that hatred is the opposite of God's love, for God's love is unconditional. And that which is unconditional can have no opposite.

Opposites can exist only in a dualistic system, where there are certain conditions that define one dualistic polarity and other conditions that define the opposite dualistic polarity. So what you see is that hatred is not the opposite of unconditional love; it is the opposite of conditional love.

What you see is that once you go into the consciousness of duality, you cannot have pure love. You can only have a love that is in a polarity with hatred. And so, you see the cause of what is sometimes called a love-hate relationship, where two people seem to love each other passionately, but then something happens and now one or both hate the other.

The reason for this is that as you go towards the lowest level of consciousness, the distance between love and hatred becomes blurred, so that you more and more easily shift from one to the other. You shift from what is seemingly love, but is selfish love, to what is seemingly hatred but is simply the expression of the fact that you oppose anything that threatens your illusion of separation.

***

Can you see, then, that there are so many things in the environmental debate that are simply reinforcing the illusion of separation, the illusion that human beings are separated from the planet upon which they live, are separated from each other, and are separated from any higher reality beyond what has been defined by the fallen beings—who have captured the privilege of formulating the problem? And who have defined the environmental debate based on the underlying philosophy that human beings are the problem.

Do you see, that the very foundation for the current environmental debate is self-hatred? Where does self-hatred come from? It comes from the fallen beings who, as they go towards the lowest level of consciousness, begin to see themselves as one outstanding individual who is set apart from all other people. Which means that this individual, then, must hate all other people. And so, this means that these individuals, as they become more and more selfish, they start promoting – without even realizing this – philosophies and thought systems that spring from hatred of human beings. And as these thought systems are accepted by people who are not quite at the lowest level of consciousness, well then you see the spread of a philosophy that is based on a hatred of the human race and causes this self-hatred to spread to many other people.

My beloved, can you begin to see, with everything we have given you, that humankind will never, ever solve environmental problems as long as they approach these problems with a philosophy that is based on and promotes self-hatred? There is only one true and real solution to environmental problems, and that is to promote a worldview based on the reality that all life is one, and that there is a fundamental oneness between human beings and the planet upon which they live.

Environmental problems are created by people; this is true. But they are created by people who are below the 48th level of consciousness and therefore have a force-based approach to everything. It is not a realistic solution to kill all these people. For who are the people who can think that the solution is to kill the people who caused the problem or to restrict their freedom? It is only people who are below the 48th level of awareness.

So can you see, that as long as you allow the environmental debate to be dominated by philosophies that spring from below the 48th level of awareness, then this debate will only perpetuate the dualistic struggle? For of course, all of the people who are below the 48th level of consciousness are not going to one day suddenly decide to commit collective suicide. They do not see what they are doing, so therefore they will appoint another group of people as the scapegoats. And they might attempt to kill that group of people, and this might result in a war between two groups of people. But nevertheless, you will never have a situation where you will overcome a problem through this perpetual dualistic struggle.

The only viable solution is that the top 10% of the people make a conscious effort to raise themselves above the dualistic thought systems and therefore create a magnetic pull on the 80% of the population. So that the population is pulled up and can now see the futility of this dualistic struggle, can now see the incredible simplicity of making one group of people the scapegoats for environmental problems. And can

Selfish love will not heal Mother Earth

even go beyond this and see the deception behind thinking that human beings can only be a problem.

***

As we have said before, the purpose of earth is to serve as a cosmic schoolroom for self-aware beings. Human beings are not the problem; human beings are the purpose for the earth, the very reason for being for the earth. It was never a goal to have a planet with a pristine natural environment untouched by man. Yet it was the original vision of the Elohim to have a balanced environment on earth, that could provide the abundant life for 10 billion people, without having the kind of imbalances you see on earth today.

Yet how can this be attained? Not by killing certain groups of people, not by forcefully restricting the activities of certain groups of people, not by humankind at large voluntarily restricting certain activities. It can be achieved only when a critical mass of people raise their consciousness beyond the 48th level, and therefore begin to see as self-evident the limitations and the futility of the duality consciousness. And then, you will see the entire planet transcend to a higher level, where gradually the environmental problems that you see today will become obsolete. Because now there will be different ways to approach the conditions that today produce many environmental problems, such as pollution.

So can you see, that if you are to be one of the forerunners for healing Mother Earth, you cannot allow yourself to be trapped in even the most subtle philosophies that are based on self-hatred or hatred of the human race? You must transcend to the higher form of love, where you love human beings. This is not to say that you need to love their egos, that you need to love the selfish expressions that they are trapped in. You do not need to love the separate self, but you need to overcome the love that is blind and that is focused on the separate self.

You need to attain the true love that opens your eyes to all, so that you can see beyond the separate self and see that there is a core of that person's being. And therefore, that person is an extension of spiritual beings in a higher realm. And there is a core of the earth that is beyond the current imbalances, and thus the earth has the potential to transcend itself as any individual has the potential to transcend itself.

Do you see, that when you lock in to love, you realize that nothing that is in existence right now is permanent or is the highest potential? Two things then happen. The Alpha aspect is that you now become willing to look beyond current conditions and reach for the higher vision, the immaculate concept. The Omega aspect is that you are no longer attached to anything that is, for you are willing to let it die, so that a higher manifestation can be brought forth. So that the current un-immaculate concept can be replaced by the immaculate concept. This is true love, the love for something more, the love for all life to become more. This is God's love.

***

If you are at the level of consciousness, where the third ray resonates with your being, then you have a higher potential. You can have a much greater impact on the environmental issue, if you will step back from the self-centered love that might have driven you to engage in this issue so far. You will have a much higher impact, if you are willing to realize that what might have driven your efforts so far has been that you were in love with a graven image, a graven image of yourself, a graven image of the world, a graven image of what nature should be like.

Realize that you have had this love because you knew – at a deeper level of your being – that current conditions on earth are not right, in the sense that they are not the highest possible. But then realize that the way to fulfill this inner knowing is not through the duality consciousness, but only by reaching beyond it. And then, be willing to look at the environmental issue with new eyes and identify the areas, where it has been polluted and perverted by people who might claim to love, but who only love these graven images that they have created, based on a state of consciousness that is trapped in duality, trapped in the force-based mindset that something has gone wrong. And we are the ones who must correct it in this epic battle between good and evil.

The epic battle between good and evil only exists in the duality consciousness, for only there can there be opposites. And when you begin to look beyond it and tune in to the reality of God's love, you know that in true love there are no opposites. There are no conditions, so how can there be opposites? And thus, when you begin to experience that love as a flowing stream coming through you, you will find that you will spontaneously begin to see the limitations of the force-based philosophies and actions that people take in the environmental debate. And then, you will find that you will spontaneously become an open door for promoting ideas and thoughts that can take this debate to a higher level.

And this, my beloved, is your highest potential. Look at the environmental debate so far, and see how it is locked in a pattern between various power elite groups who promote competing thought systems. Then, see how few people have grasped the higher vision and how few people are promoting such a vision. And then, step back and see how the current environmental debate is not actually helping to heal Mother Earth. It is only helping to rip her wounds open time and time again, by injecting negative emotional energy upon elemental life.

And then, when you begin to feel the higher love, you will find that you will spontaneously transcend any desire to perpetuate this struggle. You will spontaneously find that you will flow with the River of Life, and you will become an open door for inserting ideas and thoughts that are beyond duality.

Do you see, here, that it is not our aim with this book to give you a fixed philosophy, a new thought system to outcompete the old thought systems? For we are the Ascended Host; we have transcended duality. We have no desire to go down and battle the fallen beings by promoting some ultimate thought system. We have no desire to see our true students battle the fallen beings by promoting another thought system to outcompete the thought systems of the fallen beings.

Allow yourself to become an open door for the light of God. And as the light in the room is increased, the fallacies and the contradictions of the thought systems of the fallen beings will become more and more obvious. And then, a word here, an idea there, will be sufficient to awaken more and more people to the need for an entirely new approach. An approach that is not force-based and that does not simply promote the self-interest of certain groups among the power elite, or even certain completely self-centered individuals that have only one desire, namely to raise themselves up as gods on earth.

My beloved, allow yourself some time to step back and open your heart, mind and being to the flow of unconditional love. For once you have felt that unconditional love for yourself, you will begin to know that this is the force that drives all creation—and that there are no conditions that can prevent this flow of love from transforming the planet.

The only reason that the planet is currently in a lower state, is that unconditional love respects the free will of the inhabitants of this planet. And thus, it will not overpower them with love—if they are in love with their conditions.

And thus, your highest form of service is to be the open door for this love and to help other people recognize the difference between conditional love, that is not true love, and then the unconditional love of God that seeks only to raise up all life, based on the underlying knowledge that regardless of appearances on earth, all life is one.

My beloved, when you align yourself with this living, flowing love, the entire universe is on your side. For the driving force behind the existence and the expansion of the universe is the desire to come back into oneness, oneness between Creator and creation. And so, if you desire to have the maximum impact on healing Mother Earth, then allow yourself to flow with the River of Life, the River of Love.

Key 26
Accelerating the environmental debate to a new level

I am Serapis Bey, and I come to give you the perspective on what you can do to contribute to the environmental debate, if you feel that the fourth ray of purity is the one that most resonates with your current state of consciousness. So what can you, indeed, do? Well, you can realize what is the essence of the fourth ray, namely acceleration.

So, it is not a point to look at the current environmental debate and identify the problems, and then try to solve those problems. The point is to accelerate the entire environmental debate to the level, where there is an entirely new way to look at the problems and to look at potential ways to rise beyond the consciousness that created the problems.

If you reread my previous discourse, you will see that the fourth ray marks a turning point on the path. Students come to the fourth ray only when they have passed through the initiations of the first three rays. And they will pass the initiations of the fourth ray, only when they have found a balance between the three first rays of power, wisdom and love. So in a sense, integration between the first three rays is necessary in order to find this balance. And only when you have balance, will you be able to reach for that something higher that allows you – and that will allow humankind – to accelerate beyond the level of consciousness that has created current environmental problems.

What happens to those that have not found balance between the first three rays is, that they will inevitably go into the perversion of those rays. Thus, they will seek to solve environmental problems based on one, or even more than one, of the perversions of the first three rays. Some will think that the only solution is to use power to overpower those who are the cause of environmental problems. Others will think that it is a matter of using science to find new ways to solve the current problems. And still others will use a perverted form of love to say that it is a matter of turning the clock back to some edenic state, where all the animals ran around, unhindered by man, loving each other. And where even the wolves or the lions ate grass and did not chase other animals.

What you see in all these people is that when there is a lack of balance, they fall right into the age-old dualistic struggle. This struggle is, as we have now explained many times, based on the concept that there is something that is right and something that is wrong—and that you and your thought system have defined the ultimate standard for judging what is right and wrong. People then inevitably become seduced into thinking, that they can use their standard for right and wrong to define who is causing environmental problems. And once you have appointed another group of people as the scapegoat, as the cause, well, then it becomes obvious that the only possible solution is that those other people must stop doing what they are doing that threatens the environment. And if they will not do so voluntarily, well then inevitably it becomes necessary to use some kind of force.

You again go into the age-old struggle of fighting other human beings, seeking to force them. And this has only one effect, namely to perpetuate the struggle, put more and more negative energy upon elemental life and thereby create more and more imbalances in the natural environment.

***

How can you become a force for accelerating humankind beyond this age-old struggle? Well, you must lock in to what is the essence of the fourth ray, namely that there is something beyond the struggle and something beyond the duality consciousness that has created and that perpetuates the struggle.

This is the essence of the fourth ray. You may call it the ray of purity, as many have done. Yet you will only understand what purity is, when you understand that it cannot be defined by a standard on earth. For any standard that can be set up on earth, will – at the present level of consciousness – become just another dualistic standard for judging other people.

So, what can give you a deeper understanding of the fourth ray? Well, my beloved, my brother, Paul the Venetian, said that his love is for beauty. And indeed, one could take beauty and say that that which is pure is also that which is beautiful. Take, for example, an honest look at the animal species found on earth. You may look at the African savanna and think this represents an example of some unspoiled wilderness that should have been left as it was, untouched by the white man.

Yet is a hippopotamus beautiful? Is a rhinoceros beautiful? Is a crocodile beautiful? Is a wildebeest beautiful? Take an honest look at many of the animal species found on this planet and evaluate them based on your current sense of beauty. You will find, if you are honest, that many of them are not beautiful. You will find that there are many other things in nature that are not beautiful, even according to your current standard of beauty.

For truly, if you take a look, you will see that, of course, beauty can also be perverted and has indeed been perverted, especially by the advertising industry. Nevertheless, if you go beyond this outer, programmed sense of beauty, you will see that most people have an inherent sense of what is beautiful. And this sense is not really easy to define as an outer standard. It is ineffable, transcendental, hard to pin down. But it is an instant intuitive reaction, that you can learn to recognize whenever you view something. If you pay attention, you will find that in your heart you will have an instant sensation of whether this is beautiful or not.

And this sense can be developed, until you have a clear sense of what is pure and impure. For that which is pure, will also be beautiful. For surely, the Elohim could never envision something that was ugly, unbalanced or inharmonious. And so, you see that your intuitive sense is your connection to your I Will Be Presence. Your I Will Be Presence has a desire to express itself in the material world, but it was not the I Will Be Presence of any person that brought forth the many ugly things you currently see on earth, whether you call them natural or man-made.

The I Will Be Presence has a desire to express itself within the framework set by the Elohim and the Chain of Being, going all the way back to the Creator. And when you are in tune with this River of Life, this flowing stream of the Holy Spirit, you will bring forth only what is beautiful, what is harmonious and therefore raises the vibration of the All. When you have some sense of atunement with your I Will Be Presence, you will have that instant sense of whether something is beautiful according to the spherical sense of the Presence, or whether something is out of alignment with this universal sense of beauty, harmony and purity.

If you are willing to develop this sense – this intuitive sense of beauty, of harmony, of purity – then you can become the open door for bringing this element into the environmental debate. And when you realize that that which is not beautiful is not in alignment with the higher vision of the Elohim, then you can become the open door for bringing an impulse into the environmental debate that is sorely missing.

***

The problem is the tendency to hold on to the old, based on the idea that what existed before it was disturbed by human beings must be natural or good. Yet, as we have explained, there is hardly anything on earth that has not been distorted by the duality consciousness, by humankind going into the lower state of consciousness. Even the animal species and many conditions in nature are a product of the fact that human beings have projected negative energy and impure thoughtforms upon elemental life. And thus, what elemental life has outpictured is not the original vision of the Elohim, but the lower vision of human beings.

What is the point in holding on to the old? That which existed before your current civilization was not necessarily any purer than what your current civilization is able to bring forth. If you truly love Mother Earth, if you truly want to be a force for healing Mother Earth, it is not a matter of turning the clock back. It is a matter of turning the clock forward, of accelerating the growth of humankind. But this must be a growth in consciousness, not a growth in outer knowledge or the power to force nature into compliance with some thought system or other.

Those who are students on the fourth ray, must become a force for accelerating the environmental debate to a new level. Where you are willing to let go of, willing to question, the intellectual holy cows that have so far been running around undisturbed in the garden that many environmentally aware people as seeking to create, the Garden of Eden—but a garden based on their own definition of what should be edenic.

These are the definitions that must go. In my previous discourse I explained how, in my spiritual retreat, I put together people who have the greatest potential to clash. The only way they can move on from this is that they begin to let go of the thought systems, the philosophies, the expectations that have set them apart. They let go of all these ideas and beliefs based on the duality consciousness, and they accelerate themselves beyond that level of consciousness.

You will not solve, humankind will not solve, environmental problems as long as most human beings are trapped in this consciousness of seeing themselves set apart from other groups of people. As long as you use the environmental issue to reinforce the division between various groups of people, you will only perpetuate the dualistic struggle. So those who are on the fourth ray must become instruments for accelerating the debate beyond this need to find a scapegoat, beyond this need to reinforce divisions and conflicts.

You must become spokesmen for cooperation, but it cannot be cooperation based on the narrow self-interests that spring from those who are below the 48th level of consciousness. It must be cooperation based on what happens to those who have gone beyond the 48th level, and can therefore begin to see that there is something higher than the duality consciousness, something higher than the force-based mindset, something higher than their previous thought system.

This is what can bring new life into the environmental debate, for right now the debate is dominated by the consciousness and the philosophy of death.

***

The death consciousness is the division between Creator and creation. When you set yourself apart from the River of Life, you will inevitably go into the fear of death. You cannot – you *cannot* – go into the duality consciousness without having the fear of death as your eternal companion.

I am the hierarch of the ascension temple at Luxor. What is the main requirement you must fulfill in order to qualify for the ascension? You must overcome the consciousness of death, the illusion of death.

This illusion was originally created, when the fallen beings separated themselves from the River of Life. It has been their companion ever since, and even though we have said that they have a desire to set themselves up as gods on earth, you must realize that the deeper desire they have is to set themselves up as gods on earth because they think this will make them immortal, this will help them overcome their fear of death, the fear that is eating up their lives.

The fallen beings on earth have spread so many subtle philosophies based on this consciousness of death and the dream of some mechanical way to secure eternal life. There is no mechanical way to secure eternal life. There is only one way to become immortal, and that is to accelerate yourself beyond duality and rejoin the River of Life. Where you flow with the immortal stream of God's consciousness, that is constantly transcending itself, accelerating itself beyond its former level, whatever that level might have been.

The consciousness of death wants to stop the clock, wants to stop the flow of time, wants to raise up a standard and then make life conform to that standard. For the consciousness of death thinks, that if it can prevent things from changing, then it will have secured some form of immortality. Yet can you see, that this is actually incompatible with the true teachings behind both Christianity and science?

As we have said, these true teachings have been perverted, and have been perverted precisely because of the duality consciousness. They have been perverted because of the fear of death. And so, what did the fear of death do to Christianity? It raised up Jesus as the only son of God, as the only road to salvation. Thereby giving people the belief that if they only follow Christ, if they only declare Jesus to be their Lord and Savior, they are guaranteed to be saved, not here on earth but in a future existence.

What is the concept of materialism? Well, it is that the material world is all there is. And therefore, there is no point in even trying to go beyond a certain framework, for this framework represents the highest possible reality. And thus, it is believed that once humankind knows all the laws of nature – and learns how to make use of them through force-based technology – well then they will be able to create a society, a civilization, that can endure forever.

Yet the true teachings of Christianity is indeed what Jesus said, that those who seek to save their life shall lose it, but those who are willing to lose their lives for the sake of following Christ shall find eternal life in that self-transcendence. So, constant and perpetual self-transcendence is indeed the core of Christ's true teachings.

And then, when you look at what science has discovered about the process of evolution and the second law of thermodynamics, you see precisely the same. There has never been a static state on this planet, for as long as people have discovered fossil records, they see how one species has lived for a time and then been replaced by another species. And this has gone on for billions of years.

The second law of thermodynamics makes it clear, that no closed system can exist, for any closed system would self-destruct. And taken to its logical extreme, this law also makes it clear that the material universe cannot be a closed system, for it would surely have self-destructed. In fact, it would never even have gotten started in the process of differentiation.

***

And so, you see the reality here. There is nothing that can stand still, so it is pointless to base the entire environmental debate on the subtle concept that human beings should seek to preserve something in nature. As we have said, there is hardly anything on earth that is not affected by the duality consciousness. And this means one very simple thing. There is hardly anything on earth that is worth preserving in its current state. Anything on earth can be accelerated into a higher state, and this is the purpose of life. And thus, it should also be the purpose of the environmental debate.

You cannot become so blinded by the desire to preserve a particular species of frogs, that you think this can justify holding back the growth of human society to a higher level. Surely, there is a need, at the current level of consciousness, to limit certain activities, where those who are blinded by profit would wantonly destroy anything in nature that stands in the way of their profit machine. Nevertheless, it is not the ultimate solution that society should continue forever to put on these restrictions. For there is a way to transcend any level, and once society begins to transcend the very level of force-based technology, then it will longer be necessary to destroy natural resources in order to produce energy or anything else humankind needs.

Nevertheless, you must also understand that when humankind does transcend the level of consciousness that makes force-based technology necessary, well then humankind will also stop projecting so much negative energy upon elemental life. And this means that elemental life will inevitably be accelerated, and therefore be able to outpicture something in nature that is closer to the original vision of the Elohim. And when elemental life begins to come closer to the vision of the Elohim, then many of the conditions you currently see in the natural environment will simply disappear.

Many of the animal species that you currently see, will inevitably disappear, when elemental life is purified from the negative energy projected by humankind. And thus, instead you will see the emergence of new forms of animals and plants that are far more beautiful than what you can currently imagine.

And my beloved, those who are beginning to lock in to the fourth ray, will know that this is not a loss; this is a gain. This is not something to be resisted, this is not something to be lamented, this is not something to be postponed. Indeed, this is something to be accelerated, so that the earth can transcend, as quickly as possible, to a higher state with a more pure, with a more beautiful, expression of natural life.

***

So how can you become an instrument for this transformation? You can do so by locking in to the essence of the fourth ray, which is that you overcome the tendency to battle other people or battle other ideas. On the fourth ray you will pass the initiations only when you completely accelerate yourself beyond a negative outlook on life.

What do I mean with a negative outlook, a negative approach? I mean that you judge everything based on a standard of right and wrong, and then you think you have to somehow battle, or restrict, or destroy, or remove that which you have defined as wrong.

Those who sit at my retreat and fight – day after day, year after year, decade after decade – are all blinded by this idea that they have to prove someone else wrong and prove themselves right, or prove one idea wrong or another right. They will never move on, until they simply walk away from this entire mindset that something has to be right and something has to be wrong. They will never accelerate, until they move beyond the mindset that thinks it can only raise itself up in comparison to others, and therefore can only raise itself up by putting other people down.

When you pass the initiations of the fourth ray, you begin to realize, that there is something higher than your current worldview, than the dualistic worldview. And thus, you become willing to reach for that something higher. And this means that you go beyond the desire to put

Accelerating the environmental debate to a new level

anything down, and you begin to lock in to the pure intention of raising up all life. You are not seeking to prove other people wrong or to get society to restrict their freedom. Instead, you are seeking to inspire other people to accelerate their consciousness to the point, where they spontaneously make better choices.

Can you see the essential difference here? Those who hold on to the standard that something is right and something is wrong, are inevitably tempted into seeking to use force to control the free will and the actions of other people. Whereas those who begin to lock in to the Christ mind, will stop using force and will seek only to inspire and accelerate others. Instead of seeking to force the choices of others, you seek to help them, to inspire them, to raise their consciousness, so that they will spontaneously begin to make better choices.

Yet my beloved, what does it take to pass this initiation? It takes that you are willing to let the standard go, to let the self that is based on the standard die. And this will activate your fear of death, for you will think that if you let the self, the dualistic self, die, there will be nothing left of your identity. Or you will think that if you let some standard die, then there will be nothing left of your cause to protect the environment. And thus, you will think that the environmental issue will go downwards, because you let go of the old standard. You will think you are letting the cause down and therefore things will get worse.

Well, it is in fact possible, that as you let go of the force-based approach, things might get worse for a time. Take for example the transition from a totalitarian dictatorship to a democratic form of government. A totalitarian dictator can be a very efficient leader of a nation, because he can do anything he wants and can thus implement many things. When you give that nation free to have a democratic form of government, people might split themselves up into different factions that argue endlessly with each other, without being able to decide on anything. This is a situation very similar to what you see at my retreat in Luxor, where indeed you have people who sit there and argue endlessly, just as you see different parties in many democratic nations.

Nevertheless, even though this might seem to be a step backwards, it is not actually a step backwards. For it is still giving more people an opportunity to learn—and is that not what the purpose of the earth is all about? The earth is a schoolroom. If you let go of your force-based approach to the environmental issue, things might get worse. If enough people let go of the force-based approach to the environmental issue, things might get worse for a time. But I can assure you, that they will eventually get better. Because as people see the consequences of their actions, they will learn and they will grow.

***

Of course, this then ties in to another aspect of the fear of death, namely that the earth is on the brink of an irreversible environmental disaster. My beloved, what have we explained to you about the earth? We have explained that there is a background acceleration rate of the universe that propels all life to transcend and come closer to oneness, so that the entire sphere in which you exist comes closer to the ascension point. We have explained that because humankind has gone into the duality consciousness, the earth is lagging behind where it could have been, if humankind had not descended into duality.

How can the earth lag behind the rest of the universe? It can do so only by matter becoming more dense and therefore providing greater resistance. Yet even the material universe is expanding at an accelerated rate, which shows you that there is more and more force that is pulling on the earth to catch up with the rest of the universe, with the background acceleration rate. Greater force applied to a dense object means what? The object will be prompted to accelerate, but because of its density, the greater acceleration rate will cause greater friction.

Can you see, that there is a direct correspondence between the density of human consciousness and the density of matter on earth? And this causes friction. What does friction do? It produces heat. So if the entire planet is experiencing greater friction, is it any wonder that it is also experiencing greater heat? And thus, you see the real cause of global warming. It is not caused simply by greenhouse gases. It is, again, a product of consciousness, where the density of humankind's consciousness is lagging so far behind the growth rate of the universe that this is causing the densification of matter to the point, where it creates greater friction and thus heats up the entire planet.

Yet can you see how the fallen ones have attempted to play on the fear of death, by making so many people think that the earth is coming close to a tipping point, where the changes become irreversible? My beloved, with everything we have explained in this book, can you see

Accelerating the environmental debate to a new level

that this is simply a deliberate lie. There never is, there never has been, there never could be any changes that are irreversible.

There is nothing that cannot be accelerated into purity. This is what you begin to realize, when you lock in to the qualities of the fourth ray. You realize the lie behind the entire illusion of death, the fear of death. No matter how far you have descended into the lower state of consciousness, there is no point at which your descent becomes irreversible.

You can at any point decide to change course and start accelerating your state of consciousness. Humankind can at any point awaken and start accelerating their state of consciousness, and therefore stop putting the burden on elemental life. This will, then, lead to matter becoming less dense, and therefore the earth can begin to catch up. And when the earth begins to catch up, there will no more be the kind of friction you have seen, and thus the planet will find its rightful temperature and a greater balance in all natural processes.

***

My beloved, this is not some utopian scheme I am presenting to you. This is the deeper reality of the fourth ray, when you begin to sense, when you begin to experience, the power of the acceleration of the purity of the fourth ray.

I am Serapis Bey. I am the Chohan of a fourth ray, and I know the fourth ray better than any human being in embodiment. And I tell you with absolute certainty that I can look at this earth, and I can see – instantly – all of the impure conditions. For given that I am so one with the fourth ray, I know instantly what is pure and what is not pure. I see impurities on this planet that most human beings have not even begun to see. So if you were to step into my mind and see the impurities that I see, you would instantly be overwhelmed and become hopeless, thinking that the earth could never possibly throw off all of these impurities.

Yet you would think so only because you are looking at these impurities with your current state of consciousness. If you were to look at the impurities with my state of consciousness, you would see how unreal they are, how temporary they are. And you would see how easily the entire planet could be accelerated to a level, where these impurities would simply disappear. They would become obsolete, they would be spun off.

Have we not attempted to explain to you that the entire earth is like the image on a movie screen, projected many times every second? This image is projected through the film strips of elemental life. What happens, my beloved, to the image on a movie screen when you change the image on the film strip? Is the image on the screen not instantly replaced by the image on the film strip?

So can you see, that the moment you lighten the burden of elemental life and stop projecting these duality-based thoughtforms upon them, at that moment the earth will start accelerating. And many of the problems you currently see – and that you currently think have no solutions or could not be removed – will simply start melting away, as the dew melts away before the rising sun.

This is not utopia. This is reality.

Yes, those who are still being initiated on the first three rays and those who have not accelerated themselves beyond the fear of death, will not be able to see this, they will not be able to believe it. Yet when you truly begin to lock in to the fourth ray, you see that there is nothing that cannot be accelerated. And therefore, you have the potential to be the open door for the stream of God's light that will ultimately accelerate anything on earth.

***

And that is when you begin to go beyond a passive approach to the environmental issue and environmental problems. Surely, as my brother MORE said, those who are strong on the first ray will have a desire to express themselves and make a difference. And so, he encouraged you to use the decrees and invocations to invoke spiritual light. Of course, this can also be helpful for those who are going through the second and third ray initiations.

Nevertheless, I tell you, that when you come to the fourth ray initiations, you will go beyond this level and you will start realizing that you have an even greater potential. Instead of seeing yourself as a separate being down here, who is invoking light, you begin to see yourself more as a being who *is* light, who is the open door for the light of the Presence to shine through you. And thus, you begin to realize two things.

The Alpha aspect is that you can now begin to acknowledge that your mind has the power to be the open door for a stream of light that

Accelerating the environmental debate to a new level

will accelerate everything on earth. You can do this through invocations, but you will also begin to see that you can do it in all situations, simply through raising your awareness and tuning in to your I Will Be Presence.

The Omega aspect is that you can engage yourself in the environmental debate with an entirely new vision, an entirely new intention, of raising up all people who are concerned about the environment and using the environmental issue to show people the need to ask these deeper questions, the need to accelerate their awareness beyond the duality consciousness.

This is your true potential, the Alpha and the Omega. It is something that begins to become real to you, as you pass the initiations of the fourth ray. You begin to realize, that your highest potential on this earth is not to align yourself with one of the warring factions in the dualistic struggle. Your highest potential is to align yourself with a higher force, namely your own I Will Be Presence and the Ascended Host.

As we have said, we are not part of the dualistic struggle. We are not in opposition to the fallen beings, we are not fighting the fallen beings. This is what the fallen beings have managed to do to many people on earth. Even some spiritual people have become trapped by this, thinking that as they become more spiritual, it is their job to fight the fallen beings on earth. But it is not your job to fight anyone or anything. It is your job to accelerate yourself and to seek to accelerate all life.

We of the Ascended Host are not seeking to put down or destroy the fallen beings; we are seeking to accelerate them if at all possible. Yet of course, we respect free will. And so, we are seeking to accelerate all life. And that means that if a critical mass of people respond and accelerate their consciousness beyond a certain level, well then the law simply mandates that certain fallen beings – who are not willing to accelerate – will no longer be allowed to embody on earth. And therefore, the earth will be purified from their downward pull.

***

We have said, my beloved, that there are 144 levels of consciousness possible on earth. This is true, this will always be the case until the earth and the entire sphere reaches the ascension point. Nevertheless, this is not as static as it might seem. For you see, my beloved, when Jesus took embodiment on earth and qualified for his ascension, he raised the bar for what is the highest level of consciousness possible on earth.

Do you see what I am saying here? Take the image from physics that your eyes can detect only certain vibrations, namely visible light. So you see that the highest color that your eyes can detect is violet, but beyond it is ultraviolet. The lowest you can detect is red but below is infrared. Well, now imagine that something happened, so that the range of light that you could see was shifted upwards, so that your eyes could now see ultraviolet light but could no longer see red light. This is essentially what has happened on earth. When Jesus won the victory of his ascension, he shifted the level of consciousness that it is possible to reach on earth to a higher level. Gautama Buddha did the same and others have done the same.

So you now see, for example, that after Jesus won his victory, it was possible to go to a higher level of consciousness as the highest possible level of consciousness on earth. Yet because there can only be 144 levels of consciousness on earth, that also meant that it was no longer allowable to go to what had, up until that point, been the lowest level, what we might call the first level of consciousness. Instead, what had been the second lowest level now became the lowest level. And so, you see, that those who were not willing to accelerate their level of consciousness from what was previously the lowest level to what is now the lowest level, well those lifestreams could no longer embody on earth.

And thus, indeed, this was the judgment that Jesus came to bring, when he said: "For judgment I am come." Not that he needed to judge anyone, but that by raising the bar for what was allowed as the lowest possible level of consciousness on earth, those who would not accelerate, judged themselves by their own choosing. And so, can you see that you have the potential, either as an individual or by joining other people with like mind, to do the same?

You can be part of the judgment of Christ by raising the level of consciousness, so that the highest possible level is raised to the next step up. And therefore, those who are currently at the lowest level of consciousness, can no longer embody here—unless they are willing to accelerate themselves beyond that level. And thus, if they choose not to accelerate, that choice – that denial, that refusal to let the old die – causes them to lose their life. Not that they cease to exist but that they are no longer

Accelerating the environmental debate to a new level

allowed to embody on earth. And therefore the entire earth can be accelerated to a higher level.

This is how progress happens on earth. But it does, of course, follow the Law of Free Will. So it takes a critical mass of people to raise their awareness to the point, where the earth is truly accelerated.

***

So let me now give you the deeper understanding of what this actually means. There are certain cycles. As you are no doubt aware, they have often been called spiritual cycles. You are aware of the Age of Pisces and that the earth is moving into – and, in fact, has moved into – the Age of Aquarius. Jesus came to inaugurate the Age of Pisces. He set the pattern for the highest possible level of consciousness that was attainable by those who are willing to follow in his footsteps and therefore do the works that he did. So when Jesus won his ascension, he shifted the level of consciousness.

However, one person cannot shift the entire earth, for the Law of Free Will mandates that a certain critical mass of people, namely the top 10%, must be willing to also shift their level of consciousness. And so, even though Jesus won his victory 2,000 years ago, it was the intention that during those 2,000 years, enough people would follow in his footsteps and embody his true teachings, that they would also begin to manifest and express their individual Christhood. And therefore, the entire earth could be shifted upwards in consciousness and vibration.

Yet because Jesus' true teachings were perverted by the fallen beings, through the Catholic Church and other means, there has not yet been that critical mass of people who have attained a sufficient level of Christhood to shift the entire planet upwards. And this is indeed what causes the planet to lag behind where it could have been, and this is what causes the friction that is the cause of global warming.

Your highest potential, if you are indeed on the fourth ray or above, is to become part of this movement of those who embody the true teachings of Christ and start to manifest and express their personal Christhood. So that you can be one of the forerunners for shifting the level of consciousness of the earth, so that the earth catches up to where it should have been at the end of Pisces and therefore can enter the Age of

Aquarius without the density that should have been transcended during the past 2,000 years.

***

The Age of Aquarius is an age of freedom, of spiritual freedom. Yet you cannot attain or manifest this freedom without overcoming some of the density of matter. And thus, when the earth is still too dense, then there will be friction—and that will create heat.

There is only one possible solution. There is no technological solution that can solve the problem of global warming. There is only one possible solution, namely an acceleration in consciousness. And if you resonate with the fourth ray, then I encourage you to recognize, that you have the potential to be part of this solution and no longer be part of the problem. But you must accelerate your consciousness and come to an entirely higher level, where you begin to recognize that your highest potential is to be the Living Christ on earth.

And this will require, sometimes, a dramatic shift compared to the old state of consciousness, the state of consciousness you had when you started reading this book. And thus, we might say that I am presenting you with a crucial challenge.

Will you simply read this book as any other book? Will you say, "Ah this is interesting, but this I do not believe, or that I do not believe?" Or will you go beyond and truly let this book become the catalyst that propels you into a higher state of consciousness, because you have allowed yourself to lock in to the force of life that will accelerate you to your highest potential?

Will you let this be just another book, or will you let it be a book that accelerates you to a distinctly higher level of consciousness? From where you will shortly look back and wonder how you could stay in the old consciousness so long, when you knew that you had a purpose for being alive on planet earth at this crucial time. You knew there had to be a mission, you knew there had to be a deeper meaning and purpose—not only to life in general but to your personal life as well.

Have you not always had a sense of mission?

Well, then realize that your highest mission is to manifest your Christhood and become the open door for the River of Life to accelerate

Accelerating the environmental debate to a new level

the collective consciousness, to accelerate elemental life, to accelerate planet earth to a new and higher level, a new and higher reality.

Serapis Bey I AM, and I am already accelerated into that higher reality. And thus, I know it is real. I am not asking you to take my word for it. I am asking you to take my word and let my word accelerate you, so that you will also experience that this higher reality is real.

Key 27
The immaculate vision for the environmental debate

Hilarion I am. As the Chohan of the fifth ray, I will give you the perspective on what you can do to serve in bringing healing to Mother Earth, when you have come to and have begun to pass the initiations of the fifth ray. As Serapis Bey has explained, you will not pass the initiations of the fourth ray, until you begin to go beyond the duality consciousness and the desire to put down other people. So as you do let go of this entire desire to divide people into those who are right and wrong – and to put down those who are wrong – then you can move on to the initiations of the fifth ray.

The fifth ray has been called the ray of healing, because as you begin to pass the initiations of this ray, you seek only to heal all life. This, of course, must begin by healing yourself. Physician, heal thyself, as the old saying goes.

There is no way you can pass the initiations of the fifth ray, unless you are willing to do one simple thing: look at your own state of consciousness and take full responsibility for that state of consciousness. What is the essence of the fallen consciousness? It is that the fallen beings have gone into the consciousness of separation—but what does this mean?

When you are in separation – when you are blinded by the illusion of separation – you have a very simple division in your mind. That division is between what you consider your "self" and what you consider as being external to your self, as being "other" than "self." And now, when you have this division, you can create the mental image, the illusion, that the self is not responsible for its own state of consciousness—because its state of consciousness is a forced reaction to that which is outside the self. In other words, the self that is in division can project responsibility outside itself. It can project responsibility upon the "other," instead of accepting that the self is fully responsible for its state of self, its state of consciousness.

***

This, then, is what the fallen beings have been doing since they fell in that first sphere. They have managed to seduce numerous other people into doing the same thing. And if you will take another look at the story of how the Serpent in the Garden of Eden deceived Eve, you will – perhaps – get an important insight.

We have said how the fruit of the knowledge of good and evil is a symbol for the duality consciousness, in which you define your own truth, your own standard for what is right and wrong. Once you define this standard, you can define any problem and the solution to that problem in such a way that it will always seem as if you – meaning the separate self – are right, as if the separate self can never be wrong. For you have now defined a worldview, which is based on an underlying premise, an underlying paradigm, namely that the self can never be wrong.

Yet if you take another look, what is really being said here? What is being said is that the self is real, that the separate self is real and has some real existence. And thus, when you understand this – when you experience the reality of this – you, meaning the Conscious You, can return to the recognition that it is pure awareness. And therefore, it is not the separate self. And then, the Conscious You can begin to see, that it is not the separate self because the separate self is not. It is not real, it has no existence, it has no permanence.

What the separate self is doing – what the fallen beings have attempted to do since their original fall – is to portray the image that the separate self has reality, has existence, has permanence. Yet the deeper reality is, that everything is subject to the free will of the Conscious You. The separate self has existence, has permanence, only when the Conscious You has projected itself into the separate self, and thus looks at the world through the filter of that separate self—and thereby gives it existence and ongoingness through the power of its awareness.

Can you see, that the underlying message or belief that is being projected by the fallen beings – and by the separate selves of all beings who are blinded by separation – is that the separate self is real, has existence, has ongoingness? And the attempt to prove the separate self right, or to

The immaculate vision for the environmental debate

prove that it is never wrong, is really just a camouflage, is really just an attempt to engage you at a surface level of arguing certain points. And therefore never getting to the deeper level, where you say: "But the emperor has nothing on, the separate self has nothing on." For no matter what argument the separate self might come up with, it all springs from duality—and thus it is all unreal.

"I do not have to argue with the separate self, I do not have to argue with the separate self of other people or the fallen beings. I do not have to continue to argue back and forth in this endless dualistic struggle, that is based on the fact that the fallen beings have captured the privilege of formulating the problem. And therefore have managed to get everyone on earth to debate based on a surface understanding of life, that camouflages and hides the underlying problem. I will never win the battle with the fallen beings, I will never win the battle with the separate selves of other beings. Yet I can transcend the battle by not seeking to win, by not seeking to prove myself right or prove others wrong, but simply walking away from the struggle and instead projecting myself, my Conscious You, into oneness with my I Will Be Presence and the Spirit of Truth."

***

Yet, what will it take for you to come to the point, where you are able to do this? Well, you will have to stop seeking to win the battle that your own separate self is fighting, and is essentially fighting with you. Do you see, that your separate self is seeking to be proven right and never be proven wrong? In doing so, it is engaging in the struggle with the separate selves of other people. It is even camouflaging this struggle with the illusion that it is fighting for some greater cause. And therefore, the separate self is "truly" a spiritual self that is doing God's work or doing the work of some other cause.

Yet this is all camouflage. It has one purpose only, namely to keep the attention of the Conscious You focused on proving what you think is your self right and proving other people wrong. So that you never have the chance to stand back and say: "Is this really who I am? Do I really want to spend the rest of this lifetime – and an unknown number of future lifetimes – in this process of trying to prove my separate self right and trying to prevent that my separate self is ever proven wrong?"

You see, my beloved, we of the Ascended Host realize one simple thing: planet earth is a schoolroom. There are many lessons that can be learned, but if you step back, there is really only one lesson that is the essential lesson to learn. And that is, that you do not have to remain engaged in the dualistic struggle forever. For you have the ability to transcend it. But you do not transcend the struggle by coming to the point, where you feel you have won some ultimate victory by espousing your thought system as the superior one, or even setting yourself up in some position of superiority on earth.

You transcend the struggle by transcending the struggle.

Not by presenting the ultimate argument, but by realizing that there is no ultimate argument. And therefore, you simply drop the entire desire to argue. You walk away from the argument. And when you do this – when you walk away from the argument with others – then you can begin to take a look at yourself, to take a look in the mirror. For now you are no longer so focused on the splinter in the eyes of your brother that you have no time or attention left over to look at the beam in your own eye. And the beam in your own eye is precisely the separate self, that wants to keep you so trapped in the dualistic struggle, that you validate and perpetuate its existence.

And when you see this, you can disengage, disentangle, dis-identify the Conscious You from the separate self. And then, you can return to the state of pure awareness, where the Conscious You realizes and accepts that it is not the separate self. It is more, because it is the open door for the Presence. And when you do pass this initiation – take note, my beloved, of what I said: when you do pass this initiation and not before – then you can begin to give a service that will truly help heal Mother Earth, based on the qualities of the fifth ray.

***

Can you take what we have said and realize the dynamic here? There are many, many people who are engaged in the environmental debate – or any other area of debate in society – out of self-centered motives. Which essentially is the underlying desire of the separate self to perpetuate its existence by getting the Conscious You to direct its attention through the separate self. And it does this by projecting that there is some kind

The immaculate vision for the environmental debate

of struggle that must be won in order to bring forth the edenic state that is promised by some thought system or other.

So can you see, then, the stark – and unpleasant for many – reality that as long as you are engaged in the environmental debate based on this underlying dynamic, you are not truly helping to heal Mother Earth? You are only perpetuating the imbalances that are being projected upon elemental life and therefore causing the wounds in the body, the four bodies, of the Earth Mother. Now, when you have come to this realization – and have begun to disentangle yourself from the separate self – you can begin to step up to a higher understanding.

The higher understanding is that the entire material universe can exist for one reason only. Let us go back to the analogy of a movie theater. What you see with your physical senses and the outer mind is a material world that seems solid and seems to have an ongoing existence. Yet the reality is, that what you see is no more real or ongoing than the images on a movie screen. The particular forms you see are determined by the forms that are on the film strip in the movie projector. And as we have said, the film strip is elemental life. Yet most of the images on that film strip are projected upon elemental life through the minds of human beings who have gone into duality.

Nevertheless, those imperfect images could not be projected onto the movie screen unless there was a driving force, which of course comes from the light bulb in the movie projector. That light bulb is the beings in the spiritual realm who are allowing their own energies and beings to be the driving force that constantly upholds the material universe.

Now, as we have said, human beings on earth are truly self-aware spiritual beings. You are the ones who are sent into the material world in order to – ideally – be the open doors for the Elohim and help co-create the world. So you have the ability to be like the driving force, to be like the light bulb in the projector. You have this ability because your I Will Be Presence is constantly flowing through the open door of the Conscious You. The role of the Conscious You is to direct this stream of light, to focus it on particular forms that it wants to bring forth in the material universe.

Yet because of the Law of Free Will, the Conscious You has the ability to create any mental image it wants and to put that mental image up as a film strip or filter, through which the light from the I Will Be Presence must pass, before it is projected onto the movie screen of the

Ma-ter light, or rather the movie screen of elemental life, which then takes on the form projected upon it. And so, the question, of course, is: what is the film strip through which the Conscious You is directing the light from the Presence? What kind of role have you defined for yourself or taken on? Is it a separate self based on the illusion of separation and duality, or have you – as the Conscious You – been willing to return to the pure awareness of being the open door for the I Will Be Presence?

You see, if you go into duality and separation, you become blinded by the illusion represented by the forbidden fruit, namely that you can become as a God who can define good and evil. And therefore, you have a right to define an image through which you are projecting the light from the Presence. And my beloved, you do have a right to do this, for this is mandated by the Law of Free Will. Of course, any image through which the light from your Presence passes, will be projected onto the screen of elemental life and the Ma-ter light. And thus, you will inevitably experience – here in the material universe – conditions that are an outpicturing of the images you hold at the four levels of your mind.

You can project any image you want upon the screen of life. But you cannot escape being in the movie theater and watching the movie that you are projecting. You can project what you want, but you will experience what you project. There is no way around this. For the Law of Free Will mandates, that whereas you have the right to project any image you want, you do not have the right to project an image upon other forms of life without you yourself experiencing that image also. In other words, you do not have the right to limit or burden other forms of life without also limiting or burdening yourself with the same image.

***

When you reach the level of the fifth ray, this suddenly becomes self-evident to you. And thus, you realize the deeper truth behind the saying: "Do unto others what you want them to do unto you." You realize that what you do unto others sends a signal to the cosmic mirror, that this is what you want to experience. If you go into the consciousness of separation and create a separate self – and if you start acting as if that separate self can do whatever it wants without considering the consequences this has for others or for the All – well, then you are subconsciously sending a message to the cosmic mirror, that you want to experience a world in

The immaculate vision for the environmental debate

which everybody does the same. In which everybody is acting as if they are completely separate individuals, who have the right to do whatever they want, regardless of the consequences it has for others or for the planet upon which they live.

This is what the fallen beings have been doing for a very long time. Many, many people who did not fall with the fallen beings have been seduced into doing the same thing. My beloved, the fallen beings – most of them – have not yet had enough of this. And they may not have enough for a very long time, which is why they will eventually no longer be able to embody on this planet but will have to go to some other world, where they can outplay their selfish tendencies. So the question for you is: have you had enough of this, have you had enough of the struggle?

And when you come to the fifth ray and begin to pass the initiations of the fifth ray, then there will come a point, where you do not decide which your outer mind that you have had enough of the struggle. Instead, there comes, from deep within your being, the inner knowing that this is enough. This is all vanity. "Vanity of vanities, all is vanity."

For a time, you might feel like all life in the material world is vanity, and you want to have nothing to do with it; you just want to withdraw. This is, indeed, what I did in my last embodiment on Crete, where I was the healer, Saint Hilarion, who sought to withdraw myself from the crowds, who wanted me to do something for them instead of unlocking their own inherent abilities. Many spiritual people have come to this point, and perhaps it is healthy for a time to withdraw, at least withdraw from the environmental debate. So that you can free yourself from the subtle dualistic illusions that all people have come to accept.

Yet as you begin to truly pass the initiations of the fifth ray, you will go beyond this. You will realize that life in the material realm is not vanity. It is only the dualistic struggle that is vanity, but there is an alternative to the dualistic struggle.

You can transcend the struggle. And you can then go out and no longer engage in the dualistic struggle, but still engage in life, engage in society, even engage in debate. Yet you do so, not with a dualistic intention of proving your separate self right or proving the separate selves of other people wrong. You do so with one simple intention: to simply let your light shine, to share the individuality, the divine individuality, of your I Will Be Presence by always being just the open door and nothing more.

***

What is the essential lesson to learn on the spiritual path? It is simply this: "I have had enough of being like a God that defines right and wrong. I want to be truly divine, by being the open door for the divine individuality I already have, the immortal divine self. I want to be the open door for that divine self to express itself in this world, rather than expressing myself through this separate self that is vanity."

And when you come to this point, my beloved, then you can truly begin to give a service that will heal Mother Earth. You will be amazed at how some people will respond, when you become an open door. You will be amazed at how others will be inspired, when you become an open door. And when more and more people begin to simply become an open door for a higher perspective, a higher vision, then you will see how not only the environmental debate but the entire debate in society, will shift.

And there can come a tipping point, where the muddled, dualistic, antagonistic debate that you see today in so many democratic countries, will be irreversibly replaced by an entirely new approach that is not dualistic and antagonistic. But where people realize they need to strive for a higher vision, that is not based on separation but based on the underlying reality that all life is one. And that we will overcome the problems we have only by striving for oneness, rather than perpetuating the dualistic struggle, where one group of people must be appointed as the scapegoat and then must be forced to change or eradicated by force.

This is the shift that needs to happen, before the environmental debate begins to produce true results. You can be a forerunner for this, not only by speaking out but also in other ways. For truly, as you pass the initiations of the fifth ray, you begin to lock in to your true role as a co-creator, which is precisely that you are the Conscious You. And you are, in your highest potential, a clear pane of glass for the I Will Be Presence.

And thus, what is your potential? It is the potential to focus your attention on a particular issue, and then to be the open door for the vision of the Presence to be superimposed upon, to be projected upon, this issue.

What you will see, when you begin to sense the higher vision of your own Presence, is an immense contrast between this higher vision – this immaculate vision, this immaculate concept – and the reality of

The immaculate vision for the environmental debate 429

what is currently manifest on earth. And this is when you, then, can begin to serve in the ultimate capacity, where you never fall prey to the projections of the fallen beings. What are those projections?

***

My beloved, we have said that everything is consciousness. Can you not see, then, that everything that becomes infused with the stream of consciousness, will eventually grow in complexity and intensity or momentum, until you have created a conscious being. This is not a physical, visible being, but a being that exists in the emotional realm, or the mental realm, or even the lower etheric realm.

If you take a particular thought system and you have millions of people accept that thought system as an infallible truth, well then those millions of people will combine their mental powers. And they will allow the light from their Presences to flow through the filter of that thought system. And through their combined psychic powers, they will create a being – a beast – based on the thought system and the mental images it creates.

This is what you have in the old concept that there are two gods – Gog and Magog – who are fighting for dominance in this world. This is a symbol for the dualistic consciousness, where there must always be two opposite polarities, such as an established power elite and an aspiring power elite. But behind this – even behind the organizations or nations or people that seem to be opposing each other in the physical – well behind this, there is an emotional, mental and lower etheric component. Namely that people, through their combined consciousness, have created these huge beasts. And these beasts are constantly seeking to take over and control the minds of human beings.

What you see is that you – as a human being in embodiment – are walking around in this environment, where you are constantly being bombarded by projections from the many different emotional, or mental or etheric beings or beasts that are seeking to overpower your mind, so that you follow them.

As you are a spiritual person who is committed to healing Mother Earth, I will make the clear assumption that you are not a smoker, and that if you were a smoker in the past, you have transcended this. And thus, I think you will be able to see that people who do smoke all know that smoking is dangerous to their health. Yet they have still found a way to justify that they are still smoking. The reason why they can justify this, is that their minds have been taken over by the tobacco entity, the tobacco beast. You may talk to smokers; you present them with various arguments for why they should stop smoking, but have you ever noticed that these arguments have no effect? Because the smokers are instantly able to reject or invalidate your arguments with their outer minds.

Have you ever asked yourself why people cannot see what is so self-evident to you? Well, the reason they cannot see it, is that their minds are overpowered by these beasts, that are bigger than their individual minds. People who go below to 48th level of consciousness, do not have the individuality to avoid being overpowered by these beasts. And so, you see that even though we have said that as you go towards the lowest level of the 144 possible levels, you have people who seem to have a very strong individuality, because they are the ultimate egotists. We have given the example of Hitler, who thought he was superior to all other people and that he alone should make certain decisions. Yet when you see the deeper reality, you see that Hitler was not actually acting as an individual. For his mind was completely overpowered and controlled by an enormous beast, a conglomerate of beasts in the mental, emotional and lower etheric levels.

A thus, the Hitler that you saw as a physical person was simply a marionette for these beasts, that were seeking to use Hitler as a tool for perpetuating the ongoing dualistic struggle. And so, you see that even though people may appear to be individuals and egomaniacs, the more egotistical you become, the less of a true individuality you actually have. For you do not have the power to step back and say: "But I am not this separate self, I am not this outer beast that is seeking to take over my mind."

***

My point for giving you this teaching is to help you realize two things. First of all, that you need to free yourself from these beasts, and this is what you can do as you pass the initiations of the fifth ray. And then you, of course, need to help others do the same.

But beyond that, the second thing you can do is that you can realize that as long as you are in embodiment, you will be bombarded by emo-

The immaculate vision for the environmental debate 431

tional, mental and etheric impulses from these beasts. And their purpose is to make you believe in one simple thing, namely that the current conditions on earth are real and cannot be changed by you, by the powers of your mind or by the power of the Presence through you.

When you step back, you see that the fallen beings are only one part in a bigger conglomerate. This conglomerate is what Jesus referred to as the prince of this world. It is what the Buddha referred to as Maya, the demons of Maya, the forces of Maya, the veil of Maya. This entire conglomerate has one purpose, one message: It wants to perpetuate its existence.

It is, of course, completely unreal; it has no reality and no permanence. But it wants to perpetuate its existence by making you think it has reality and permanence. And so, what is its aim? Its aim is to get you to shut off the flow of light from your Presence, to get you to turn down this flow of light, or to get you to direct the flow of light through the filter of the separate self. The separate self, of course, is built on the illusion of separation, so the separate self believes that the basic structure of this world is real and has permanence.

The separate self will believe in the illusion of Christianity, that the current conditions on earth were created by God and that there is a devil, which has some real power over them—unless they uncritically adhere to the doctrines of the church. Or the separate self will believe in the illusions of materialism, that it is no more than a sophisticated monkey, and therefore could not possibly have the powers of mind to have control over matter. So can you see, that both orthodox Christianity and materialistic science are projecting the image that you, as an individual, do not have power over matter? You do not have the power to be the open door for a force, that can transform this world and therefore shatter the false images projected upon this world through the duality consciousness.

The entire force – the prince of this world, the illusion of Maya – wants you to believe that you are not a Conscious You that has the potential to be a clear pane of glass for the power of your Presence, the power that can transform any condition in this world. This is what Maya wants you to believe: that you cannot be an open door for the Spirit while you are still in embodiment. And so, when you realize this – and when you begin to go beyond this illusion – then you can indeed become an open door for the Spirit.

You can look at any condition on earth, and you can know with absolute certainty that it is not real, it is not permanent. It is only a temporary image projected upon elemental life. And then, you can know that you have the potential, you have the power of the mind, to be the open door for your Presence projecting a higher image onto that condition, so that elemental life will be set free to outpicture the higher vision, rather than the dualistic vision.

Take the situation where Jesus – who had at that point attained a high degree of Christhood – meets a man with a withered hand. The man himself believed that his condition was permanent, that the hand was dead and would remain so for the rest of his lifetime. Everybody who knew this man believed the same thing. Can you see, that they had all fallen prey to the illusion that this condition, that was manifest in matter, was real and was permanent and that there was no power that could change it?

Can you see, that Jesus did not accept this illusion? He saw the withered hand, yet he did not see it as permanent or unchangeable. And thus, he was willing to be the open door, whereby the power of the Spirit could work through him and replace the dualistic image projected upon this man's body elemental with a higher image. And thus, the body elemental instantly outpictured the higher vision projected upon it by a person who was the open door. Because Jesus was the open door, the power from his Presence could overpower the collective vision of all of the people who thought the withered hand was permanent.

***

This is the power of true individuality, as opposed to the false individuality of the egomaniac who thinks he is superior to all others. Jesus did not think he was superior to anyone else. He saw the basic oneness between himself and all other people. And that is why he only attempted to raise up all life, in whatever way that could possibly be done, based on the state of consciousness of the individuals he encountered.

Jesus did not accept the belief of the man that his hand was withered permanently. Yet he did not overpower the free will of the man either, which is why you see that he would often ask people: "Believest thou that I have the power to do this?" And if they believed that Jesus had the

The immaculate vision for the environmental debate

power to heal them, then they would be healed. Because thereby, they demonstrated that they were willing to be healed.

Nevertheless, Jesus did not come to do something for others. He performed his miracles only to demonstrate the power of mind over matter. And then, he did everything possible to attempt to make people see, that that power was not exclusive to him, for everyone has that same power within them. Did he not say, "The kingdom of God is within you?" Did he not say, "Those who believe on me, the works that I do shall they do also, and greater works shall they do." For as more and more people begin to accept their true potential to be the open door for the Spirit, then they will build a momentum. And this collective momentum will then be able to produce even greater miracles than Jesus was able to produce 2,000 years ago.

This was indeed what was meant to happen during the Age of Pisces. It has not yet happened, but there are enough people in embodiment who are close enough to manifesting this Christhood and acknowledging and accepting this Christhood, that they could very quickly build a momentum that would make this start to happen. Whereby you would see many changes in the consciousness of humankind. And as you begin to see changes in the consciousness of humankind, well then, of course, humankind will begin to project different energies and different images upon elemental life. And then, you will see that, almost instantly, elemental life will begin to conform to these higher visions, these higher images.

For I tell you, that elemental life is obedient to the Law of Free Will. The elementals will take on any thoughtform projected upon them by human beings. But those who are the more complex elementals will also know, when they are not taking on the highest possible thoughtform, and they will suffer under it.

Take a look at yourself. You as a human being have the ability to sense when something is pleasant and when something is not pleasant, because you are being forced to take on something that you know is not right. You may not be able to formulate with your mind why it is not right, but you sense that this is unpleasant.

Of course, elemental life can also sense when something is unpleasant. And thus, I assure you that elemental life would rejoice – would be exceeding glad – in throwing off the imperfect energies and thoughtforms, and instead outpicturing thoughtforms that would make elemental life feel free and unburdened, and feel that they are part of this great, wondrous symphony of life. Each little elemental would rejoice, if it was free to play its role in the symphony of life, and thereby experience the fullness of that symphony. Truly, each human being would also feel the same, if they were free to play their role in the symphony of life.

For thereby, all human beings would begin to experience that planet earth does not have to be this ongoing dualistic struggle. Instead, planet earth could be this wonderful sphere, this wonderful concert hall, where each of the 10 billion people on this planet would play an individual role, an individual instrument. Yet instead of these individualities clashing and destroying each other, they would all combine to form this wonderful symphony orchestra. And then, the entire earth would begin to vibrate with the rhythmic cadences of this cosmic symphony, unlike anything that most human beings can currently envision.

My beloved, just imagine listening to the radio, and at first there is nothing but static, an unrhytmic, disturbing, jarring static that truly goes on your nerves after just a few seconds. And yet, suddenly, the dial of the radio is turned and the static begins to decrease in intensity, until it begins to fade away. And now, suddenly, you can begin to hear the music underneath the static. And as the static decreases, the music tones forward more and more powerfully.

And suddenly, the room and your mind is filled with the wonderful rising and falling of this fantastic symphony, that suddenly makes you feel like you are transported into another realm. And instead of all the problems and conflicts, there is now peace, there is now a calmness, there is now harmony. And you are flowing with the stream of this music. You are rising and falling with the music, and you feel that you are one with the music and one with all other beings who are part of this grand symphony.

***

Truly, the earth that was envisioned by the Elohim could best be compared to a concert hall, with a giant symphony orchestra all playing the same tune — and therefore, each individual instrument adding its power to the wholeness of the music performance.

Ahh, what an incredible beauty envisioned by the Elohim. And as you pass the initiations of the fifth ray, you will not only begin to under-

The immaculate vision for the environmental debate 435

stand this beauty, you will begin to experience and feel the symphony. And thus, you will know that this is reality. And therefore, you will never again be deceived by the prince of this world, by the demons of Mara, the illusion of Maya, that this world – in its present imperfect state – is real and that there is no force that could overturn the current state of affairs, there is no force that could take power away from the prince of this world.

You will never be deceived by this illusion. You will know its un-reality, and therefore you will play your instrument. You will begin to be emboldened to stand forth in the midst of the dualistic debate and simply play your individual instrument, and let other people respond however they will respond. You will not be overpowered or convinced by their negativity and by their projections. For truly, the separate self of various people, and truly the demons and beasts working through them, will attack you and will howl at you – as they did with Jesus – that you have no right to be in this world. You have no right to be the open door for the Spirit. You have no right to play your instrument. You should conform to them and play the same disharmonious instruments that they are playing.

But my beloved, as you pass the initiations of the fifth ray, this will mean nothing to you. You will see it as complete unreality. And you will see, that free will mandates that they have no right to demand, that you conform to their choices. For you have a right, as a divine individual, to make your own choices. You have a right to make the choice to be the open door for your I Will Be Presence to play its instrument in this world. And thus, you will be unmoved, you will be non-attached as the Buddha, and you will stand upon the rock of Christ and you will play your instrument. And you will let that instrument spread its harmonious sound waves, and you will be content by just playing, as the sun is content with shining its light.

Eventually, some people will respond to your harmonious waves. They will be inspired, they might even be transformed. They might even begin to play their own instrument. And certainly, you will then rejoice in this, and you will come together with these people and you will start playing an instrument as a group. And therefore, you will have more power and more momentum. But you are still non-attached. You do not put any expectations or demands upon others. You do not demand that they should conform to some new vision. You are the open door for the

Spirit, and you are just flowing with whatever your I Will Be Presence wants to express through you. You are playing the tune of the Presence, and you are content with continuing to be the open door, who places no expectations or demands on what should or should not happen.

For you no longer have any standard for what is right and wrong. You are not judging other people, you are not judging yourself. You are simply focused on one thing and one thing only: to be the open door for the Presence, so that the Presence is free to express itself through you in its ongoing desire to raise up all life. Not by seeking to change other forms of life, but by simply giving them a frame of reference that there is a higher choice than the choice they are making right now. There is a higher state of consciousness. There is a higher state of being than what they are outpicturing right now.

This, then, is the highest service of those who are on the fifth ray. And as you pass the initiations of the fifth ray, you can go beyond to even higher levels of service. And this, of course, will be the joy of Nada and Saint Germain. And so, I gratefully and lovingly end this release. And I then allow my beloved brother and sister to add their melodies to my own and those who have played before me in the symphony of this book.

Key 28
Being the open door for peace through oneness

I am Nada, the Chohan of the sixth ray. One of the qualities of the sixth ray is indeed peace. What does this mean for your potential to give service in the environmental debate, or in any other part of the debate that can bring humankind forward?

Imagine yourself in a situation, where you are debating in some kind of public forum. Imagine that there are several political parties, or organizations, or representatives from various groups. Can you see, that what happens in most of such situation is that the various groups will each have their own agenda, and their entire purpose for entering the discussion is to further their particular agenda? And so, is it not easy to see, that this is why there is so often simply an endless discussion about what to do, and it is so hard to come to a consensus upon which all can agree?

Can you see, that this tendency to look at only a specific interest – and to even think that this is more important than the interests of any other people – is indeed what has caused most human conflicts? It is clearly the dualistic struggle outplayed in the political arena. This has led to many forms of violence, even wars. But in democratic nations it has been replaced, so that there is at least no longer violence. And indeed, this is a step forward, but what you see today is still that many democratic nations are trapped in these endless discussions and struggles between different political parties, who claim to be representing separate interests. But is it not because even in democratic nations, there is still the illusion that people can be divided up into particular segments and groups that have different interests?

Yet is not one of the principles of democracy that "all men are created equal" and that all people are endowed by a higher authority with the same basic rights? So if all are created equal and if all are supposed to have equal rights, how can it be impossible to reach a consensus? It can happen only when people are focused on a surface level, an illusory problem, an illusory division, that seems to split them into separate groups and segments that have opposing or contradictory interests.

***

Yet what are some of the most basic rights upon which democratic nations are founded: life, liberty and the pursuit of happiness. Do not all people have an interest in being alive, in being free and in being free to pursue happiness? So how can it be impossible to find consensus? Well, it can be impossible only, when people are blinded by the illusions of duality — that inevitably divide everything into opposing polarities and segments.

And, of course, as we have said, when people are below the 48th level of awareness, they are inevitably blinded by these divisions. When you look at the 144 levels of consciousness that are possible on earth, you will see, that as you go towards the lowest level, you find people who are more and more blinded by divisions, who are more and more convinced that divisions are real — and that therefore it has some ultimate, epic importance that one particular group gains superiority over all others.

As an example of a person who was at the lowest level of consciousness, take Adolph Hitler, who trusted no one, not even his closest advisers. It was him against everybody. So it was with Stalin, Mao Zedong and many other dictators that you see around the world. This is the ultimate state of division.

So what happens, when you go in the other direction and approach the 144th level of consciousness? Well, what happens is that you go through the process that you see in Jesus, of coming first to see "I and my father are one" and then to see your oneness with all life here below. First you attain the vertical oneness with your Presence and then the horizontal oneness with all life.

So when you reach that 144th level, you see yourself as a completely open door, for you are one with the Presence. And the Presence is an expression of God, and everything else is an expression of God. And thus, you see the oneness of all life. At that point – or even as you begin to approach these higher levels of awareness – you can begin to serve

Being the open door for peace through oneness 439

this greater cause, this non-dualistic cause, of promoting and furthering the oneness of all life.

This, then, is the ultimate service. But how do you further this cause? By having no cause, my beloved!

How do you ultimately prove anything? By not seeking to prove anything. By having no agenda, no expectations, no structures in your mind that you are seeking to prove right and get other people to accept. The way to the ultimate service is to be the open door.

***

Right now, it is very possible that as you read these statements, you will notice that somewhere inside of you is a voice screaming that this is false, this cannot be right. What is screaming is your ego. Because your ego knows that when you become the open door, it will die, it will lose its hold over you.

Your ego has enough awareness that it does not want to die, it has a survival instinct. So it wants to keep deceiving you into thinking, that you have to have personal opinions, you have to have personal interests, you have to have expectations, you have to have a goal for your life, you have to have a mission in life. You have to find meaning in life, and therefore you are here to promote some kind of change, to save the world, to save the environment, to save the whales, to save the frogs — or whatever cause human beings define for themselves.

How do you promote the ultimate cause? The ultimate cause is the non-dualistic cause of the oneness of all life. How do you promote his cause? By letting go of all lesser causes!

If you think the goal of saving some species is worthy and can justify you struggling against another group of human beings, then you are not furthering the ultimate cause. You are only furthering the dualistic struggle.

I am not saying that you should withdraw from debate. But I am saying that if you want to raise your service to its highest potential, to the level of the sixth ray, then you do indeed need to go through a process of freeing your mind and being from these dualistic causes that you might have espoused at some point in your life. And this will require you to go through a period of fasting, as Jesus demonstrated when he walked into the wilderness and stayed there for 40 days and nights. This is a symbol, in its deepest sense, of Jesus withdrawing from his previous view of what was his mission in life, his previous ideas, expectations and attachments to giving a service and having a purpose for his life.

He withdrew from his previous consciousness. And then, for 40 days and nights, he examined his motives, his expectations. He gave them up, he surrendered them, and he let them go. And he got himself into a state of consciousness, where he was empty. He had no agenda, desires, no expectations. And as he became the open door, then he saw a vision of his highest service in that lifetime.

As long as you think you have to throw yourself into the public debate by furthering a particular cause, then you will not give the highest service. Go back to my image of a public debate, where each group is seeking to further a particular interest. Now imagine that you step into this arena, but instead of fighting for a particular cause, you are seeking to use the public debate only as a tool to further the ultimate cause of oneness among all people and oneness between people and Mother Earth. And thus, you look beyond the narrow interests of each group.

This is not to say, that you do not speak about or to these groups and address their concerns. But you do it with the deeper awareness, that behind the debate is the deeper cause of oneness. And thus, can you see, that you have the potential here to provide a higher vision?

You might be able to be the open door for ideas that none of the people who are so focused on a narrow interest could even fathom. These people are so focused that they are not the open doors; they are the closed doors or even only the half-open doors. For they have a screen in front of their door that filters out certain ideas, which they cannot fathom based on their preconceived structure.

Once you are the open door and bring forth an idea, then many of the people will be able to see and embrace this idea. Only, they could not have been the open doors for bringing it into the debate. Yet even beyond being the open door for new ideas, you can be the open door for something else, namely a stream of high-frequency spiritual energy—namely the active, bubbling stream of peace.

***

If you will listen to my voice and vibration, you will sense here that vibration of the active, bubbling stream of peace. You may think this is

Being the open door for peace through oneness

not your normal concept of peace. For you may have been deceived into thinking that peace is what? Peaceful—meaning passive, soft, gentle, non-disturbing. Yet peace has an Alpha and an Omega side. And the Omega side is indeed soft and soothing, but the Alpha side of peace is strong, is active, is flowing. And it will not leave "in peace" those who are blinded by duality and therefore can never find true peace.

The Alpha aspect of peace will indeed go into a debate, not to soothe and gloss over problems. The active aspect of peace will enter a debate precisely with the purpose to stir the pot, to stir up the problems, to provoke the conflicts and contrast, so that they can come out in the open and thereby become visible to those who have not acknowledged the ultimate consequence of duality.

For have we not explained to you, that there are those who form one polarity that is obviously seen as evil, but the greater problem is those who are the subtle ones, who claim to be good but are not good in an ultimate sense but only according to their own dualistic definition. And so, those who are the ultimate servants of peace go into an area precisely to flush out the serpents, who are seeking to hide or appear as being benign. This is what you saw Jesus do on many occasions, many more than are actually recorded in the Scriptures.

Why do you think Jesus directly sought out confrontations with the scribes and Pharisees? Why do you think he in many cases provoked them by calling them hypocrites, by pointing out their hypocrisy or their contradictions, or even by calling them the sons of the devil? You may think that this could not be a representative of peace, who would do this. But it is, indeed, a true representative of the Alpha aspect of peace. And of course, you also saw that Jesus had mastered the Omega aspect, which allowed him to comfort people that deserved comfort, even to calm the waves of the angry sea, as a symbol for his ability to instantly calm the turbulent emotions of other people.

Jesus had mastered both the Alpha and the Omega aspect of peace. And whereas many people look at Jesus and understand and see his Omega aspect – and think that in order to be good Christians they have to be like him – there are indeed few who see the Alpha aspect. Can you not see Jesus walking into the temple and overturning the tables of the moneychangers? Do you think he did this calmly and peacefully? No, but he did not do it angrily either. He did it with the vibration of absolute determination, that would not leave alone those who were trapped in illusion—and therefore was willing to stir up these illusions, to stir up the hidden feelings so that their anger came out. Even to the point, where they became so angry that they demanded that he be executed. And this was, indeed, what led to the killing of Jesus: the anger that was brought out.

And thus, can you see, that when you are a true representative of peace, you are willing to be like a mirror that mirrors back to people what they are not willing to see in themselves? Only it gives it back to them in a more extreme form, that they might have an opportunity to see what they have not been willing to see, while it was still hidden under the veil of being good.

I am not thereby saying, that you need to do what Jesus did and provoke the power elite, so that they will end up killing you. For we have entered a different age. Nevertheless, you need to be – if you are willing to be a true representative of the sixth ray – willing to be that open door, so that the active stream of peace can flow through you and indeed stir up what needs to be stirred up. By provoking those who are the ultimate hypocrites of thinking they are working for a good cause, while they are truly working to promote the dualistic struggle.

***

This is your higher potential of service. Many well-meaning people, both in the environmental debate and elsewhere, have not reached the point, where they are willing to be the open door for the active flame of peace. They think that in order to be spiritual, they have to be calm, they have to be gentle, they have to be soothing, they have to always be in control—or at least appear to be in control.

But you cannot, my beloved, become an instrument for the active stream of peace unless you have dealt with your own hidden emotions, unless you have been willing to flush them out in yourself—to let the flame of peace flush it out in yourself, that you may see these emotions and deal with them. And thereby gradually overcome them, to the point where, again, you have no emotions of a lower sort, because you have no agenda, no expectations, you have no cause for which you think you have to fight.

Do you see, again, that the one thing that has trapped most of the well-meaning people on this planet is that they have fallen prey to the

Being the open door for peace through oneness 443

dualistic illusion created by the fallen beings? Namely, the illusion of the epic battle and the need to win an ultimate cause, an ultimate battle. Do you see how easy it is for the fallen beings, once they have conquered the privilege of formulating the problem? If you can make people believe that within a few years the earth will pass some point of no return – some tipping point, from which the ultimate environmental disaster will be irreversible – well, then can you not see, that you can get many well-meaning people to put their efforts into seeking to force society into compliance with some kind of agenda?

Yet can you see, that by doing this, you are giving your light to the fallen beings? But you are also reinforcing your own illusion that you are here to fight some ultimate cause, and that this will give you some ultimate reward. Why did the Christian Crusaders kill Muslim men, women and children? Because they thought they would score points – Brownie points, as the Girl Scouts say – that would give them entry into the kingdom of heaven.

They thought that by doing this, they would be redeemed in the eyes of God—and thus God simply had to accept them into his kingdom. This is the illusion that the fallen ones have believed in since their original fall—that if they go into the unascended realm and force all other people to be saved according to their definition, then they will have redeemed themselves in the eyes of God—and God will be forced to accept them into his kingdom. And not only that, God will be forced to accept that he was wrong all along and that the fallen beings were right. This is their dream, and they think they can achieve it by getting everyone on earth to follow them, or at least submit to them.

There are those among the fallen beings who want everyone to submit, and they seek to attain it through force. There are those who want everyone to be converted, and they seek to attain it through deception. But both are deceiving themselves, for there is no ultimate cause that could guarantee you entry into the kingdom of God. For the kingdom of God is a state of consciousness, where you have transcended duality. And how do you – as we have now attempted to explain to you many times – ultimately transcend duality? By simply walking away from the dualistic struggle!

***

So do you see the dilemma that many spiritual, well-meaning people are facing, as they work their way up through the first five rays? Do you see, that many of the people on earth are indeed trapped in indifference or a focus on their specific personal interests? This is what you see in many of the people who are below the 48th level of awareness; they are completely focused on what they see as their own narrow personal interests. How do you pull yourself beyond that level? Well, you do so by beginning to look to something that is beyond your personal interest. And what is beyond? Well, obviously some greater cause of improving society and even improving the earth.

There is a point on the spiritual path towards higher levels of awareness, where you do indeed need to embrace a cause. And of course, you must embrace it based on your current level of consciousness. And so, it is inevitable that as you begin to embrace a cause that goes beyond yourself, you will be pulled into embracing one of the causes defined by the fallen beings. However, the trick is to understand, that this can indeed give you a growth in consciousness. Because it does expand your awareness beyond that of narrow self-interest.

You begin to look beyond narrow self-interest to a cause that is beyond yourself, your separate self. And this helps you grow in awareness. However it only helps you grow in awareness up to a certain level. And if you do not take the next step, you will stay at that level. And you can, even for many lifetimes, be completely absorbed in this epic illusion of the epic battle, the epic cause. Many spiritual people, many sincere and well-meaning spiritual people, have been absorbed in this for lifetimes. I have talked about those who were the leaders of the Inquisition or the Crusades. They thought they were doing God's work, but they were not willing to step back and see, that as long as you see yourself in opposition to anyone, you are not doing God's work. For God's cause it to promote the oneness of all life, the awakening of human beings to the highest level of self-awareness, where you experience the oneness of all life.

So can you see, that it is perfectly in order, it is perfectly natural – and given the current state of the earth, perfectly unavoidable – that as you begin to rise above the levels of narrow self-interest, you will go through an interim period, where you will fight for – or at least seek to further – causes that are not ultimate causes, because they are defined by the fallen beings according to the dualistic consciousness? But this

Being the open door for peace through oneness

is not "wrong" because it is part of your growth. However, it would be unfortunate if you became stuck in this dualistic struggle. And that is, indeed, why one of the main messages in this book is the need to transcend it.

This is why we say this so many different times, because each Chohan provides a perspective for those who are currently vibrating with that specific ray. And so, do you see, that there comes a point where, in order to grow further on the path, you must begin to look beyond duality, the dualistic struggle? And this happens as you approach and reach the 96th level of awareness, where you must begin to lock in to the Christ perspective that is beyond duality. And you must begin, then, to open yourself up to the ultimate form of service, which is to be the open door for both the Alpha and the Omega aspect of peace, meaning the force of oneness.

For what is peace? It is oneness, my beloved. For what is the cause of conflict? It is division, is it not?

***

There is a way to speak out, where you speak openly and honestly about issues and problems, but you do not do it in a way that is dualistic. You are not seeking to raise up some people or some cause by putting other people or other ideas down. You are speaking in a way that is neutral, yet active; not passive. You are speaking in a way that may stir things up in those, who are not willing to look at the beam in their own eye, but always want to focus the debate on the splinters in the eyes of others.

The grand illusion embraced and promoted by the fallen beings is that there is an inherent flaw in God's design for the universe. Something has gone wrong, and it needs to be corrected—and someone needs to correct it. And we are the ones, because we are the ones who have the only truth about what has gone wrong. This is the grand illusion.

When you reach the 96th level of awareness, you begin to see this; it begins to become self-evident. And then, you can be the open door for challenging this illusion in many different ways, and doing so in a way that will sometimes seem like it is leading to more chaos and division and conflict. For you are seemingly flushing out the differences, the conflicts, the animosities.

Yet do you really think that true peace on earth can come about by ignoring or glossing over the many problems and divisions created through duality? Or do you think true peace can come about only through the difficult process, whereby people are confronted with their divisions, whereby these divisions are flushed out in the open, so that people can finally see them—and then have the ability or the opportunity to make the choice to let them go?

There are few people who are more blinded than those who think they are working for a good cause. For there are few people who are less willing to take a look at themselves and acknowledge, that they are not working for an ultimately good cause. For they are only working for a good cause as defined by a dualistic thought system, and their efforts are not helping to bring peace on earth. They are only helping to further the dualistic struggle and to help it camouflage itself in more and more subtle forms.

You may think, that many of the activities that take place in the environmental debate or among environmental activists are helping to further a good cause. But if they are motivated by the illusions that further the dualistic struggle, then they are not helping to heal Mother Earth. So how do you bring peace? You do not bring peace by regurgitating oil upon the troubled waters, so that they are forcefully calmed. You bring peace by becoming the open door for the stream of peace.

Sometimes it might soothe and calm the emotions. But in many cases, there must first be a period, where the emotions and the conflicts and the contrasting ideas are stirred up and brought to the surface. So that people can no longer ignore them, can no longer gloss them over, but indeed must confront them.

And in many cases, people are so blinded by the dualistic mindset, by the veil of Maya, that the only way they can come to see their own illusions is by acting out those illusions in an extreme manner. And then, when they have finally – perhaps after a long time – acted out their illusions to some extreme level, then they will be awakened and say: "Why are we doing this? Why are we continuing to do this? Have we not had enough of this? Is there not an alternative to this? Is there not a better way?"

***

Being the open door for peace through oneness 447

What is it that the Ma-ter light has done, what is it that the Earth Mother has done, what is it that elemental life has done? They have recognized the reality that the earth is a schoolroom, and they have then made themselves available to outpicture in physical form the subtle, unrecognized, subconscious mental images that humankind is projecting out. They have done this in order to mirror back to human beings what is in their own consciousness and what they have not been willing to see.

The universe, then, is the cosmic mirror. And so, when you come to the level of the sixth ray, what is your ultimate service on the sixth ray? It is to serve as a personal extension of the cosmic mirror, and therefore go into situations and relationships for the purpose of mirroring back to people what is unresolved in their own state of consciousness. This, among many other things, means that you sometimes allow people to project upon you. You allow them to even abuse you in various ways, as Jesus told you to do when he said: "Resist not evil, but turn the other cheek."

You are not resisting evil in a dualistic manner; you are allowing evil to outplay itself, so that people might have an ability to see this. Or if they are not willing to see it, they might be judged by violating the innocents who are turning their cheeks—and in turning the other cheek brings about the judgment from the cosmic mirror.

But there are also some times, where you do not allow people to abuse you, but where you challenge them openly by being the open door for the active, the Alpha, aspect of peace. That will not leave them alone in their illusion that they are good, but will force them to act out their subconscious tendencies and beliefs, until it becomes obvious to everyone – and eventually to themselves – that they are not as good, or as benign, or as peaceful as they thought.

No one becomes peaceful by being forced to become peaceful—this I think should be self-evident to those who are on the level of the sixth ray. So you cannot go in and force someone to be calm and peaceful. But you can go in and, so to speak, force out the divisions in their subconscious minds, so that they can see them. And now that they see them, they have an opportunity to choose, whether they will continue to embody them – and therefore reap the return current from the universe – or whether they will see them and transcend them by changing their state of consciousness.

Can you see, that sometimes the road to true peace goes through chaos? What did many of the people around Jesus say to him? What did the demons say to him, when he approached the man who was possessed? "Leave us alone, thou son of God!" Many of the people who met Jesus were disturbed by him, by the light of the Alpha aspect of peace streaming through him. And many of them, either directly or indirectly, said: "Leave us alone!" But what is the entire purpose of the incarnation of the Christ? It is precisely to not leave people alone in their illusions.

For their illusions will eventually cause them to self-destruct. So the Christ is willing to go into this world, to stir things up and disturb people in their illusory sense of peace. And why do people have this illusory sense of peace? Because they have used a dualistic mindset to become as gods, defining good and evil. And according to their definition of good and evil, they always appear to be good.

And therefore, they are completely trapped into thinking they are good, and that they are guaranteed to be saved. But in reality, they are making no progress, they are standing still. And meanwhile, the rest of the universe is moving on, and there will come a point, where they will be faced with the choice to either move on or go to some lower level than the earth. Go to an even lower level than the earth, we might say, for truly, this is not a very high planet.

***

So what does the Christ do? Does the Christ sit up there in heaven and leave these people alone in their illusions? Nay, the Christ says: "I will go down there and take on a physical body, and I will get in their face, so they cannot ignore me. And therefore, I will force them to act out what they refuse to see in their own subconscious minds. And then, perhaps, when they do see it, well then perhaps they will choose to transcend it. And if not, then they will be taken from the earth, and thus the entire planet will transcend that level of consciousness."

This is what the Christ does, and this is true love. It is also what brings true peace. "Peace, peace but there is no peace." Men may cry out for peace, but until they are willing to look at the beam their own eye, to look in the mirror and face the warring in their own members – in the subconscious mind – there will be no peace on earth. There will be no good will among men, until there is good will within men—and

Being the open door for peace through oneness

women. And there will not be peace within until you have looked at the divisions in your own mind.

This is what you have become an instrument for, as you pass the initiations of the sixth ray. You can be willing to do what Jesus did: stand in front of those who need to be provoked and stand on the rock of Christ. You can be willing to let them attack you, to accuse you and say all manner of false things against you. But you are unmoved.

You are not fighting them in a dualistic manner, you are not seeking to prove them wrong. You are not seeking to put them down. But neither are you letting them intimidate you into not disturbing them. And certainly, you are not letting the fallen beings project upon you their own mindset, and therefore put you down to the point, where you think you have no right to be the Christ on earth.

When you are at lower levels of consciousness, you should not attempt to challenge the power elite on earth. For you will either be destroyed by them – destroyed emotionally and spiritually – or you will be engaged in the dualistic struggle. And either way, the devil wins and will laugh all the way to the bank—where he will deposit your light, that you have given him.

***

Yet when you do reach a certain level – when you have overcome your expectations, your attachments, even your sense of having to fight for some cause – then you can, as Jesus demonstrated, be the open door for a more direct challenge to the power elite and the false gurus and false teachers that are found in every area of society—those who promote their false dualistic ideas as if they were true ideas with some ultimate authority.

This is the potential you have, when you are willing to go through the initiations of the sixth ray, which is, as I have said, to be willing to let the stream of peace stir up anything that is anti-peace in your own being. This takes courage, great courage. But once you have passed the initiations of the fifth ray, you will have that courage. And thus, you will not see it as something you have to go through that is threatening, or dangerous, or scary. You will embrace the opportunity. And therefore, you will not engage in a dualistic battle with the fallen beings or the power elites out of an enjoyment of the battle. But you will find a certain enjoyment in being completely calm inside, while watching how other people are outplaying their subconscious divisions until they become more and more obvious.

And you will find a certain appreciation in seeing how – without you having any outer intention – your Presence will suddenly interject an idea, a saying, that will cause people to stop in the middle of a heated debate and discussion. This one idea will cause them to fall silent, and now they are thinking. Now they are suddenly seeing the contradictions in their viewpoints. Now they are suddenly beginning to see how their very approach to the debate can never achieve the end they claim they want to achieve. They are suddenly beginning to see, that they can never bring peace as long as they think they have to fight other people. And they can never actually further the cause of the environment as long as they are trying to fight other people.

For "other people" are not the problem. It is the illusion that there are "other people" that is the problem.

If you want to overcome "the problem," you need to overcome the illusion that human beings can be divided up into factions, based on the standard that something is right and something is wrong—and therefore some people are good and some people are evil. When you overcome that illusion, then you see what the problem is. The problem is the consciousness of separation, that makes it seem like there are "other people" that are separate from "us" and thereby obscures the underlying reality that all life is one. And therefore, there cannot be "other people."

When you embrace that reality, then you can begin to give true service. Then you can begin to minister unto life. And then you can be the open door for true and lasting peace.

This is the peace that I AM. And before Abraham was, I AM.

Key 29
Individuality is the key to the Golden Age

Saint Germain I AM. In my first discourse, I attempted to give you the vision that there is indeed a potential that the earth can transcend its current level of struggle and conflict, of limitations and lack, and go into what I called a Golden Age. This is an image that I have attempted, through various messengers and organizations, to give to humankind since the 1930s. And indeed, there has been much progress since that time. And some of that progress has indeed been caused by the fact, that so many of my students have taken this vision and projected it into the collective consciousness. Thereby freeing other people to become the open doors for the bringing forth of new ideas and technology, that helped bring about the progress you have seen.

Nevertheless, there are also many of the students who have looked at my vision and have misunderstood the central point. For they have been so colored by the fallen consciousness, that they have actually transferred the fallen consciousness to the vision of Saint Germain. So even though I know, that many of these students are still so trapped in the fallen consciousness, that they will be unwilling to even acknowledge the validity of what I will say, I will still say what I will say. For I know, that there are students who will indeed be able to grasp the central point, that I will give you in this message.

***

You see, my beloved, there are many people on this earth who are what you might call futurists and who have a vision that the earth is on the way to a better society. Yet there is indeed also many among them, who are still so colored by the fallen consciousness, that they think that this utopian future society can be achieved only by either forcing or persuading all people to come into compliance with a specific thought system or standard, defined on earth.

This is precisely the dream of the fallen beings, that they have projected out since their original fall. And it will never – my beloved, did you hear me, it will NEVER – bring forth the Golden Age of Saint Germain. I am not in compliance with the age-old, idolatrous image of the external God in the sky, who is sitting up here with a fixed standard, according to which I judge everything and everyone on earth. I am not sitting up here with a vision of the Golden Age that is defined in every detail.

Certainly, I have certain principles and ideas and visions, certain sketches and blueprints, for the Golden Age, but it is not set in stone. For I know something that the fallen beings also know, but that they do not want you to know. I know that the Golden Age will be manifest not through forcing or deceiving people into giving up their individuality, but only through allowing and encouraging people to express that individuality.

For you see, my beloved, we have so far attempted to give you a gradually increasing awareness of the problem represented by the fallen beings. That is, it might be a problem seen from your viewpoint, whereas it is truly not a problem seen from the viewpoint of the ascended masters—who know what is real and what is unreal, and know that that which is unreal has no power over that which is real.

What we have said so far is, that what the fallen beings rebelled against was that the Creator created self-aware extensions of itself and gave them free will. You might therefore surmise, that what the fallen beings rebelled against was free will. This is not incorrect, my beloved, but it is not the complete picture. For we have attempted to give you the understanding, that there is an Alpha and an Omega in everything.

Free will, therefore, is the Omega aspect. So what is the Alpha? Well, it is what we have called self-awareness. What do you need in order to have self-awareness? You need two components: awareness and self. Meaning that there has to be an individuality that can give you the sense of self, which is the basis for you having self-awareness.

Now my beloved, this is truly a subtle understanding, so be willing to stretch your mind. Or rather, be willing to go into your heart and let the Conscious You become an open door, so that you might receive an

Individuality is the key to the Golden Age

inner understanding from your I Will Be Presence, rather than seeking to understand my words through the outer mind.

***

What the Creator has done is the seemingly impossible task – but of course, with God all things are possible – what the creator has done is to create innumerable self-aware extensions of itself, and each of these extensions is endowed with an absolutely unique individuality. And then, each extension has been given free will to express and expand that individuality. So can you see, that individuality is the Alpha and free will is the Omega?

Of course, from the perspective of the fallen ones, the real problem is free will. Because individuality is not a problem for them until it is expressed. So if they can either forcefully take away people's free will, or if they can deceive people into not exercising their free will, well then individuality is not really a problem.

Yet from a deeper level, the fallen beings are indeed rebelling against both the Alpha – that the Creator gave each being individuality – and the Omega—that the Creator gave them free will. What the fallen beings want you to do, is to restrict your free will, so that you cannot express your individuality—because you are limiting your free-will choices to a set of predefined choices, that are defined according to a standard set up by the fallen beings.

So the real plan of the Creator is to create all of these self-aware extensions of itself, and to send them into a certain environment, where they are, then, in much the same situation as the students in Serapis Bey's retreat. They will inevitably clash, because in the beginning – as they are new co-creators – they will have to experiment with their free will. And thus, they will inevitably bring forth expressions that will clash with those of other beings.

The challenge that the Creator has put before all is this: will you see your individuality as being in conflict with the individuality of others, or will you transcend this limited, dualistic, separatist view and see that your individuality is unique. And therefore, it can never be in conflict with the individuality of others.

My beloved, was this a sentence that was difficult for you to understand? If it was, it is because you have not yet locked in to what it means that you have individuality.

My beloved, it is difficult to give you a linear illustration of this. But as one illustration, let us take a diamond that is created in such a way that it has a number of facets. Each of the facets of the diamond is, so to speak, a little mirror. It can reflect light.

Now you know, that if two light beams oppose each other, they might create an interference pattern and annihilate each other. Yet what happens, when you shine light on a diamond? Each of the facets will reflect the light, but none of the beams from the facets will actually cross each other. For the diamond is shaped in such a way that the mirror of each facet points in a unique direction. And thus, it will not send the reflection of itself into the path of any other facet. And this, of course, is what gives the diamond is unique beauty.

Imagine that the facets annihilated each other, so there was no shine in the diamond. The diamond would then not be beautiful. So what makes it beautiful is, that it has a number of facets, and each facet is unique, so that they all enhance each other instead of annihilating each other.

So can you begin to see, that the Creator's plan is to create an incredibly beautiful universe with myriads of unique facets, that are each shining their unique light. But all of them are combined in such a way, that the unique expressions do not annihilate each other; they enhance each other. And together they create a whole that is far more than what any of the parts could express alone, but even far more than the linear sum of each part. The whole is more than the sum of the parts.

***

Can you see, that this is the very key to understanding the Creator's plan and vision for the universe? Individuality is the building block of the Creator's vision.

Yet in order for individuality to come to shine, there must be an interim period, where there is seemingly chaos. Where it seems like the individualities clash and where the individual self-aware beings are outplaying their individualities in ways that do clash with each other. Yet as each individual facet raises its awareness from the 48th level through

Individuality is the key to the Golden Age

the 96th level, and begins to approach the 144th level, something unique will happen.

As you, as an individual, begin to come more and more into oneness with your I Will Be Presence, you become more and more able to simply be the open door for the Presence. So what you will express is the individuality of the Presence. And that individuality was created in such a way, that it cannot conflict with the individuality of any other self-aware being.

Do you see, that as more and more people raise their level of awareness towards the 144th level, then they magically begin to form this diamond, where each facet is shining its light without interfering with the light of any other facet? And where all of the facets together form this incredible whole, where each facet is the open door for a unique manifestation of the Creator's total Being.

And can you see, that when you have this free expression of the creative flow of the Creator – flowing through the I Will Be Presence of each of the self-aware beings living on earth – well, when that happens, my beloved, then the earth will truly outpicture the abundant life of the Golden Age. For there will be such an expression of creativity that society will go through a transformation, that will be far more dramatic than what you have seen between the society of the caveman and current civilization.

You may think there has been immense technological progress, compared to the difference between the caveman and today's technology. But it will be dwarfed by what will happen in the Golden Age, as humankind first goes beyond force-based technology, where there is always conflict. And then even goes beyond non-force-based technology to the technology of the mind.

***

What happened to the fallen beings was, that they became so focused on the chaos, that they were not able to see the chaos as what it truly is, namely the initial creative tension that was meant to bring forth the higher vision of the diamond. Is not a diamond dug out of the ground? Does it not have a rough shape in the beginning and needs to be cleaned and then polished into various facets, before it becomes the shining diamond? But if you did not see a vision of the end goal, then you might think that what was being done to the diamond was wrong, or chaotic, or violent.

Yet what happened was, that the fallen ones began to see individuality as a threat. They began to see the individuality of other beings as a threat to the expression of their own individuality. And even when their entire sphere came closer and closer to the ascension point, they refused to shift out of this illusion and simply shift their attention, whereas they could instantly have shifted into seeing, that individuality and differences is not the threat. It is the potential of becoming more, for many individual beings create more as a whole than any of them could create alone.

So instead, the fallen beings became trapped in the quest of seeking to raise their separate individuality into some ultimate state, instead of letting the separate individuality die and becoming one with their divine individuality, whereby they could have found their place as facets on the diamond. But they were not happy to be just one among many facets. They wanted to have some ultimate status, where their individuality was raised beyond the individuality of others to some ultimate or superior validation or recognition.

Yet, the sun does not find its joy in being worshiped by human beings on earth. The sun finds its joy in shining its light. When you reach the 144th level of awareness, you have no desire whatsoever to be admired, or raised up, or idolized by other people. For you are so in bliss of feeling the creative flow of your I Will Be Presence through the open door of the Conscious You, that you need nothing else.

And so, it is, that you find your place as a facet in the diamond of humanity. And when that diamond is complete, you will see that each individual being on earth will have complete creative freedom. For can you not see, based on what we have told you earlier, that the lie of the fallen beings is that you can find freedom only in rebelling against God's plan and expressing your separate individuality, your separate self, in an extreme form.

This is what happened to Hitler and other egomaniacs throughout history. They thought they were free, because they had the power to do whatever they wanted without reaping the consequences. And yet, just as they thought they had reached some ultimate status on earth, things began to crumble or their bodies began to give out and the dream collapsed.

Individuality is the key to the Golden Age

***

What the fallen ones want you to think is, that in order for you to either be saved or serve some ultimate cause, you should suppress the individuality, your creative expression of that individuality, in order to follow the fallen beings and comply with their standard. Which they want you to believe will bring about the ultimate utopia, which is their false version of the Golden Age.

They think that they can sit here on earth and define the matrix for the Golden Age. But I tell you, you cannot create a committee of even the wisest people on earth and have them sit here and look at current knowledge and current technology, and then use that to create a blueprint for the Golden Age. It cannot be done, my beloved!

For the Golden Age will be based on such creativity, that it cannot even be imagined based on current technology. And thus, the only way is that the Conscious You projects itself out of identification with the outer, linear, analytical mind. The only way is that you become the open door for the creative flow of the I Will Be Presence. It is when you dare to express your individuality – your divine individuality – that you become an instrument for bringing the Golden Age into manifestation.

Have I not talked about the need to unlock, to free, your imagination? How are you ultimately free as an individual self-aware being? You are ultimately free, when the Conscious You has disentangled itself from the separate self, so that you are no longer perceiving everything through the filter, the colored glasses, of the separate self. And then, the Conscious You – still tied to the physical body – can look up at the I Will Be Presence and the I AM Presence. And then, the Conscious You can come to the recognition: "I am *that* I am; I am THAT I am up there, and not the separate I am down here."

At that moment, the Conscious You can say with Christ: "I and my father – meaning I and my Presence – are one." Then, you can also say with Christ: "I can of my own self – meaning the separate self and the physical body – do nothing; it is the father – meaning the I Will Be Presence – who is the true doer."

And then, you can find your rightful place, where you realize: "My father – my Presence – works hitherto and I work." For it is truly the flow of the I Will Be Presence that can be the key to bringing forth new manifestations on earth. But you also work, because as a Conscious

You, you choose where to focus your attention. You only have a certain amount of attention, you only have 24 hours a day, there is only so much you can do in one lifetime. So you choose what you will focus on, and then your I Will Be Presence will be happy to express its creativity in the field that you have chosen to focus on.

You see, my beloved, your I Will Be Presence is multifaceted. It is not that your I Will Be Presence is an artist, or a scientist, or a musician. Your I Will Be Presence can express its creativity through any role that you choose here on earth—as long as you choose to be open door.

So your I Will Be Presence does not force you to become a musician, for example. It does not make that choice for you; it allows you – as the Conscious You – to make that choice. Because you are the one who has the right to say: "I want to experience what it is like to see the earth from the perspective of that role, and I want to experience what it is like to express my creativity through this outer vehicle." And then, the I Will Be Presence is more than happy to let its light and its creativity flow into the outer vehicle that you have chosen. And that is how your father works hitherto and you work.

***

Now, of course, there are certain lifestreams who have chosen to come into a particular embodiment for a particular purpose. Jesus had made the choice to fulfill his mission before he came into embodiment. The Conscious You of Jesus had made that choice. So we might say that after taking embodiment, the Conscious You of Jesus was not entirely at liberty to choose another course of action, for it had already made a higher choice [although it had the free will to ignore that previous choice].

So do you see here, that there is a distinction that must be made. When you take embodiment, you will go through a certain forgetting. You forget your divine plan, you forget the choices you made before taking embodiment, you forget your identity. And so, as you grow through childhood into adulthood, you are indeed meant to gradually reconnect to your Presence and rediscover your divine plan.

Nevertheless, there is still plenty of room within that divine plan for you to make many choices, based on your current embodiment. It was not that Jesus was a marionette that followed some predefined plan. But he did come to rediscover his divine plan, the plan that he had chosen,

Individuality is the key to the Golden Age

and he accepted that. But even in accepting it, there were many creative decisions that he could make as to how to express it in the particulars of that embodiment.

Even though you might say, that Jesus had a certain limited mission – for it was almost guaranteed that he would have to provoke the power elite to such an extent that they would kill him – he still had great creative freedom in how he talked and interacted with people during the three years of his mission, and the 30 years that were a preparation for his mission. And of course, in today's age you will not have to be killed in order to fulfill your mission. For the entire idea and plan is that at this particular time, there are 10,000 people in embodiment who have the potential to acknowledge and express the same level of Christhood as Jesus. And of course, the idea is that the power elite cannot kill all of them.

There are also millions of other people who can express a high degree of Christhood, beyond the 96th level. And thus again, they cannot all be killed, when they all dare to express their Christhood at the same time, so they supplement and reinforce each other.

As I am giving this discourse, there has been a period of the people in certain Muslim nations in Africa rising up against the dictators that have been there for decades. Throughout the previous decades, those dictators had ruled through fear, because as one or a few individuals dared to stand up against the dictator, they were instantly killed or imprisoned. But what happened now was, that so many people decided to stand up to the dictator, that the dictator realized he could not kill or imprison all of them.

***

For indeed, the power elite, the fallen beings, face a very simple equation. It is a mathematical equation, for the fact is that they are vastly outnumbered on this planet. And so, the only way that the fallen beings can use force to suppress the population is not actually through physical force, but through the fear that is generated by the threat of physical force. And as long as the people accept that threat, well then the fallen beings will stay in power.

But realize, my beloved, a very simple equation. The fallen beings are so few, that they cannot physically suppress the entire population.

So they need to have a segment of the population act as their henchmen, in the form of soldiers and police officers and what have you. Yet the simple problem is, that those who are acting as extensions of the power elite have friends and family members among the population. And so, there comes a point, where people are not going to be willing to imprison or kill their own family members or friends. And thus, when enough people stand up against the power elite, there is nothing the power elite can do about it except retreat.

And my beloved, this is the power of the Age of Aquarius. Jesus came as an individual to show the ultimate power of individuality. Jesus was one facet shining bright, but he was the only one at the time. So where was the diamond? The plan for this age is, that there are so many Christed beings expressing their Christhood, that they do indeed form the diamond. And when the diamond is formed, people will see the matrix. And they will see the power of community, of coming into unity around a greater vision, a unified vision, based on the reality that all life is one. And that each individual is an expression of the one, and therefore cannot be a threat to other individuals who are also expressions of the one.

For the reality is, as Nada so eloquently said, there are no "other" individuals. For you can have self-awareness only because you have an individual self, but you can have awareness only because your awareness is the Creator's omnipresent awareness, expressing itself through your individual self.

When you reach that 144th level of consciousness, you experience this as a living reality. I realize, that those who are below that level, will not lock in to what I am saying, for it will just be a theory, a mental image for them. But when you reach the 144th level, it is no longer a theory, it is no longer a mental image. For you have now reached gnosis, where you experience it, you are one with it. You are one, my beloved, with the oneness of the Creator. You know you are an expression of the Creator, and nothing can threaten your expression.

***

There is, of course, a fundamental difference between expressing your light and going into the fallen consciousness of seeing the light of others as a threat—and then seeking to restrict their light through force or

Individuality is the key to the Golden Age

deception. But when you reach the 144th level, you will no longer see the fallen beings as a threat to you.

At lower levels, you go through a period, where you begin to recognize as self-evident the presence of the fallen beings and their consciousness. And in the beginning of this period of transition, it is inevitable that you will come to see the fallen beings as being somewhat of a threat to you. Because, after all, they are seeking to limit your freedom.

There are so many things in current human society that seek to limit or even destroy the creative freedom of the individual. And as you begin to see this, you must go through a period, where you rebel against this because you are seeking to free yourself from the influence.

But then you come to a point, where you begin to realize, that it is not a matter of rebelling, in a physical outer way, against these external restrictions. The real key to freedom is to take command over your state of mind, so that you are not allowing the fallen beings to intimidate you into voluntarily restricting the expression of your individuality, your Christhood.

For do you not see what I said before? The fallen beings do not have the physical power to suppress the population, but neither do they have the physical power to suppress you as an individual. They cannot exercise power over your mind. Even if they could exercise total power over your body – which is becoming increasingly difficult for them in modern society – they still could not restrict your mind. And thus, you could be imprisoned in a cell, but you could still sit there, in the total bliss of oneness with God, and radiate a light that would gradually add to the momentum that will inevitably overthrow the fallen ones and their reign on this earth, by shifting the 144 levels of consciousness upwards, as we have already explained.

You see, that there comes a point, where you realize that even though the fallen ones are present on earth and have a certain power over your physical body, they have no power over your mind. And thus, the real key to freedom is to free your mind, to where you are no longer either intimidated by the force of the fallen beings or deceived by the deception, the serpentine lies, of the fallen beings. And then, when you begin to see through even the most subtle serpentine lies, then you will gradually – one by one – discard those lies, discard those facets of your separate self and let that separate self die.

And as you do this, you come closer and closer to the ultimate freedom, where you are the open door which no man can shut. Meaning that no force on earth, no expression of the fallen consciousness coming from the illusion of separation, can cause you to stop being the open door for the creative flow of your Presence.

That, my beloved, is total freedom. That, my beloved, is the key to overcoming current environmental problems, current problems in any aspect of society. And it is the key to manifesting the Golden Age, because it is the key to bringing forth the ideas that will manifest the Golden Age.

**

The fallen beings want you to believe that a Golden Age – their version of the Golden Age – can be brought by suppressing individuality, so that all people are made to be the same, so that they are mindless minions, marching to the drumbeat of the fallen beings. This is their dream. Look at Nazi society, look at communism under Stalin, look at communism under Mao, and see how they were attempting to turn the population into mindless robots, who would march without thinking—without thinking individually but only thinking the thoughts programmed into their minds by the party apparatus. So that they would mindlessly and without question follow the orders of the leaders.

This is how they attempted to create a Golden Age, through forcing the suppression of individuality. Or even seducing those who were the intellectuals, and who were indeed seduced. Look at how many people in the Western world were seduced into believing in the potential to bring forth a Golden Age through communism, or through limiting the growth of the population or the growth of society.

Can you not, then, take everything we have given you in this book and use it to free yourself from these illusions of lack and force and deception? Can you not, then, come to the realization, that the real key to overcoming the problems and manifesting the Golden Age is to be the open door for the creative flow of the Presence, yourself choosing where to focus and where to direct that flow? And as you direct it and focus it, you will see how the creativity of the Presence will bring forth, through you, new ideas, new thoughts. And this will magically transform the

Individuality is the key to the Golden Age

earth. When enough people become the open doors for new ideas, then the fallen beings will not be able to hold back the creative flow.

The creative flow of the individuals that are currently in embodiment has already created a combined momentum. What the fallen beings have done with their structures, their thought systems, is to build a dam. But I tell you: the dam is beginning to buckle under the pressure. It is waving back and forth, and it is even beginning to crack, and the water is beginning to squirt through.

And my beloved, when you accept who you are and enough other people accept who they are, then the dam will suddenly burst and the floodgates will be opened. And the earth will be flooded with such an overwhelming force of creative ideas and inventions, that what today seem as insurmountable problems will become seen for what they truly are: lack of knowledge, lack of creativity, shadows that disappear as soon as the light is turned on.

The light of the creative sun of the presences of individual beings are ultimately expressions of the ultimate creative sun of the Creator itself. You are the Creator expressing itself. You are the Creator looking at itself. When you recognize this, my beloved – as I have recognized it and as all members of the Ascended Host have recognized it – then you will know the truth in the statement: "As Above, so below."

Then, you will be the open door for manifesting the vision of Above here below in the physical frequency spectrum on planet earth. And then, you will realize the reality that as people become the open doors, then what is here below will be a reflexion, a mirror image, of what is Above. And then, you will have "as Above, so below."

And then comes the ultimate state, where the below is no longer below. For the below has been raised in vibration, so that it becomes part of what is Above. And the earth ascends, and the entire material universe ascends, and your sphere becomes the latest addition to the spiritual realm, where all self-aware beings know the one underlying reality that all life is one.

And in knowing that reality, they experience ultimate freedom, the ultimate freedom that I AM.

Key 30
Transcending hatred of the Mother

Gautama I AM. Gautama is my name, the Buddha is my title.

What does the Buddha have to do with a book, that is primarily given for people, who have grown up in what is normally called the Western world? Has not one of your major poets once written, "East is East, and West is West—and never the twain shall meet." Well, my beloved, what exactly is East and what exactly is West? You live on a spherical globe. How can you divide that globe up by drawing an artificial line and saying: What is on one side of that line is East and on the other side is West? Does this not show exactly what the chohans and the Blessed Mother have attempted to explain throughout this book: the tendency to set yourself up as a God who says, "Where I am is the center of the world. And thus, everything is defined based on its position to where I am."

This is what has created the division among human beings. And it was, indeed, one of my principal drives – when I walked the earth 2,500 years ago – to help people overcome this divisive consciousness, which is precisely what I called the veil of Maya.

Maya is often translated as illusion, but it is a specific kind of illusion, namely the illusion of separation, the illusion that reality – that what exists – can be divided into these segments. And that those who have set themselves up as gods have the power and the right to define the divisions based on some thought system or other.

***

When you have passed the initiations of the seventh ray, you understand freedom, you experience freedom, you have become one with freedom. Yet what does it take to come to that point? It takes that you actually face and transcend every fear found on this planet.

There is, of course, a fear for each of the seven rays, and you can go through the discourses by each of the chohans and you can identify those fears. But in the end, there is really only one underlying fear, and that is what we might call the fear of freedom.

For have we not said, over and over and over again, that God has given you free will, and that you live in a universe in which everything is subject to free will? What does this actually mean? It means that you – as an individual self-aware being – have the capacity and the right to define your sense of self any way you want.

Yet can you perhaps sense – if you tune in to your own conscious and subconscious mind – that there is a certain fear associated with this? Before you reach the 144th level, you will go through a period, where you must face this fear—the fear of freedom, the fear of having the complete freedom to define who you are. And in order to help you face and walk through this fear of freedom, let me give you some thoughts.

***

It is important for you to understand – as has been said before but as I will say again – that all fear is a fear of the unknown. What you fear is not reality; it is an illusion. So, all of your fears spring from the fact that you have come to identify yourself as a separate self. You have come to believe in the illusion of separation. And as we have said, the inevitable companion of this illusion is the fear of death, the fear that the separate self could be no more.

So as the Conscious You begins to free itself from identification with the separate self, the Conscious You faces the fear of freedom. Because the Conscious You begins to realize, that it is not the separate self. But the question then becomes: "Well, if I am not the separate self; what am I, what do I want to be?"

You now face the eternal dilemma, that has been faced by all spiritual seekers throughout history. The dilemma is this. While you are looking at the world through the filter of the separate self, you cannot fully see your I Will Be Presence. Therefore, you cannot come into full identification with the Presence. And this means that from your viewpoint – where you are looking through the filter of the separate self – it will seem as if letting the separate self die means that there will be nothing left.

Just look at how many people on earth fear physical death, because they fear there will be nothing left of them after they die. Then look at the many, many near-death experiences that people have had. And what is the one message underlying all of them? It is the message of continuity.

There is, indeed, awareness – there is consciousness, there is self-awareness – after the death of the physical body. Yet while you are still in a body, you are looking at the world through the filter of the outer mind that is associated with, and to some degree produced by, the body and the brain. And thus, you tend to cling to this life. You cannot know for sure that there is life after death, while you are still looking at the world through the body.

If you actually observe people who are dying, you will see that there are two basic reactions. There are people who keep fighting death to the very end, but then there are people who, when death nears, come to a sort of inner resolution, an inner peace, where they surrender unto death. Those who come to this inner resolution and surrender unto death are those, who have used the Conscious You's ability to project itself outside the filter of the physical body.

Thus, instead of perceiving life through the filter of the body, they have gained at least a glimpse of how it is to perceive life from outside the body. They have gained an inner knowing, that there will be some part of them, that will continue an existence after the physical body dies. And this is why they can surrender to death and let go of the body and the one lifetime among many, that they are now coming to the end of.

***

You see, when you come to the initiations of the seventh ray, you will have to face this fear. It is very similar to the fear of the death of the physical body. It is also the fear that if you let the separate self die, there will be nothing left of you. The way to conquer this fear is to realize, that it is based on the illusion of separation—and be willing to actually use the Conscious You's ability to project itself anywhere it wants.

If you will take an honest look at yourself and many other people, you will see, that there is a tendency for people to avoid, to seek to avoid, that which they think will be unpleasant. People spend enormous amounts of money or mental and physical effort trying to avoid things.

In fact, one might say that the main industry in the Western world is precisely the avoidance industry, where people are seeking to avoid this or that, from physical labor, to growing old or to death. Anything that people think will be unpleasant, they are willing to pay to avoid—and somebody is willing to sell them the illusion that they can avoid it, at least for a little time longer.

If you, then, take an honest look at students who are on the spiritual path – or claim to be on the spiritual path – you will see, that a substantial part of them have used the spiritual path precisely as another way to avoid. What did Jesus say, when he walked the earth? He said: "Stop looking at the splinter in the eyes of your brothers and sisters, and start looking at the beam in your own eye." What has been described throughout this book is that the fallen ones have been doing this from the very beginning—refusing to look at themselves and projecting blame outside themselves based on a standard they have created.

As a result, they have created the illusion of the epic struggle, where in order to be a good or spiritual person, you have to fight this battle or the earth will somehow go down. Yet this is all avoidance. And this has caused millions of sincere spiritual people to go into the blind alley of seeking to avoid looking at themselves, looking at their egos, looking at their fears. So you cannot pass the initiations of the seven rays if you are unwilling to look at your fears.

**

So what is fear? Well, as I have said, it is an illusion. And this is why fear forms what we have called a catch-22. There is something you fear. And as a result of fearing it, you try to avoid having to confront it. Yet my beloved, if the something you fear is a complete illusion, how will you come to see that it is an illusion as long as you are seeking to avoid it?

When you were a child, you might have feared that there were monsters under your bed. And you might have been afraid to look, because if you looked under the bed, you would see the monsters. But then, there came a point, where you actually realized, that there were no monsters. Or you actually gathered up the courage to look under the bed and see, that there were no monsters. And when you looked, and saw that the

Transcending hatred of the Mother

condition you had feared did not exist, well then, you realized that what you had been fearing was a mirage, a mental image, an illusion.

This is the one underlying realization that can save you untold grief on the spiritual path: if you will simply determine, that you will take an honest look at your fears. And whenever you discover a fear, then you use the Conscious You's ability to mentally project yourself into the fear, even into the condition that you fear. And then you ask yourself: "Does this fear really have any power over me? If the condition that I fear did come to pass as a physical reality, would it really have any power over me? Could it change me, as a spiritual being? Could it change my state of mind? For is it not, after all, a temporary condition?"

When you know that you will survive physical death, then is there really any condition on this earth that you need to fear? For after all, how could it be any more than temporary? And when you begin to realize that you are an immortal spiritual being, how can that which is temporary, measured by earth time, have any power over you and your ongoingness in the River of Life?

There is nothing you cannot transcend, there is nothing you cannot free yourself from. There are people who have experienced very difficult physical conditions on earth but have still attained peace of mind.

***

As you have passed the initiations of the seven rays, there is one more ray that you come to, which is called the eighth ray of integration. And as you begin to lock in to the energies of integration, you begin to realize, that you are indeed a spiritual being who can never, ever, be affected by anything on earth. You begin to realize, that you are the Conscious You. You are pure awareness. You are an open door.

You can go in and identify yourself as a separate being, but that will not change you. Because you are pure awareness. There is nothing in the world of form that can change pure awareness. And there is nothing in the material universe that can change your I AM Presence and your I Will Be Presence. And when you know, and begin to experience as a living reality, that nothing on earth can change you, then why would you fear anything on earth? You begin to realize, that whatever might happen to you on earth, it is simply an experience.

And then, when you are willing to confront the fear of death and the associated fear of failure, you can realize that even the idea that something is unpleasant – and something else is pleasant – is an offspring of the consciousness of separation, the consciousness of duality, where there must always be two polarities. You can come to a point, where you have attained what I attempted to explain to my disciples 2,500 years ago.

You have attained a state of complete non-attachment. You are non-attached because you no longer need to divide experiences on earth into that which is pleasant and that which is unpleasant. Whatever happens to you on earth is neither pleasant nor unpleasant—it simply is.

A condition simply is. And you realize you are more. And therefore, the condition does not have power over you. Instead you – meaning your Presence – has power over the condition. But you cannot come to that point through an intellectual understanding. You can come to that point only when the Conscious You stops identifying itself with the separate self. But as I have just explained, you can stop identifying yourself with the separate self only when you are willing to face all of the fears of the separate self.

You must go into these fears, experience them from the inside, experience mentally the condition that you fear. So that you can come to see it as an illusion, or at least see it as an illusion that this condition could have any power over you as pure awareness, as an extension of the Presence.

***

Do you see, my beloved, when the Conscious You sees itself as pure awareness, as an open door for the flow of the Presence, then you are like the sun? As we have hinted at before, nothing can approach the sun. You can unite all of humankind with all of their sophisticated technology in building the biggest spaceship you could ever imagine. You could fill it with all of the nuclear bombs in the world, and then you could send it towards the sun in a prideful attempt to somehow hurt the sun.

But what would happen as that giant spaceship came closer to the sun? The very mass that it has would be exposed to the rays of the sun, and what would the rays of the sun do? The rays of the sun demand that matter be accelerated into a higher state of vibration. And so, the

Transcending hatred of the Mother

spaceship would have two ways to go. It could either be accelerated into the same vibrational level as the rays of the sun, which means it would obviously transcend its destructive form and matrix. Or it could be exposed to the sun's heat rays, that would heat up the matter in the spaceship, until it would start breaking apart, disintegrating and melting, so that no organized structure was left.

When you begin to see yourself as the open door for the Presence, you experience the flow of the Presence. And thus, you experience that there is no power on earth that can stop that flow, because the flow is strong enough to transform any condition on earth. And thus, you begin to realize that you are the open door which no man – which no power on earth – can shut.

Yet there is a power on earth that can shut your open door, and that is you, your free will. When you identify yourself as a separate being, you think that the flow of your Presence should be subject to certain conditions on earth. And thus, you voluntarily shut the door for the flow of the Presence. And this is when you become subject to the fear, that something on earth has power over you, or could change you against your will, or could destroy you against your will. And this is when a very subtle change happens to your worldview.

***

Instead of seeing yourself as the open door for a greater force – that is beyond anything on earth – you now see yourself as a limited being, who is subject to the forces on earth. And this means, that you begin to see yourself as a victim of conditions on earth, even a victim of conditions in the universe.

This is what happened to the fallen beings in that first sphere. This is what has caused the fall of all beings since then. There are, as we have said, two kinds, two divisions, among the fallen beings. There are those who use force and those who use deception. Those who use force have what we might call a hatred of the father, whereas those who use deception have what we call hatred of the mother.

There are those who hate God for giving them self-awareness and individuality. Yet the reason they hate God is that they are not willing to take responsibility for their own choices.

What have we said throughout the book? You have free will. You have the free will to make the choice to rebel against God's plan. God has given you that right. God does not even judge you for doing so. You are the one who judges yourself, because as you rebel against God's plan, you must adopt a dualistic standard, according to which your choices are now seen as bad. And so, you seek to compensate for this by proving God wrong.

But this is futile. What you need to do is to simply look at yourself and say: "Oh, but I was the one who made the choice to rebel against God's plan. So I am the only one who can change that choice. And I have the right to change that choice." And thus I have a right to say: "I will no longer identify myself as a separate being and rebel against God's plan. I will choose to rejoin the River of Life."

But you see, as long as you are not willing to take full responsibility for the fact, that it was your choices that separated yourself, then you must reject that it was your choices. It was God who somehow unjustly cast you out of heaven, because he would not see the wisdom of your dualistic worldview. And this is what, then, keeps these fallen beings trapped in their hatred against the father.

***

Now, in a sense, we need to say that all fallen beings have hatred against the father. But the ones that use deception, are seeking to get all human beings on earth to go into the state of hatred against the mother. They claim, in many cases, that they are the true representatives of the father. But they are seeking to get you to believe, that the father has created a world that is the way it is right now. And thus, it is God that has created the world, that gives you all of these unpleasant experiences. It is God's fault, that you have to fight Mother Nature to scratch out a living at the sweat of your brow. It is God's fault, that the universe acts like a mirror that returns to you what you send out.

And this is precisely what has caused many, many people to go into this state of hating the mother aspect of creation. They hate the world of form, they hate planet earth, they hate the physical universe, they hate that they have unpleasant experiences, that they have to work for a living, that they get old, that they get diseases, that they reap what they sow. And so, they take this hatred out upon the mother.

Transcending hatred of the Mother

And truly, if you want the real, underlying cause of environmental problems and natural disasters on earth, it is precisely that so many people on this planet have this unrecognized hatred of the mother. And they are constantly directing these hateful energies through their emotional bodies upon elemental life.

And elemental life becomes so burdened by these energies, that they eventually become so agitated, that they cannot fulfill their function. And so, their only way is to try to throw off this hateful energy, and this is what leads to many imbalanced conditions, such as natural disasters or erratic weather patterns. Have people not for a very long time talked about the "fury of the storm." Because when you go out in a storm, it feels like the air is angry, and it is lashing you with its power.

But it is not that elemental life is angry. For elementals do not have self-awareness and thus cannot feel anger. They simply take on the anger, but they have no conscious thought that "I am angry at this or that." It is not that the elementals are consciously thinking, "We are angry at human beings and we are going to punish them." Elementals are simply forced into shaking off the energy. So what human beings feel as the fury of the storm is their own anger, their own hatred against the mother, that is coming back to them.

***

My beloved, as long as this hatred of the mother continues to exist, without being recognized or addressed by human beings, then there is little realistic hope of truly healing Mother Earth and overcoming environmental problems. Thus, as the final chapter in this book, I appeal to you as a spiritual person, as one of the forerunners for healing Mother Earth, to take a look at yourself and the collective consciousness. Be willing to acknowledge this hatred of the mother, and then be willing to face it. Be willing to mentally go into this hatred of the mother and sense how it hates the mother plane. But what it really hates is that the mother is what returns to you the consequences of your own choices.

There is only one way to overcome this, and that is to recognize, that you have made those choices yourself, and that there is nothing wrong – according to a standard created by God – in you making those choices. It is only the dualistic, unreal standard of the fallen beings that makes it seem wrong. God has given you the right to make any choice you want, and the mother element simply reflects back to you the mental images you send out. So if you do not like what comes back, there is only one logical conclusion: send out something different. If you do not like the images on the movie screen, change the images on the film strip in the projector.

***

Now, of course, when you begin to realize this as an individual being, you also need to look at the fact that you cannot override the free will of the rest of humankind. And thus, neither Jesus nor I could go in and be the open door for changing the entire planet. And that is why we did not come to change the planet; we came to inspire people to transcend their level of consciousness—which would then indirectly change the planet.

And thus, you need to realize, that as you work your way towards the 144th level of consciousness, you must do the same. You must stop being focused on producing particular outer results, such as a particular result in the environmental issue. Instead, you must begin to focus on the overall goal of raising people's awareness, individually and collectively.

You realize, that the key to your freedom is to change the choices you have made. And this means you also realize, that there is nothing gained by you forcing other people to change their behavior. There can only be gain, when you inspire people to change their state of consciousness. And thus, based on their new state of consciousness, they will spontaneously make better choices.

This is the only way that change has ever been brought forth on this planet, and it is the only way it can ever be brought forth. No amount of force can bring the Golden Age, as Saint Germain has said. When you realize this, you realize why Jesus and myself did not primarily battle outer conditions but attempted to inspire people to open their eyes and see something beyond their current mental box, their current level of consciousness. And at that point, you begin to lock in to the underlying reality that we have descried: that the purpose of the entire universe is the growth in self-awareness.

The Golden Age of Saint Germain is not an age, in which people will find ways to create force-based technology, that can give them this hugely advanced civilization. What you see in many of the science-

Transcending hatred of the Mother

fiction movies is the dream of the fallen beings, whereby they can use force-based technology to conquer the universe. This is not the dream of the Elohim and the Ascended Host. Our vision is, indeed, that people transcend the force-based mindset, which of course springs from the illusion of separation.

***

It is the father's good pleasure to give you the kingdom. When you learn to work with the laws of nature, God will give you everything you desire. It is only when you set yourself apart, that you have to work against the laws of nature and therefore use force to get what you want. So the key is to realize, that you do not further God's cause by fighting these dualistic battles against other people. You further God's cause by being willing to let the separate self die, even if you do not know whether there will be any self left.

You go into this state, where you say: "God, you can take me home right now." And you know that if you die at this moment, you would have no regrets, you would have nothing you felt you had to do on earth. You would have no cause, no battle, you had to win before you could leave. You are ready to leave this very second. And in having this willingness to let the separate self – the separate self that does have ambitions and goals and battles it must fight – die – finally – then you set yourself free to return to the pure awareness, where you are an open door for the Presence.

My beloved, the separate self is separated from the Presence Above, which is the father element. But it is also separated from the mother below, which is the mother element. How, then, does the separate self relate to the material world? Well, as we have attempted to explain, the separate self is not actually seeing the material world. The separate self is seeing everything through the filter of the mental images it has created. And thus, when the separate self is fighting something, what is it fighting? It is fighting itself! It is fighting its own mental images, like Don Quixote was fighting the windmills, who in his mind appeared to be knights opposing his quest.

You can – because you have free will – continue to fight the windmills for an indefinite period of time. It is your right. But if you have had enough of fighting your own self-created windmills, then we have offered you an alternative. And if you had not had enough, why would you have endured reading this long book up until this point?

What is the key to stopping this fight? It is to realize, that what is fighting is the mind itself. And it is doing so in a desperate attempt to preserve itself, to preserve the hold it has over you, the hold it has by capturing, by fascinating, the attention of the Conscious You. The separate self, the ego, is seeking to maintain its own relevance, its own existence, by fascinating the Conscious You to look at the world through it. And it wants to continue doing that by creating these artificial battles.

***

If you will look honestly at your own thought process – as I encouraged people to do 2,500 years ago – you will see this pattern. There is an element of your mind that is going on 24 hours a day with these mental arguments. Oh yes, this mind may claim that it is arguing against other people or other ideas and thought systems, and that it is doing this for a greater cause. But the reality is, that the mind is arguing against its own mental images. And it is doing so for one purpose only: to maintain its own relevance and thus its own existence, because it has captured the attention of the Conscious You.

The mind wants you to believe, that you cannot leave it behind, that you cannot stop thinking, you cannot stop analyzing, you cannot stop caring and being engaged in the struggle to create a better earth.

But you *can*, my beloved!

Do you know when you will be free of this mind? The mind wants you to believe, that you will be free when you win some final battle, when you come up with some final argument. But there is no final battle to be won. There is no final argument to come up with.

My beloved, the central feature of the fallen consciousness is that it has defined its own image of reality. It has set itself up as a God, defining good and evil. Yet what have we said about duality: there must be two opposite polarities. So can you see, that in the dualistic mind, there can never be a final argument? You can argue convincingly for one issue, for one idea. But other people can come up with other arguments against that idea. What will determine whether people accept one argument or the other? It is simply a matter of which of the dualistic polarities they are polarized towards.

Transcending hatred of the Mother

Can you not look at the debate in society and see how many times, for example, in democratic nations you have two political parties arguing about the same issue. Take the United States, where you have the Republicans and the Democrats. Should one not think that in a particular issue, such as the economy, there would be one decision that was best for the greatest number of people? And therefore, it should be possible to come to a consensus.

Does it really make sense that a particular issue is completely different when viewed through Democratic glasses, as opposed to being viewed through Republican glasses? So can you not see, that the Democrats represent one dualistic extreme, and those who are polarized towards that extreme will always agree with the arguments advanced by the Democratic Party. The Republicans, of course, represent the other dualistic extreme, and those who are polarized towards that will always agree with the Republican arguments.

It is that simple, my beloved. Because all of the people involved with the debate are only seeing their own mental images, and none of them can see beyond it to see the deeper reality of what is actually best for all people. And so, those who will become the forerunners for healing Mother Earth, and changing the debate in all areas of society, are those who can lock in to this deeper reality. But you can lock in to the deeper reality only, when you start freeing yourself from this incessant, never-ending battle that is going on in your own mind.

***

You must begin to do what I encouraged my students to do 2,500 years ago. You must begin to question your perception and realize, that the mind that is always thinking and analyzing, forms a filter for how you look at reality. Twentyfivehundred years ago, my beloved, I started the Dhammapadha with the words: "Preceded by perception are mental states, for them is perception supreme."

Based on the understanding we have given you in this book, you can arrive at a deeper appreciation for these cryptic words. We have told you, that you have four levels of the mind. The highest is the identity level.

It is at the identity level, that you can go into the state of seeing yourself as a separate being. Yet how do you go into this state, how do you go into separation? Separation is based on a dualistic polarity between two opposites. You cannot go into separation and remain neutral. You go into separation by choosing one of the two polarities. You go into either one polarity or the other.

And once you have made the choice to go into a particular dualistic polarity, then you will create a mental state. In other words, the fundamental division in your mind, that takes place at the identity level, will be transferred into your mental body as a particular mental state. And the mental state, of course, is then also translated into a particular emotional state, that then becomes translated into actions.

But now listen carefully, my beloved. Preceded by perception are mental states, for them is perception supreme. The vast majority of human beings on earth are not aware of the division at the level of their identity mind, their identity body. Why are they not aware of this? Because they perceive the world through the mental states, namely their mental and emotional bodies.

This means, that their perception of the world is colored by the mental state. But the mental state is a product of the division at the identity level. Which means that as long as you are perceiving the world through the perception created by the [etheric] state, you cannot question the mental state. And therefore, you cannot even perceive the division at the identity level.

Your perception of the world around you is a product of your [etheric] state. And therefore, you are not able to question your perception. You think that what you see is not a mental image created in your own mind. Nay, you think that what you see is reality the way it is. But can you see, that your mental state and your perception was set on a certain track already at the identity level, when you had to go into one or another dualistic polarity?

So when you, again, look at the United States, you see that the Republican Party represents a certain dualistic polarity, and the Democratic Party represents the opposite polarity. What determines whether people are Republicans or Democrats? It is the division at the identity level, that makes them prone to being polarized towards this or that polarity. And as long as they cannot question that division, they will remain Democrats for life, and they will look at life through the filter of the Democratic arguments.

Of course, my beloved, if you do look at the United States, you will see, that more and more people are starting to no longer see themselves as strictly Democrats or strictly Republicans. They are becoming more centrist, they are looking for what I 2,500 years ago called the middle way.

***

The middle way is not a compromise between the two dualistic extremes. It is realizing that your perception is not accurate as long as it is colored by the dualistic extremes. And thus, what I told my students to do was; not to find a compromise between the extremes, but to transcend the entire consciousness in which there must be extremes, there must be polarities. The middle way, then, is not truly the middle between the two extremes; it is transcending the entire level of consciousness, where there are opposites, divisions—pairs, as I called it.

So can you see, that there are already millions of people on this planet, who have reached the level of consciousness, where they are becoming open to the middle way? And what they need is simply people who can go out and clarify this, and act as the leaders who can speak the kind of truths, the kind of ideas, that will make these people say: "Yes, I see that this is a higher approach; this is what I have been looking for. I knew there was something wrong in the political debate, but I could not put my finger on it. But here it is. We need to go in an entirely new direction, we need to take a new approach to solving our problems, for the old combative approach is no longer working."

Millions of people are ready for this. If enough people will become the open doors for their Presences to speak these new ideas, then there is a potential that there can be a grand awakening, beyond anything you have seen in known history. And this can, indeed, lead to a process that will become like a giant river, that washes away all opposition to the manifestation of a new and better age, a Golden Age.

I am Gautama Buddha, and I am in complete oneness with Saint Germain, who has also reached the state of Buddhahood. I am in complete oneness with Jesus, who has also reached the state of Buddhahood. I am in complete oneness with Mother Mary, who has also reached the state of Buddhahood. Together, we four represent the father, the mother, the son, and the Holy Spirit. We are, along with many among the Ascended Host, the sponsors of the Golden Age of Aquarius.

We are willing to work with anyone who is willing to be the open door. But you cannot be the open door until you have let the separate self die. And this includes letting go of the epic dream, that you are here to promote some ultimate cause, to win some ultimate battle. And it also requires that you have let go of the mind, that just wants to make itself relevant, by continuing these arguments 24 hours a day, seven days a week.

Be willing to first die; die to the world, so that you can be reborn to the Spirit. Be willing to let all of your ambitions die, so that you can be the open door. And in being the open door for the Presence finding that ultimate peace, ultimate fulfillment, ultimate bliss. The bliss that I AM.